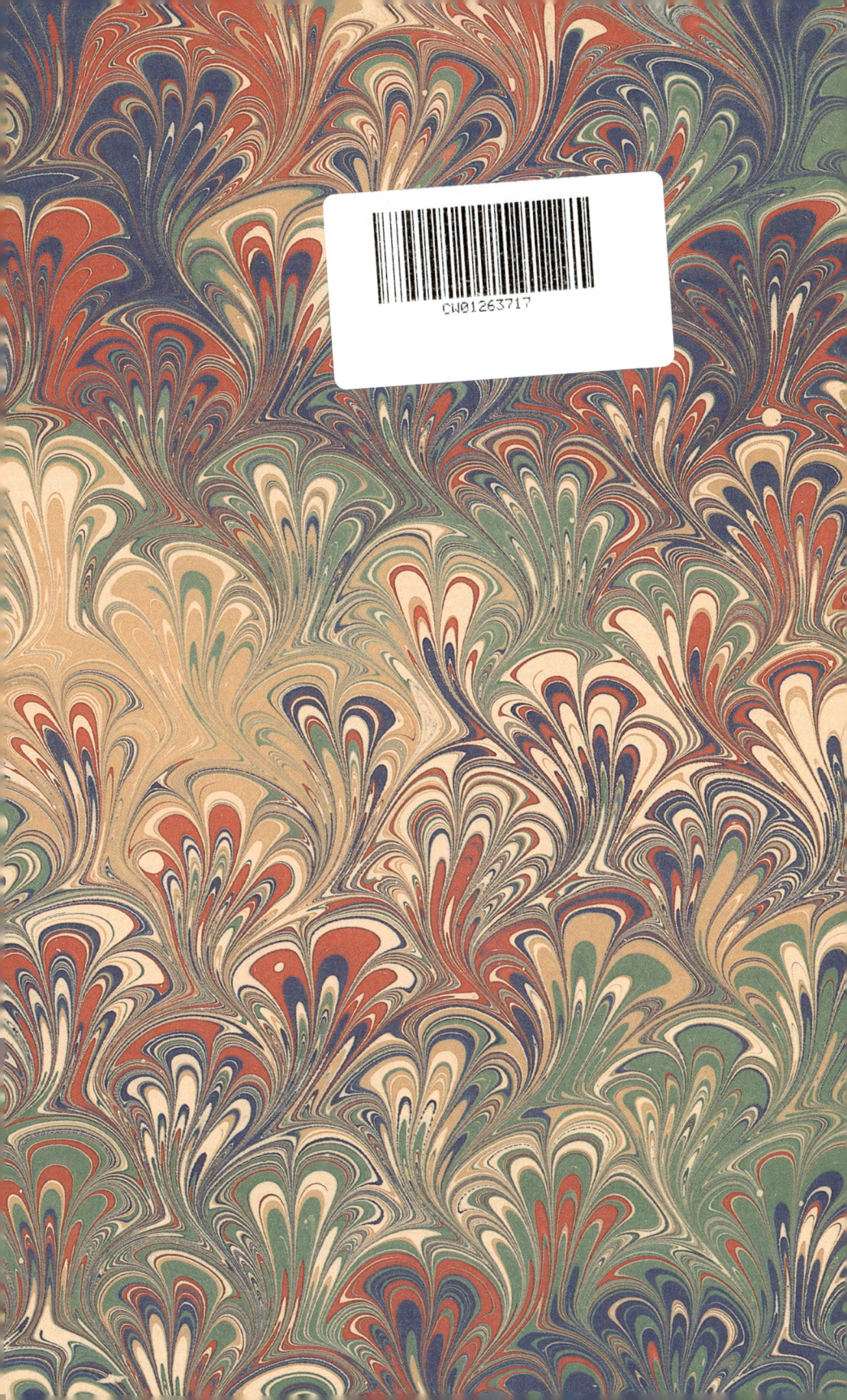

ARMY GROUP CENTER
The Wehrmacht in Russia
1941-1945

Also by Werner Haupt
ARMY GROUP NORTH
ASSAULT ON MOSCOW 1941

ARMY GROUP CENTER
The Wehrmacht in Russia
1941-1945

WERNER HAUPT

Schiffer Military History
Atglen, PA

Book Design by Robert Biondi.
Translated from the German by Joseph G. Welsh.

This book was originally published under the title,
Heeresgruppe Mitte,
by Podzun-Pallas Verlag, Friedberg.

Copyright © 1997 by Schiffer Publishing Ltd.
Library of Congress Catalog Number: 97-65443.

All rights reserved. No part of this work may be reproduced or used in any forms or by any means – graphic, electronic or mechanical, including photocopying or information storage and retrieval systems – without written permission from the copyright holder.

Printed in the United States of America.
ISBN: 0-7643-0266-3

We are interested in hearing from authors with book ideas on related topics.

Published by Schiffer Publishing Ltd.
77 Lower Valley Road
Atglen, PA 19310
Phone: (610) 593-1777
FAX: (610) 593-2002
E-mail: Schifferbk@aol.com.
Please write for a free catalog.
This book may be purchased from the publisher.
Please include $2.95 postage.
Try your bookstore first.

Contents

	Preface	7
Chapter 1	The Theater of War	9
Chapter 2	The Deployment	15
Chapter 3	The Attack	26
Chapter 4	The Defense	110
Chapter 5	The Retreat	139
Chapter 6	The Defeat	182
Chapter 7	The Interior	231
Chapter 8	The Surrender	258

Appendixes

Appendix 1: Organization of the Army Group 1941-1945 326

Appendix 2: Organization of the Luftwaffe in the Central Area 1941-45 331

Appendix 3: Organization of the Navy in the Northern Areas 1945 333

Appendix 4: Organization of the "Red Army" 1941-1943 335

Appendix 5: Commanders of the Army Group and Armies 338

Appendix 6: Chiefs of Staff of Army Group Center and Weichsel 340

Appendix 7: Duty Positions in the Army Group Staff 1941-1945 342

Appendix 8: Commanders of the Rear Area 344

Appendix 9: Senior Artillery Commanders 1945 345

Appendix 10: Duty Positions of the Luftwaffe Operations Staff 346

Appendix 11: Duty Positions of "Red Army" Senior Commands 1941-45 348

Appendix 12: Commitment of Air Defense Divisions in the Central Area 351

Appendix 13: Highest Awards in the Central Area 352

Appendix 14: Combat and Battle Calendar 353

Appendix 15: Generalkommissariate Belorussia 1943 354

Appendix 16: Abbreviations 355

Preface

The "History of Army Group Center" is the next book of a trilogy covering the Eastern Campaign. The publisher and the author believe that the horrible war against the Soviet Union in the years 1941-1945 has now been generally described.

The present work will again bring to life the combat operations of Army Group Center – and from 1944/45, also Army Groups North and Weichsel, which were created from it – to life for all who belonged to this the strongest German army group; to life for the student of military history; to life for all readers who can learn from the history of this war that power and blood, shells, and bombs cannot make the world a better place.

The book is ultimately a monument to the soldiers of friend and foe who gave their lives to their Fatherland, as well as to the memory of the German and Russian civilians who were sacrificed to the war.

In 1941, Army Group Center assaulted up to the gates of Moscow only to end up before those of Berlin in 1945. Therefore, their history is plainly the history of the German front line soldier.

The author has related the battles, victories, and defeats of Army Group Center on the basis of the available archives, publications, and special studies. He hereby thanks everyone that has helped and advised him!

Werner Haupt
Waiblingen, Summer 1968

1

THE THEATER OF WAR
The Land - The People - The History

During the Eastern Campaign of 1941-1945, Army Group Center of the German Army was to defeat the metropolis of the Soviet Union, while it ended up defending its own capital. Therefore, the history of Army Group Center can serve as a symbol for the struggle of the Wehrmacht in the vastness of Eastern Europe.

The armies of the army group began their fateful offensive, which would lead them from the Vistula to Moscow, during the hot summer of 1941. Here, the attack ebbed under the weight of the "Red Army" counterattack, as well as the merciless winter. The German divisions had to withdraw from central Russia and, from this time on, hold the region of the former Belorussian Socialist Soviet Republic for almost 2 1/2 years. The last months of the war were again played out on Polish territory and, finally, in the German homeland from the Baltic Sea to Upper Silesia.

The great differences between the German Reich and the Soviet Union were not only a test of strength between their armies, but a struggle having an economic and ideological basis. The horrendous struggle was also influenced by the land on which it took place.

The Army Group Center Theater of War encompassed the enormous area between Berlin and Moscow, as well as between the Baltic Sea and the

Army Group Center

Pripet Marsh. The German soldier endured the struggle against a courageous, if merciless, enemy, primarily in Belorussia.

• • •

Belorussia, or Ruthenia (as the German occupation authority called it) is the enormous land complex tying Central and Eastern Europe together. There is no natural boundary to the east. Therefore, the cruel wind, which whistles over the steppes of central Russia, reaches the Belorussian marshes and forest-lands unhindered. The winter is much colder and longer – often down to minus 40 degrees – than it is in Central Europe. The summer is moderately warm, however, and more persistent than in Poland or the Baltic Provinces. Therefore, there is frequent precipitation in June and July. The transition from a land to a sea climate dominates the terrain.

This is a wide plain that is separated by the western Russian ridge into a northern and a southern zone. The ridge itself boasts wide rolling hills that stretch from east to west. Three great ridges are formed, including the Minsk Hills with the Lysaya Gora (at 343 meters the highest point in Belorussia). At the same time, this is the watershed between the Dnepr and the Nieman/Memel. Then there are the Dnepr Hills in the Orsha area and, finally, the Vitebsk-Nevel Hills, which form the watershed between the Duena and Finish Gulf.

The large area of 125,000 square kilometers is flat in the south, while the northern ridges fall off sharply. The northern land bridge – the so-called "gate of Smolensk" – offers the most favorable line of communication to central Russia.

The plain in the north around Vitebsk and Polozk is hilly. The lakes here are drained by the Duena, which forms a natural boundary to the north.

The southern plain, on the other hand, is almost flat and consists of 50% marsh and moor. This characteristic of the terrain is especially noticeable in the Pripet Marsh. Here the ground is water-tight, forming a permanent marsh that marks the border with the Ukraine.

The rivers are another characteristic of Belorussia. The total length of the waterways is 32,000 kilometers. Four water systems characterize the terrain. First is the powerful Dnepr, with a length of 2,150 kilometers. It

Chapter 1: The Theater of War

emerges in the Waldai Mountains and runs 470 kilometers through the land before leaving Belorussia. It is navigable from Orsha. The river reaches a width of 75 to 320 meters, and a depth of up to 8 meters. Its largest tributaries are the Drut, Berezina, Sozh, and Pripet. The second largest system is the 1000 kilometer long Duena, which had dug a deep bed through the land 75 to 250 meters wide. Its tributaries are called the Obal, Drissa, and Luchosa. A third river system is the Lovati, which flows from south to north into Lake Ilmen. The fourth and smallest system is formed by the Nieman/Memel.

To the left and right of the rivers are often endless and impassable forests. Belorussia consists of about 2 million hectares of forest, so that 25% of the total land is forest. The most forest-rich area is the Polesse Forest with its tall birches and pines. Here, traffic is only possible on corduroy roads. These embankments were built in the time of the Tsars and had been improved and widened since then. In the Belorussian forests we find 56% spruce, 11% fir, 10% birch, 9% alder, and 6% oak. These enormous forests supported industries such as sawmills, matches, paper, and furniture.

The most important industry for the 10 million inhabitants was agriculture. The people struggled with meager tools to make the ground fruitful. In 1941, there were approximately 10,000 kolkhozes and 1000 sovkhozes. Their most important crops were oats, barley, and potatoes. Belorussia was the potato capital of the Soviet Union.

As German tanks, vehicles, and the high-tech combat aircraft of the Luftwaffe traveled through Belorussia or took off from its airfields, the native peasants were still wearing the same clothes worn by their great-grandfathers: trousers and skirts of coarse homemade linen, handmade shoes from birch, and, in the winter, overcoats and capes from the skins of their own sheep.

The peasants between the Duena and Pripet, whose lives consisted of poverty and hard work, saw no change in their existence to be derived from the German war machines in 1941. As soon as the campaign began, they had to go into the fields to sow. The winter is long here and the summer short.

Army Group Center

The ground of Belorussia did not produce much other than grain and potatoes. In the north, flax was still grown.

Another industry was provided by the rich animal life. In the forests and marshes lived animals that had long died out in Europe. Here were bears, foxes, wolves, elk, badgers, beaver, fish, and marsh otters. Animal trapping was lucrative. There were many breeding farms run by the large Moscow and Leningrad fur firms.

The Belorussian Socialist Soviet Republic consisted of an area as large as Bavaria, Brandenburg, Wuerrtemberg, and Baden put together; however, there were only five major cities. The most important of these was Minsk, with 240,000 inhabitants. Then followed Vitebsk (167,420), Smolensk (156,670), Mogilev (99,440), and Bobruisk (84,110). The only lines of communication tying Belorussia to Central Europe and central Russia lead through these large cities. This vast area could only be crossed quickly and securely on the railroad lines and highways, which were called "rollbahns" by the German soldiers. Otherwise, the terrain was like the people – hostile.

The people here were hostile throughout most of history. Their origins lay in the dark reaches of time and are still not clearly known today. The ancient population came from a base Slav root. They arrived from the east and advanced into the valleys of the Duena, Berezina, Sozh, and Pripet. Thus, they dislodged the people already living here, most likely Lithuanians and Fins.

In the following centuries, the Slavic people settled in the area between the Nieman, Pripet, and Dnepr. Therefore, this region became the ancestral home of the Slavs.

The various tribes did not join together. It was not until the 9th Century that a powerful state emerged under the princes of Novgorod.

In later centuries, the great princes of Kiev dominated the region between the Duena and Pripet.

The arrival of the Mongols in the 13th Century only affected Belorussia up to the border. Then the Lithuanian tribes took over the land. However, several hundred years later the Poles showed up and defeated the Lithuanians in 1386, thus attaching the land to their own kingdom. Lithuanian traces

Chapter 1: The Theater of War

can still be discerned today, as in the ruins of the castle in Lida. The epoch of the Lithuanians was also when a native culture developed.

On the other hand, the Poles tried to do away with the local culture. They forced Polish culture on the local population with draconian measures. The population, however, did not relent.

At this time, the land was already known as "Belorussia" or "White Russia." The first such reference was in the map of Cardinal Nikolaus of Cusa in 1491. The map indicated the region west of the Dnepr with this name. The areas east of the river were called "Red" and "Black Russia." The great princes of Moscow, which had achieved power at the end of the 15th Century in Eastern Europe, also designated the eastern Slavic region of their kingdom with the same names.

In 1655, Alexei Mikhailovich declared himself "autocrat of all Greater, Lesser, and White Russia, Lithuania, Volhnia, and Podolia."

The division of Poland in 1772 and 1793 finally brought Belorussia under the realm of the Tsar.

On 6/2/1774, the newly acquired area was designated by Tsarina Katherine as the new province of "Belaya Rossiya" (White Russia). The residents were referred to as Ruthenians. The word is the latinized form of the old Slavic name "Russian."

The Belorussian region remained pretty much unchanged. The influence of the crown only reached the cities. The people of the land lived pretty much as they had under the Poles or the Lithuanians.

When the Emperor Napoleon entered Russia with his army in 1812, he published an order of the day, saying, "Belorussia is to be treated not as a conquered land, but as an ally!"

The middle of the 19th Century brought the first indications of the unrest of the people against the upper classes from Western and Central Europe. In 1863, Kalinovski planned an uprising, which was bloody and suppressed. It was 42 years before the Belorussians organized a second rebellion.

World War I flowed over wide sectors of the land. German and Russian shells plowed up the earth – and the defeat on the Russian side increased the anti-Tsarist forces. Mikhail Vassilevich Frunze, the "Clausewitz" of the Soviets, founded the Bolshevik movement in Belorussia. On 4/3/1917, the

Army Group Center

Council of Workers Deputies met in Minsk and abolished Tsarist authority.

The Belorussian Socialist Soviet Republic was founded on 12/30/1918 by Frunze. However, the new republic never knew peace. Polish troops and formations from the "White Army" invaded the land and fought the Soviet militia.

This struggle was ended by the Treaty of Riga, which gave a portion of Belorussia to Poland and the eastern provinces to the new USSR. The unity of Belorussia, was, therefore, destroyed. Russian was still spoken in the Belorussian towns that now belonged to Poland.

After the introduction of Sovkhozes and Kolkhozes, the Soviet authority no longer concerned itself with the cultural development of the peasants. However, the main centers of Soviet power remained in the cities. Here, enormous construction projects were undertaken (such as the 1500 seat opera house in Minsk).

The "Red Army", in accordance with Moscow's agreement with the German Reich, again occupied the former Belorussian region of Poland in 1939. Within a short period of time, the Soviets stamped their imprint on the land – and 1 1/2 years later, a new army returned; these were the troops of Army Group Center.

2

THE DEPLOYMENT
German and Soviet Measures

The 1940 Western Campaign defeated the British-French Alliance on the continent. After achieving this objective, Hitler believed that Great Britain would give up the war and submit to the German peace proposals. The military catastrophe in Flanders would practically force England to make peace with Germany.

The German Wehrmacht stood at the height of its power when its tanks reached the Channel. Their were no more enemies on the continent for the armies of Hitler. The pact with the Soviet Union in 1939 had secured their rear. So, at the time of the Western Campaign, they only had to leave a security force in the Generalgouvernement.

In mid-June of 1940 there were only five infantry divisions to protect the newly-won eastern territories, and they were not altogether combat capable. The Senior Commander in the East – the highest military authority stationed with the German forces in Poland – General of Cavalry Baron von Gienanth, commanded the 209th, 365th, 372nd, 379th, and 393rd ID. Luftwaffe formations did not exist in the Vistula area, except for a few training units.

After the end of the Western Campaign, the OKH [Army High Command] transferred the 18th Army and several infantry divisions from France to the east. These formations were primarily quartered in East Prussia. This measure was taken because of the unexpected occupation of the Baltic Republics by the 8th Soviet Army!

This "Red Army" advance was a result of the German-Soviet Pact of 8/23/1939. This was one of the secret protocols:

> "In case of a territorial-political alteration in the region of the Baltic States, the northern border of Lithuania will form the boundary of the spheres of influence between Germany and the USSR."

The Soviet Union digressed from this as they sealed the German-Lithuanian border with their motorized forces on the first day of the occupation!

The Moscow government, therefore, had created a "fait accompli" that Germany had to take into consideration, because, at the same time, the Soviets had intentions in Finland and Rumania. The extension of Soviet power indicated an indirect threat to the German Reich by threatening its source of oil in Rumania and its shipping lanes in Scandinavia. Both had significance for the conduct of the war if Hitler wanted to eventually bring Great Britain to its knees.

This situation was first discussed by German commanders and general staff officers on 7/13/1940. On 7/21/1940, Hitler had ordered the OKH "to attack the Russian problem." This meant that, from now on, German general staff officers had to think about and plan for an attack against the "Red Army!"

Major General Marcks, Chief of Staff of the 18th Army, was charged with developing such a plan. On 8/5, the General presented his draft, which proposed:

> "The purpose of the campaign is to defeat the Russian armed forces and make Russia incapable of being an enemy of Germany in the near future. To protect Germany against Russian bombers, Russia must be occupied up to a line on the Lower Don-middle Volga-northern Duena ... Moscow forms the economic, political, and spiritual center of the USSR. Its conquest will destroy the unity of the Russian Empire. ...

Chapter 2: The Deployment

The German Army strikes with its main forces into the elements of the Russian Army located in northern Russia and captures Moscow!"

At this time, Moscow stood at the center of the so-called "Marcks Plan." However, Hitler, who required placing political – economic interests before military, turned down the draft. With the approval of the OKH, he tasked Major General Paulus to come up with a new plan.

In the summer of 1940, the Army directed more and more formations from the west to eastern Germany and into the Generalgouvernement. The Luftwaffe, as before, left its air squadrons in France, where they were engaged in the bitter "Battle of Britain."

On 9/20/1940, the commander of Army Group B, Field Marshal von Bock, was established as the senior commander in the east. On this day, he had 25 infantry, 3 panzer divisions, one motorized, and one cavalry division available. The commander established his headquarters in Posen and, on 10/15/1940, transferred his operations staff to Warsaw.

In December, Major General Paulus completed his attack plan, which was approved by Hitler. On 12/18/1940, the OKW [Wehrmacht High Command] published Instruction Nr. 21 under the designation "OKW/WFSt./ Abt. L (I) Nr. 33408/40", also known as "Plan Barbarossa."

The plan began:

> "The German Wehrmacht must be prepared to defeat Soviet Russia in a quick campaign, even before the war against England is over..."

Further on it said:

> "The majority of the Russian Army, which is located in western Russia, is to be destroyed by bold operations utilizing well advanced panzer wedges, and the withdrawal of combat capable elements into the vastness of Russian territory is to be prevented..."

The operation plan for the central German army group was as follows:

Army Group Center

"...In the center of the entire front falls the mission of breaking through out of the area around and to the north of Warsaw with particularly strong tank and motorized formations, to destroy the Russian forces located in Belorussia. Conditions must be created for the penetration of strong mobile elements to the north, in order to destroy enemy forces fighting in the Baltic Provinces, in cooperation with the northern army group, which will be operating out of East Prussia in the general direction of Leningrad. After achieving these most important missions ... the attack operation will be continued to occupy the important communications and armament center of Moscow...."

In contrast with the "Marcks Plan", the plan did not hold Moscow as the most important objective of the German offensive. Therefore, the force group committed in the center of the front only had the mission of defeating the Soviets in Belorussia and then advancing in the direction of Leningrad. Moscow – the most profitable objective of the campaign – was not even to be thought of at the beginning of the offensive!

At the beginning of 1941, the German Wehrmacht leadership energetically made preparations for the planned conflict with the USSR. On 2/20/1941, the Luftwaffe formed a working staff in Berlin under Colonel Loebel, which was to bring the preparations of the Luftwaffe on line. At the same time, the Army General Quartermaster established the first supply bases in former Poland. The Senior Quartermaster of Army Group B moved to Warsaw in order to establish stores for the divisions on the border. The Dienststelle des Generals z.b.V.II (Hannover) became the "Staff of the 102nd Army Rear Area Command." This staff later had to secure the deployment of the rear area of the army group.

The deployment of the Eastern Army began in February 1941. Seven infantry and one motorized division rolled to the east on the railroad. The units remained in the Generalgouvernement. Border security was, as before, entrusted to a few widely scattered forces.

In the meantime, however, the German long range reconnaissance pilots flew deep into Soviet territory. In October 1940, the OKL [Luftwaffe High Command] established a special purpose air reconnaissance group

Chapter 2: The Deployment

under Lieutenant Colonel Rowehl. This group was ordered to photograph Russian territory with four special squadrons and determine the eventual deployment of the "Red Army."

Two squadrons were committed over the area into which Army Group Center was to advance. The 1st Squadron flew the "He-111." This aircraft was equipped with a special high altitude engine. The squadron took off from Seerappen/East Prussia and reconnoitered over Belorussia. The 4th Squadron flew "Ju-88-B" and "Ju-86-P" aircraft from Krakau and Budapest. The aircraft took photos of the area between Minsk and Kiev at an altitude of 12,000 meters.

Because the deployment of divisions increased during the following weeks – alone from mid-March to mid-April 18 large formations rolled into the Generalgouvernement – the agencies of the reichsbahn had to make an enormous effort. The 2nd Field Railroad Direction (Dresden) was tasked with increasing the capacity of railroad transport in Poland by 100% by the beginning of May! In addition, 30,000 railroad engineers and civilian construction troops were subordinated to the Field Railroad Direction.

In mid-April, the German deployment increased from week to week. The garrisons in East Prussia and the Generalgouvernement were so full that the land appeared to be an armed camp. 16 divisions arrived in the army group area. The army commands and the corps staffs took up their sectors and played out the initial plans with the unit commanders.

The troops themselves were kept in the dark as to the objective and purpose, while the general staffs of the senior commands were working out the particulars of the operation order. The army group, which was to receive the designation "Center", had the following mission:

> "Army Group Center destroys – driving strong forces in front of its flanks – the enemy forces in Belorussia, promptly reaches the Smolensk area by concentrating its mobile forces south and north of Minsk, and thereby creates the conditions necessary to have strong elements of its mobile forces cooperate with Army Group North..."

The army group command assigned its army commands and panzer commands their initial objectives:

Army Group Center

4th Army = Dnepr crossing near and north of Mogilev,
9th Army = Dnepr crossing near and southeast of Polozk,
2nd Panzer Group = area near and south of Smolensk,
3rd Panzer Group = area near and north of Vitebsk.

The "Aussenstelle OKH/Generalquartiermeister Befelsstelle Mitte" (Major Eckstein) established supply points behind the army and panzer group sectors, from which the supply columns of the combat groups could obtain the necessary supplies. The distribution points had 20,000 tons of transport capacity available, which they received from three truck transport regiments and one NSKK Brigade.

On 6/14/1941, Hitler ordered all of the commanders of the army groups, armies and luftflotten committed in the east to Berlin. He gave them their last instructions for the attack against the USSR.

The deployment in the Generalgouvernement and the German war preparations could not remain hidden from the Soviets. They continued to fulfill their economic agreements with the German Reich – for example, from 2/10/1940 to 6/22/1941, the USSR delivered 1 1/2 million tons of grain, 1 million tons of mineral oil, 2,700 kilograms of manganese, chrome, platinum, etc. – however, they had also been preparing for conflict with the German Reich for months.

In the "Red Army" field orders from 1939 it was stated:

> "The USSR will answer any enemy attack with a destructive strike of the entire weight of its armed forces. Our war against the attacker will be the most justifiable war in the history of mankind!"

Even at this time, this threat was directed at Germany.

Consequently, the Russian economy was based on a war economy since 1939. 26.4% of the national budget went to defense in 1940.

The Soviet armed forces had learned from their unfortunate winter campaign against Finland and, in particular, from German operations in the west in 1940. The production of heavy weapons was increased enormously from summer 1940. The number of new tanks – principally heavy types –

Chapter 2: The Deployment

totaled 358 in 1940, and a year later it was 1503, including 1110 "T-34's." Aircraft production increased six-fold, artillery seven-fold, and anti-tank weapons 70-fold!

The deployment of the "Red Army" on its western border had a considerable influence on the beginning of the conflict. The dislocation of Soviet troops in western Russia, according to German intelligence, was as follows:

9/1/1939: 44 rifle divisions
20 cavalry divisions
3 motorized brigades

3/12/1940: 90 rifle divisions
22 cavalry divisions
22 motorized and tank brigades

5/1/1941: 118 rifle divisions
20 cavalry divisions
40 motorized and tank brigades.

According to this report, there were 45 rifle divisions and 15 motorized or tank brigades in front of Army Group Center. The majority of these divisions, including two tank and six motorized brigades, were located far to the west between Bialystock and Brest-Litovsk. The second largest grouping of 16 rifle divisions, two cavalry divisions, and three motorized brigades was in second echelon between Novogrudek and Baranovichi.

At the beginning of May 1941, the government of the USSR prepared the population and, in particular, the Army, for war with its propaganda. On 5/5/1941, Stalin gave an important speech in Moscow, in which he said:

> "The situation is extremely serious. We must count upon a German attack in the near future."

Army Group Center

War between Germany and the Soviet Union seemed remote at the beginning of April 1941. The Wehrmacht entered Yugoslavia and Greece. Weeks went by, then the German soldiers stood on the Peloponnese and in Crete. The increase in power Hitler acquired seemed unimaginable. However, valuable time was lost.

Quickly, the final preparations for war were made. The 2nd Air Command, under Field Marshal Kesselring, which had formerly been responsible for the conduct of the air war against England on the Channel coast, left the west and arrived in Warsaw several days later. The air formations of the VIII Air Corps took off from southern Greece and Crete for transfer to central Poland.

During the nights of 6/19 and 6/20, the attack divisions moved into their assembly areas directly behind the border.

On this day, from north to south, Army Group Center had the following formations:

3rd Panzer Group:
VI Army Corps, with 26th, 6th ID;
XXXIX Motorized Army Corps, with 20th, 7th Panzer Divisions;
V Army Corps, with 35th, 5th ID;
LVII Motorized Army Corps, with 12th, 18th, 19th Panzer Divisions.

9th Army:
VIII Army Corps, with 161st, 28th, 8th ID;
XX Army Corps, with 256th, 162nd ID;
XLII Army Corps, with 129th, 102nd ID.

4th Army:
VII Army Corps, with 221st Security Div, 23rd, 258th, 7th, 268th ID;
IX Army Corps, with 263rd, 137th, 292nd ID;
XLIII Army Corps, with 252nd, 134th, 131st ID;
XIII Army Corps, with 17th, 87th ID.

Chapter 2: The Deployment

2nd Panzer Group:
XLVII Motorized Army Corps, with 17th Panzer Division, 167th ID, 18th Panzer Division, 29th Motorized ID;
VII Army Corps, with 31st, 45th, 34th ID;
XXIV Motorized Army Corps, with 3rd, 4th Panzer Divisions, 1st cavalry Division, 267th ID;
XLVI Motorized Army Corps, with "Grossdeutschland" Infantry Regiment, 10th Panzer Division, SS "Das Reich" Division.

The army group had the following reserve formations available:
LII Army Corps, with 293rd ID behind the 4th Army;
286th Security Division behind the 4th Army;
403rd Security Division behind the 9th Army;
255th ID behind the 2nd Panzer Group.

During the night of 20 June 1941, the last preparations were made on both the German and the Russian sides. In Moscow, intelligence arrived from Agent Central "Red Chapel" in Switzerland that the German attack was expected on 6/20!

On the evening of the next day – the last hours before the most horrible war in history began – Field Marshals von Bock and Kesselring conducted their last briefings. The commander of Army Group Center felt despondent; responsibility for the future lay heavily on his shoulders.

In the headquarters of the commands east of the Bug, the telephones also rang shrilly. Final instructions were given by Moscow:

> "During the night, the firing positions on the fortified zones on the national border will be occupied. All units are to be combat ready..."

The clocks indicated 0030 hours on 22 June 1941, when the Soviet liaison officers received these instructions. There was no more time to do anything further. Indeed, 90 minutes later, the last grain train passed the German border station in Brest-Litovsk. The German assault troop leaders, however, in assembly areas on the Bug, glanced at the illuminated dials of

Army Group Center

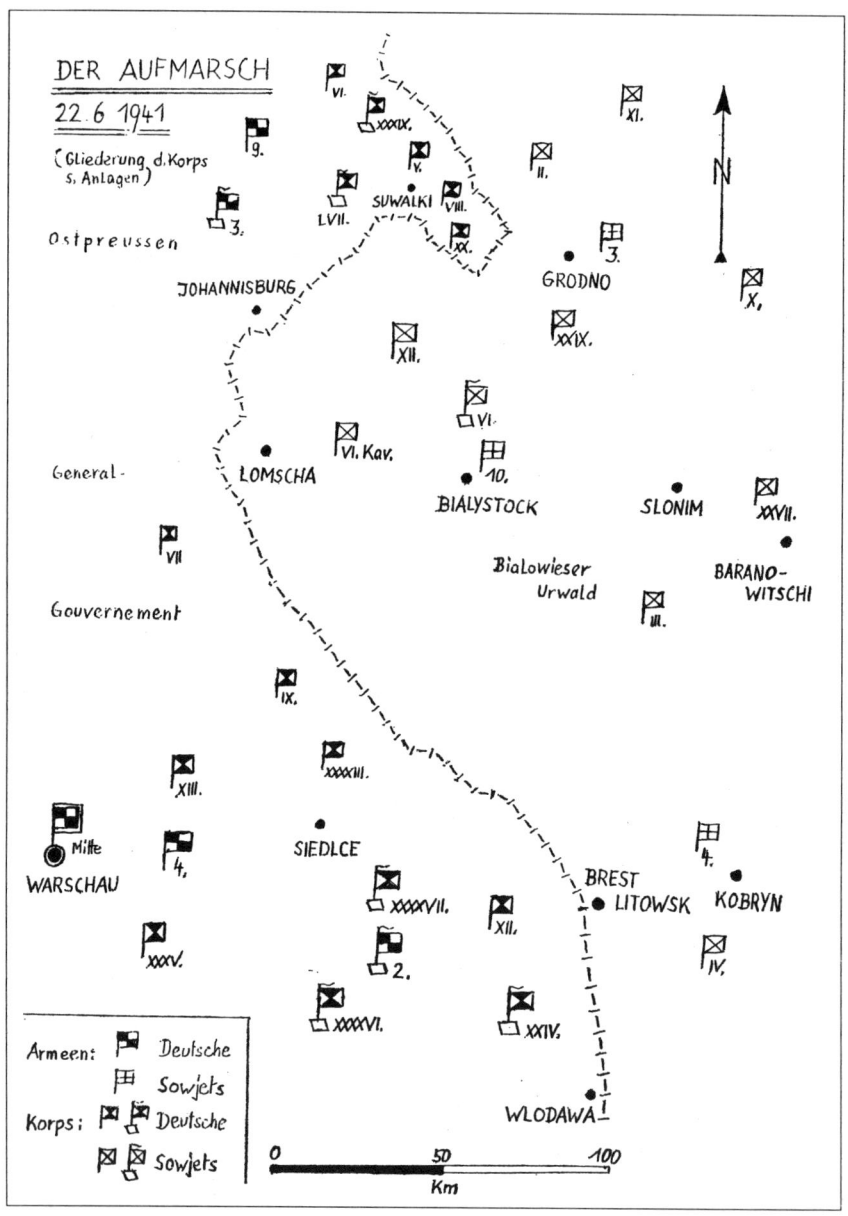

The Deployment 6/22/1941

Chapter 2: The Deployment

their wrist-watches and the men of the XXIV Motorized Army Corps heard the last words of their commanding general: "Forward!"

The German ambassador in Moscow, Count von der Schulenburg, left the embassy in the Kremlin at 0400 hours:

> "...In view of the intolerable pressure of the Russian troops on the demarcation line, which divides them from the German troops, the order has been issued to advance into the USSR!"

As the first rays of morning appeared over the distant horizon in the east, the war had begun...

3

THE ATTACK
The German Offensive 1941

It was Sunday, as the German attack against the Soviet Union was launched on 22 June 1941.

The hour of its start was established by order. Before this time, however, aircraft from the Luftwaffe and assault troops from the Army were already in USSR territory.

Six combat aircraft of the 2nd, 3rd, and 53rd Combat Squadrons took off 40 minutes before the official start from their airfields in central Poland. The crews were specially trained in night flying for their missions. The aircraft immediately rose to high altitude and flew across the border, in order to be over their targets at the exact time the artillery fire began. Their mission was to bomb the most important Soviet airfields and prevent the Russian pilots from taking off.

On the border itself, it was still quiet at 0300 hours in the morning. In fact, the night was not completely still. The motors of vehicles droned, tracks rattled over asphalt, horses whinnied, entrenching tools clinked, the metal of weapons twinkled, the breeches of guns snapped shut, and the boots of marching soldiers plodded through marshy fields. The German Eastern Army was ready.

Located on the Bug, opposite the bridge near Koden, was an engineer assault troop of the Berlin-Brandenburg 3rd Panzer Division. These men

Chapter 3: The Attack

were to assault across the bridge at the beginning of the attack and clear the way for the following motorized troops.

Then the sounds of engines from the German combat aircraft approached from the west. Lieutenant Moellhoff, from the 3/39 Engineer Battalion, glanced at the dial of his watch. Dammit, its only 0300 hours. The noise of the aircraft will alert the Soviet border guards. Therefore, the engineer officer raised his arm; his people jumped from their cover, advanced, overran the sentries, and took up positions on the far side of the bridge. The Bug bridge was in German hands, and the first four Russian soldiers were marched away to captivity – before the war had started.

Then it was 0315 hours:

Hundreds of guns of all calibers opened fire on known Soviet border fortifications and watch towers along the wide front from East Prussia to central Poland. The roar of fire pierced the morning fog, which had just begun to lift. At the time the engines of the motorcycles, trucks, and tanks roared to life, the assault engineers jumped up, directing their flame-throwers on the enemy's wire obstacles, while others pushed the first rafts into the waters of the Bug and the Nieman and the infantry tightened their grip on their carbines and hand grenades – and the first bombs of the German combat aircraft fell on the Russian airfields.

The officers in the main headquarters of the Western Military District in Minsk still did not know, at this time, that their armies were already defending. A few minutes after 0300 hours, the telephone rang.

Lieutenant General Kuznetsov, commander of the 3rd Army, reported from his main headquarters in Grodno:

> "Germans crossing the border, Grodno being bombarded. Telephone contact with the border interrupted, two radio stations have fallen..."

And from now on, one bit of bad news followed the other. The local commanders of Bialystok, Grodno, Lida, Brest, Volkovysk, and Slonim reported the bombardment of their cities. The combat squadrons of the Luftwaffe, the aircraft of the II and VIII Air Corps, dived onto the airfields, traffic intersections, and bridges with their engines screaming.

Army Group Center

Then, it was the hour of the "Landser."

The infantry and engineer assault troops rushed forward. Senior Lieutenant Zumpe from the 3/135 IR [Infantry Regiment] of the 45th ID assaulted across the Bug bridge near Brest-Litovsk with his group, only a few minutes after the last Russian grain train had passed.

It was the same all over.

The soldiers of the 3rd Panzer Division boarded rafts five minutes after the beginning of the attack, crossed the Bug, and entered Russian territory. The motorized columns rolled across the bridge won in the daring raid.

The commanders were forward with their troops, perhaps anticipating the difficulties of the next weeks, months, and years.

The Soviet border guards were taken by surprise, captured, and thrown back. Before they could even think of resisting, the German motorcyclists, scouts, and assault engineers were long gone. However, the enemy was there! The sun had not peeked over the horizon yet as Soviet hand grenades detonated and machine-guns and rifles rattled in fire. The German assault troops were suddenly stopped, and they had to await reinforcements.

The reinforcements arrived only slowly. They still could not find solid crossings over the Bug. Indeed, the engineers were busy constructing bridges, though valuable time was being wasted. At 0900 hours, the first bridge was established in the 4th Army area. The 178th Engineer Battalion of the 78th ID had constructed it near Drohizyn. The new amphibious tanks – there were four battalions of them in the German Army – crossed the border rivers. Particularly impressive was the 1/18 Panzer Regiment under Major Count von Strachwitz. The battalion crossed the Bug near Pratulin north of Brest-Litovsk. Sergeant Wierschin was the commander of the first tank on Russian territory. Suddenly, their appeared two enemies that the German General Staff officers had not counted. These were sand and marsh. In the first hours of 22 June, the "Landser" ran into quite enough of them. The 3rd Panzer Division, under its active commander, Lieutenant General Model, became hopelessly bogged down in the moor near Stradecz south of Brest-Litovsk. By the afternoon, the division had gained only 20 kilometers of the assigned 80! The infantry had gone just as far at some loca-

Chapter 3: The Attack

tions, as they too had to cross this morass of marsh and sand. Therefore, the right flank of the 2nd Panzer group lay immobile for hours – and Generaloberst Guderian had expected success here. The commander of the XXIV Motorized Army Corps, General of Panzer Troops Baron Geyr von Schweppenburg, therefore, ordered a halt at 1500 hours. He diverted the 3rd Panzer Division to the north. Now they could finally advance.

However, on other sectors, the tanks did not bog down because of sand and mud, but because the enemy was too strong. Thus, the 25th Panzer Regiment – whose commander was the winner of the "Pour le merite" and Knight's Cross, Colonel Rothenburg – lost half of its vehicles from enemy fire in front of Olita. Also on this sector, a gap was located during the evening. At 1900 hours, Rittmeister Niemack established the first bridgehead across the Nieman east of Seirijei with the advance detachment of the 5th ID. Therefore, the breech was formed for the 3rd Panzer Group of Generaloberst Hoth.

The greatest surprise to the German command on this day was the defense of the fortress of Brest-Litovsk. On 21 June, the German long range reconnaissance and observation posts reported that the Russians were not expecting an attack in the citadel. Then, 24 hours later, the unexpected occurred – the Soviets were prepared for combat.

The 45th ID (Major General Schlieper) was ordered to capture the city and the citadel. At exactly 0315 hours, the 98th Artillery Regiment and the 4th Rocket Launcher Regiment began their destructive fire. In one half hour, the rocket launchers alone fired 2880 rounds. Then the attack followed. The daring raid of the 3rd Company of the 135th IR succeeded. The bridge was captured.

The companies of the 130th and 135th Regiments crossed the Bug. The 3/135 IR, under Captain Praxa, assaulted the western island and into the center of the city. However, the attack failed in front of the citadel. The artillery fire had no effect on the defensive works. The defenders fired from all of the windows and gaps in the walls. The 130th and 135th Regiments had to work their way up to the citadel – however, they could get no further. Thus, in the evening twilight, the 133rd IR had to be committed to support the attack on Brest.

Army Group Center

The 45th ID registered a high loss of blood on this first day of the war: 21 officers and 290 non-commissioned officers and men lay dead on the battlefield.

So, as the Soviet soldiers defended here in the citadel of Brest-Litovsk, the Russian pilots made an effort, in spite of their inexperience and old aircraft. They bravely attacked German columns and were shot down in the air by fighters bearing the iron cross.

On the morning of 6/22, six Russian combat aircraft tried to attack the Biala Podlaska airfield, which was the staging area of the 77th Stuka Squadron. Fighter aircraft of type "Me-109" were on guard and shot down all six enemy aircraft. However, the Russians did not give up. In the afternoon, they repeated the attack and lost 15 aircraft.

During the afternoon, another group of 12 combat aircraft attacked a column of vehicles, in which General Guderian rode. Again German fighters were there. This time they were aircraft from the 51st Fighter Squadron of Colonel Moelders. All 12 Russians were sent burning to the earth. At a third location, the Soviets had some success. The commander of the 27th Fighter Squadron, Lieutenant Colonel Schellmann, was killed in air combat over Grodno.

Night slowly descended over Russia.

The German leadership reviewed the outcome of the first day. It was a successful outcome, even if everything that was anticipated was not accomplished. Luftflotte 2 had destroyed a total of 528 enemy aircraft on the ground and 210 in the air. Field Marshal von Bock could also be satisfied with the success of his army group. The border was crossed at all locations and the lead elements stood 40 kilometers deep in enemy territory. The most successful was the attack of the 3rd Panzer Group, which forced the Nieman. Therefore, they had outflanked the Soviet 3rd Army on the right flank and had torn an almost 100 kilometer wide gap between the fronts of the Western Military District and the Russian Northwest Front. The enemy 27th, 56th, and 87th Rifle Divisions were defeated and withdrawn to the southeast. Grodno was burning.

The result was expressed in a report from the commander of the IX Army Corps, General of Infantry Geyer, which was transmitted to the army commander on the evening of 6/22:

Chapter 3: The Attack

"The troops were assisted in their commerce with the population by German speaking prisoners of war. ... In other locations, there was no interaction with the population, because they could not understand each other and because the German soldiers did not understand the customs of the land and people. In addition, there are many demoralized people everywhere. The pressure of the demoralized is increasing, many of the houses have burned down. ...In many of the former Polish areas, the German soldiers were greeted as liberators. However, even in old Russia, they come with flowers and friendly greetings. ..."

The second day of the war began as the previous did. In the very early morning, the combat and reconnaissance aircraft took off, the reconnaissance squadrons set in march, and the batteries fired their early morning greetings where the enemy was believed to be.

The army group attacked along the entire width of the front.

The 2nd Panzer Group of Generaloberst Guderian not only covered the right flank, but also advanced quickly on the roads east of Brest-Litovsk, in order to get to Smolensk as quickly as possible.

The greatest success of this day belonged to the XXIV Motorized Army Corps on the right. The 3rd and 4th Panzer Divisions attacked vehemently. The lead groups of the division of Lieutenant General Model reached Kobryn at 1100 hours. Here, only yesterday, was located the headquarters of the 4th Soviet Army. The first tank battle occurred on this sector, as the Soviet XIV Mechanized Corps (Major General Oborin) launched a counterattack. However, after losing 36 "T-26's", the Soviets withdrew. Model gave his soldiers only one order: "Forward!" In the evening, the advance detachment, under Major Biegel (commander of the 39th Engineer Battalion), stood in the Szczara sector. On 6/23, Model's tanks destroyed a total of 107 Russian combat vehicles and found itself located 150 kilometers east of the border. An incredible achievement! Major Biegel was the first officer in Army Group Center to receive the Knight's Cross for this action.

The 2nd Panzer Group attacked deep into the enemy's front, and thereby advanced into the rear of the defenses in the Bialystok bend. The Russian leadership realized this fatal situation and ordered a breakout. This occurred

Army Group Center

on 6/24, with the full weight on the left flank of the XLVII Motorized Army Corps. Soviet armored combat vehicles broke through the thin German security lines and advanced to Slonim.

The news caused a great sensation at Führer Headquarters. For the first time in this campaign, Hitler was nervous. His entourage thought that he was going to issue another order to halt, like he did at Dunkirk.

The 3rd Panzer Group of Generaloberst Hoth received the following mission for this offensive:

> "The 3rd Panzer Group, subordinated to Army Group Center, breaks through the enemy's border forces in the area north of Grodno in cooperation with the 9th Army and, by quickly advancing into the region north of Minsk, makes contact with the 2nd Panzer Group, which is advancing on Minsk from the southwest, to create conditions for the destruction of those forces located in the Bialystok and Minsk region."

On 6/22, the panzer group set out with the XXXIX Motorized Army Corps along the Suvalki-Olita road. Here, the Nieman was forced by the 7th and 20th Panzer Divisions, while the V Army Corps and the 12th Panzer Division also crossed the river south of there. Contact between the right flanking armies of the Western Military District and the troops in northern Russian was thereby severed. The main Soviet positions north of Grodno were outflanked. The panzer group attacked further to the east, encircling enemy forces in the forest and marsh region of the Puszca-Rudnika. The left flank penetrated to the north.

On the morning of 7/24, the soldiers of the 7th Panzer Division (in the Western Campaign, they had earned the name "Phantom Division") stood in front of the former capital of Lithuania, Vilnius. The division attacked from the move. The 7th Motorcycle Battalion, under Major von Steinkeller, advanced to the airfield at 0300 hours in the morning, captured 50 enemy aircraft, and entered the city at 0500 hours. The population greeted our troops with enthusiasm, threw flowers, and offered drinks.

The Soviet divisions in front of the left flank of the army group were defeated!

Chapter 3: The Attack

The panzer group, however, could not rest.

The 25th Panzer Regiment (Colonel Rothenburg) and the 1/6 Infantry Regiment (Major Stroebe) formed the new lead element. Both units reached the Minsk-Moscow highway 20 kilometers northeast of Minsk in a forced march on the night of 6/25 at 2200 hours!

Field Marshal von Bock believed he could utilize the favorable situation and wanted to divert the panzer group directly to Polozk. Then the OKH interfered. It categorically ordered the panzer group be held on the high ground near Minsk, in order to await the 2nd Panzer Group to close ranks. The OKH further instructed the army group commander to continue the operation only on special orders of the OKH. Field Marshal von Kluge was to take command of both panzer groups.

Therefore, the army group's first phase had ended within three days. Now they had to regroup and draft new plans. They did not want to give the Soviets any time to react...

The Russian leadership did not have time. They were still suffering from the shock of the powerful Wehrmacht attack. The first 72 hours of the war bought only defeat on the entire front. Foreign Commissar Molotov gave a harmonious speech that did not concur with the actual events of 6/22. He said:

> "The government requires that you rally to the Bolshevik Party, in order to protect the Soviet government and its great leader Stalin. Our cause is just. The enemy will be destroyed..."

However, on this day, Soviet troops were being severely beaten. The V Soviet Rifle Corps gave up its positions near Bialystok, and the VI Cavalry Corps had to withdraw to the east. The entire northern flank of the Western Military District was shaken on the first day of the war. The commander, Army General Pavlov, had no information on the situation of his armies. Somehow he knew that his 10th Army was the most threatened. Therefore, he dispatched his 1st General Staff Officer, Colonel Boldin, to Bialystok by plane. When the colonel landed, he got caught up in the panic of the fleeing army. He arrived at the headquarters during the evening and passed on the categorical order to counterattack.

Army Group Center

Major General Golubev, the commander of the 10th Army, transmitted this order to his corps over radio. He could not carry it out. Indeed, Russian regiments did set out from several locations – as far as the commissars could force them. Then they ran into the German 4th Army. The XIII Mechanized Corps (Major General Akhlyustin) was destroyed in the meeting and forced to withdraw. The counterattack of the 10th Army was over before it began.

On 6/23, the center of the Soviet front was in retreat.

The day before, the southern flank was torn by the 2nd Panzer Group. Guderian's tanks rolled over the 6th, 42nd, 49th, and 75th Rifle Divisions, destroyed the counterattack of the XIV Mechanized Corps near Kobryn, and gained freedom of maneuver on the Brest-Litovsk-Smolensk rollbahn.

On 6/23, on the basis of the alarming reports from all sectors of the front, the government in Moscow decided to reorganize the senior commands. The formation of a Supreme Command of the Armed Forces (STAVKA) was ordered. Marshal Timoshenko took command of this high post; Army General Zhukov was named as his deputy and Chief of the General Staff.

On 6/23, the STAVKA issued its first instructions to coordinate the various frontal sectors. The commander of the Western Military District was ordered to immediately launch a counterattack. Moscow ordered attacks in two directions, in order to stop Army Group Center or to at least harass it. The first attack was to be in the direction of Lublin, the second in the direction of Suvalki.

Army General Pavlov ordered the main effort be in the Grodno area. In addition, he deployed the XI Mechanized Corps (Major General Khazkelevich) and the VI Cavalry Corps (Major General Nikitin) during the night. As the morning of 6/24 dawned, only the XI Mechanized Corps attacked. The VI Cavalry Corps was dispersed by German combat aircraft, whereby the 6th and 36th Cavalry Divisions suffered so many losses that they were no longer combat capable.

Army General Pavlov then ordered the suspension of the attack. The 3rd and 10th Soviet Armies withdrew to a line Lida-Slonim-Pinsk.

The front of the Western Military District had lost its striking power. Marshal Timoshenko established a new army command near Minsk. The

Chapter 3: The Attack

13th Army command (Lieutenant General Filatov) received troops from reserve formations of the "Red Army." Its mission was to prevent the collapse of the Military District!

The only bright spot for Moscow during these turbulent days was the exemplary combat of the defenders of Brest-Litovsk. Elements of the 6th and 42nd Rifle Divisions could not hold off the attack of the 45th German ID and withdrew into the citadel of the fortress. Here they dug in behind the strong walls that held up to shells and even stuka bombs. Captain Zubachev and regimental commander Fomin took command in the citadel.

The three regiments of the 45th ID conducted bitter and costly combat for each square meter of ground in the old fortress during the first week of the war. These days did not agree with the term "War of Flowers" used to describe this campaign. Artillery fire and bombing attacks broke off one piece after another from the citadel. On 6/29, seven "Ju-88's" of the 3rd Combat Squadron attacked the eastern front of the position with 1800 kilogram bombs, and the resistance of the Russian defenders collapsed. 400 men surrendered. However, combat continued within the citadel. Fanatic officers and commissars barricaded themselves within the officers' club building. These were men from the 44th Rifle Regiment, under Major Gavrilov, and they surrendered after they were dead.

The battle for Brest-Litovsk was over on 6/30. 7000 Russians were captured by the Germans. The losses, however, of the 45th ID were equally as heavy. The Austrian regiments lost 40 officers and 442 men dead and 1000 wounded during this battle.

The front, meanwhile, stood between 150 and 200 kilometers further to the east.

The wedges of the two panzer groups raged deep into Russian territory. The majority of the Western Military District was encircled in the Bialystok area. The advanced panzer divisions closed the encirclement themselves. Now it was the job of the infantry divisions of the 4th Army (Field Marshal von Kluge) and the 9th Army (Generaloberst Strauss) to reinforce the ring and make the breakout of the Russians impossible.

The infantrymen had accomplished considerable marches during the past few days, which were complicated by the searing heat of the summer sun and the dry dust of the roads.

Army Group Center

The OKH then decided that the Bialystok pocket must first be eliminated, while Field Marshal von Bock wanted to yield to the pressure of his panzer generals. The OKH, naturally, won out. Therefore, the panzer forces of the army group remained in position from 6/25, so that the infantry divisions could catch up and finish the battle in the pocket.

The Soviet divisions tried to break out of the encirclement in all directions. The German army corps, therefore, had to repulse strong attacks. The VIII Army Corps was able to hold northwest of Novogrudek. On the other hand, the situation on the south of the pocket came to a head. There, the Soviet 10th Army wanted to break through to Slonim. The encirclement front here was still not solid because, at that moment, only the XLVII Motorized Army Corps (General of Panzer Troops Lemelsen) was deployed there on a wide front. The Soviet breakout attempt hit on 6/25 with its full weight on the 17th Panzer Division (Lieutenant General von Arnim), which held on with much difficulty. After the deployment of the 29th Motorized Infantry Division (Lieutenant General von Boltenstern) the crisis was resolved. The XII Army Corps (General of Infantry Schroth), which followed behind the motorized corps, was still tied up in combat on the Tselvianka. The encirclement front solidified quickly only on the extreme western tip of Bialystok. From north to south stood the XX, XLII, and VII Army Corps on a solid front, and they slowly pressed the encircled enemy forces to the east.

The OKH continued to concentrate on the pocket. In the three encircled armies it saw a latent threat to the far advanced panzer groups, which, for the three days of the war, had no contact with the neighboring armies in the south and the north.

Therefore, on 6/25, the OKH established the 2nd Army command, under Generaloberst Baron von Weichs, as the senior command authority for the encirclement front. The 2nd Army command was now responsible for the battles at Bialystok-Novogrudek. The 4th and 9th Armies were released from their former missions and could now devote their energies to pursuing their infantry divisions in the Minsk-Smolensk direction.

The 9th Army immediately set its two corps in march to the east in the direction of Lida-Vilnius. The VI Army Corps (General of Engineers

Chapter 3: The Attack

Foerster) followed the XXXIX Motorized Army Corps with the 26th (in the north) and 6th ID (in the south). The V Army Corps followed with the 35th and 5th ID. Nevertheless, on 6/26, the 5th ID (Major General Allmendinger) had to be diverted to the south when the Soviets tried to break out of the Bialystok pocket to the northeast.

On the evening of 6/26, it was established that the enemy's breakout attempts were disconnected and being conducted without a unified command. The first indications of demoralization were noticeable, and more and more deserters reported to the German troops. Many of them brought their personal weapons with them. In addition, the enemy was suffering from supply problems.

The OKH realized that the pocket no longer represented a threat to the panzer groups and gave its permission for their further commitment.

The newly committed 13th Soviet Army entered an assembly area on either side of Minsk with the II, XLIV Rifle Corps and XX Mechanized Corps. However, before its divisions were ready, the panzers were there! The XXXIX Motorized Army Corps (General of Panzer Troops Schmidt) penetrated from the north toward Minsk. The enemy withdrew to Borissov. The 7th Panzer Division (Lieutenant General Baron von Funk) pursued them. Colonel Rothenburg fell here. The two remaining divisions of the corps – 14th Motorized Infantry Division (Major General Krause) and the 20th Panzer Division (Lieutenant General Stumpff) – attacked to the south. Before the eyes of the German reconnaissance battalions appeared the towers of the capital of Belorussia.

The army group continued the attack. The 2nd Air Command committed a reconnaissance squadron to establish whether the Russians would defend in the Orsha-Vitebsk-Smolensk area. On the morning of 6/26 at 1130 hours, the army group command ordered the two panzer groups to attack with the majority of their formations as quickly as they could toward Minsk to encircle the Soviet formations located to the west of there – this would take care of almost all of the remaining combat capable formations of the Western Military District.

The 12th and 20th Panzer Divisions (Lieutenant Colonel Stumpff) approached Minsk from the north, while the lead elements of the 2nd Panzer

Army Group Center

Group advanced from the south. On 6/27, the 17th Panzer Division (Lieutenant General von Arnim) reached the southern edge of Minsk with its advance detachment. The 12th Panzer Division of Major General Harpe was the first German division to enter the Belorussian capital. On the next day, the Reich battle flag flew from the city's towers.

The flank protection of the two panzer groups was handled independently, even though the main effort changed.

In the north, the 20th Motorized Infantry Division (Major General Zorn) covered the left flank of the 3rd Panzer Group alone east of Vilnius. The 900th Training Brigade was inserted next to them by the OKH. The XXIV Motorized Army Corps (General of Panzer Troops Baron Geyr von Schweppenburg) secured in the south. An unexpected breakthrough occurred here. On 6/26, the 3rd Panzer Division captured the heavily defended Sluzk and, therefore, stood 300 kilometers east of the Reich border! Lieutenant General Model gave his soldiers no rest. He continued to drive the division forward. Two days later, the men of the 6th Panzer Regiment, under Lieutenant Colonel von Lewinsky, raised their flag on the Bobruisk citadel. The Berezina was reached!

Moscow recognized the terrible danger on their central sector. The STAVKA immediately ordered the formation of new combat units, committed militia formations, and gathered all available troops from the interior of central Russia. The army group "Reserve Front" was organized under Marshal Budenny. The Marshal established his headquarters in Smolensk. He had three new armies. They were the 16th, 24th, and 28th Armies. They were ordered to occupy and secure the Polozk-Vitebsk-Orsha-Dnepr sector.

If the Soviets were able to effectively reinforce this line, then they would have been able to stop the offensive of Army Group Center. The front of Army Group Center was still widely dispersed at this time, because only its motorized divisions were advancing to the east. The majority of the infantry divisions were still committed on the pocket front near Bialystok, Novogrudek, Minsk, and west of Slonim.

The dispositions of Army Group Center reflected the following picture on the evening of 6/28:

Chapter 3: The Attack

The 3rd Panzer Group stood on either side of Minsk with the XXXIX Motorized Army Corps and continued to attack. On the other hand, the LVII Motorized Army Corps had to cover the pocket front northeast of Novogrudek with its three divisions (from left to right: 12th and 19th Panzer Divisions, and 18th Motorized Infantry Division). Here attacked the remnants of the 3rd and 4th Soviet Armies, in an attempt to break through to the northeast. Behind the LVII Motorized Army Corps marched the VI Army Corps (6th and 26th ID) and the V Army Corps, which had already penetrated to the south with the 5th ID.

The wide bend of the pocket ran to the corner of Bialystok, which was occupied by elements of the 23rd (Major general Hellmich) and 87th ID (Lieutenant General von Studnitz). The front was held from left to right by: VIII Army Corps (161st, 28th, 8th ID), XX Army Corps (256th, 162nd, 102nd ID), XLII Army Corps (87th, 23rd ID), VII Army Corps (7th, 268th ID), and the IX Army Corps (137th, 292nd ID).

The pocket front between the Szczara sector and Minsk was not so thickly occupied. On this almost 150 kilometer wide front stood only the XII Army Corps, with the 29th Motorized Infantry Division and the 34th ID at this time.

The second, smaller pocket during these first days of the war was formed west of Slonim. Here the XVII and XLII Army Corps were committed with (from left to right): 17th, 78th, 134th, 131st, 45th, and 31st ID.

The 2nd Panzer Group no longer participated in the pocket battles. Its northern corps – XLVII Motorized Army Corps with the 17th, 18th Panzer Divisions, and 10th Motorized Infantry Division – found itself advancing south of Minsk. The right corps – XXIV Motorized Army Corps, with the 4th and 3rd Panzer Divisions – marched to the Berezina. The 1st Cavalry Division penetrated into the marshes of the Pripet.

In light of this situation – the motorized troops advancing forward, while the infantry divisions remained tied down – the army group ordered all available reserve formations to the east. The LIII Army Corps was ordered to the south as flank protection. The XLVI Motorized Army Corps followed the 2nd Panzer Group with the 10th Panzer Division, 60th Motorized Infantry Division, and the SS Division "Das Reich." The 258th, 252nd,

Army Group Center

and 167th ID were rushed to the pocket west of Slonim. The 129th ID was inserted between the XX and VIII Army Corps.

The battle in the thick forest region east and southeast of Bialystok made enormous demands on both sides. It proved that the Russians were already masters in camouflage and were able to always find gaps through which they could slip away. The troops suffered considerable losses. During this time, losses totaled, for example: 340 men from the 78th, 550 from the 292nd, 650 from the 263rd, and 700 men from the 137th ID!

However, slowly the pocket front was compressed. The encircled Soviets began to suffer from the shortage of ammunition and rations. The lack of discipline lead to panic. The soldiers of the 12th, 89th, and 103rd Rifle Divisions shot their commissars and crossed over to the Germans.

A special report of the OKW for 6/29 read:

"In spite of hopeless breakthrough attempts, the ring of German armies drew narrower. In a few days, two Soviet armies either surrendered or were destroyed!"

That was the balance sheet for Army Group Center after the first week of the Eastern Campaign.

Luftflotte 2 did not let the Army down.

Field Marshal Kesselring, who directed the commitment of the Luftflotte from his command train near Brest-Litovsk, had two air corps available, which were the most successful in the Luftwaffe. The II Air Corps (General of Aviation Loerzer) had previously crossed swords with the Royal Air Force at the Channel. The VIII Air Corps – the close combat corps – of General of Aviation Baron von Richthofen previously fought in the Balkans and in Crete. It deserves credit for a considerable portion of the success of the Balkan campaign. The I Air Defense Corps (Lieutenant General von Axthelm) supported both panzer groups.

The commitment of the two air corps has to be considered independently from the ground operations. It was not only the mission of the air formations to eliminate the Soviet Air Force early on, but also bomb the way clear to the east for the motorized divisions.

Chapter 3: The Attack

The first mission: Destruction of the enemy Air Force, was executed with great success in the first hours of the campaign. The Russian airfields near the front were destroyed by bombing as the German infantrymen approached. The Russian fighter and combat aircraft were shot down in great numbers by the experienced German fighter pilots. The enemy's tactics changed at the end of June. Then the Soviet combat aircraft flew in tighter formations with considerable fighter cover and enjoyed success against the columns of the army group.

The air combat was different than either that of the Western Campaign or the air battle for England. The greatest success for the German fighters was on 6/30 in the air battle over Minsk. Soviet combat, fighter-bomber, and fighter aircraft tried to help their formations, which were located west of Minsk, to break out. The 51st Fighter Squadron under Colonel Moelders shot down the groups of aircraft with the red stars. As the day ended, the 51st Fighter Squadron had shot down a total of 114 enemy aircraft and registered its 1000th air victory. Captain Joppien and Lieutenant Baer were the most successful pilots on this day with enemies shot down each. Colonel Moelders shot down two Russians.

The support of the ground troops – the second mission of the Luftflotte – was arranged so that the VIII Air Corps was active in the 3rd Panzer Group sector. The II Air Corps formed a special combat group under Colonel Fiebig for commitment in the 2nd Panzer Group area of operations.

The formations of the I Air Defense Corps served independently in the front line of the air defense. Thus were they committed and thus did the regiments of Lieutenant General von Axthelm shoot down their first 28 aircraft by 6/25. However, more and more the air defense batteries proved to be of considerable help to the infantry during the counterattacks of motorized Soviet forces. By 7/11, the air defense corps had shoot down a total of 100 aircraft and, during the same period of time, had reported the destruction of 100 enemy armored combat vehicles.

The month of June slowly came to an end. The Soviet Union and its "Red Army" had suffered great setbacks, and the German leadership had believed that the campaign was already half won. The Soviets were not defeated! They found the time, opportunity, and men to reorganize their formations, refit them, and direct them to battle.

Army Group Center

On 6/28, Moscow named the commander of the 1st Far Eastern Army, Lieutenant General Yeremenko, as commander of the Western Military District. Lieutenant General Malandin was assigned as the new Chief of Staff. Lieutenant General Yeremenko relieved his predecessor at his headquarters near Mogilev. The first meeting was conducted by the new commander in the presence of Marshal Voroshilov and the capable Chief of the General Staff, Colonel General Shaposhnikov, as well as the Secretary of the Central Committee of the Communist Party of Belorussia, Ponomarenko. General Yeremenko's first order was short and to the point:

"Halt on the Berezina and defend!"

This order was transmitted to the troops at the same time that Hitler was considering the continuation of operations by Army Group Center in his far off East Prussian headquarters. The OKH itself was against a continued advance to the east, and the Chief of the General Staff Halder proposed on 6/30 that, after Smolensk was reached, the tanks of the army group had to be diverted north, because the infantry corps could reach Moscow on their own!

The Soviet leadership concentrated new formations in the Smolensk-Orsha-Mogilev area, while the German leadership was still not sure as to how to continue the campaign!

The Army Group Center commander hoped to relieve the insecurity of the OKH by turning the command of the two panzer groups over to Field Marshal von Kluge (against the will of Generalobersts Hoth and Guderian!), in order to centralize the direction of the motorized forces under one command to the Dnepr. Then the army group command would have the time to concentrate on eliminating the pockets behind the front.

The battle for the Bialystok pocket came to an end on 7/2. Enemy forces still held out, however, in the Novogrudek-Volkovysk area. Here the Soviets continuously tried to break out to the east. At some points things had reached a crisis, but they were mastered when the entire V Army Corps and the 900th Training Brigade, which had just arrived from Vilnius, were committed. The Russians surrendered on 7/5.

Chapter 3: The Attack

Field Marshal von Bock issued the following order of the day from his new headquarters in Baranovichi:

"Commander
Army Group Center Headquarters, 7/8/1941

Order of the Day
The double battles of Bialystok and Minsk are over. The army group combated 3 Russian armies in the strength of approximately 32 rifle, 8 tank divisions, 6 motor-mechanized brigades, and 3 cavalry divisions. Of these, the following were destroyed:

22 rifle divisions
7 tank divisions
6 motor-mechanized brigades
3 cavalry divisions

The remaining units, that were able to avoid encirclement, have weakened combat strengths.
The bloody losses of the enemy are very high. The number of prisoners and captured equipment as of yesterday is:

287,704 prisoners, including several corps and division commanders
2,585 captured and destroyed tanks, including heavy combat vehicles
1,449 guns
245 captured aircraft...
Our own losses were not so high.

This success, achieved against a strong enemy, who often fought bitterly to the last man, is thanks to your courage and bravery!
...Now we must take advantage of this victory! I know that the army group will make further efforts; we cannot rest before complete victory is achieved!"

Army Group Center

The termination of this major pocket battle marked the end of the first phase of the campaign. Now Soviet resistance stiffened throughout. In addition, it began to rain during the beginning of July. Therefore, a new enemy showed up that had not been anticipated by the German General Staff: rain and mud!

Still, the advance continued without pause.

The panzer groups attacked into the depth of Russian territory, while in the west the infantry divisions regrouped after the end of the pocket battle. The army group command established a supply center for 73,000 tons of goods in Minsk under the Oberquartiermeister of the 4th Army, Lieutenant Colonel Krumpelt; this was a five-day supply of fuel, rations, and ammunition.

The 3rd Panzer Group was ordered to advance its two corps from Minsk to the northeast, in order to establish contact with the right flank of Army Group North and, at the same time, open the way for the neighboring army group to the east. The 2nd Panzer Group, on the other hand, advanced to the east toward the Dnepr.

However, the Soviets did not waste the time the Germans allowed them. Their informant in Switzerland reported on 7/2:

> "German Operation Plan I, with the objective of Moscow, is still valid. Flanking operations are a diversion, the main effort lies on the central front."

The Moscow government took rigorous measures to reinforce the defenses on the central sector. The failures of its military commanders were severely punished. The commander of the 4th Army, Major General Korobkov, who escaped from the pocket, was court-martialed with several other commanding generals, condemned to death, and hanged.

Marshal Timoshenko himself took command of the Western Military District. Marshal Budenny and Lieutenant General Yeremenko were his deputies. Therefore, the former defense minister of the USSR had received unlimited powers. He could rely on his experience and his ability to access

Chapter 3: The Attack

all military equipment and reserves and committing them all in the battle against Army Group Center.

On 7/3, Stalin gave his first speech on the radio since the beginning of the war, and in it he explained:

> "The enemy is pitiless. He is determined to occupy our territory, take our grain, use our oil, the fruits of all our labor. ...
>
> The life and death of the Soviet state is at stake, the life and death of the people of the Soviet Union; this will determine whether the people of the Soviet Union will be free or enslaved. It is necessary for the men of the Soviet Union to be concerned with mobilizing themselves and all of their labor for war, they must show no compassion for the enemy!"

These demands on the people of the Soviet Union – the Ukrainians, Belorussians, Lithuanians, Uzbekians, Armenians, etc. – to defend their homeland was, at the same time, used to strengthen the will of the soldiers to resist on all frontal sectors. An order of the day from Stalin, issued on the same day, was distinguished by some noteworthy sentences (which were also written by Hitler four years later):

> "... We must take all of the railroad rolling stock with us. ... Not one kilo of corn, not one liter of fuel must fall into the hands of the enemy. ... Anything of value, metal, grain and oil, must be destroyed if it cannot be withdrawn."

The commander of the two panzer groups pressed on to reach the new objectives of the Dnepr and Duena as quickly as possible. Field Marshal von Kluge, the commander, was not enthusiastic about these plans. Nevertheless, he had to give in when the forward battalions reached the river bank and established bridgeheads.

The 2nd Panzer Group in the south of the army group front committed the XXIV Motorized Army Corps through Bobruisk in the direction of Mogilev. On 6/30, the 3rd Panzer Group reached the east bank of the

Army Group Center

Berezina. Lieutenant General Model immediately continued the attack. Three days later, the tanks of the 6th Panzer Regiment waded the Drut, and the infantrymen of the 3rd and 394th Regiments assaulted Rogachev, reached the Dnepr, and crossed the river. The first bridgehead was, however, destroyed by the enemy. A second bridgehead, which was established on the following day, could also not be held. The enemy counterattacked.

The XLVII Motorized Army Corps was moved from Baranovichi to Minsk and from there to attack along the highway to Smolensk. The 18th Panzer Division (Major General Nehring) formed the lead element. Their 3/18 Panzer Regiment (Major Teege) and elements of the 52nd Infantry Regiment (Colonel Jollasse) captured the undamaged Berezina bridge near Borissov in a daring raid. Therefore, the departure base for an attack into the Smolensk area was won.

The 3rd Panzer Group was also committed from the Minsk-Moledechno area to the northeast. The XXXIX Motorized Army Corps reached the east bank of the Berezina west of Lepel on 7/3 with the advanced 7th Panzer Division after heavy combat, and the 20th Panzer Division was following close behind. Further to the north, the LVII Motorized Army Corps broke through between Molodechno and Vileka. Its 18th Motorized Infantry Division (Major General Herrlein) approached Polozk on 7/3, while to the northwest, the 19th Panzer Division (Lieutenant General von Knobelsdorff) approached the Dissna.

It also appeared here that the enemy was getting stronger, and the LVII Motorized Army Corps had to stop. Only the 7th Panzer Division was able to make it through Lepel to the lake passage near Senno, where they were attacked by strong enemy forces from Vitebsk. Now all of the lead panzer elements ran into enemy forces that were locally superior in men and material, and the divisions, which had been in combat for a week – the 3rd Panzer Group, for example, only had 50% of its vehicles available – were in trouble.

In the meantime, Marshal Timoshenko was able to construct a new front between the Duena and the Dnepr. He had realized that the worst threat to his sector was in the Polozk-Orsha area. Here he committed the majority of his newly arrived forces. The 22nd Army, under Major General Yershakov, took over the sector on either side of Polozk. The 20th Army,

Chapter 3: The Attack

under Major General Kurochkin, joined ranks at Orsha. The 21st Army (Lieutenant General Yefremov) was established at Mogilev. However, that was not enough for Timoshenko. He formed a new 16th Army, under Lieutenant General Lukin, in the Smolensk area, which was considered a reserve army. Additionally, he summoned the 19th Army, under Lieutenant General Konev, from the southern sector of the Eastern Front into the Vitebsk area. Therefore, he had closed the front!

Then he ordered a counterattack!

The 22nd Army committed the V Mechanized Corps, with 300 tanks, and the VII Mechanized Corps, with 400 tanks, to attack against the 3rd Panzer Group. Here it appeared that the breakthrough of the 7th Panzer Division had located the seam between the 22nd and the 20th Armies. The attack of the superior Russian forces had a severe effect on the XLVII German Motorized Army Corps. The 17th and 18th Panzer Divisions were not only stopped, but thrown back. On the Soviet side, the 1st Motorized Rifle Division, under Major General Kreiser, particularly distinguished itself. This division, with its "T-34's" – against which there was still no defense – gave the 18th Panzer Division a hard time for several days near Borissov.

Luckily, German aircraft arrived in the nick of time and helped the panzer divisions. The II Group of the Training Squadron under the command of Senior Lieutenant Meyer – at this time, the only fighter-bomber group in the Luftwaffe – attacked the "T-34's" that had broken through and drove them into the marsh. During this first major attack of aircraft against tanks, 47 "T-34's" and "Kv-I's" were destroyed!

Now the German panzer divisions transitioned to the counterattack themselves. They were able to partially surround the V Mechanized Corps and destroy it. However, the threat was still not eliminated. The 19th Army now hit the battlefield from the Ukraine. The XXIII Mechanized Corps advanced on the hills southwest of Vitebsk. However, it was boxed in by the Luftwaffe, stopped, and destroyed. Thus, the last Soviet attack in the north collapsed.

What was happening in the south?

Here, the Soviets registered a surprise success. The Russian attack – particularly that of the 117th Rifle Division – was directed against the 10th Motorized Infantry Division, which had penetrated into the Shlobin area.

Army Group Center

They were to cover the right flank of the panzer group. They had to withdraw before the superior attack of the enemy. Nevertheless, the neighboring 3rd Panzer Division was able to clear up the situation, under heavy losses, and re-conquer Shlobin. In this manner, the 1/6 Panzer Regiment alone had lost 22 combat vehicles. The advance of the XXIV Motorized Army Corps had to be halted. The corps could not advance any further at this location and had to withdraw behind the Dnepr. In contrast, the 4th Panzer Division (Major General Baron von Langermann und Erlencamp) anticipated crossing the river northeast of Bobruisk near Stariy Bykhov and gaining ground to the east.

Therefore, the Soviet counterattack had failed here.

Marshal Timoshenko still did not give up the battle for lost.

On 7/10, Moscow again reorganized its entire army. Now three command authorities were inserted, which were responsible for the center, the north, and the south of the vast front. Marshal Timoshenko took command of the central sector – designated as the "Western Front" by the Russians. His deputy remained Lieutenant General Yeremenko. Lieutenant General Malandin held the post of Chief of the General Staff. The political leadership was taken up by member of the Central Committee of the Communist Party of the Soviet Union Bulganin, the later President of the USSR.

The Soviet Army Group "Western Front" was organized as follows on 7/10/1941:

Right flank:
22nd Army (Major General Yershakov) with LI and LXII Rifle Corps;

Center of the front:
20th Army (Lieutenant General Kurochkin) with II, XX, LXIX Rifle Corps, V and VII Mechanized Corps;
19th Army (Lieutenant General Konev) with XLIII Rifle Corps;
13th Army (Lieutenant General Remesov, from 14/7 Lieutenant General Gerassimenko) with XX Mechanized Corps;

Chapter 3: The Attack

Left flank:
21st Army (Colonel General Kuznetsov) with LXIII, LXVI and LXVII Rifle Corps.

Reserve:
4th Army near Krichev;
16th Army (Lieutenant General Lukin) near Smolensk.

The air formations of the "Red Army" – the Soviet Air Force was not a separate branch of service – in the area of Army Group "West Front" were subordinated to Colonel Naumenko. On 7/10, he had 339 combat and fighter aircraft available.

Marshal Timoshenko issued an order of the day to his armies, which ended with the words: "Anyone who retreats will be shot!"

He could not stop the catastrophe. It was too late! The tanks of Generaloberst Hoth had found a gap through which they advanced on a wide front to the Duena. The 22nd Soviet Army, which was to defend between Idritsa and Vitebsk, could not hold the lake passage near Sebezh, in spite of a gallant defense. Thus, the divisions of the XXXIX and LVII Motorized Army Corps reached the foreground of the Duena on 7/8.

Stuka attacks smashed the temporary fortifications of the so-called "Stalin line" in front of the river. The main effort lay here in the Ulla area, west of Vitebsk. The XXXIX Motorized Army Corps (General of Panzer Troops Schmidt) crossed the Duena on 7/8 at 1000 hours. The 20th Panzer Division (Lieutenant General Stumpff) was the first division of the army group to cross the river, and the 18th and 20th Motorized Infantry Divisions followed.

The 20th Panzer Division penetrated directly northeast of Ulla along the Polozk-Vitebsk railroad to the southeast and, on the following morning, reached Vitebsk, which was burning from being hit by hundreds of bombs. The advance detachment of the division, under Senior Lieutenant Sahmel (2nd Company of the 21st Panzer Regiment) entered Vitebsk along with elements of the 92nd Anti-tank Battalion and the 92nd Motorcycle Battalion.

Army Group Center

On 7/10, the XXXIX Motorized Army Corps stood on the north bank of the Duena with two divisions. The 20th Motorized Infantry Division was crossing and the 7th Panzer Division reached the high ground south of Vitebsk.

Therefore, the Duena block of the Soviet "West Front" was breached. At the same time as the XXXIX Motorized Army Corps, the LVII Motorized Army Corps approached the Duena near Dissna. Directly behind them followed the XXIII and VI Army Corps. The latter was stopped by heavy enemy resistance in front of Polozk. Nevertheless, the enemy's resistance had decreased noticeably. The majority of the 22nd Soviet Army began withdrawing across the Duena.

The first operational objective of Army Group Center appeared to have been achieved. The Smolensk land bridge was to be the departure base for the conquest of Moscow, but it had to be utilized before the wet weather period arrived.

Unfortunately, the two neighboring army groups did not advance as far to the east. They were still standing in front of their first operational objectives. Therefore, this posed a problem for the OKH, which eventually came up with new plans. The Chief of the General Staff of the OKH noted in his personal diary on 7/12:

> "I don't support the idea of continuing the advance of the two panzer groups to the east. I believe that Hoth must turn to the north with considerable elements, in order to fix the newly committed 19th Army and Group Nevel in the rear, and Guderian must turn to the south, in order to encircle the enemy forces on his southern flank, perhaps he should advance as far as the Kiev area..."

Nevertheless, these new ideas could not be brought to reality. The Soviets had something to say about it. The German soldier realized that the enemy's resistance stiffened from week to week. The Soviet leadership ordered its armies not to allow the German panzer forces to advance further to the east.

Lieutenant General Lukin, the commander of the 16th Army, was ordered to establish a defense of the Smolensk land bridge. On 7/13, a new

Chapter 3: The Attack

army group was formed, which was designated "Central Front." Colonel General Kuznetsov was its commander, while Colonel Sandalov was the Chief of Staff and Party Secretary Ponomarenko was the advisor. The "Central Front" was to secure the left flank of "West Front" with the 13th and 21st Armies between the Berezina and the Dnepr.

In the rear of these forces, a new "Reserve Front", under Lieutenant General Bogdanov, emerged. It had six armies and strong air forces (Major General Pogrebov). The armies deployed into the following areas (from north to south):

29th Army in the Ostachkov area
30th Army in the Velikie Luki - Rzhev area
24th Army in the Yartsevo - Viazma area
28th Army in the Briansk area
31st and 32nd Armies remained in reserve for the time being.

Therefore, it was still not over. Five additional groups were created in the threatened areas of Rosslavl, Beliy, and Yartsevo to improve combat operations. They were commanded by generals who would play a major role during the war. The commanders of these groups were: Lieutenant Generals Kalinin, Masslennikov, Kachalov, Major Generals Rokossovskiy, and Khomenko.

Moscow ordered the transition to a counterattack and the closing of the existing frontal gaps. In the north, the 22nd Army had the objective of Gorodok, the 19th Army had Vitebsk, and the 20th Army Orsha Shklov. In the south, the "Central Front" was to prevent the 2nd Panzer Group from crossing the Dnepr. In the center – in the Smolensk area – strong forces had, in the meantime, been deployed in departure positions for an offensive to the west.

The attack of the "Central Front" hit Guderian's three corps during their deployment on the Dnepr. Only the XXIV Motorized Army Corps was able to make it across the river near Stariy Bykhov. The XLVI Motorized Army Corps on the left reached the Dnepr with the SS Division "Das Reich" opposite Shklov. The XLVII Motorized Army Corps, attacking south of the highway, established a bridgehead with the 17th Panzer Division

Army Group Center

(Major General von Weber) between Kopys and Orsha, but they could not hold it.

The German troops held their river positions. On 7/13, the 17th Panzer Division destroyed 500 tanks! The front of the panzer group slowly stabilized as the infantry divisions approached from the rear. The enemy was still basically in the rear of the panzer divisions. The offensive of the 13th Soviet Army (Lieutenant General Gerassimenko) was parried at Mogilev, where three divisions – in particular the 3rd Panzer Division and the "Grossdeutschland" Motorized IR – blocked it, and it was later encircled by the VII Army Corps (General of Artillery Fahrmbacher). The battle of Mogilev lasted another week. The enemy knew he had to defend and could not be influenced by artillery nor bombs. The four divisions of the VII Army Corps – the 7th, 15th, 23rd, and 78th ID – did not give up, and, on 7/26, launched a concentrated attack. The 15th ID (Lieutenant General Hell) occupied the city on the following day.

After the attack of the 21st Soviet Army (Lieutenant General Yefremov) on Rogachev and Shlobin was stopped, Generaloberst Guderian ordered his divisions to continue the attack. Now the infantry divisions had also closed ranks on the Dnepr. The IX Army Corps (General of Infantry Geyer) was inserted on the left flank. Its 137th ID relieved the 17th Panzer Division in front of Orsha. When the 2nd and 3rd Panzer Groups gained ground to the east, the battle for Smolensk began.

The 2nd Panzer Group continued to attack the XXIV Motorized Army Corps to the east. On 7/18, the 3rd and 4th Panzer Groups reached the Sozh and the region south of Krichev. The XLVII Motorized Army Corps advanced to Orsha, which was captured by the 17th Panzer Division on 7/15. When the XLVI Motorized Army Corps made it to Kopys, forced the crossing of the Dnepr, and captured Gorki, the way to Smolensk was open.

The 29th Motorized Infantry Division (Lieutenant General von Boltenstern) was ordered to break through to Smolensk. Soldiers of the 15th and 71st Infantry Regiments, the 29th Anti-tank Battalion, and the 1/29 Artillery Regiment accomplished this mission. Indeed, they received heavy artillery fire. The infantry troops, however, were able to make it into the southwestern quarter of the city by the evening of 7/15. The battle to occupy the city began on the next morning at 0400 hours. Fierce street

Chapter 3: The Attack

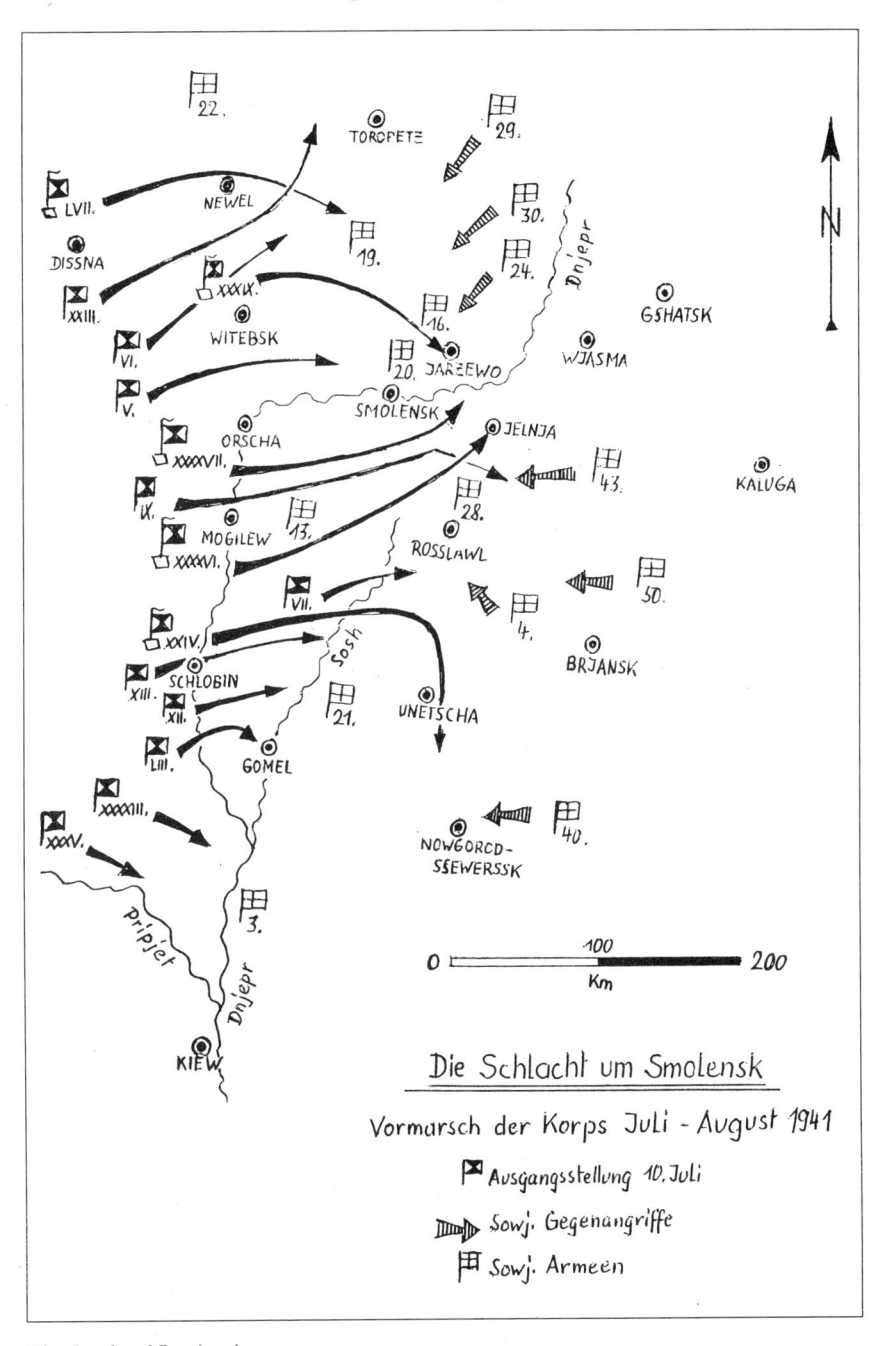

The Battle of Smolensk

battles erupted in the heavily damaged city. However, in the afternoon the Dnepr, which divides Smolensk in two, was reached and crossed. At 2000 hours, the 29th Motorized Infantry Division controlled the city!

The 2nd Panzer Group drove a wedge to the northeast into the enemy front. Now the 3rd Panzer Group came from the north, and a new pocket appeared to be forming.

The XXXIX Motorized Army Corps had thrown back the enemy and was breaking through from Vitebsk to the southeast. The last Soviet counterattack – conducted by the 1st Motorized Rifle Division of the 20th Army – did, indeed, stop the 20th Panzer Division, but the 7th Panzer Division was not hindered in its advance. Its 1/25 Panzer Regiment (Captain Schulz) and a combat group of the 7th Infantry Brigade (Colonel Baron von Boineburg) reached the Smolensk-Moscow highway near Yartsevo on 7/15.

Marshal Timoshenko had to hastily evacuate his headquarters in Yartsevo and withdraw to Viazma.

Again the majority of three Soviet armies were encircled, and elements of the 16th, 19th, and 20th Armies sat in the "trap."

Unfortunately, the encirclement front of the two panzer groups was very thin, and then their fronts were further dispersed by the OKH. The left flank of the 3rd Panzer Group was diverted to the north to assist Army Group North to advance into the Nevel passage. The LVII Motorized Army Corps could not follow the XXXIX Motorized Army Corps through Vitebsk toward Yartsevo, but had to turn 180 degrees. Luckily, on 7/15, the XXIII Army Corps had captured Polozk and, therefore, overpowered the last Soviet bridgehead on the southern bank of the Duena.

The panzer divisions – being far advanced – had to open a new battle. The infantry formations marched – often more than 150 kilometers to the rear – at quick-time. The march-route of the foot troops was just as strenuous in the year 1941 as it was 130 years before when Napoleon's armies passed over the same routes. With few exceptions, the roads had not changed much! Thus, Napoleon's regiments in 1812 had needed only 30 days longer from the border crossing to Smolensk as did the formations of the two panzer groups!

Chapter 3: The Attack

The diary of a soldier of the 5th Infantry Division describes the efforts of the Landser while advancing through the vast expanse of central Russia during these hot and dusty days:

> "We were in Belorussia. During several break periods, we had the opportunity to examine the Soviet villages. What a foreign, destitute world this was, was the thought of each soldier, as he remembered his own Schwaebisch homeland. Here, all of the houses, barns, and stalls were made of wood, most with straw roofs; they were fire traps; there were no front gardens with flowers. The houses had been unchanged for hundreds of years, there were no door handles, no window frames, no beds or chairs. Only the large stalls for the cattle in the Kolkhozes were somewhat newer. ..."

The infantry corps of the 4th Army were subordinated to the 2nd Army command, after Field Marshal von Kluge had taken command of the two panzer groups. Generaloberst Baron von Weichs was ordered to march as quickly as possible behind the panzer groups with his 2nd Arm to free up the far advanced motorized divisions for further commitment as soon as possible.

The additional instructions from the OKH, however, could not be executed until mid-July 1941. Then the battle for Smolensk developed, which is given little consideration in the German literature, while it was considered a great battle in the Soviet historical descriptions, since it was the first time that "the German Blitz was stopped."

The OKH had assigned the land bridge of Smolensk to Army Group Center as its initial operational objective, and from there an attack was to follow on Moscow, where the offensive would then turn to the north or the south, depending upon the situation. The Soviet leadership also understood these possibilities. The land bridges between the Dnepr and Duena, as well as between Orsha and Vitebsk, were the invasion routes to Moscow since antiquity.

The "Red Army" command knew that the capital of the USSR could be a battlefield by mid-July!

Army Group Center

On 7/18, Stalin ordered the formation of the "Moscow Front" (Army Group Moscow) under the command of the former commander of the Moscow Military District, Lieutenant General Artemev. To him were subordinated the newly created 32nd, 33rd, and 34th Armies. The troops of these armies, along with thousands of conscripted civilians, were committed to the construction of a defensive system in the Nudol-Lake Trostenskoe-Dorokhovo-Borovsk-Vyssokinichi area.

The situation around Smolensk, in the meantime, had considerably worsened. The 29th Motorized Infantry Division, as the lead element of the XLVII Motorized Army Corps, was still the only formation located in Smolensk, whose outer districts were tenaciously defended by the regiments of the Soviet XXXIV Rifle Corps. The 18th Panzer Division had still not arrived at Smolensk. They had been directed to the south on the highway directly west of the city, where they were engaged in fierce defensive combat with forces withdrawing from the west into the Smolensk area. The 17th Panzer Division was engaged in similarly fierce combat to their left. Their commander, Major General Ritter von Weber, fell during this combat. The division's communications battalion alone registered 31 dead in just a few days!

The Smolensk pocket was still not completely closed. Only the widely dispersed 7th Panzer Division fought on the highway near Yartsevo in the east, while the 20th Motorized Infantry Division and 12th Panzer Division held the pocket front on an almost 80 kilometer wide front from southeast of Demidov to Rudnya. The 3rd Panzer Group had to divert the rest of its divisions to protect these forces to the northeast. Thus, the 20th Panzer Division was fighting on practically four sides in the Prechistoe area, the 18th Motorized Infantry Division marched on Kresty, and the 900th Training Brigade advanced toward Demidov. Because the LVII Motorized Army Corps was tied up far to the north in the Nevel-Velikie Luki sector, it was unavailable for the battle for Smolensk.

Thus, on the evening of 7/18, six German divisions were in combat with 12 encircled Soviet divisions!

Then the Russian attack to liberate Smolensk broke loose! Lieutenant General Yeremenko concentrated all available divisions and brigades and,

Chapter 3: The Attack

on 7/18, launched them in an attack to the west. Their objective was the liberation of the encircled forces of the 16th, 19th, and 20th Soviet Armies! Because only the 29th Motorized Infantry Division was deployed around and near Smolensk, a decisive defense could not be organized to counter these superior forces. In spite of this, the German soldiers fought in their positions.

The 129th Soviet Rifle Division (Major General Gorodnyanski) and the 57th Tank Brigade (Colonel Mishulin) reached Smolensk, captured several blocks of houses in fierce combat, and broke through to the encircled troops!

This success compelled Moscow to name Lieutenant General Yeremenko commander of the "West Front" (Chief of Staff Lieutenant General Malandin), in order to guarantee a unified command in the Smolensk area.

However, General Yeremenko had already reached the zenith of his success.

The German infantry Divisions and panzer forces were now being quickly double-timed to the Smolensk area to relieve the German forces and choke off the Soviet attack with a counterattack. The 2nd and 3rd Panzer Groups approached ever closer, as did the army corps.

The V Army Corps (General of Infantry Ruoff) was the first to reach the battlefield from Vitebsk (Here, on 7/16, Stalin's son, Yakob Dzhugavili, was taken prisoner. He was a senior lieutenant and chief of a battery in the VIII Soviet Rifle Corps). The 5th ID and the 35th ID launched a concentrated attack on Rudnya, in order to relieve the 12th Panzer Division.

The enemy recognized the threat posed by this attack and threw the 23rd, 46th, 134th, 144th, 153rd, and 229th Rifle Divisions against the two German divisions. The battle here was fiercely fought around individual strong points, and it reminded older officers of the battles during the 1st World War. The 5th ID alone, in five days, lost 91 dead, 306 wounded, and 3 missing.

Slowly, the German front was reinforced around the pocket. The VIII Army Corps (General of Artillery Heitz) had closed ranks along the highway from the west. The 8th ID (Major General Hoehne) closed the pocket directly on the highway, while the 137th ID (Lieutenant General Bergmann) brought the 29th Motorized Infantry Division welcome relief in Smolensk. When the 129th ID (Major General Rittau) finally arrived from the north, the 20th Motorized Infantry Division and 12th Panzer Division were freed up for further commitment.

The 3rd Panzer Group advanced its panzer and motorized divisions to the Vop, in order to establish a solid defensive front northeast of Smolensk against new Soviet flare-ups. Thus, in the last weeks of July, from north to south, from Lomonosovo up to the confluence of the Vop into the Dnepr south of Yartsevo, stood the following: 18th Motorized Infantry Division, 20th Panzer Division, 900th Training Brigade, 12th Panzer Division, and the 7th Panzer Division.

At this time, the enemy tried to penetrate the German positions and threw their rifle divisions into the fire daily. Alone in the approximately 50 kilometer long Vop River sector, the 220th, 251st, 69th, 144th, 91st, 129th, 133rd Rifle Divisions, and the 101st Tank Brigade attacked from right to left. The main effort of the attack was near Yartsevo, from where the Soviet troops were the closest to Smolensk. The 7th Panzer Division took the main brunt of this attack. The Soviet troops committed the first "Stalin Organs." These were multiple rocket launchers that could fire 320 rockets within 26 seconds. Alone the 7th Infantry Regiment registered 410 losses and the 7th Motorcycle Battalion reported 70 dead.

At the end of July, the 2nd Panzer Group closed the gap between their north and south motorized corps. The VII Army Corps (General of Artillery Fahrmbacher) and the IX Army Corps (General of Infantry Geyer) were inserted between the XXIV and XLVI Motorized Army Corps.

The XLVI Motorized Army Corps (General of Panzer Troops Vietinghoff) moved closer to the XLVII Motorized Army Corps located south of Smolensk and gained ground to the east. On 7/18, its 10th Panzer Division (Lieutenant General Schaal) was able to occupy Yelnya and, therefore, achieve the farthest point to the east during the German summer offensive. With the capture of Yelnya, the Smolensk pocket was finally closed!

The Soviet leadership still did not give up. They wanted badly to hold onto the Smolensk area. The commanders of the 16th (Lieutenant General

Chapter 3: The Attack

Lukin) and 20th Armies (Lieutenant General Kurochkin), who were encircled in the pocket, were strictly ordered, "Hold!" At the same time, all troop commanders in the Dnepr sector between Yelnya and Yartsevo were ordered to attack to the east. A special attack group was formed under Major General Rokossovski, which was to be on the main effort of this counterattack, while to the right and the left of it, the 24th Army (Major General Rakutin) was to attack Yelnya, and the 28th (Lieutenant General Kachalov) and 30th Armies (Major General Khomenko) had to attack Yartsevo and up to the Vop. The air forces under Major General Voreizhkin joined in the battle with 138 combat aircraft.

Defensive combat developed on the entire front before the two panzer groups, which were able to overcome all crises! The German front solidified considerably in spite of the losses. The Soviet counterattack could not make progress to the west. Elements of the 28th Soviet Army were even cut off and wiped out. Then the enemy finally deployed the forces of the 43rd Army; however, even they could not advance.

Moscow now gave up on the relief attempt and ordered the encircled armies to break out to the east! Lieutenant General Kurochkin committed the V Mechanized Corps (Major General Alekseenko), with the 14th (Colonel Vassilev) and 17th Tank Brigades (Colonel Kortshagin), as the breakthrough group. The breakthrough to the east was only partially successful – the majority of the 16th and 20th Armies remained in the pocket.

The Soviets later confirmed that they had lost 32,000 prisoners, 685 tanks, and 1178 guns in the battle. On the other hand, the OKW reported 348,000 prisoners, approximately 3000 tanks, and approximately 3000 guns. The actual numbers lie somewhere in the middle!

The battle of Smolensk was over. Army Group Center had the decision in its favor – however, the Soviets were able to stop the German offensive on Moscow and disrupt OKH plans to remove the 3rd Panzer Group to the north!

The battle of the Vop and Dnepr continued.

The fierce combat of the Army around Smolensk was supported by the air formations of the Luftwaffe. On 7/8, in view of the delay in the German

Army Group Center

offensive, Hitler had categorically ordered that Moscow and Leningrad not be attacked by the Army, but "be bombed into the ground by the Luftwaffe!"

Luftflotte 2, therefore, had to fly a major attack on Moscow, even though all of its squadrons were tied down around Smolensk by tenacious enemy defensive forces. The 3rd, 53rd, 54th, and 55th Combat Squadrons, as well as the 100th Combat Group and 3/26 Combat Squadron, took off on the evening of 7/21 for the first attack on the Soviet capital. 127 combat aircraft reached the air space over Moscow without incident and dropped 104 tons of high explosive bombs and 40,000 incendiary bombs during this night. The 2/55 Combat Squadron received the Kremlin as its target, but they missed it and dropped their bombs on a sports stadium whose outline looked like that of the seat of Stalin's government from a high altitude!

Moscow was taken by surprise by the attack. On the following days, the commander of air defense, Major General Gromadin, had to considerably reinforce his defensive forces. Elements from the ground air defenses were assembled as quickly as possible. Soon, the German aircraft returned. They flew a second attack on the night of 7/23 with 115 aircraft – not quite as strong as on the previous night.

The Luftflotte also had to attack the armaments centers at Voronezh, Tula, and Briansk with its combat squadrons at this time. The combat aircraft suffered losses, because the range of the fighter aircraft did not permit them to escort the bombers for the entire distance. In July, the German attacks on the various works in central Russia compelled the Moscow government to transfer the industrial installations to the Urals, on the Volga, to western Siberia, and to Central Asia.

Because the fighter squadrons were lacking and could not support the long range bombers, they were used more and more to protect the ground divisions from the attacks of Soviet fighter-bombers. Here the German fighters proved to be far superior thanks to their experience and superior aircraft.

Lieutenant Colonel Moelders, commander of the 51st Fighter Squadron, achieved his 101st air victory on 7/15 and, therefore, was the first German pilot to shoot down 100 enemy aircraft in combat. He was thereby named General of Fighter Aviation and removed from the front. His squad-

Chapter 3: The Attack

ron was turned over to Major Beckh. At that time, the 51st Fighter Squadron led all of the German fighter squadrons, closely followed by the 27th Fighter Squadron under Major Woldenga.

However, the Army received its best support from the formations of the air defense artillery, in particular the 8.8 cm gun, which proved to be one of the most successful weapons against the new and improved heavy Russian armored combat vehicles! Thus, the air defense batteries came to be used less in defense from enemy air formations and more for the protection of important strong points, or for securing the advance detachments.

The most successful of Lieutenant General von Axthelm's air defense corps performed the following missions in July 1941:

"7/2 - Defense of the Borissov bridgehead by the 1/12 Air Defense Regiment;

7/10 - Defense of the Vitebsk bridgehead by the 1/36 Air Defense Regiment;

7/23 - Commendable commitment of the 2nd Battery of the 36th Air Defense Regiment on the Vop;

7/24 - Defense of the Orsha bridgehead by the 1/22 Air Defense Regiment;

8/5 - During the defense of the Orsha bridgehead, particularly the Dnepr bridges, the 4th Battery of the 24th Air Defense Regiment destroyed five tanks, 13 guns, 80 trucks, and captured 200 prisoners."

The success of Army Group Center at Smolensk was not sufficient to achieve operational freedom for the Germans to the east. Now Hitler and the OKH applied the brakes. The reason was the poor German supply situation.

The total transport capacity of Army Group Center on 7/15 was approximately 45,450 tons, of which approximately one-third was immobile due to poor roads and the wear and tear on equipment.

Army Group Center

The railroad transported 6300 tons on 14 trains daily and, therefore, could not meet the requirements of the armies. Eight days later, this shrunk to 8 trains. The effect of this was so catastrophic that the divisions on the Dnepr and Vop were soon short of ammunition.

The second reason for the German High Command delaying the continuation of the offensive was the situation of the two neighboring army groups, which were still far to the rear. In mid-July, a serious crisis developed on the northern flank of Army Group South, which compelled the OKW to issue Instruction Nr. 33 (441 230/41) on 7/23:

> "As soon as operations and supply allow, the 1st and 2nd Panzer Groups will be subordinated to the 4th Army, in order to advance into the industrial region from Kharkov across the Don to the Caucasus, followed by infantry and mountain divisions!"

This imaginary objective was believed by the OKH to allow the forces of Army Group South to advance through Kharkov-Kursk, in order to provide flank protection for the operations of Army Group Center toward Moscow. Therefore, for the first time, a wide gap surfaced in the strategic concept between Hitler/OKW and the OKH, and it was never closed.

The German General Staff realized that the Russian enemy was being underestimated and would only be defeated by a quick conquest of the Soviet capital. Hitler and the OKW, however, believed more in the economic-political sphere. On 7/28, General Halder wrote in his diary:

> "...the splitting up of the panzer groups...leads to a dispersal of the forces and their bogging down in the decisive direction of Moscow."

The subordination of the two panzer groups to the 4th Army was now canceled. The 3rd Panzer Group was transferred to the 9th Army, while the 2nd Panzer Group remained independent as "Army Group Guderian." The 4th Army retained command over its old divisions, while the 2nd Army command took over the forces deployed on the Pripet front, which were to protect the flank of the army group.

Chapter 3: The Attack

At the end of July, the southern flank of Army Group Center was in danger of being penetrated by the Soviets, because Army Group South hung back so far that no support could be expected from it.

Field Marshal von Bock summoned his commanders to a meeting at his headquarters in Orsha. Here he made Hitler's instructions known, that the army group would no longer be executing any large scale outflanking maneuvers, but only forming smaller pockets. Therefore, the freedom of maneuver of the panzer groups was limited.

In fact, freedom of maneuver no longer existed. The 3rd Panzer Group had to turn its attention to the north, where the Russians were able to cross the Kholm-Toropets line to the west. "Army Group Guderian" stood with its left flank in heavy defensive combat near Yelnya and had to remove the crisis on the southern flank with its right flank!

"Army Group Guderian" was reinforced with infantry forces. At the end of July, it received the VII Army Corps, with the 7th, 23rd, 78th, 179th ID; the IX Army Corps, with the 137th, 263rd, and 292nd ID; and the XX Army Corps, with the 15th and 268th ID. To remove the flank threat in the Roslavl sector, Generaloberst Guderian deployed his right flank as follows:

XXIV Motorized Army Corps, with the 10th Motorized Infantry Division and the 7th ID to protect the flank near Klimovichi, 3rd and 4th Panzer Divisions in front of Roslavl;

VII Army Corps, with the 23rd and 197th ID behind the 3rd Panzer Division.

Therefore, these two corps had to be removed from the previous front. If the planned attack did not go smoothly, the army group would be in danger, the extent of which one could not yet determine. The Chief of the General Staff noted, "Army Group Center remains our problem child!"

The front of the army group had become extended, but it could only be secured in a strong-point manner with the forces available. At the end of July, the 42nd ID, 9th Panzer Division, 7th Motorized Infantry Division,

Army Group Center

and 1st Cavalry Division became available to Army Group Center. The losses of the army group since 6/22 totaled 74,500 men. The 23,000 replacements did not make up for these losses. Losses by army were the following:

2nd Army = 30,000 men,
9th Army = 15,000 men,
2nd Panzer Group = 5,000 men,
3rd Panzer Group = 4,000 men.

In spite of the ideas of the High Command, the German offensive continued to advance wherever the panzer divisions found gaps in the slowly strengthening Soviet front. Such a gap existed at the location where there was a threat to the army group – namely on the southern flank.

Generaloberst Guderian, whose XXIV Motorized Army Corps had reached Sozh in mid-July, was given the task of clearing up this situation. He ordered the XXIV Motorized Army Corps not to stop advancing, but instead to take Roslavl. This mission was accomplished on 8/1 by the 4th Panzer Division and 23rd ID. Two days later, the advance detachments of the 35th Panzer Regiment (4th Panzer Division) and the 507th IR (292nd ID) closed the small pocket northeast of Roslavl.

Only five days later, Generaloberst Guderian drove the corps of General of Panzer Troops Baron Geyr von Schweppenburg to the south. It turned out that strong enemy forces stood in front of the 7th ID near Krichev and they could attack from there to the north at any time. The tried and true 3rd and 4th Panzer Divisions attacked from Miloslavichi to the southwest on 8/9 – it was almost to the rear(!) – and defeated the enemy in a classic armored attack (the companies advanced on a wide front).

Therefore, the threat from the south was finally removed!

Guderian now had an open road – however, the OKH interfered. The Chief of the General Staff, Generaloberst Halder, had not agreed with this independent conduct of the war by Guderian for some time now. Arguments occurred, in which Field Marshal von Bock often acted as referee, even though he often agreed with Guderian.

Chapter 3: The Attack

Then, on 8/4, Hitler arrived at Army Group Center headquarters in Borissov, accompanied by Colonel Huesinger, Chief of the OKH Operations Branch. Hitler summoned the army commanders to this meeting. Stormy arguments occurred, and Hitler categorically forbid any further attack on Moscow until the flanks were secured. Hitler also issued far reaching missions to the army group, which would further fritter away the forces of the army group instead of concentrating them. Among other things, he ordered the 3rd Panzer Group to take the Valdai Hills in the north, not to help Army Group North, but to create a departure base for further operations. The right flank of the army group must first clarify the situation in the Gomel area and near the Pripet Marsh.

On 8/6/1941, the situation of Army Group Center was reflected on the OKH map as follows:

The 9th Army (headquarters in Vitebsk) stood with the subordinate 3rd Panzer Group north of the Smolensk-Moscow highway up to the edge of the marsh region south of Kholm. The L Army Corps (General of Cavalry Lindemann) was deployed by Army Group North as a flanking corps and maintained contact with the northern neighbor. It was the same with the right neighbor, the XXIII Army Corps (General of Infantry Schubert). On 8/10, this corps deployed. It was exhausted and had neither sufficient rations nor ammunition. The 3rd Panzer Group, as before, held the Vop sector with its two motorized corps, as well as the V and VI Army Corps, and had to repulse continuous enemy attacks from the east.

"Army Group Guderian" stood with the infantry divisions of the 4th Army between the highway and Krichev. The XLVII Motorized Army Corps defended in the north, the XX Army Corps fought in the Yelnya bridgehead, the XLVI Motorized and the Army Corps and IX Army Corps stretched from here to Roslavl, while the VII Army Corps and XXIV Motorized Army Corps oriented their front to the south. On this sector, the positions of the army group were almost oriented to the west.

The 2nd Army (headquarters in Mogilev) had control of this flank. From left to right they slowly inserted the following into the impassable region of the Pripet Marsh: XIII, XII, LIII, and XLIII Army Corps. The extreme right flank of the army group was formed by the XXXV Corps

Army Group Center

with the 45th and 293rd ID. These two divisions were deployed on their own and had no contact with the left flank of Army Group South, where there was a 150 kilometer wide gap.

In view of the constantly strengthening enemy resistance, Army Group Center could not accomplish all of the missions assigned by the OKH. The front of the army group appeared – as Generaloberst Halder once noted – dispersed. There was no trace of a main effort – and one could not be established.

In the summer of 1941, the German Eastern Army was no longer in a position to accomplish the most basic principles of strategy!

On 8/8, Generaloberst Hoth wrote to the army group command:

> "The combat strength of the Russian leadership is still not broken and tenacious resistance can still be expected!"

Only during the first weeks of August was it possible to slowly relieve the panzer divisions of the 3rd Panzer Group in defensive positions on the Vop River with the advancing infantry divisions. However, the Soviets still did not give up. They still crashed rifle divisions of their 24th (left), 32nd (center), and 30th (right) Armies against the German positions. The defenders received no rest, day or night. A division sector was often 24 kilometers wide, so that the area could only be secured in a strong point manner.

For the first time, the Soviet artillery proved to be superior not only in quantity, but also in quality. In addition, our batteries suffered from chronic ammunition shortages. The enemy air force continued to strengthen its commitment in the battle. This was particularly noticeable when, on 8/3, the VIII Air Corps of Generaloberst Baron von Richthofen was transferred from the north of the army group to Leningrad. Therefore, the German lines were practically without fighter protection!

A particularly unhappy situation occurred in mid-August when superior enemy forces succeeded in penetrating into the 161st ID sector. The division was no longer capable of defending and withdrew to the west. The panzer group committed all available combat groups to clear up the situa-

Chapter 3: The Attack

tion near Yartsevo. Elements of the 7th Panzer Division, the 5th ID, the 900th Training Brigade, and the 643rd Heeres Anti-tank Battalion were brought up.

In pouring rain, the German side did not succeed in the battle, but only made further sacrifices. The 7th Panzer Regiment, for example, lost 30 combat vehicles. On 8/20, it was clear that the Soviets were the stronger. The 3rd Panzer Group ordered the withdrawal. It was the first – if only on a local basis – retreat in the Army Group Center sector.

The battle on the left flank of the panzer group developed more favorably than here on the Vop. The XL Motorized Army Corps (General of Cavalry Stumme) drove the German front further to the northeast. The 19th and 20th Panzer Divisions drove the Soviet 22nd Army through Velikie Luki. As the 1/21 Panzer Regiment (Lieutenant Colonel von Gersdorff) of the 20th Panzer Division established contact with the 1/73 Infantry Regiment (Major Koehler) and the 27th Panzer Regiment (Colonel Thomale) of the 19th Panzer Division east of Velikie Luki on 24/8, the enemy was trapped and there was no way out. So, here the attack could be continued.

On 8/29, the 21st Panzer Regiment (20th Panzer Division) enjoyed the last success with the capture of the Toropets communication hub.

Then the army group ordered:

"Cease all movement, move on order of the OKH only!"

What had happened?

The confused situation in Army Group Center in August required the German leadership to make a decisive decision as to how the campaign was to be continued. The OKH worked out a proposal that was signed by Field Marshal von Brauchitsch on 8/18. This memo proposed continuing the offensive on the center of the front. The operational objective was ultimately the destruction of the enemy forces on the front, the disruption of his defensive lines, and the capture of Moscow.

Hitler turned down this proposal three days later. On 8/21, he issued basic instructions (WFSt. L. Nr. 44141/41):

Army Group Center

"The 8/18 Army proposal for the continuation of the operations in the east does not agree with my intentions:

I order the following:

1) The most important objective to achieve before the outbreak of winter is no longer the capture of Moscow, but the capture of the Crimea, the industrial and coal region on the Donets and the disruption of the Russian oil deliveries from the Caucasus. ...

2) The operationally favorable situation, that was achieved by reaching the line Gomel - Pochep, must be taken advantage of by a concentrated operation with the inner flanks of Army Groups South and Center. ...

3) Without regard to future operations, Army Group center must commit sufficient forces to achieve the objective of destroying the 5th Army, which will allow the army group to protect its front from all enemy attacks. ..."

These instructions caused the former plans of the army group to be changed. Field Marshal von Bock immediately called OKH and sharply informed them that the army group front could only be maintained by attacking Moscow! On 8/23, Generaloberst Halder arrived at the army group headquarters, in order to transmit the new missions of the army group in relation to the south.

Here, in the meantime, "Army Group Guderian" and the 2nd Army were attacking the Soviet forces between the Dessna and Pripet. On 8/17, the XXIV Motorized Army Corps (General of Panzer Troops Baron Geyr von Schweppenburg) had already outflanked the left flank of the "Briansk Front" under Lieutenant General Yeremenko with the 3rd Panzer Division (Lieutenant General Model), without the Soviet leadership knowing it. Moscow and the headquarters of the "Briansk Front" believed that the armored attack was only a diversion at this time to mask the Army Group Center offensive on Moscow.

Chapter 3: The Attack

When the Soviet leadership realized their error, it was already too late. The XXIV Motorized Army Corps severed the Briansk – Gomel rail line near Unecha and attacked the 3rd Panzer Division through Starodub to the south. After that, by 8/20, (from right to left) the 10th Motorized Infantry Division, and the 4th and 17th Panzer Divisions also reached the railroad line, and the Soviet front was torn.

The violent attack of the panzer divisions to the south inevitably forced the withdrawal of enemy formations, which were located in front of the 2nd Army, to the south. Therefore, the 2nd Army now had freedom of maneuver. Their left flank – 17th and 260th ID – occupied the most important city in the combat region, Gomel. The left neighboring divisions: 1st Cavalry Division, 131st, 112th, 167th, and 31st and 34th ID, forced the Soviet divisions to the east between Klintsy and Novosybkov. Here, the Russians fell into the pincer movement of the XXIV Motorized Army Corps and were encircled or forced to withdraw to the southeast, leaving behind their heavy equipment!

The XLVII Motorized Army Corps (General of Panzer Troops Lemelsen), which was in second echelon behind the XXIV Motorized Army Corps on the left, established flank protection to the east, because pressure from the "Briansk Front" was more noticeable there. Lieutenant General Yeremenko wanted, with all of his might, to catch Guderian in his pincer. On 8/21, the 17th Panzer Division occupied Pochep, while to the north, on a widely dispersed front, the 18th Panzer Division and 29th Motorized Infantry Division held thin defenses up to the Dessna.

On 8/13, the "Briansk Front" was assigned the mission of covering the southwestern flank of Moscow. They assembled two armies with 20 divisions. (During the summer of 1941, the STAVKA did away with corps, because they lacked the necessary number of staff officers and corps troops! Thus, during mid-August, large formations only included brigades, divisions, and armies!) The organization of the "Briansk Front" reflected:

50th Army in the north (Commander: Major General Petrov) with the 217th, 279th, 258th, 260th, 290th, 278th, 269th, 280th Rifle Divisions, and 55th Cavalry Division;

Army Group Center

13th Army in the south (Commander: Major General Golubev) with the 6th, 12th, 148th, 132nd, 155th, 317th, 285th Rifle Divisions, 21st and 52nd Cavalry Divisions, and 50th Tank Brigade.

On 8/17, Lieutenant General Model's tanks had already defeated the front of the 13th Army and, on 8/23, Lieutenant General Yeremenko had to issue strict orders: "50th Army must not take one step backward! 13th Army recaptures Starodub and Unecha!" However, they could no longer do this. Guderian's tanks rolled further. Moscow now decided to remove the 3rd and 21st Armies from the "Central Front" and subordinate them to the "Briansk Front." The commander of the 13th Army was relieved and, on 8/24, replaced by Major General Gorodnynski. This was the day on which the 3rd Panzer Division reported its greatest success, which led to the battle of Kiev. An advance detachment of the division – 1st Company of the 6th Panzer Regiment (Senior Lieutenant Vopel) and an engineer platoon from the 394th Infantry Regiment (Lieutenant Stoerck) – captured the 700 meter long Dessna bridge near Novgorod-Seversk in a raid on 8/24 at 1000 hours. The first bridgehead on the southern bank of the Dessna was established and could not be taken away from Lieutenant General Model's soldiers, in spite of the rigorous commitment of Soviet infantry and air formations. The 1st Reconnaissance Battalion of the 3rd Panzer Division, under Major Ziervogel, captured Shostka on the Kiev-Moscow rail line on the following day.

Therefore, the Ukraine was isolated from central Russia!

"Army Group Guderian" attained freedom of mobility to the south!

It was a freedom of mobility which was, nevertheless, examined by the army group command with great concern. The situation on the front of the army group – with the exception of the south – was not very rosy. A crisis of the first order was still facing the Yelnya bridgehead. Here, during the month of August, several German divisions found themselves in defensive combat similar to that of the battle of Verdun during the 1st World War.

Moscow had ordered Army Groups "West Front" and "Reserve Front" to recapture the general line Velizh-Smolensk-Yelnya-Roslavl. The "Re-

Chapter 3: The Attack

serve Front" committed the 28th and 43rd Armies against the Yelnya bridgehead alone, supported by strong air forces.

The SS Division "Das Reich" (SS Obergruppenfuehrer Hauser), which held the bridgehead, was bloodied here and had to be replaced by infantry divisions on 8/17. Subsequently, fighting in the trenches near Yelnya, were the following: 10th Panzer Division, SS Division "Das Reich", 268th, 292nd, 263rd, 137th, 87th, 15th, 78th ID, and the "Grossdeutschland" Motorized Infantry Regiment. The 263rd ID, for example, registered a total of 1200 casualties during the time period 8/20-8/27, and the 137th ID reported 2000 casualties from 8/18 to 9/5.

On 8/28, Field Marshal von Bock called headquarters OKH and reported:

"The end of the resistance strength of the army group is at hand! It is impossible to hold the eastern front!"

Generaloberst Halder could only answer that the surrender of the Yelnya salient would eventually have to be considered! The battle of Yelnya continued. The IX Army Corps (General of Infantry Geyer) had taken command here. At this time, located in the bridgehead, from right to left, were: 268th, 292nd, 78th, 15th, 137th and 263rd ID. The latter closed its left flank on the Dnepr, where the VIII Army Corps stood on the opposite bank.

The Soviets now deployed the 24th Army and also committed it against Yelnya. On 8/30, the 50th and 64th Rifle Divisions achieved a deep penetration with the support of the 47th Air Division and several tank regiments. Three days later, the OKH decided to evacuate the Yelnya salient under energetic pressure from the army group command.

On 9/6, the Soviet 24th Army occupied the ruined city!

The eastern front of the army group, which stretched from Toropets in the north to Roslavl in the south, was static. The main effort was decisively transferred to the south. At the beginning of September 1941, the army group had neither sufficient men nor equipment to continue activities in the east. The situation was especially catastrophic with the panzer formations and the operational forces of Luftflotte 2. All of the operational troops were, strength-wise, incapable of beginning an offensive.

Army Group Center

General air superiority in the area had shifted to the Soviets. According to the Luftwaffe High Command, operational air forces on 9/7/1941 were:

	German	Soviet
Fighters	151	373
Combat Aircraft	281	158
Reconnaissance	25	18
Transports	–	136

Indeed, German success against Soviet air forces were enormous. In the meantime, however, the enemy was able to duplicate the experience of the German pilots. Most of the successful German fighter pilots realized that "many hounds kill the rabbit." Thus, on 8/25, among others, the commander of the I/51 Fighter Squadron, Captain Joppien, was shot down in air combat over Briansk. At that time, with 70 air victories, he led all fighter pilots.

The successes of the I Air Defense Corps (Lieutenant General von Axthelm), which was committed in the Army Group Center sector, from the beginning of the Eastern Campaign to the beginning of September totaled: 314 aircraft shot down and approximately 3000 armored combat vehicles destroyed.

In mid-September 1941, the army group had to transition to positional warfare. The front east of Smolensk was defended on a 120 kilometer width by the XX, IX, and VIII Army Corps (from right to left). Six Soviet armies continuously assaulted their positions here – (from right to left) the 29th, 30th, 24th, 28th, 43rd, and 50th – without being able to influence the general front situation.

The government in Moscow preached to the people about a war of liberation. This was an attempt to get the varied peoples of this vast land to fight against the German armies. Stalin threw all of the former Bolshevik requirements "overboard" and allied himself with the traditions of "Mother Russia." On 9/18, he reinstated the old Tsarist designations of "Guards Divisions." On this day, the first four rifle divisions were re-designated as guards divisions. It turned out that these divisions had been committed

Chapter 3: The Attack

against Army Group Center since the beginning of the war. They were the former 100th, 127th, 153rd, and 161st Rifle Divisions.

Army Group Center was to temporarily attack its right flank to the south. This flank was organized on 9/3 as follows:

2nd Army: XXXV Corps command with the 112th, 45th ID;
XIII Army Corps with the 134th, 17th 260th ID;
XLIII Army Corps with the 131st, 293rd ID.

"Army Detachment Guderian":
XXIV Motorized Army Corps with the 3rd, 4th Panzer Divisions, 10th Motorized Infantry Division, "Grossdeutschland" IR;
XLVIII Motorized Army Corps with the 17th, 18th Panzer Divisions, 29th Motorized ID.

At this time, the front line ran from the area north of Chernigov to the northeast, bent west of Novgorod-Seversk sharply to the south to Krolevets, and ran from here directly to the north through Voronezh and Shostka and back toward Novgorod-Seversk.

The attack of the two armies to the south was launched simultaneously. The Dessna was reached on 9/9 by the 2nd Army, and the XIII and XLIII Army Corps bypassed Chernigov almost on the entire breadth. The XXIV Motorized Army Corps cut through the area between Korop and Krolevets and attacked Konotop.

Therefore, the 5th Soviet Army, which had fought so bravely and successfully in the Pripet region, was threatened with being encircled. Its formerly solid front fell apart on 9/9. Chernigov was occupied on this day by the 17th Panzer Division (Lieutenant General Loch), 134th ID (Lieutenant General von Cochenhausen), and 260th ID (Lieutenant General Schmidt).

Generaloberst Baron von Weichs, commander of the 2nd Army, issued an order of the day on 9/10:

Army Group Center

"With this attack, you have created the prerequisite for a destruction battle of great import, which will begin immediately. The enemy will be encircled from all sides by us and destroyed. ..."

Marshal Budenny, the commander of all of the Soviet troops on the southern sector of the Eastern Front, lost sight of his armies in the area north and east of Kiev on 9/10/1941. There was no longer centralized command and control. On 9/12, German air reconnaissance determined for the first time that the Soviet troops were withdrawing along the entire front.

Field Marshal von Rundstedt, commander of the German Army Group South, asked OKH to subordinate the 2nd Army and "Army Detachment Guderian" to him for the purpose of simplifying command and control. However, the OKH turned down this request in view of their further plans. Thus, the 2nd Army and "Army Detachment Guderian" remained under the control of Army Group Center.

The lead division of "Army Detachment Guderian" was, as before, the 3rd Panzer Division. On 9/12, Lieutenant General Guderian dispatched an advance detachment to the south from Romny with the mission of establishing contact with Army Group South. The combat group under Major Frank reached the area north of Lokhvitsa on the evening of the same day. On the next day, the city was in German hands. The lead elements of Army Group South were only 40 kilometers away to the south!

Lieutenant General Model did not quit. A small combat group, consisting of two officers and 45 men, launched a daring raid to the south on the morning of 9/14 – and, by 1820 hours, established contact with the 2/16 Engineer Battalion of the 16th Panzer Division. Therefore, the pocket around Kiev was closed!

The battle of Kiev began – it would be the greatest pocket battle in military history!

The resistance strength of the encircled Soviet armies – the 5th, 26th, 37th, and 38th – had noticeably decreased and collapsed within a few days. The pocket front was hermetically sealed from all sides by the German divisions and the Russian troops were compressed.

On 9/16, the OKH removed the 2nd Army and transferred it to the eastern front of Army Group Center. Only the staff of "Army Detachment

Chapter 3: The Attack

Guderian" (headquarters Romny) remained as the senior command authority of the army group on the southern flank. On 9/18, Generaloberst Guderian commanded the following units:

The XXXV Corps command was on the right flank. Its 262nd, 134th, and 292nd ID attacked east of Yagotin to Orsha. The 45th ID followed in second echelon. The XXIV Motorized Army Corps controlled the left sector. SS Division "Das Reich" occupied Priluki and, therefore, established contact with the XXXV Corps command. The 4th, 3rd Panzer Divisions and 25th Motorized Infantry Division attacked from the west to Piryatin. Flank protection to the east between Romny and Lokhvitsa was provided only by the 10th Motorized Infantry Division.

Combat here was fierce. The Soviets had formed two combat groups that were to close the gap in the front between the "Briansk Front" and the "Southwest Front." These combat groups, three rifle, two cavalry divisions, and two tank brigades, under the leadership of Major General Yermakov and Colonel Akimenko, continuously advanced against the positions of the 10th Motorized Infantry Division (Lieutenant General von Loeper), which was able to hold on with the support of the 104th Air Defense Regiment (Colonel Lindenberger) and the "Hermann Goering" Air Defense Regiment (Colonel Conrath).

The battle for Kiev came to an end on 9/20 for "Army Detachment Guderian." The divisions were removed from the front, one after the other, and assembled. The wheeled infantrymen of the 3rd Panzer Division captured the brave commander of the Soviet 5th Army, Major General Potapov. A medical officer from the 3rd Panzer Division wrote in his diary on 9/21:

"It is a picture of horror. Corpses of men and horses scattered among vehicles and equipment of all types. Ambulances are turned over. Heavy air defense guns, cannons, howitzers, tanks, trucks, some are stuck in the marshes, some were driven into the houses or trees. It is chaos."

In September 1941, the Red Army's "Southwest Front" was in utter chaos. The classic pocket battle of the 2nd World War – in 1944 there would be another, only this time Army Group Center would be the loser – was over. "Army Detachment Guderian" reported 82,000 prisoners.

Army Group Center

Time was working against the German Army. It was already the end of September, but the end of the campaign was nowhere in sight. The OKH wanted, in any case, to gain as much territory to the east and force a decision before the onslaught of winter. On 9/6, the OKW ordered in Directive Nr. 35:

> "The initial success against the enemy forces, which were located between the inner flanks of Army Groups South and Center, in conjunction with the continued encirclement of Leningrad, have created the basis for a decisive operation against Army Group Timoshenko, established in front of Army Group Center. In the time available before the outbreak of winter, they must be destroyed. In addition, Army Group Center must attack as soon as possible with the objective of defeating the enemy east of Smolensk in a double envelopment in the direction of Viazma, with strong panzer forces on each flank. After this encirclement operation, the Army's center will set out in the direction of Moscow – the right adjacent to the Oka, the left adjacent to the upper Volga."

That was the order according to which Army Group center was to regroup its troops, while the battle of Kiev was still ongoing. The OKH now brought forward the forces from other theaters of war, which were needed so badly in the past few months. Thus, the 4th Panzer Group (commander Generaloberst Hoepner, Chief of Staff Lieutenant Colonel Chales de Beaulieu) was deployed from the northern sector of the Eastern Front through Nevel to the army group. From 9/18, one after the other arrived: the LVI Corps command, 3rd Motorized Infantry Division, LVII Corps command, 20th Panzer Division, XLI Corps command, 6th, 1st Panzer Divisions, 36th Motorized Infantry Division, and the 8th and 19th Panzer Divisions.

From the Reich came the 5th Panzer Division.

The Luftwaffe also deployed strong forces. The VIII Air Corps (Generaloberst Baron von Richthofen) transferred back to the Luftflotte 2 area of operations from the northern sector. The II Air Defense Corps (Lieutenant General Dessloch) was transported from the south.

Chapter 3: The Attack

On 9/23, "Army Detachment Guderian" left the Kiev battlefield and prepared for the new offensive in the Glukhov area. The organization of Army Group Center at the end of September was, from south to north:

"Army Detachment Guderian" (Generaloberst Guderian):
XXIV Mot AC (General of Panzer Troops Baron Geyr von Schweppenburg)
with the 3rd, 4th Panzer Divisions, 10th Mot ID, "Grossdeutschland" IR
XLVIII Mot AC (General of Panzer Troops Lemelsen)
with the 17th, 18th Panzer Divisions, 29th Mot ID;
XLVIII Mot AC (Lieutenant General Kempf)
with the 9th Panzer Division, 16th, 25th Mot ID;
XXXIV Corps (General of Infantry Metz)
with the 45th, 134th ID;
XXXV Corps (Lieutenant General Kempfe)
with the 95th, 112th, 293rd ID, 1st Cav Div.

2nd Army (Generaloberst Baron von Weichs):
XII AC (General of Infantry Schroth)
with the 34th, 52nd, 258th ID;
XIII AC (General of Infantry Felber)
with the 17th, 260th ID;
XLIII AC (General of Infantry Heinrici)
with the 31st, 131st ID;
LIII AC (General of Infantry Weisenberger)
with the 167th, 296th ID.

4th Army (Field Marshal von Kluge):
VII AC (General of Artillery Fahrmbacher)
with the 23rd, 197th, 267th ID;
IX AC (General of Infantry Geyer)
with the 15th, 137th, 263rd ID;
XX AC (General of Infantry Materna)
with the 7th, 78th, 268th, 292nd ID.

Army Group Center

4th Panzer Group (Generaloberst Hoepner):
XL Mot AC (General of Cavalry Stumme)
with the 2nd, 10th Panzer Divisions;
XLVI Mot AC (General of Panzer Troops von Vietinghoff)
with the 5th, 11th Panzer Divisions, 252nd ID;
LVII Mot AC (General of Panzer Troops Kuntzen)
with the 19th, 20th Panzer Divisions, 3rd Mot ID,
SS Division "Das Reich."

9th Army (Generaloberst Strauss):
V AC (General of Infantry Ruoff)
with the 5th, 35th ID;
VIII AC (General of Artillery Heitz)
with the 8th, 28th, 87th ID;
XXIII AC (General of Infantry Schubert)
with the 86th, 206th, 251st, 253rd ID;
XXVII AC (General of Infantry Waeger)
with the 106th, 129th, 161st ID.

3rd Panzer Group (Generaloberst Hoth):
VI AC (General of Engineers Foerster)
with the 6th, 26th ID;
XLI Mot AC (General of Panzer Troops Reinhardt)
with the 1st Panzer Division, 36th Mot ID;
LVI Mot AC (General of Panzer Troops Schaal)
with the 6th, 7th Panzer Divisions, 14th Mot ID.

Generaloberst Halder, Chief of the Army General Staff, arrived at army group headquarters in Smolensk on 9/24 to meet with Field Marshal von Bock and the army commanders. Two days later, the army group command issued the attack order:

"1. After a long waiting period, the army group will again attack.

Chapter 3: The Attack

2. 4th Army, with the subordinate 4th Panzer Group, attacks with its main effort on either side of the Roslavl-Moscow road. ...

3. 9th Army, with the subordinate 3rd Panzer Group, breaks through enemy positions between the highway and the Beloi area and advances up to the Viazma-Rzhev rail line. ...

4. An attack will be simulated on the inner flanks of the 4th and 9th Armies, in order to tie up as many enemy forces as possible.

5. 2nd Army protects the southern flank of the 4th Army. In addition, they breakthrough the Dessna positions...and advance in the direction of Sukhinichi....

6. The 2nd Panzer Group advances – two days prior to the beginning of the attack of the other armies–across the line Orel-Briansk. ...

...

9. The reinforced Luftflotte 2 will defeat the Russian Air Force facing the army group. ..."

The army group organized according to this overall offensive plan. The three infantry armies and the 3rd Panzer Group were in their departure positions during the last week of September. The newly inserted 4th Panzer Group deployed into the 4th Army sector. "Army Detachment Guderian", without giving its divisions one day rest, turned 180 degrees and moved into the Glukhov sector. The right flank, where the army detachment stood, was assigned the most far reaching attack objectives and, therefore, would have to begin the attack a few days earlier (The motorized army corps were redesignated panzer corps on 10/6).

During the last four weeks, while the offensive of the army group did not drive any further to the east, the "Red Army" also rearranged itself and deployed the following armies, which were newly organized, regrouped,

Army Group Center

or brought up from the interior, from north to south: 22nd, 29th, 30th, 19th, 16th, 20th, 24th, 43rd, 50th, 3rd, 13th, and 40th Armies.

"Army Detachment Guderian" set out on 9/30 as ordered in a thick morning fog. Indeed, all of the corps were not yet in their departure positions and the right flank could not be immediately protected – however, the attack rolled.

The tried and true XXIV Panzer Corps set out on either side of the Sevsk-Orel road, with the 3rd and 4th Panzer Divisions in the front lines, taking the enemy by surprise. On the following day, the corps was able to capture Sevsk, while the 10th Motorized Infantry Division was committed in flank protection on the right. The XLVII Panzer Corps, with the 17th and 18th Panzer Divisions, also advanced quickly and drove north of Sevsk into the Karachev area west of Orel. The two corps achieved unbelievable gains in two days. They broke through the Soviet front and drove 130 kilometers deep – then they ran out of fuel.

The protection of the right flank of the army group was secured! The unit commanders were informed of Hitler's order of the day during the night of 10/2 – the day on which "Operation Typhoon" began:

> "The last great decisive battle of this year will deliver a destructive blow to the enemy. ...We will remove the threat to the German Reich and all of Europe, which has existed since the time of the Huns and the Mongols, of an invasion of the continent. ...The German people will be with you in the coming weeks as they were before!"

The offensive against Moscow began on 10/2 in sunny autumn weather. On the first days, the combat squadrons of Luftflotte 2 flew repeatedly and cleared the way. The troops were pretty much filled with men and equipment – and the German soldier still felt superior to his Russian enemy.

On 10/2, "Army Detachment Guderian" battered the opposing 13th Soviet Army. The 21st and 55th Cavalry Divisions and the 121st and 150th Tank Brigades, which were launched in counterattack by the enemy, were thrown back by the 4th Panzer Division (Major General Baron von Langermann und Erlencamp). The division reached the paved road to Orel.

Chapter 3: The Attack

The tanks, supported by the 543rd Anti-tank Battalion (3rd Panzer Division), entered Orel on the following day. The great railroad and road hub was energetically defended by the troops of the Orel Military District under Lieutenant General Tyurin. However, the 4th Panzer Division was the stronger.

The left neighboring 2nd Army had to make a frontal attack. They ran into an enemy force that had entrenched in solid bunkers and could not be driven out by German artillery fire. The army could not achieve even a small local penetration into the initial enemy defensive positions.

On 10/2 at 0530 hours, the 4th Panzer Group opened its attack. Two hours later, its corps had established bridgeheads on the eastern bank of the Dessna. XII Army Corps and XL Panzer Corps threw the enemy back. During the evening, the 10th Panzer Division (Major General Fischer) stood 30 kilometers deep behind the Dessna and had broken through the Soviet front. There were no longer any unified Russian formations in front of it!

The infantry divisions of the 4th Army were not shown up by the tanks. The engineer troops set out across the Dessna in rubber rafts during the German artillery barrage, suppressed bunkers, and removed mines. Thus, the way was cleared for the infantry. The enemy was thrown back here as they were by the motorized troops on the right. The 78th ID (Lieutenant General Gallenkamp) broke through the river positions to a depth of 10 kilometers. The attack was continued on the following day with similar success. Each enemy counterattack – even with heavy tanks – was repulsed.

The left flank of the army group – 9th Army and 3rd Panzer Group – overran the initial Soviet positions on a wide front. The center and the right flank of the army advanced furthest, thanks to the support of the VIII Air Corps. The Votrya was quickly overcome and the Vop was reached, on which so much blood had flown. The LVI Panzer Corps broke through the enemy front first and advanced to the southeast toward the Dnepr. 6th (Major General Rauss) and 7th Panzer Divisions (Lieutenant General Baron von Funck) reached the Dnepr on 10/3!

The troops of Generaloberst Guderian had advanced the furthest during the last few days. On 10/3, the XLVII Panzer Corps was diverted and assigned Briansk as an objective. The 18th Panzer Division advanced across the Orel-Briansk road and, on 10/5, occupied Karachev with the 3/18 Panzer Regiment (Major Teege). The 17th Panzer Division was given the mission of advancing to Briansk and capturing the Dessna bridges there. They achieved their mission! On 10/6, Briansk was taken in a daring attack and Lieutenant General von Arnim's 17th Panzer Division captured the Dessna bridge!

The XXIV Panzer Corps advanced as a sword point toward Mzensk. Here the attack had to be temporarily halted because, firstly, they ran out of fuel, and secondly, the 26th Soviet Army appeared on the battlefield and, with superior tank forces, severely threatened the far advanced 4th Panzer Division.

"Army Detachment Guderian", which was redesignated as 2nd Panzer Army on 10/6, had achieved its first objective as "programmed." The enemy front was broken through and, with the attack on Briansk, the first pocket operation was initiated. Unfortunately, 2nd Panzer Army did not have the use of all of its panzer forces, because the XLVIII Panzer Corps was committed to the south in flank protection and was advancing toward Kursk almost unhindered by the enemy.

The left neighboring 2nd Army, which during the first days of the offensive did not achieve initial success, achieved freedom of mobility when the attack of the 17th Panzer Division became noticeable. The 43rd and 50th Soviet Armies withdrew to the west. The infantry divisions of the 2nd Army closely pursued the enemy, crossed the Dessna on 10/5, and approached the Briansk-Roslavl road on the following day.

The pocket around Briansk began to be closed.

Elements of the 13th Soviet Army (in the south), 3rd (in the center), and 50th Armies (in the north) fell into the pincers of the panzer and infantry divisions. The Soviet commander, Lieutenant General Yeremenko, was able to escape from his headquarters in the Sveni railroad station on 10/6 – then the tanks with the iron crosses arrived!

The 4th Panzer Group of Generaloberst Hoepner attacked the center and southern flank further to the east on 10/4. The 10th Panzer Division took Mozalsk on this day. At the same time, the 2nd Panzer Division approached the Yukhnov-Viazma road from the south. The 10th Panzer Divi-

Chapter 3: The Attack

sion (Major General Fischer) gained 40 kilometers on 10/5 and captured Yukhnov. The XL Panzer Corps sent its two divisions from here to the north, in order to reach Gzhatsk. Then the OKH intervened and demanded that the pocket not be closed there, but near Viazma, in accordance with the "Führer Directive"!

The commander of the Soviet "Reserve Front" reported to Moscow on 10/5:

> "Situation on the left flank extremely serious. There are no forces available to block the penetration on the Moscow highway. ...The strength of the front is not sufficient to stop the enemy attack in the direction of Spas-Demensk, Yukhnov, Medyn."

Moscow then ordered "Reserve Front" to withdraw to a line 25 kilometers east of Viazma-Zhisdra. At the same time, the commander of the 32nd Army (Major General Vishnevskiy) was ordered to secure the withdrawal route. However, before the 32nd Army could prepare to execute this mission, German tanks appeared on either side of Viazma!

The 10th Panzer Division advanced to Viazma directly from the south and entered the city on 10/6!

The divisions of the 4th Army followed close behind the advanced panzer divisions. On the 3rd day of the attack, the army stood in the rear of the Soviet front east of Yelnya! Here, the enemy gave up the fight. The 292nd ID (Major General Lucht) captured Yelnya on 10/6.

The 9th Army, with the subordinate 3rd Panzer Group, executed the great turning maneuver between Yartsevo and Beloi on 10/4. The LVI Panzer Corps (General of Panzer Troops Schaal) crossed the Dnepr, throwing back the 103rd Soviet Tank Brigade (which was equipped with US tanks). The 7th Panzer Division (Lieutenant General Baron von Funck) attacked through to the highway to Viazma from the northwest. The division occupied 15 kilometers of the road and established contact with the 10th Panzer Division in Viazma.

Therefore, the second large pocket was closed.

Elements of the Soviet 16th, 19th, 20th, and 32nd Armies were encircled between Yartsevo and Viazma.

Army Group Center

The OKH believed that this indicated the successful completion of its plans and, on 10/7, ordered:

"2nd Panzer Army will attack through to Tula as soon as possible. They will take part in the attack on Moscow from the south.

2nd Army, closing from the north, will, for the time being, remain tied up with the encirclement and destruction of the enemy in the Briansk area.

4th Army will immediately attack across the line Kaluga-Mohaisk, with the subordinate 4th Panzer Group taking the Viazma-Moscow highway.

9th Army, with the forces of the subordinate 3rd Panzer Group, achieves a line Gzhatsk-Sychevka to isolate the pocket battle from the north. All elements of the 3rd Panzer Group freed-up will be assembled as soon as possible for an attack in the direction of Kalinin or Rzhev."

This order, which was transmitted by the OKH, Field Marshal von Brauchtisch, to the army group headquarters on 10/7, regulated the deployment of the armies for the decisive attack on Moscow.

However, the government in Moscow and the STAVKA had not given up. The commander of the "Reserve Front", Marshal Budenny, who had already lost the battle of Kiev, was dispatched to a command in Asia. His replacement on 10/8/1941 was Army General Zhukov. The staff of the "Reserve Front" was disbanded two days later and combined with that of the "West Front." Army General Zhukov took command over both "fronts." His deputy was Colonel General Konev, and his Chief of Staff was Lieutenant General Sokolovskiy.

Army General Zhukov immediately took control over the "front", and he regrouped. From the north to the south, he now commanded the 16th Army (Lieutenant General Rokossovskiy) near Volokolamsk, 5th Army (Major General Lelyushenko, from 10/18 Major General Govorov) near Mohaisk, and the 49th Army (Lieutenant General Sakharkin) near Kaluga.

Chapter 3: The Attack

The troops of the Moscow Military District, under Lieutenant General Artemev, were alerted on 10/9 and occupied positions on either side of Mohaisk, where the newly organized 26th Army (Major General Kurkin) was assembling.

However, the battles in the two pockets near Briansk and Viazma continued.

The 2nd Army command (Generaloberst Baron von Weichs) took control over the Briansk area on 10/7. On 10/8, the pocket was temporarily closed by the arrival of elements of the XLVII Panzer Corps from the north and the XLVIII Panzer Corps from the south, while the divisions of the XXXV Corps command (left) and XXXIV Corps command approached slowly from the west. The pocket was first split on 10/8. The battle grew more difficult day by day, because the weather sided against the Germans.

The first snow fell on 10/6/1941. It did not remain long. Soon wet weather arrived. Then came the mud. The mud remained one day, then two days, then three days. There were no longer any solid roads – all had turned to mud. Men, animals, and vehicles all sank into the mud and were stuck. The XXIV Panzer Corps was stuck fast in the mud. Its 4th Panzer Division frantically held on near Mzensk. The 3rd Panzer Division fought around Orel and Bolkhov. The 9th Panzer Division of the XLVIII Panzer Corps stood east of Dmitriev.

The 2nd Panzer Army had no divisions left to fight to the east!

On the other hand, the Soviets attacked from the east!

Further to the west, the battle continued around towns and forests. The 16th Motorized Infantry Division, 25th Motorized Infantry Division, 95th, 134th and 45th ID closed a solid ring around the 13th Soviet Army between Sevsk and Dmitriev. The 3rd Army, which wanted to break out to the east through Orel, was attacked by the 17th Panzer Division, 10th Motorized Infantry Division, 1st Cavalry Division, 296th, 262nd, and 293rd ID, and compressed west of Kromy. East of Briansk, the fate of the 50th Soviet Army was sealed by 10/15, as its breakout through Karachev was stopped by the 18th Panzer Division and "Grossdeutschland" Motorized Infantry Regiment.

The Viazma pocket also slowly burned out. The infantry divisions of the 4th Army followed the 4th Panzer Group closely. The 258th ID reached

Army Group Center

Yukhnov on 10/6. At the same time, the SS Division "Das Reich" continued to advance on Gzhatsk. On the following day, the 3rd Motorized Infantry Division arrived near Yukhnov. Therefore, the eastern front of the pocket was solidified.

The divisions, which were to arrive from the west, bogged down, however, from the flooded routes and the start of the enemy's breakout attempts. Finally, however, on 10/8, contact was established with the forces of the 9th Army near Dorogobush as they deployed from the northwest.

The 9th Army, with the subordinate 3rd Panzer Group, moved slowly, however, along the flooded roads, constantly opposed by the enemy and suffering a chronic fuel shortage. The VI Army Corps captured Beloi. The XLI Panzer Corps secured the northern front of the pocket on either side of Sychevka. The V Army Corps gradually relieved the divisions of the LVI Panzer Corps, which were in heavy defensive combat on the highway.

After a few days had passed, there was no longer a 19th, 20th, or 32nd Soviet Army. Their commanders, Lieutenant General Lukin, Lieutenant General Yershakov, and Major General Vishnevskiy were taken prisoner by the Germans, along with hundreds of thousands of their soldiers.

The OKW reported on 10/19:

"A special report informs us that the double battles of Briansk and Viazma have ended victoriously.

Under the command of Field Marshal von Bock, troops of the German Army in close cooperation with the Luftwaffe of Field Marshal Kesselring have destroyed the Soviet army group of Marshal Timoshenko in strength of eight armies with 67 rifle, 6 cavalry, 7 tank divisions, and 6 tank brigades. The mopping up of the combat area is essentially finished. The special report informs us that the number of prisoners has reached 657,948; 1241 armored combat vehicles and 5396 guns were also captured. ..."

The "Red Army" had lost a battle in front of the gates of its capital. The official Russian report described this loss in these words:

Chapter 3: The Attack

"... With great sacrifice, the enemy has been able to achieve gains in terrain, however, the enemy paid for it dearly."

The war had reached Moscow.

The Moscow government tried everything it could to prevent chaos in the capital. Militia units were deployed in the city during the summer, and they also began the initial work on planned defensive positions. At the beginning of October, the entrenchment work continued feverishly. On 10/12, the National Defense Committee issued a decree to the population: construct a protective wall outside of the city and directly at the city boundary. The work was conducted with spades and pick-axes. Daily, between 85,000 and 100,000 people, of which one-third were women, worked on these positions. Thus, in several weeks, 361 kilometers of anti-tank trenches, 366 kilometers of anti-tank obstacles, 106 kilometers of dragons' teeth, and 611 kilometers of wire obstacles appeared west of Moscow. In addition, within the city was constructed: 30 kilometers of concrete obstacles, 10 kilometers of barricades, and 19,000 cheval de frise.

The regional committee of the Communist Party published a letter in which they said:

"We must construct such a strong defensive network that no enemy can penetrate it. ...Men and women come out to build the fortifications! We will surround the glory of the Russian People – Moscow – with a fortification belt. ..."

At the same time, the government began to relocate the most important industries. By the end of November, 498 operations, with 210,000 workers, were transported to central Russia or Siberia in 71,000 railroad wagons. At the same time, the foreign missions, embassies, etc. were directed to Kuibyshev, 850 kilometers distant from Moscow. The most important ministries had already been underway since 10/15. At this time, Lenin's coffin was also removed from the mausoleum in "Red Square."

These preparations led to great unrest among the population. The first shops were stormed in Moscow by women and children on 10/19. Panic

Army Group Center

appeared to be inevitable. Then the government intervened. On 10/19, Stalin announced the siege! Army General Zhukov received unlimited powers. The war counsel of Army Group "West Front" issued a decree to the population:

> "Comrades! During the hour of highest danger for our country, the lives of the soldiers belong to the fatherland! The homeland demands the greatest efforts from each of us, all of our strength, courage, bravery, and steadfastness! The fatherland calls on us to establish an insurmountable wall."

Moscow had become a fortress city at the end of October. Indeed, the celebration of the October Revolution was held. However, the ceremonies were not conducted on "Red Square", but in the "Mayakovskaya" Metro Station, where Stalin made a speech. After the celebration, the soldiers moved directly to the front.

The battle for Moscow began!

The battle for Moscow gave no time for pause.

The STAVKA united the fighting divisions in the Kalinin area into a new army group, "Kalinin Front." The commander was the effective Colonel General Konev, and the Chief of Staff was Major General Ivanov. The 3rd Panzer Group, which was attacking here, had to overcome constantly stiffening resistance in order to continue to gain ground to the east. Luckily, the flank was secured to the north. The important communications center of Rzhev was captured on 10/15 by the 206th ID (Lieutenant General Hoefl) and elements of the 26th ID (Major General Weiss).

"Kalinin Front" was ordered to make the 3rd Panzer Group and the infantry divisions of the 9th Army pay dearly for each meter of ground with its armies – 22nd, 29th and 30th Armies, and Army Detachment Lieutenant General Vatutin. The majority of the panzer group bogged down because they did not have sufficient fuel to advance, and the panzer divisions could only form combat groups. However, these were able to break through every small gap in the enemy's front.

Chapter 3: The Attack

Thus, on 10/14 a combat group of the 1st Panzer Division, under Major Eckinger, assaulted Kalinin and captured the undamaged road bridge there. The new commander of the XLI Panzer Corps, Lieutenant General Model, quickly shoved everything into the Volga bridgehead which emerged. Behind the 1st Panzer Division hurried the 900th Training Brigade, followed by the 36th Motorized Infantry Division. Behind them the soldiers of the 6th, 26th, and 162nd ID marched through the mud and slush.

This bridgehead, however, was oriented to the northeast and not to Moscow! At this time, from the 9th Army, only the V Army Corps (General of Infantry Ruoff), with the 35th and 129th ID, fought to the east. Both divisions approached the Mohaisk-Volokolamsk line after unspeakable bravery and heavy losses.

This line formed the rear edge of the Soviet defenses. The rifle divisions in the Mohaisk area were absorbed by the new 5th Army, under Major General Govorov, which fought bitterly along with the 16th Army of Lieutenant General Rokossovskiy. The advance troops of the 4th Panzer Group and the 4th Army perceived the tenacity of the enemy to decrease day by day.

The XL Panzer Corps (General of Cavalry Stumme) slowly closed ranks to the east after the Viazma pocket was mopped up. The first division freed-up – the SS Division "Das Reich" (SS Obergruppenfuehrer Hausser) – captured Gzhatsk and continued to advance. The 2nd, 5th, and 10th Panzer Divisions were not able to follow until six days later. The Division "Das Reich" stood alone against two Russian armies!

On 10/19, the XL Panzer Corps captured Mohaisk. Here the corps stopped, until the first infantry combat groups of the VII Army Corps finally arrived. Then the XL Panzer Corps set out again. The resistance of the enemy and the lack of cooperation from Mother Nature made things much more difficult. The Soviet defenders no longer withdrew from in front of the tanks, and they literally had to be shoved out of their covered trenches.

The 316th Rifle Division (Major General Panfilov) fought on the Volokolamsk highway until the last German armored combat vehicle was destroyed in close combat. The 32nd Siberian Division engaged the SS

Army Group Center

Division "Das Reich" and the panzer brigade of the 10th Panzer Division on the Borodino Heights – once Napoleon's fateful battlefield. The Siberians fought until there were none left alive!

On 10/25, the panzer brigade of the 10th Panzer Division (Colonel von Hauenschild) captured Russa. Then they bogged down; ammunition and fuel was at an end. The IX Army Corps (General of Infantry Geyer) closed ranks, inserting themselves between the XL Panzer Corps and the VII Army Corps. However, the infantrymen could also advance no further. Finally, the 195th IR (Colonel von Neufville) of the 78th ID reached Lokotnya. Therefore, on 10/26, the grenadiers stood right next to Moscow! The road sign indicated only 80 kilometers! However, they did not make it...

The center of the army group froze into positional warfare! On the roads to Moscow stood the VII Army Corps with the 7th, 197th, and 267th ID. The IX Army Corps lay east of Russa with the 78th and 87th ID. The XL and XLVI Panzer Corps closed to the north. On either side of Volokolamsk, on the left flank of the army, the soldiers of the V Army Corps (2nd Panzer Division, 35th, and 106th ID) entrenched. The Landser learned about trench warfare, as their fathers had 25 years before. Not a house stood standing, the roads were a morass, and no supplies came forward. At the end of October, five men shared one loaf of bread for two days! With positional warfare came hunger, sickness, and death.

Technology surrendered to the power of Mother Nature!

The southern flank of the army group – 2nd Army and 2nd Panzer Army – was also not spared. The divisions of the 2nd Army mopped up the pocket and then marched to follow the 2nd Panzer Army. The march of the infantrymen was tormenting. The men had to drag their weapons and equipment through thick mud. No vehicles could make it through the mud. The horses were fed the straw from roofs. On 10/26, the lead elements of the army reached the Oka.

The 2nd Army command was taken from the front and transferred to the southern flank. They were to take command of the XLVIII Panzer Corps, as well as the XLIV and XXXV Corps commands, in order to secure the extended flank in the Livny area.

At the beginning of October, the 2nd Panzer Army organized all operational panzer forces under the XXIV Panzer Corps. The corps was to break-

Chapter 3: The Attack

through toward Tula, in order to be able to defeat the corner-stone of the Moscow defense. The XXIV Panzer Corps fought its way around Mzensk. Finally, when Colonel Eberbach's tank brigade was able to cross the Suzha north of the city, the resistance of the 52nd, 55th, and 283rd Soviet Rifle Divisions collapsed.

Colonel Eberbach's combat group – 6th and 18th Panzer Regiments – won freedom of maneuver to the east. They were able to throw back the 6th Guards, 41st Cavalry Divisions, and the 4th Soviet Tank Brigade near Chern and gain additional ground toward Tula. The 3rd Panzer Division, which was now led by Major General Breith, after Lieutenant General Model left, was ordered to capture the large industrial city of Tula. However, the division bogged down! 2000 of its vehicles became stuck in the mud! Only the "Ju-52" transports could bring fuel forward.

The attack on Tula began on 10/29. The lead group of the 3rd Panzer Division under Major Franck was still five kilometers from Tula that evening! During the night, the 6th Panzer Regiment (Lieutenant Colonel Munzel) closed ranks. The assault on Tula began on 10/30 at 1100 hours in the afternoon. However, only 60 men from the "Grossdeutschland" Regiment were able to enter Tula in a raid, and then they were thrown out. The Russians were the stronger.

On the next day, two battalions of the "Grossdeutschland" Motorized Infantry Regiment (Colonel Hoernlein) were located on the southern edge of Tula. Behind them were the tanks of the 6th Panzer Regiment without one liter of fuel. They could go no further...

Tula was not reached.

The infantrymen, engineers, artillerymen, and radiomen of the XXIV Panzer Corps slowly fought their way forward through the mud. A medical officer wrote in his diary:

> "... The mud is getting thicker. We are sweating in spite of the cold. We break for 10 minutes, then we start to freeze immediately. Everybody is sick and weak. Then one lays in the mud. He can go no further. ..."

Army Group Center

Stalin pointed out the danger represented by the German attack on Moscow to the people through decrees, proclamations, and instructions. He spoke on the occasion of the 24th anniversary of the October Revolution:

> "...If the Germans want a war of destruction, then so be it. From this time on, it will be our mission, the mission of all of the people of the Soviet Union, the mission of the fighters, the commanders, and the political functionaries of the armies and fleets, to destroy all Germans, who have entered our homeland as occupiers, to the very last man! ..."

On the other hand, there are the words written by the commander of the 2nd Panzer Army to his wife in Germany on the very same day:

> "...It is troublesome for the troops if the enemy gains time and we have to continue our plans in the winter. ...How this will turn out, only God knows! ..."

The Russian winter, feared by the leadership and the troops, was approaching. At the beginning of November, frost set in. The land was covered with a thin layer of snow. The ground hardened. The vehicles could move again. However, in just a few minutes, the icy east wind covered men, horses, vehicles, and weapons with a thin coating of ice. The war crept into the poor huts of the villages...

On 11/12, the Chief of the General Staff, Generaloberst Halder, arrived at the army group headquarters in Orsha. He had summoned all of the army chiefs to a meeting to point out the final objectives of the offensive. The Generaloberst assured them that Army Groups North and South had suspended their advance and that only Army Group Center had to continue the offensive. He said:

"Attacking is a better solution than wintering in the wilderness."

Field Marshal von Bock was of the same opinion. He established the reaching of the Moskva in Moscow and the Volga Canal as the operational

Chapter 3: The Attack

objective. However, the OKH went further; it still dreamed of the successes of the summer. Generaloberst Halder ordered that the 2nd Panzer Army – which, on this day, had only 50 operational combat vehicles (they were supposed to have 600) – was to reach Gorki! This was 400 kilometers behind Moscow!!! A request that the Chief of Staff of the 2nd Panzer Army, Colonel Baron von Liebenstein, could only acknowledge by shaking his head without speaking.

The thermometer fell and fell...

The army group needed 32 supply trains per day if it was to remain combat effective. However, only 20 per day were arriving in Smolensk. The highest number was achieved on 11/24, with 24 supply trains. Thus, the first winter clothing only trickled forward. When the temperature registered 20 degrees below zero, the first winter overcoats reached the infantry divisions. However, at first, there was only one coat for every fifth man!

Thus, the army group attacked...

In addition, it had been considerably weakened...

Luftflotte 2 was ordered by OKW to immediately transfer to Italy. Here, the German-Italian troops in North Africa were severely battered and needed active air support if North Africa was to be held. The entire II Air Corps left for Italy and Sicily at this time. The German 27th and 53rd Fighter Squadrons, which had been so successful against the Soviet combat squadrons, as well as the 26th Interceptor Squadron, was lost in a moments notice, just as the final attack was to be launched on Moscow.

Luftflotte 2 reported the following successes during the time period from 6/22 to 11/30/1941:

"Shot down or destroyed: 6670 aircraft, 1900 tanks, 1950 guns, 26,000 vehicles, 2800 trains."

The VIII Air Corps (Generaloberst Baron von Richthofen) took command of all German air forces in the army group sector.

Since 11/14, the Soviet leadership had realized that the German troops were preparing for a new attack on Moscow. Therefore, the STAVKA organized six new armies and immediately inserted them in the front of Moscow's second line of defense. From north to south were deployed: the

Army Group Center

31st Army near Kalinin, 1st Shock Army near Dmitrov, 60th Army west of Moscow, 33rd Army near Naro-Fominsk, 49th Army west of Tula, and the 10th Army east of Tula.

The Soviet defenders occupied their positions. These ran from Rzhev directly to the east up to Klin, then to the south across the Istra Reservoir through Istra, Svenigorod, Kubinskoe, Naro-Fominsk, Zerpukhov, and from here in an arc to Tula.

The army group crashed against this front.

The 9th Army secured the left flank to the north with infantry divisions. Its front stretched from the Kholm area to the west and up to the Volga near Rzhev. The army drove its right flank to the east as soon as the attack of the 3rd Panzer Group was effected.

The 3rd Panzer Group, which was led by General of Panzer Troops Reinhardt since 10/5, was located with the bulk of its forces in and around Kalinin. Only the LVI Panzer Corps (General of Panzer Troops Schaal), with the 6th, 7th Panzer Divisions, 14th Motorized Infantry Divisions, and the XXVII Army Corps (General of Infantry Waeger), with the 86th and 162nd ID, were available north of Volokolamsk. The XXVII Army Corps attacked on 11/15 and reached the southern edge of the Volga Reservoir on the fourth day, behind which the Soviets had withdrawn.

On 11/16, the LVI Panzer Corps attacked across the Lama against the positions of the 30th Soviet Army. The 7th Panzer Division hit the exact seam between the 30th and 16th Armies, overran the 17th Caucasian Cavalry Division after fierce combat and, on 11/20, stood at the Kalinin-Moscow rail line and, several hours later, on the Kalinin-Moscow road. The city of Klin fell into the hands of the 7th Panzer Division and 14th Motorized Infantry Division on 11/23. The 6th Infantry Regiment and elements of the 25th Panzer Regiment, under Colonel von Manteuffel, captured the bridge across the Moscow-Volga Canal near Yakhroma on 11/27 and established a bridgehead. A panzer company under Senior Lieutenant Ohrloff occupied the electric power station that provided Moscow with electricity. The 7th Motorcycle Battalion assaulted the canal locks!

This incredible success, nevertheless, could not be utilized, because the army group ordered that they were to go no further, but were to attack

Chapter 3: The Attack

along the western side of the canal to the south. Therefore, on 11/29, the bridgehead was evacuated. The LVI Panzer Corps took charge of screening the front to the northwest. On the other hand, the XLI Panzer Corps (General of Panzer Troops Model) ordered the continuation of the attack to the south with the 1st, 6th Panzer Divisions, and 23rd ID.

The corps slowly advanced in icy cold, driving snow and against tenacious enemy resistance. The divisions penetrated into the residential suburbs of Moscow. However, then the troops bogged down, and they advanced no farther. On 12/5, the corps combat diary reported:

"... completely exhausted and, for the first time in this campaign, combat incapable. ..."

General of Panzer Troops Reinhardt ordered the suspension of the attack!

The order of the day of the 4th Panzer Group for 11/17 read:

"The time for waiting is over. We can attack again. The last Russian defense before Moscow is defeated. We must stop the beating of the heart of the Bolshevik movement in Europe. ...The panzer group has the good fortune of leading the decisive attack!"

On 11/18, the panzer group attacked between Volokolamsk and Naro-Fominsk. To the left was the V Army Corps (2nd Panzer Division, 35th, 106th ID), which closed on the XLVI Panzer Corps (5th and 11th Panzer Divisions), XL Panzer Corps (10th Panzer Division, SS Division "Das Reich"), and IX Army Corps (78th and 87th ID), and on the right flank marched the VII Army Corps with the 7th, 197th, and 267th ID.

The V Army Corps (General of Infantry Ruoff) had the furthest distance to cover and, therefore, attacked 24 hours earlier than the neighboring corps in the direction of Klin. The Soviets energetically took up the defense. The 44th Siberian Cavalry Division rode in close order with drawn sabers against the Mussino Heights and the 106th ID. The last classic cavalry attack in military history came to a bloody end in the fire of German guns. Then the way to Klin was open. The 106th ID (Major General Dehner) reached the area in front of Klin on 11/23. The 2nd Panzer Division (Lieutenant General Veiel) severed the Leningrad-Moscow rail line near Solnechnogorsk on the same day. The division attacked north past the Istra Reservoir together with the 35th ID (Lieutenant General Fischer von Weikertsthal), bypassed it, and then penetrated to the south. The 2nd Panzer Division reached the Klaisma Reservoir on 11/27.

The sign indicated: "Moscow = 35 kilometers!"

The infantrymen, engineers, and tankers did not give up. In spite of the driving snow and icy cold east wind, they attacked further. The 106th ID (Major General Dehner) reached Krasnaya Polyana, 27 kilometers in front of Moscow. The 35th ID – whose command was taken over by Major General Baron von Roman on 12/2 – was able to reach Kryukovo and Matushkino, in cooperation with the 11th Panzer Division (Major General Scheller). From there, it was another 22 kilometers to the Kremlin! The 2nd Panzer Division, fighting on the left flank of the corps, approached even closer to the Russian capital. The 62nd Engineer Battalion advanced up to Khimki, a Moscow suburb, which lay a distance of 16 kilometers from "Red Square." Individual assault troops of the battalion worked their way an additional eight kilometers further.

These were the soldiers that stood the closest to Moscow!

The two panzer corps, which formed the main effort, made a frontal attack against the Soviet defensive positions west of the Istra. The XLVI Panzer Corps (General of Panzer Troops von Vietinghoff) reached the Istra Reservoir on 11/23. Without stopping, the advance detachments of the two divisions attacked across the ice of the 18 kilometer long and 2 kilometer wide reservoir. The 61st Motorcycle Battalion (11th Panzer Division), under Major von Usedom, was the first across, directly followed by the 1/89 Engineer Battalion (5th Panzer Division). Senior Lieutenant Breitschuh's engineers removed 1100 mines and 40 fused explosives in a short period of time.

The XL Panzer Corps (General of Cavalry Stumme) fought against bitter resistance on the Volokolamsk-Istra road. Neither side would give

Chapter 3: The Attack

any quarter. On 11/25, the 10th Panzer Division (Major General Fischer) and the SS Division "Das Reich" (SS Obergruppenfuehrer Hausser) stood on the Istra. The combat group of Lieutenant Colonel Dr. Mauss (10th Panzer Division) assaulted Istra on the following day, which was bitterly defended by the 78th Siberian Rifle Division. The Siberians did not give way and had to be forced out individually. The men of the "Das Reich" Motorcycle Battalion, under Sturmbannfuehrer Klingenberg, were only able to create a passage to the citadel with their side arms and spades.

The strength of the corps was exhausted after the capture of Istra. Only individual SS assault troops continued to advance to the southeast. On 11/28, in -32 degree cold, they were able to capture Vykovo and, three days later, Linino. Only 34 kilometers separated the SS men from the Kremlin!

The IX Army Corps (General of Infantry Geyer) advanced north of the Moskva to cover the flank. The corps had contact neither on the left nor the right. On 11/24, the 78th ID (Colonel Weber) bogged down in the Moskva Valley. The 87th ID (Lieutenant General von Studnitz) and the 252nd ID (Lieutenant General von Boehm-Bezing) continued to struggle through -34 degree cold and an icy snow storm. The 461st IR (252nd ID), under Colonel Karst, stood alone on the front. The advance combat group of the 87th ID made it to Chernaya Gryas, 35 kilometers from Moscow. Then they went no further.

The VII Army Corps (General of Infantry Fahrmbacher), attacking south of Moscow, pressed against ice and snow and against the heavy attacks of the 20th Soviet Army, which was led by one of the best minds in the "Red Army", Lieutenant General Vlassov. The 267th ID (Major General Wachter) took up the protection of the frozen Moskva. The 197th ID (Lieutenant General Meyer-Rabingen) attacked in the center, while the 7th ID (Lieutenant General Baron von Gablenz) attempted to protect the open right flank with the subordinate French volunteer regiment.

The advance of the panzer group became more difficult, strenuous, and costly day by day. Therefore, on 12/3, Generaloberst Hoepner ordered a three day halt on his own!

Field Marshal von Kluge's 4th Army, which closed on the right, did not take part in these attacks! During the mud period, the army remained in

Army Group Center

favorable positions from Naro-Fominsk to northwest of Aleksin. The army had committed, from right to left: XIII Army Corps (260th, 52nd, 17th ID), XII Army Corps (137th, 267th, 98th ID), LVII Panzer Corps (19th Panzer Division, 258th, 15th ID), and the XX Army Corps (292nd, 183rd ID, 3rd Motorized Infantry Division). The immobility of the army was caused by an enemy attack, which hit the XIII Army Corps (General of Infantry Felber) particularly hard. The corps was in crisis and could only be extracted from its unpleasant situation by combat groups of the XII Army Corps. Field Marshal von Kluge held up his army as long as the situation could not be mastered. On 12/1, it was. Then the XX Army Corps (General of Infantry Materna) and LVII Panzer Corps (General of Panzer Troops Kuntzen) attacked. The XX Army Corps advanced the quickest. It reached the highway east of Naro-Fominsk on the first day with all of its divisions – 3rd Motorized Infantry Division, as well as the 183rd, 258th, and 292nd ID – and penetrated into the enemy defensive positions with the support of the 27th Panzer Regiment. The 3rd Motorized Infantry Division (Lieutenant General Jahn) assaulted Naro-Fominsk in -38 degree cold! Elements of its 29th IR and the 2/479 IR of the 258th ID penetrated into the city, but they could go no further. Only the 258th ID (Major General Pflaum) reached Yushkovo – 44 kilometers from Moscow – with the 58th Reconnaissance Battalion, 1/258 Anti-tank Battalion, and the 1/611 Air Defense Battalion.

At this time, the 4th Army command suspended further attacks and withdrew all of the advanced divisions back to the departure positions behind the Nara. Therefore, the frontal attack of the 4th Army and 4th Panzer Army had failed decisively!

The 2nd Panzer Army (Generaloberst Guderian) was to roll from Tula to the Moscow defensive positions and cut off Moscow in the east from the interior. This offensive sacrificed the army.

The strong points in front of Tula, which were gained in a raid by formations of the 3rd Panzer Division and the "Grossdeutschland" Motorized Infantry Regiment, had to be evacuated on 11/9. The resistance of the 50th Soviet Army, under Lieutenant General Boldin, was too much for the exhausted German infantrymen and tankers. In the meantime, Tula was turned

Chapter 3: The Attack

into a fortress. Colonel Melnikov supervised the defensive preparations. A militia regiment, under the command of Gorshkov, had repulsed the first German attacks. Then the 4th Tank Brigade (Colonel Katukov) arrived, and it immediately counterattacked the advanced elements of the 3rd and 4th Panzer Divisions. (The tank brigade was redesignated as the 1st Guards Tank Brigade on 11/11.)

Generaloberst Guderian committed the XLVII Panzer Corps (General of Panzer Troops Lemelsen) on the right flank with the mission of reaching the line Yefrimov-Mikhailov, east of Venev. The LIII Army Corps (General of Infantry Weisenberger) advanced in the direction of Venev. The main effort again lay with the XXIV Panzer Corps (General of Panzer Troops Baron Geyr von Schweppenburg), which was to capture Tula in a flanking attack. The XLIII Army Corps (General of Infantry Heinrici) had to advance through Kaluga toward Aleksin to secure contact with the 4th Army.

The troops advanced slowly to the northeast in the icy frost – the temperature fell several degrees daily. The 18th Panzer Division (Major General Nehring) captured Yefremov on 11/20. The division continued to advance combat groups further to the northeast. In this manner, the 88th Reconnaissance Battalion (Major von Seydlitz) reached the town of Skopin near Gorlovo. It was the eastern-most point soldiers of Army Group Center were to occupy in Russia!

The 10th Motorized Infantry Division (Lieutenant General von Loeper) penetrated to Mikhailov on 11/26 and was able to blow up the railroad bridge on the Voronezh-Moscow line with an engineer assault troop. Then the division had to entrench on a 60(!) kilometers wide front into the snow and ice. The 29th Motorized Infantry Division (Major General Fremery) occupied Yepifan, south of Mikhailov, but it then had to turn elements to the west, because the 239th Siberian Division was threatening from that direction.

The XXIV Panzer Corps reached Tula for the second time. Generaloberst Guderian wrote:

> "The icy cold, the wretched shelters, the shortage of clothing, the high losses in men and equipment, the lack of heating fuel made the conduct of battle a chore. ..."

Army Group Center

On the left flank of the corps, the 296th ID (Lieutenant General Stemmermann) held the southern edge of Tula. Its front stretched far to the west and east. Northeast from them the 3rd Panzer Division (Major General Breith) labored its way to the west through snow and ice. The one time successful division fought against the 154th, 299th, 413th Rifle Divisions and 31st Cavalry Division. The 4th Panzer Division (Major General Baron von Langermann and Erlencamp) fought on the Vashana. On 11/24, the 17th Panzer Division (Colonel Licht) entered Venev. Its reconnaissance battalion advanced from here 20 kilometers to the north and reached the area 3 kilometers south of Kashira. Then they had also reached the end of their strength. From this point the objective, Moscow, was still 80 kilometers away.

The LIII Army Corps (General of Infantry Weisenberger; from 11/28 Lieutenant General Fischer von Weikersthal) followed in second echelon on the left, closing the gap between the XXIV and XLVII Panzer Corps with the 167th ID and 112th ID.

The XLIII Army Corps, which was on the left, fought alone on a wide front. The left division – 131st ID (Major General Meyer-Burgdorf) – no longer had contact with the right flanking division of the 4th Army. On 1/27, the 131st ID was able to capture Aleksin from the south. Then the strength of the corps was exhausted. General of Infantry Heinrici suspended the attack.

The army group command was not satisfied. On 11/29, it ordered the 2nd Panzer Army to execute the battle of Tula under all circumstances! The 2nd Panzer Army command now planned to attack the XXIV Panzer Corps from east to west and the XLIII Army Corps from west to east, in order to have them meet north of Tula and, therefore, cause the fall of the city and the fortress.

The last phase of the battle of Tula began on 12/2. On the very next day, the last tanks of the 3rd and 4th Panzer Divisions crossed the Tula-Moscow rail line near Revyakino. The 4th Panzer Division was even able to take Kostrovo on 12/4. Their lead panzer elements now stood 15 kilometers from the 131st ID!

Then the temperature sank again during the night. It was -37 degrees! On the morning, none of the tank engines started and none of the gun

Chapter 3: The Attack

breeches opened. On the other hand, the winter mobile Soviet battalions attacked near Venev and blew the 17th and 4th Panzer Divisions apart! In spite of this critical situation, Generaloberst Guderian continued to attack the XLIII Army Corps. The corps now shifted the main effort to the 31st ID (Major General Berthold) on the right. The division attacked in the grim cold, broke through the first enemy positions, and then bogged down. Losses were enormous. The 82nd IR registered 100 dead and 800 frost bite cases in one day! The 3/17 IR – the Goslarer Jaeger – were bloodied.

Generaloberst Guderian ordered: "Halt! Defend!"

He broke off the battle of Tula.

The combat diary of the 2nd Panzer Army reported on 12/5:

"The combat strength of the brave troops has come to an end after an enormous effort! The troops must now stop! The army will gradually withdraw to the Don-Shat-Upa positions!"

It was now the hour of the "Red Army"!

The military leadership of the Soviet Union had been planning to decisively stop the German offensive since October, and they had a force potential available. The industries, which were transferred to Siberia, began to turn out their first products. By the rigorous measures of the political and economic functionaries, they were able to deploy the manpower and material of the enormous empire. The agents in Moscow reported that Japan was not going to join in the war against the Soviet Union. Therefore, the STAVKA immediately ordered that the troops of the Far Eastern armies be quickly transported to the Western Front.

Thus, during the first days of December, 30 rifle, 3 cavalry divisions, 33 rifle, and 6 tank brigades rolled fresh on to the front, while the German Army received neither supplies for the men and weapons nor rations or fuel!

The STAVKA reorganized the troops in front of Moscow. They formed strong assault combat groups from their armies. The plan foresaw:

1. The cutting off of the two German panzer wedges in the north and south before Moscow,

Army Group Center

2. Attacks through the open flanks,
3. The destruction of Army Group Center.

The attack wedges were to be met near Viazma. Therefore, the entire army group would be encircled and the Eastern Army would suffer catastrophic defeat. The Russian Army marched to this enormous counter offensive from north to south as follows:

    Army Group "Kalinin Front" with 22nd, 29th, 31st, 39th and 30th Armies;
    Army Group "West Front" with 1st Shock, 20th, 16th, 5th, 33rd, 43rd, 49th, 50th and 10th Armies
    Army Group "Southwest Front" (from 25/12 "Briansk Front") with 3rd, 13 and 61st Armies.

The Soviet air forces remained subordinate to the armies as before. In comparison to the weak forces of the VIII German Air Corps, they were far superior. On 12/5/1941, they were organized as follows:

Army Group "West Front":
10th, 46th Fighter Divisions,
12th, 23rd, 28th, 31st, 38th, 43rd, 47th, 77th, 146th,
Combat Air Divisions;
Army Group "Southwest Front":
11th, 61st Fighter Divisions;
Directly subordinate to STAVKA:
26th, 40th, 42nd, 51st, 52nd, 81st, 133rd
Long Range Air Divisions.

This enormous deployment was neither recognized nor expected by the Germans. Only the officers and soldiers at the front had a presentiment that "something was cooking" in the east. On 12/1, Field Marshal von Bock implored the Army Chief of the General Staff from his headquarters in Orsha:

Chapter 3: The Attack

"The attack now appears to make no sense and have no purpose, the time is fast approaching when the strength of the troops will be completely exhausted!"

The strength of the troops was already exhausted. The German Eastern Army had suffered, up to this point in time, 158,773 dead, 563,082 wounded, and 31,191 missing. Even worse were the losses in vehicles and weapons. The panzer army of Generaloberst Guderian had only 25 tanks left – it was supposed to have 600!

Then the "Red Army" hit!

They launched their offensive on the morning of 12/5. Hundreds of combat and fighter-bomber aircraft attacked the freezing and hungry German soldiers with bombs and machine-gun fire, thousands of shells smashed into their shelters, and guns and thousands upon thousands of voices yelled "Hurrah!"

The attack hit the German front with its full weight.

Army Group "Kalinin Front" attacked on a wide front to the south in between the Valdai Hills and Kalinin. Army Groups "West Front" and "Southwest Front" followed on 12/6 with 88 rifle, 15 cavalry divisions, and 24 tank brigades. The temperatures averaged under 30 degrees [below zero]. The Russian troops were 100% equipped for winter warfare.

The German front withdrew in disarray. Only the 4th Army held temporarily in their favorable positions behind the Nara.

The attack of Army Group "Southwest Front" in the extreme south threw back the front of the 2nd Army in the first assault. The 3rd, 13th, and 61st Soviet Armies attacked through the lines of the defenders between Livny and Yefremov.

Field Marshal von Bock reported to the OKH on 12/9:

"The army group is no longer in the situation to withstand the enemy attack!"

On the following day, he telephoned again:

Army Group Center

"2nd Army is broken through near Livny. 45th and 134th ID are overrun!"

On 12/12 at 1130 hours, von Bock called a third time:

"Situation critical!"

The three armies of the "Southwest Front" had attacked through the German front. The 45th ID (Major General Schlieper) was swept aside near Livny, in spite of bitter resistance. The neighboring 134th ID was dispersed during the maelstrom of the withdrawal and died on the battlefield in front of Orel. Its commander, Lieutenant General von Cochenhausen, fell with hundreds of his soldiers.

General of Panzer Troops Schmidt, who led the 2nd Army since 11/15/1941, could do nothing more than order a withdrawal to rear area positions that had not yet been prepared. On 12/14, he was ordered by the OKH to do the following:

"The 2nd Army will be subordinated to the commander of the 2nd Panzer Army. Both armies will hold positions forward of the line Kursk-in front of Orel-Plavskoe-Aleksin!"

However, this order was already overtaken by events on the following day. The left flank of Army Group "West Front" attacked the 2nd Panzer Army. The I Guards Cavalry Corps (Major General Belov) advanced toward Venev, the 10th Army (Lieutenant General Golikov) captured Kashira and Yepifan, and the 50th Army of Lieutenant General Boldin drove the XXIV Panzer Corps and the XLIII Army Corps apart south of Tula. The XXIV Panzer Corps evacuated Chern on 12/17 and withdrew to Mzensk. The 10th Motorized Infantry Division was partially encircled near Chern, but it was able to fight its way out with great difficulty. The gap to the XLIII Army Corps grew to a width of 40 kilometers within a few days!

Through this gap alone attacked 22 rifle divisions and the I Guards Cavalry Corps. The commander of the Smolensk rear area, Lieutenant

Chapter 3: The Attack

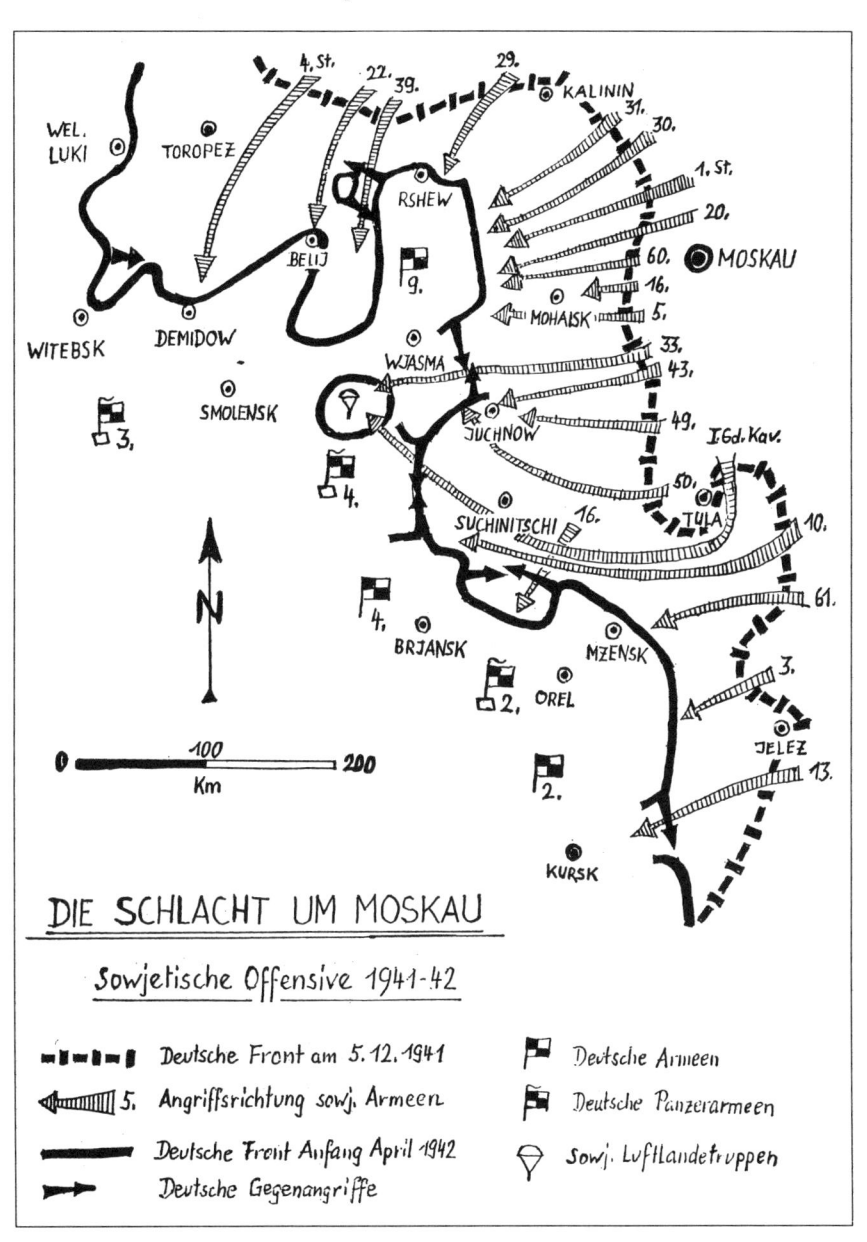

*The Battle of Moscow
Soviet Offensive 1941-42*

Army Group Center

General von Unruh, was designated combat commandant and received construction battalions and other supply troops, with which he was to close the gap. However, it was too late!

The XLIII Army Corps (General of Infantry Heinrici) was split off from the 2nd Panzer Army, and it fought its way back to Kaluga. Here it defended the city with its three divisions (31st, 131st, and 137th ID) until 12/30. Therefore, the corps protected the right flank of the 4th Army and helped to stabilize the German front!

On Christmas Day 1941, the 2nd Panzer Army was also separated from the 2nd Army. The Soviet troops broke through on a 70 kilometer front southeast of Orel and assaulted toward the Dessna. During these hours of crisis, Generaloberst Guderian ordered the surrender of the Oka-Suzha line, which was still being held in the east, and its withdrawal to the west. This decision was particularly difficult for the Generaloberst to make. He did, however, save his army by making it.

The right flank of the army group now practically hung in the breeze. Contact with Army Group South was decisively lost. In the Maloarkhangelsk area, the LV Army Corps (General of Infantry Vierow) was able to construct a temporary front line with all available troops, so that the Russian breakthrough would not lead to total chaos.

The catastrophe of the army group, however, was not only on the right flank, but along the entire front. The OKH energetically interfered in the command and control. Field Marshal von Bock fell seriously ill on 12/17 and had to relinquish command. Field Marshal von Kluge took over command of the army group. The command of the 4th Army went to General of Mountain Troops Kuebler.

On 12/19, Hitler relieved Field Marshal von Brauchitsch and took over the OKH himself. He issued Basic Order Nr. 442 182/41:

> "Any large withdrawal is inadmissable, because this will lead to the loss of heavy weapons and equipment. The senior commanders, commanders, and all officers must insure the occupation of positions by their personal example to the troops, disregard the enemy troops that have broken through on the flanks and into the rear of our troops, defend with fanatical tenacity!"

Chapter 3: The Attack

The Soviets now frontally attacked the 4th Army and 4th Panzer Army west of Moscow. The withdrawal of the 4th Army cost much blood and many lives. Losses were caused less by wounds than by freezing. The troops registered 90% of their losses from frost bite. The 5th, 33rd, and 43rd Soviet Armies attacked through the front of the 4th Army on 12/12 and pushed them back between Yukhnov and Mohaisk. The II Guards Cavalry Corps (Major General Dovator) tore the front of the 4th Army and 4th Panzer Army apart in an attack across the Moskva southwest of Svenigorod. The gaps between VII Army Corps in the south and IX Army Corps in the north could not be closed.

The IX Army Corps (General of Infantry Geyer) fought back to the Rusa and finally held off the attacks of the Cossack regiments here. Therefore, a fiasco on the right flank of the 4th Panzer Army was averted!

The 3rd Panzer Army was attacked frontally by the 30th, 1st Shock, 20th, and 16th Soviet Armies. The 30th Army attacked through the seam between the 14th and 36th Motorized Infantry Divisions toward Klin. The city could only be held by the quick intervention of elements of the 1st Panzer Division. However, the entire LVI Panzer Corps (General of Panzer Troops Schaal) was, therefore, now in danger of being encircled. Klin was the center point of the army's defense. The LVI Panzer Corps entrenched here in the ice and snow and made it possible for the other divisions of the army to withdraw to the west. On 12/14, Klin was given up.

Two days later, Klin fell. Therefore, the 3rd Panzer Army was defeated and had to quickly withdraw to the west. The combat report of the 3rd Panzer Army on 12/21/1941 read:

> "The picture of the withdrawal route was not a pretty one, discipline began to relax. ... Often leaderless convoys took to the roads, while the fighting troops from all branches of arms, including the air defense troops, held forward with their last ounce of strength. The convoys were taken by panic. ... Without rations, they fled leaderless. ... Road ice, up-slopes, long bridge ramps all slowed the march tempo. ... This is the worst hour of the panzer group!"

Army Group Center

Christmas Day 1941 would determine whether or not the army group would survive. Finally, the OKH intervened. On 12/20, Hitler ordered all available Army reserves to be sent to the army group. The message from OKW to OKH read:

> "Hold and fight until the last. Do not take one voluntary step backward. ... Construct a rear area line in a strong point-like manner. ... Assemble stragglers and send them forward. ... Prisoners and inhabitants will be relieved of their winter clothing. Burn down valuable farms!"

This message was passed on in sharper form by the OKH on the same day in Nr. 3208/41 gKdos. The new commander of the army group, Field Marshal von Kluge, explained this "Führer Order":

> "Everyone must hold where he stands! ... My personal approval must be received before any withdrawal of a division formation!"

The Field Marshal found fault with the arbitrariness of the order from his superior, but passed it on. Thus, at the moment the two outstanding panzer leaders, Generalobersts Guderian and Hoepner, had to engage in a hopeless battle with their troops, and Guderian was relieved of his post. Two days later, on 12/28, the commander of the army group received a letter from Hitler:

> "Strip Generaloberst Hoepner of his shoulder boards and send him home. Effective immediately, he has been discharged by me from the Wehrmacht!"

At this time, Army Group Center was defending on a 780 kilometer wide front. Its six armies were fighting – without any Luftwaffe support, without heavy tanks, without supply – against 16 Soviet armies and two cavalry corps that were much better equipped for winter warfare.

Chapter 3: The Attack

The Chief of the General Staff of the "Red Army", Colonel General Shaposhnikov, told the army commanders:

> "We must first gather our experience in modern warfare. We have, indeed, driven the enemy from in front of the capital; however, the war will not be decided here. It will take time!"

4

THE DEFENSE
Positional Warfare 1942

The winter was merciless.

At the end of the year, the temperature registered between -20 and -30 degrees. The snow lay on the roads, fields, and in the thick forests up to one meter deep. The houses in the poor towns were burned down. The soldiers had to seek temporary cover from the icy east wind behind walls of snow. They had no winter clothing. Frostbite increased dramatically and far surpassed the number of bullet wounds.

The soldiers of the army group continued on in spite of this. They were now on their own. The horses fell into the snow from hunger and disease. Wherever they fell in the snow, they were covered with a thick coating of ice in minutes. The motorized battalions were stuck as fast as the infantry battalions. They lacked antifreeze for the fuel and the oil. They had to warm the engines before they could start them. The artillery had to blow up their guns. There were no more prime movers and even if there were, they could not fire the guns, since the breeches were frozen.

The evacuation of the wounded on stretchers and in ambulances became a race against their freezing to death. And all too often, the cold was the winner. The shadow of the "Grande Armee" of Napoleon stretched over the army group – if one could still call it an army group! Then ... the enemy

Chapter 4: The Defense

hit unmercifully. On 7 January 1942, the High Command of the "Red Army" issued new objectives to its armies and "fronts" for the second phase of the offensive:

The "Briansk Front", which hitherto had recaptured 1100 towns and villages and completely defeated the right flank of Army Group Center with a cleverly executed attack, was to advance toward Orel.

The "West Front" was ordered to advance on Yukhnov and, in cooperation with the "Kalinin Front", encircle the German troops in the Mohaisk-Gzatsk-Viazma area. In addition, Army General Zhukov ordered his armies:

1st Shock, 20th, 16th Armies: Syschevka-Rzhev;
5th, 33rd Armies: Mohaisk-Gzhatsk;
43rd, 49th, 50th Armies: Yukhnov-Viazma;
I Guards Cavalry Corps: Viazma;
10th Army: Kirov.

The "Kalinin Front" was to attack Rzhev with the 29th and 31st Armies, the 30th and 39th Armies were to attack west of there toward Sychevka, while the 22nd Army had to sever the Rzhev-Velikie Luki railroad line.

The "Northwest Front" on the extreme right flank had the mission of separating Army Group Center from Army Group North with the newly formed 3rd and 4th Shock Armies, included in this front were offensives against Kholm, Velikie Luki, Toropets, and Velizh.

On 2 January, Field Marshal von Kluge, commander of the army group, requested an immediate withdrawal of the armies, after the Soviet penetrations and breakthroughs were noted near Maloyaroslavets and Staritsa. However, the OKH held fast to the viewpoint that the existing gaps were to be closed before the surrender of any positions could be considered.

How were things going on the front at this time?

Army Group Center

The "Briansk Front" (commander: Colonel General Cherevichenko, Chief of Staff: Major General Kolpakchi) had thrown the right flank of the army group far back to the west by the end of the year. Its 40th Army broke through the thin front of the XLVIII Panzer Corps (General of Panzer Troops Kempf) southeast of Kursk on 1/6. At this time, the lead motorized rifle and ski regiments reached the Kursk-Oboyan road and penetrated into the suburbs of Oboyan.

The German forces here – the 239th, 299th ID, and 16th Motorized Infantry Division – stood against the crashing waves of Soviets in -40 degree temperatures. Because the combat groups of the 3rd Panzer Division were brought up in time, the positions on the Seim were held.

The situation was in no way alleviated. Several days later, the III Guards Cavalry Corps, with the 5th, 6th Guards Cavalry Divisions, 32nd Cavalry Division, and 34th Rifle Brigade, broke through the German front between XLVIII Panzer Corps and the LV Army Corps, the flanking corps of Army Group South. The Soviets crossed the Tim, advanced on Shchigry, threw back the 9th Panzer Division and 95th ID, and threatened Kursk. Again, the 3rd Panzer Division was brought up, thrown against the III Guards Cavalry Corps, and was able to defeat them in a daring attack. Major General Breith, commander of the 3rd Panzer Division, was the first officer to receive the Oak Leaves to the Knight's Cross during the new year. He had saved the right flank of the army group with his combat groups.

At the end of January, combat here slackened off.

The attack of the "West Front" had torn through the front of the 2nd Panzer Army and the 4th Army between Belev and Kaluga four weeks before. The 10th Soviet Army attacked into this gap with six rifle, 4 cavalry divisions, and 1 tank brigade, in order to advance on Yukhnov.

The 80 kilometer wide front was completely lost to the German troops. The only large formation standing here was the combat inexperienced 216th ID under Major General Baron von und zu Gilsa. The division was just sent from France. When it was unloaded in Sukhinichi, the Soviets arrived! Sukhinichi was encircled.

Then a Führer Order arrived: "The town is to be held under all circumstances!"

Chapter 4: The Defense

Major General Baron von und zu Gilsa held Sukhinichi as a breakwater with the 396th IR (Lieutenant Colonel Schaer) and stragglers – approximately 5000 men. The 10th Soviet Army and the I Guards Cavalry Corps were already far to the west, as Sukhinichi was still being fought over.

The commander of the 2nd Panzer Army decided to relieve Sukhinichi. A combat group consisting of elements of the 18th Panzer Division and the 208th ID, under Major General Nehring, was prepared for this operation around Zhisdra on 14 January. The combat group set out two days later. The center, elements of the 208th ID under Colonel Jolasse, hit the 323rd Soviet Rifle Division on 1/17, and the Soviets were beaten back in fierce combat. Major General Nehring continued to march with four detachments. The march route of the columns was the front line. The enemy was on all sides.

In the meantime, the High Command in Moscow removed the 16th Army from the Moscow area to Sukhinichi to finally eliminate the German strong point. The commander of the army, Lieutenant General Rokossovskiy, was severely wounded at this time. Because of his loss, the army was leaderless.

Combat Group Nehring penetrated through the center of the 16th Soviet Army. The 5th Panzer Regiment (Colonel Kuzmany) established contact with the encircled troops on 1/24 at 1230 hours. While the 1000 wounded of the 216th ID were being transported to the west, another Führer Order arrived: "Hold at all costs!"

Major Generals Nehring and Baron von und zu Gilsa did not uphold this order. They ordered a breakout! Hitler and the OKH gave in. Major Generals Nehring and Baron von und zu Gilsa received the Oak Leaves to the Knight's Cross; Major General Nehring was assigned as commander of the "German Afrikakorps" on 2/1. Hitler issued an order of the day:

"This action had great significance for the entire situation!"

The 49th and 50th Soviet Armies had blown through the front of the XLIII Army Corps (General of Infantry Heinrici) and encircled them. The corps did not give up. A first attempt to break out to the west failed. The

Army Group Center

second, on 14 January, succeeded. The infantry regiments fought to the north, suffering heavy casualties. The enemy attacked the combat groups from all sides unmercifully. The fight was conducted with extreme bitterness and without quarter. The 31st Anti-tank Battalion (Lieutenant Colonel Ulrich) defended Kostino as the rear guard. On 1/29 at 1455 hours, the last radio message arrived from them:

"The right quarter of the town is lost ... Kostino!"

Then nothing further was heard from the battalion.

The breakout of the XLIII Army Corps succeeded! General of Infantry Heinrici was entrusted with the defense of Yukhnov. The lead elements of the 43rd, 49th, and 50th Soviet Armies attacked the city on 3 February. However, the mixed combat groups of General Heinrici held their positions around Yukhnov and, therefore, so did the front of the 4th Army and 4th Panzer Army (On 1 January, the former panzer groups were redesignated into panzer armies).

On 20 January, General of Infantry Heinrici had taken command of the 4th Army. At the same time, two other commands were changed. The former commander of the 9th Army, Generaloberst Strauss, became severely ill on 1/15. General of Panzer Troops Model was his replacement. A day earlier, General of Infantry Ruoff took command of the 4th Panzer Army after Generaloberst Hoepner was discharged from the Wehrmacht.

On 15 January, the OKH ordered a general retreat to a line Rzhev-Gzhatsk-Yukhnov, which was held to some extent.

The Soviets reinforced their attack in the sector of the "West Front." Here the I Guards Cavalry Corps was advanced between Sukhinichi and Yukhnov to the northwest and had reached the area south of Viazma. At the same time, the 33rd and 5th Armies broke through between Yukhnov and Mohaisk (Mohaisk was occupied by the 5th Army on 1/20) and they approached Viazma from the west.

On the same day, the STAVKA ordered the I Guards Cavalry Corps to capture Viazma in cooperation with the 4th, 8th, and 201st Airborne Brigades. The three airborne brigades were dropped between Viazma and

Chapter 4: The Defense

Yartsevo and were to fall onto the rear of the German front from the west.

The left flank of Army Group Center – 3rd Panzer Army and 9th Army – were also battered in mid-January and pushed back to the west. The 20th Soviet Army, under Lieutenant General Vlassov, advanced into the Volokolamsk sector on 1/13 and opened the way for the II Guards Cavalry Corps (Major General Pliev), which was also advancing on Viazma from the northeast.

Therefore, it appeared that the strength of the "Red Army" was weakening. At the end of January, the front of the German armies stabilized. The Soviets suspended their offensive between Kalinin and Kursk!

This new strategic situation meant that the far advanced Army Groups "Kalinin Front", "West Front", and "Briansk Front" had to overcome their supply problems, which could not be mastered with the means available. The "History of the Great Patriotic War" – the multi-volume work of the Soviet General Staff – described the bogging down of the winter offensive 1941/42 as follows:

> "The overestimation of our success was not in tune with reality. The splintering of the strategic reserves led to a lack of the necessary forces in the breakthrough gaps. The frittering away of the tank and cavalry formations did not allow for the establishment of a main effort. The failure of the High Command ultimately allowed the Germans to establish their defense."

On the German side, it must be admitted that the strict Führer Order to "Hold at any price" was, in fact, correct in this situation and in the extreme cold. An unplanned retreat through the ice and snow would have led to the destruction of the army group within a few days. In addition, the will of the individual soldier to survive cannot be forgotten, since this had much to do with the stabilization of the front!

At the beginning of February, it appeared the army group had survived the crisis. Now the commanders energetically assembled their troops for counterattack, not only to throw back the widely separated enemy forces, but to encircle them.

Army Group Center

Generaloberst Schmidt, the commander of the 2nd Panzer Army, conducted a concentrated counterattack with mixed combat groups out of the Mzensk area in the east and Zhisdra in the west against the 61st Soviet Army, which had driven a deep wedge into the German front northwest of Orel.

The German attack achieved complete success. Elements of the 61st Army were encircled northeast of Zhisdra and systematically destroyed. The frontal salient was removed. The German main combat line again shifted back to the east between Zhisdra in the south and Spas Demensk in the north. The second deep enemy penetration in the German front existed west of Yukhnov. Troops of the 4th Army and 4th Panzer Army attacked out of the north and south on 3 February against the 33rd Army. In spite of their courage, the Soviets could not prevent their being compressed into a small area and having the front straightened out here.

The situation on the Eastern Front was considerably improved.

After spring arrived, the snow melted and the roads were turned into mud puddles, and all combat activity ceased.

In April 1942, the 4th Panzer Army was removed from the front and directly subordinated to the OKH as reserve. In June, the 4th Panzer Army was transferred to Army Group South to participate in the Stalingrad offensive here.

Long before – at the end of January – the command of the 3rd Panzer Army was taken from its former area of operations. General of Panzer Troops Reinhardt and his staff took command of all German troops on the left flank of the army group.

Here lay the main effort of the Soviet offensive. Here it appeared that a catastrophe was being prepared for the army group. Perhaps it would come to its end in this sector of the front. ...

At the end of December 1941, Soviet Army Group "Northwest Front" was ordered to separate Army Groups North and Center with its two shock armies. The 3rd Shock Army was to strike the right flank of Army Group North between Demyansk and Kholm. The 4th Shock Army had to destroy the left flank of Army Group Center.

Chapter 4: The Defense

The 4th Shock Army – this was the former 27th Army – attacked on 9 January 1942 with 8 rifle divisions, 4 independent artillery regiments, 3 tank battalions, and 10 ski battalions against the left flanking division of Army Group Center (253rd ID). This one division could not hold up against this superior force by itself. They lost the town of Peno to the 249th Rifle Division (Colonel Tarasov).

The OKH quickly recognized the danger here and ordered elements of the LIX Army Corps, which had just arrived from France, to immediately stop the gap between Army Groups Center and North. This was the Silesian 189th IR from the 81st ID that was thrown directly from the railroad cars into the battle between Anreapol and Okhvat.

"The regiment's winter equipment was laughable."

This harsh sentence was logged in the combat diary of the corps. It simply meant that the Silesian infantrymen had to do battle without any winter equipment against the excellently trained for winter combat and better equipped Soviet ski battalions and motorized infantry battalions!

The battle resulted in the sacrifice of the 189th IR. The regiment, under Colonel Hohmeyer, was bloodied in the forests around Okhvat. 1100 officers and soldiers, including the regiment commander, did not return. The Silesians had held off an entire army for four days!

The next strong point was Toropets. The 85th IR, 207th Anti-tank Battalion, and a wheeled company were encircled by the 360th Rifle Division. The defenders were, nevertheless, able to fight their way to the southwest.

Losses on both sides were heavy. The 4th Shock Army was subordinated to the "Kalinin Front" on 1/22 and was ordered: "Attack into the rear of Army Group Center!" The army had neither contact with the 3rd Shock Army on the right, which had bogged down in front of Kholm and Velikie Luki, nor with the 22nd Army on the left.

The 4th Shock Army reached the Velizh-Kresty area on a wide front. Then the tenacious German defense became noticeable. The LIX Army Corps (Lieutenant General von der Chevallerie) arrived with the 81st (Colonel Schopper), 83rd (Major General von Zuelow), 205th (Lieutenant General Richter), and 330th ID (Major General Count von Rothkirch). The corps established a defensive block in the first weeks of February between Vitebsk and Demidov. From the left to the right, the 277th, 416th, 556th, 552nd, and 555th Infantry Regiments opposed the enemy. The 257th IR and the 183rd Engineer Battalion defended Velizh.

The attack of the 4th Shock Army stalled at these positions. The 360th Rifle Division and the 48th Rifle Brigade captured the northern portion of Velizh. However, they went no further. The German regiments transitioned to the counterattack and, on 6 February, forced the 4th Shock Army onto the defense!

The Soviet offensive had, indeed, torn a 125 kilometer gap between Army Groups Center and North. Now the strength of the attack armies was exhausted. The left flank of the army group stabilized under the circumspect command of Generaloberst Reinhardt (since 1/1/1942), as did the eastern front of the army group.

Now there was another source of danger, and it is was the most critical: Rzhev.

With its three armies (from left to right: 29th, 39th, 22nd), the "Kalinin Front" had the mission of overrunning the 9th Army and the 3rd Panzer Army from the north. The 9th Army, which was gradually withdrawing from Kalinin to the southwest, received a Führer Order on 3 January:

"9th Army does not take one step backward. The line achieved on 1/3 is to be held!"

However, on the next day, this order was already overtaken by events. The Soviet troops of the 39th Army attacked across the frozen Volga, tore through the thin defensive lines of the 256th ID (Lieutenant General Kauffmann), and broke through into the forested region southwest of Rzhev. In a short time, there was a 15 kilometer gap to the neighboring 206th ID (Lieutenant General Hoefl). Therefore, the XXIII Army Corps was isolated from the front of the 9th Army!

The motorized and winter mobile Soviets pressed further to the south and stood 8 kilometers west of Rzhev on 1/5. Major General Lindig, 122nd

Chapter 4: The Defense

Artillery Commander, formed an initial blocking position here with hastily thrown together combat groups. In light of the threatening situation, the 9th Army command removed one regiment each from the 86th, 129th, and 251st ID on the eastern front and transported them into the Rzhev area. The OKH subordinated the 3rd Panzer Army command to the 9th Army and entrusted Generaloberst Reinhardt with the leadership on the eastern front of the army.

The 39th IR of the 26th ID counterattacked under Colonel Wiese on 7 January from Grishino toward Molodai Trud to close the frontal gap. The regiment captured six towns in the bitter cold. Nevertheless, it could not close the gap. Then the breakthrough of the 4th Shock Army on the left flank became noticeable. The 9th Army had to take energetic measures to prevent the threatened encirclement.

On 1/11, the Soviets reached the Sychevka area and, therefore, attacked toward the only rail line that connected Rzhev with Viazma – as well as with the interior. Alert units under Colonel Kruse, the 9th Army artillery commander, opposed the Russians here. They held out bravely, but they could not prevent them from advancing up to the freight railroad station at Sychevka.

The army hastily assembled combat groups, which had made it to the west, southwest of the Rzhev front, in order to open the rear for the majority of the army. Major General Lindig led the group near Rzhev, which was composed of supply troops, convoys, and Luftwaffe units. A combat group of the 129th ID (Colonel Danhauser) closed to the south. Then followed units of the 86th ID (Colonel Weidling). Near Sychevka the situation began to stabilize, as the first companies of the 1st Panzer Division (Major General Krueger) arrived from the eastern front.

The Soviet formations did not stop their advance to the south. The 39th Army already had the majority of its troops far in the rear of the 9th Army. The 29th Army followed and attacked Rzhev, while the XI Cavalry Corps broke through in the direction of Viazma and the autobahn.

General of Panzer Troops Model, who was the new commander of the 9th Army, ordered a counterattack of the German formations between Rzhev and Sychevka. The 1st Panzer Division attacked from Sychevka to the north on 1/21 in -45 degree cold. A reinforced combat group of the VI Army

Army Group Center

Corps under Major General Recke, commander of the 161st ID, attacked from Rzhev to the west on the following day. The isolated XXIII Army Corps dispatched a mixed combat group (elements of the 206th ID, elements of the SS Cavalry Brigade, and the 189th Assault Gun Battalion) to the east. Both combat groups met near Solomino on 1/23 at 1245 hours.

Therefore, the forces of two Russian armies and the XI Cavalry Corps, that had broken through to the south, were cut off from their rear areas! The XXIII Army Corps had again made contact with the army!

General of Panzer Troops von Vietinghoff, commander of the XLVI Panzer Corps, took command of the Sychevka area on 1/25. The 1st Panzer Division and 86th ID were subordinated to him. It was high time. The Soviets had been trying since 1/26 to open the pocket front of the 206th and 256th ID by launching continuous attacks.

However, General Model did not intend to allow the encircled enemy forces to escape. He decided to remove a regimental strength combat group from all of the army's sectors and organize it into an attack formation. The German attack to destroy the encircled enemy forces began on 29 January.

The following large formations participated:

XLVI Panzer Corps with 1st Panzer Division, 86th ID, SS Division "Das Reich";
Combat Group VI Army Corps under Major General Burdach;
Combat Group XXIII Army Corps under Colonel von Raesfeld;
6th Panzer Division, 246th ID, SS Cavalry Brigade.

The German attack advanced only slowly, however, it had to be conducted against a bitterly fighting enemy and against deep snow drifts. On 3 February, the attack momentum of the Soviets began to weaken. The lead elements of the 1st Panzer Division and the SS Cavalry Brigade reached Cherdino on 2/5. Therefore, the pocket was closed for a second time! There was no escape for the encircled formations of the 29th and 39th Armies! Within fourteen days, the resistance of the enemy collapsed. 4833 prisoners fell into German hands, and 187 tanks and 343 guns were abandoned on the battlefield next to 26,647 dead Red Army soldiers.

The great threat to the 9th Army was removed!

Chapter 4: The Defense

However, the crisis of the army group was still not completely overcome. On 16 February, the "Red Army" High Command ordered its Army Groups "Kalinin Front" and "West Front" to take up the offensive again to decisively destroy the German armies between Yukhnov and Rzhev. Both army groups received two guards corps, 10 rifle divisions, 2 airborne brigades, and four air regiments. The initial objective of these forces was to be the reinforcement of the 33rd Army and the I Guards Cavalry Corps, which had broken through near Yukhnov.

The I Guards Cavalry Corps (Lieutenant General Belov) reached the Viazma area from the south on 2 February. It was supported by the 8th Airborne Brigade, which had been flown into the Oserechnaya area four days earlier. These forces in the rear of the 4th Army were cut off from their rear areas on 2/3 by German attacks.

As General of Panzer Troops Model was able to encircle two armies near Rzhev, General of Infantry Heinrici likewise encircled a strong combat group near Viazma.

The STAVKA ordered the breakout of the encircled formations. Only 5200 men, however, were able to escape to the south from out of the Rzhev pocket, and they were able to join up with the I Guards Cavalry Corps. Another general breakout failed under German defensive fire.

Combat continued on all sides; in individual farms, around forests, and at intersections. Neither side could make any gains. The strength of friend and foe was coming to an end. At the end of February, Moscow committed the 50th Army on the front near Yukhnov to establish contact with the encircled formations – that were now lead by Lieutenant General Belov. However, this attempt also failed!

The German front held!

On 20 March, the STAVKA issued another order and assigned the armies new objectives:

"1. "Kalinin Front" and "West Front" reach a line Beliy-Dorogobush-Yelnya-Krassnoe by 4/20.

2. "West Front" is to make contact with the encircled forces with the 43rd, 49th, and 50th Armies by 3/27, at the latest.

Army Group Center

3. 5th Army occupies Gzhatsk by 4/1.

4. 16th and 61st Armies attack and capture Briansk.

5. "Kalinin Front" destroys the Olenin Group of the 9th Army with the 30th and 39th Armies by 3/28.

6. 29th and 31st Armies occupy Rzhev by 4/5."

This order was far reaching and had the destruction of Army Group Center in mind. However, none of the objectives were achieved by the Soviet armies. The German defenders dug into the snow covered ground. After the spring sun began to shine at the end of March and the snow began to melt and the land was turned into a marshy morass, the soldiers of the army group continued to hold their positions against enemy attacks as tenaciously as before!

Combat on the Eastern Front became positional at the beginning of April 1942. Nowhere was the "Red Army" able to achieve an additional penetration into the German main combat line. The battle in the rear of the front against the encircled Soviet formations continued with bitterness.

Generaloberst (since 2/1/1942) Model ran into the machine gun fire of the encircled forces during a flight in a "Fieseler Storch" on 23 May. The wounded pilot was able to bring his aircraft with the severely wounded Generaloberst to Beliy with his last ounce of strength. Generaloberst Model only survived because of a blood transfusion. The command of the army was temporarily taken over by General of Panzer Troops Vietinghoff.

The battle against the encircled forces of Lieutenant General Belov died out at the end of May 1942. The Soviets were compressed ever further. In spite of this, large elements of the I Guards Cavalry Corps and the 4th Airborne Brigade, including Lieutenant General Belov, were able to break out to the south on 6/9. The 7th ID, which was supposed to block the Soviets near Kirov, was overrun.

In spite of this, the last threat to the army group was removed, which could now orient itself again to the east and north. Field Marshal von Kluge

Chapter 4: The Defense

and his new Chief of Staff, Major General Woehler, regrouped their forces. On 16 June 1942, the army group had the following forces available:

42 three-regiment infantry divisions,
6 two-regiment infantry divisions,
4 motorized infantry divisions
8 panzer divisions,
6 security divisions,
1 SS division.

The month of June passed on the front without any decisive events. Various assault and scout troop operations were conducted by both sides, as well as daily artillery fire strikes. The typical characteristics of positional warfare were reminiscent of World War I. The front in the central sector began to petrify.

The emphasis on the Eastern Front had shifted decisively to the south in June, where Army Group South launched an offensive against Stalingrad and the Caucasus. The Soviets removed more and more forces from their central front.

Rzhev, as before, was still not quiet, since there was no pause in the firing here. Here, new German and Soviet commands continued to try to change the course of the front. The large frontal salient, which terminated in Rzhev, had to be held by the 9th Army if the army group was not to be outflanked in the rear. The Soviets had to do all they could to compress this sector, which was a "boil" on their front.

On 2 July, the 9th Army began "Operation Seydlitz." It had the objective of clearing up the situation in the rear of the army.

The XXIII Army Corps (General of Infantry Schubert) attacked on the morning of 2 July at 0300 hours with two combat groups. The western group was composed of the 1st Panzer Division (Major General Krueger), the 102nd (Major General Friessner), and the 110th ID (Lieutenant General Gilbert). The eastern group consisted of the 5th Panzer Division (Major General Fehn) and the Cavalry Group (Colonel von der Meden). The 2nd Panzer Division (Major General Baron von Esebeck) and the 246th ID

Army Group Center

(Major General Siry) attacked from Beliy to the north and east, in order to march opposite the XXIII Army Corps.

The 102nd ID made the best progress on this day. Its 84th IR made into the Luchessa sector. The 2nd Panzer Division forced the crossing of the Nacha near Bossino. The Soviets recovered very quickly and brought up their tanks on the first day. Fierce combat ensued, which forced the German divisions to suspend the attack because they lacked friendly air support. The German attack gained momentum again, when, on 7/4, the XLVI Panzer Corps joined in the battle with the 86th, 328th ID, and 20th Panzer Division. The corps pulled the stagnant XXIII Army Corps further forward. The 1st Panzer Division and the 102nd ID finally overcame enemy resistance and broke through the front of the 39th Army!

The lead attack elements of the 1st Panzer Division (coming from the north) and the 2nd Panzer Division, coming from the south, met on Sunday, 5 July, in Pushkari. Therefore, the initial objective was achieved. The enemy front was split! The Soviets recognized the danger and conducted a fierce counterattack.

The German front held!

The XLI Panzer Corps (General of Panzer Troops Harpe) formed a unified front in the northwest of the new pocket from the 1st, 2nd, 5th Panzer Divisions, and the 102nd and 246th ID. The 2nd Panzer Division advanced further and, on 7/7, made contact with the 20th Panzer Division. Therefore, the pocket was divided in two.

Large elements of the 39th Army (Lieutenant General Masslennikov) were caught in the "trap." In spite of dare-devil breakout attempts, they could not break through the German front. On 10 July, the first signs of disintegration were noticeable in the pocket.

The 1st Panzer Division and 86th and 102nd ID attacked again on 7/11, compressing the enemy even more. Then the enemy's resistance collapsed. Two days later, the battle was over. The Soviets surrendered.

The 9th Army had cleared up their rear area!

The STAVKA tried to help its 39th Army. From 5 July, they conducted small diversionary attacks continuously. All of the attacks were repulsed and pushed back.

Chapter 4: The Defense

The 2nd Panzer Army had to suffer most at this time. A crisis erupted in its area of operations, when strong enemy armored forces with air support crashed against the northern front of the army for seven days. The formations of the LIII Army Corps (General of Infantry Cloessner) and the XLVII Panzer Corps (General of Panzer Troops) located here had to ultimately commit their last clerks and drivers in the front line for defense. The 18th Panzer Division (Major General von Thuengen), 19th Panzer Division (Major General Schmidt), and 52nd ID (Lieutenant General Rendulic) stood at the focus of the battle, which had reached its climax near Belev and Zhisdra. On 7/13, the crisis was over. The Soviets suspended their attack after they had lost 446 tanks and 161 aircraft!

However, the Soviet leadership did not give up. They badly wanted to force a decision at Rzhev. The 30th Army attacked to the north of Rzhev on 7/30, after a 1 1/2 hour barrage fire. Thanks to superior air and tank support, the enemy was able to split the front between the 87th and 256th ID on the first day. The VI Army Corps (General of Infantry Bieler) "scraped together" the last reserves.

Movement suffered on the withdrawal roads, so that the German combat groups could not prevent the further advance of the Soviets. Every meter was bitterly contested. A combat group under Colonel Furbach (1/58 IR, 743rd Engineer Battalion, 328th Reconnaissance Battalion, and a Reichsarbeitdienst (RAD) [Reichs Labor] Detachment) was able to close the gap in the front, near Polunino, after fierce combat.

The 9th Army command inserted the 6th ID (Major General Grossmann) between the 87th and 256th ID. Therefore, the situation on this sector was stabilized. The attacks of the tank and rifle formations continued without pause, but were repulsed by the men of the 6th ID.

The commander of the "Kalinin Front", Colonel General Konev, issued an order of the day on 27 July, in which he said:

"I order the officers, political workers in all branches of arms, infantrymen, artillerymen, members of the tank branch, pilots, mortarmen, machine-gunners and tank destroyers, to attack the enemy quickly

Army Group Center

and with courage, to break through the enemy's defensive lines, as well as to destroy his technical weapons and energetically pursue the bandits before they can recover.

I order the city of Rzhev to be captured. ... Forward for Stalin! Forward brave soldiers! Win back the land of the ancient city of Rzhev! Bravely on to Rzhev! ..."

That was the order which would lead to the next phase of the battle of Rzhev on 4 August. The Soviets planned to advance frontally against the city with the 29th and 30th Armies from the north, while the 20th (left) and 31st Armies (right) were to attack from the east in the direction of Sychevka, in order to cut off the defenders of Rzhev in the rear. Here, the main effort lay in the 20th Army area, Lieutenant General Reiyter, with two tank and one cavalry corps.

The major attack was launched on 4 August at 0615 in the morning, after a long barrage fire and simultaneous air attack. Seven rifle divisions and one tank brigade attacked on a narrow axis into the XLVI Panzer Corps sector. The 161st, 342nd ID, and 14th and 36th Motorized Infantry Divisions, which were located here, were not able to stand up to the superior force. The Soviets penetrated into the German main combat line in the afternoon.

During the night, the 20th Army committed the two tank corps of Major Generals Hetman and Slomatin, as well as the cavalry corps (Major General Kryukov). At the same time, the 9th Army command ordered the removal of the 1st, 2nd, 5th Panzer Divisions, and 102nd ID from their former sectors to support the XLVI Panzer Corps. Then, on 5 August, the 31st Army (Major General Polenev) was able to break through the German front on the seam between the 14th Motorized Infantry Division and the 161st ID southeast of Zubtsov. Only the 36th Motorized Infantry Division (Major General Gollnick) was in the position to offer any resistance and, therefore, prevent the collapse of the front near Zubtsov.

In this dangerous situation, the 5th Soviet Army arrived on the left flank of the "Kalinin Front" and frontally attacked Sychevka. The situation was mastered by the last commitment of the German divisions. The XXXIX

Chapter 4: The Defense

Panzer Corps took command of the south Zubtsov area. Here fought the 36th Motorized Infantry Division and 342nd ID against the VIII Soviet Tank Corps.

Slowly the front stabilized everywhere. The 1st, 2nd Panzer Divisions, and 78th and 102nd ID were brought forward and, with the brave RAD Detachments, repulsed all of the Soviet attacks against the Rzhev-Sychevka rail line. In this manner, for example, the 2nd Panzer Division destroyed a total of 64 enemy combat vehicles on 8/9. The 10th Air Defense Regiment destroyed more than 50 tanks with its 8.8 cm batteries.

The main effort of the Soviet attack was shifted further to the south. Here, the 3rd Panzer Army was able to hold only after committing all of its forces. Generaloberst Model returned on 10 August from the hospital and went to the front line on the same day. However, this time he could not influence fate. 47 rifle, 5 cavalry divisions, 18 independent rifle, and 37 tank brigades were a few too many!

The right flank of the 9th Army and the left flank of the 3rd Panzer Army had to withdraw. Karmanovo, east of Sychevka, fell into the hands of the Soviets on 8/22. The battle used up the last reserves of the armies. Losses exhausted the troops.

The Soviet attack in front of Sychevka died out. The "Kalinin Front" did not reach the desired rail line at any location. Colonel General Konev, therefore, ordered the main effort shifted to the north. The city of Rzhev, on which shells and bombs rained down endlessly, was in ruins. The 29th and 30th Soviet Armies crashed ceaselessly against the German positions on the northern bank of the Volga. Here, on 22 August, stood only the 6th, 87th, and 129th ID. These three divisions experienced the fiercest defensive combat in their history. Gradually, they had to withdraw. Losses were too great. The Soviets split the 6th and 87th ID on 8/24. The 87th ID withdrew to the south back across the Volga.

The Rzhev bridgehead became smaller and smaller. On 26 August, the defenders were located on the edge of the city. Major General Grossmann took command of the bridgehead. He had the following units available on this day:

Army Group Center

18th, 37th IR (both from the 6th ID), 428th IR and 1/430 IR (129th ID), 473rd IR (253rd ID); artillery regiments from the 6th and 129th ID; 2/57, 808th, 884th Heeres Artillery Battalion; 180 Assault Gun Battalion; 561st Heeres Anti-tank Battalion; 4th Air Defense Regiment; 2/49 Air Defense Battalion and a combat group from "Grossdeutschland."

Rzhev was on the front. Generaloberst Model ordered that no command post be allowed to withdraw and that the last clerk and cook must take up their carbines. The Generaloberst was the master of improvisation. He brought in forces from all possible sectors and threw them wherever there was a crisis. No commander knew the units that were subordinated to them, since he held them for only a few days or even just several hours; then he would have to give them up or get new ones; or he might also be sent to a different sector. The soldiers nicknamed this type of combat "Vermodelung [Model-ization]."

The battle of Rzhev continued another four weeks. They were weeks full of bitter combat and heavy casualties. Field Marshal von Kluge arrived at Führer Headquarters on 22 August. He proposed a limited withdrawal of the 3rd Panzer and 9th Armies to an abbreviated position. However, Hitler refused categorically and reproached the Field Marshal because all of the counterattacks did not result in territorial gains!

The OKH deployed only two divisions to the threatened front around Rzhev. These were the "Grossdeutschland" Armored Infantry Division and the 72nd ID. Both were immediately thrown into the battle and were able to help hold the front until the end of September!

The enemy offensive then ebbed in the Rzhev area. The XXVII Army Corps (Lieutenant General Weiss) withstood all attacks. The 29th Soviet Army tried again at the beginning of October to capture Rzhev with the 52nd, 215th, 220th, 369th, 375th Rifle Divisions, 30th Tank, and 32nd Anti-tank Brigades. However, the German defenders held and did not withdraw!

By the Beginning of October, the "Kalinin Front" had lost 460 tanks. Therefore, its strength was exhausted. The Soviets suspended the battle in the second week of October.

The German Offensive

In the early morning of 22 June 1941, the first assault troops cross the Bug. The war with the Soviet Union had begun. No one knew how it would end.

The 3rd Panzer Group captures Grodno on the second day of the war. Therefore, the Soviet troops in central and northern Russia are separated.

...e charred citadel of ...e fortress of Brest-...tovsk, whose defend-...s held out for ten ...ys against all attacks ...om the air and the

Smoke and fire mark the advance of the troops. There is no rest for the mounted reconnaissance detachments.

The battlefield of Bialystock. German tanks advance through a thick forest, while destroyed Soviet tanks line the edge of the road.

Infantrymen from the 3rd Panzer Group enter the burning Vitebsk in the north of the front. The lead elements of the 2nd and 3rd Panzer Groups reach Minsk, the capital of Belorussia, in the center of the front (below).

The 2nd Panzer Group crosses the Berezina in the south of the front. The advance continues... But how far?

The Soviet airfields were heavily bombed by the Germans on the first days of the war. The Russian Air Force suffered heavy losses.

Two Bf 109 fighter aircraft over Smolensk; the cathedral is at right. The German fighters were far superior to the Russian Air Force at the beginning period of the war.

The commander of the 2nd Panzer Group, Generaloberst Guderian, speaking with the commander of the 51st Fighter Squadron, Colonel Moelders. In the background is Captain Joppin, who was shot down several weeks later.

The Battle for Smolensk

A tank company in combat for a town near Smolensk. The Soviets had now lost their fear of tanks.

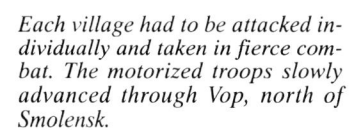

Each village had to be attacked individually and taken in fierce combat. The motorized troops slowly advanced through Vop, north of Smolensk.

Smolensk is captured by the 29th Motorized Infantry Division. In spite of fierce combat, the cathedral remains undamaged in the background.

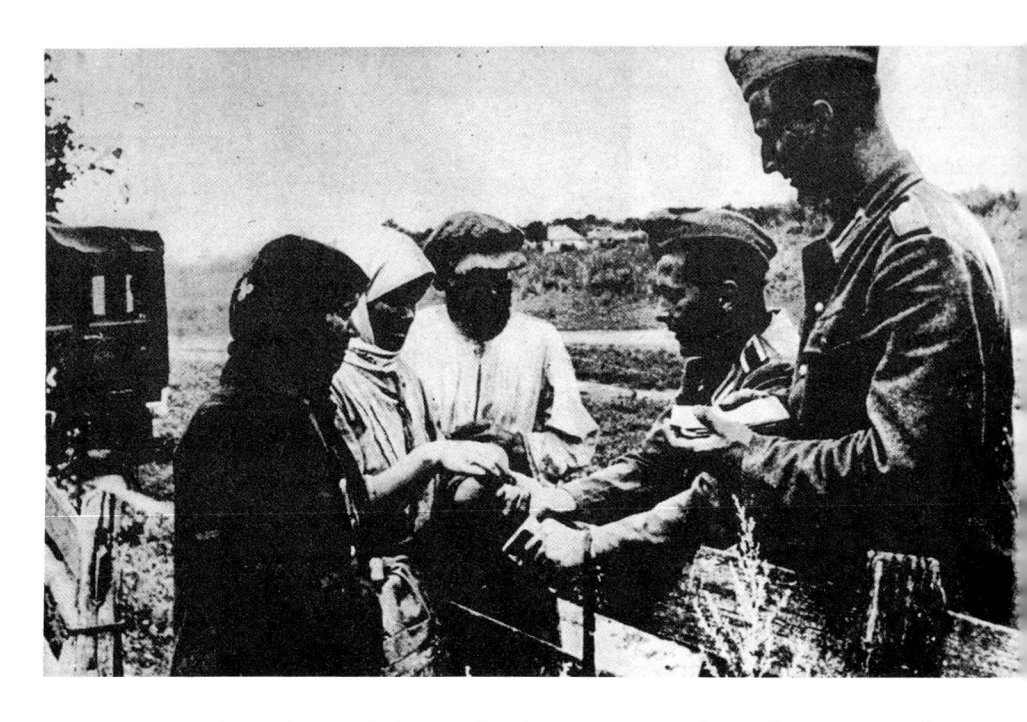

The meeting of "Landser" with the poor Russian peasants – an impressive occurrence these days. With dictionary in hand, eggs are bought; both parties make out well.

The wretches of war. A Russian family lost father and home. It was the same here in Smolensk as it was in Polozk, Bobruisk, Mogilev and other places...

The Battle of Moscow

On 10/2/1941, Hitler issued a decree to the "soldiers of the Eastern Front." Thus began the battle of Moscow. Soon it would be autumn...

Several days later, the frost and the first snow fall arrived. The weather worsened and delayed all movement.

The early onslaught of a strong winter found the German Army unprepared. They had neither winter clothing, protection from the cold for vehicles and weapons nor solid shelter.

The 3rd Panzer Group reached the Volga in the north of the front between Rzhev and Kalinin.

The soldiers of the 2nd Panzer Group advance on Tula through ice and snow. Will the ring around Moscow be closed?

Combat around Kaluga, in the middle of the front before Moscow.

September/October 1941. Two large Russian defensive positions emerged around Moscow, they were constructed in particular by women.

The Russian capital was attacked several times by combat squadrons of Luftflotte 2. However, the defenses became ever stronger and the attacks were suspended in November.

The Soviet Counterattack Winter 1941/42

Soviet tank formations roll through the snow covered streets of Moscow, in preparation for the great counter offensive.

The "T-34", the best tank in the "Red Army", defensive weapons were powerless against it in 1941.

The great, costly retreat across the snow covered plains begins.

The Front Holds

At the beginning of February 1942, the German front solidified everywhere. Enemy forces, that had broken through, were encircled north of Yartsevo.

Reserves from the homeland and from France were rushed to the east, in order to reinforce the front.

As spring arrived on the land, the German front was stable. Infantrymen in a firing position near Rzhev.

View of the Volga from Rzhev. The battle for this city and its interior proved the defensive will of the German soldier. The 9th Army stopped the great Soviet offensive here and, therefore, saved the army group.

German Commanders

Field Marshal von Bock

Field Marshal von Kluge (left) with Generaloberst Model, then commander of the 9th Army, at a command post during "Operation Citadel."

Generaloberst Heinrici (center), long time commander of the 4th Army, took over Army Group Vistula in 1945, which had to fight the final battle of the war (Berlin).

"Operation Citadel" 1943

The 9th Army attacked the hills north of Kursk with strong panzer forces on 12 July 1943. New tanks – here a "Panther" – penetrated into the initial enemy positions.

"Operation Citadel" was to change the tide of the war in summer 1943. However, in spite of the commitment of new weapons, the Soviets proved to be the stronger. German armored infantrymen take cover behind one of their own combat vehicles – here a P-IV – advancing against Russian positions near Ponyri. A Soviet soldier surrenders and crawls toward the germans.

The Great Withdrawal 1943

The Soviets seized the initiative on the entire front in mid-July 1943. German armored infantrymen occupy a temporary defensive front, while the heavy weapons – here a 7.5 cm anti-tank gun – are withdrawn.

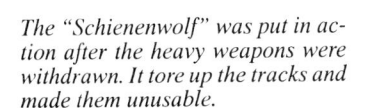

The "Schienenwolf" was put in action after the heavy weapons were withdrawn. It tore up the tracks and made them unusable.

*The blowing of the r[ailway]
road bridge over the [Oka]
near Orel. This was d[one]
to all of the bridges...*

Chapter 4: The Defense

The defensive combat of the 3rd Panzer and 9th Armies was supported by the few Luftwaffe elements as best as they could. The majority of the air formations were flying their sorties over Stalingrad and over the Caucasus at this time. The VIII Air Corps of Generaloberst Baron von Richthofen, who was the senior Luftwaffe command authority in the Army Group Center area of operations since November 1941, was transferred in Spring of 1942. The tried and true VIII Air Corps and the I Air Defense Corps (Lieutenant General Reimann) went to the southern front.

"Air Command East" was established as the new command authority. It was formed out of the former command of the V Air Command (General of Aviation Ritter von Greim) and transferred from Brussels to Smolensk.

General of Aviation Ritter von Greim (Chief of Staff: Major General Plocher) also took over the missions of the former Luftwaffe Commander (Koluft) in April 1942. This concerned the troop services provided for the Army, such as reconnaissance, courier, and air defense batteries. In its stead was created the Air Liaison Officer (Flivo), which, however, had no command authority.

"Air Command East" only had a few air formations available. Only the 51st Fighter Squadron, under Major Nordmann, remained in the central sector. To them alone was tasked the clearing of the air space, which was insufficient in view of the steadily increasing enemy superiority. It required great sacrifices. For example, on 14 February 1942, the commander of the 1/51 Fighter Squadron, Captain Eckerle – winner of the Swords and Oak Leaves – died in air combat over Velikie Luki.

The air defense artillery was the most important branch of arms in "Air Command East." The former II Air Defense Corps was disbanded. The staff and formations had formed the 18th Motorized Air Defense Division since 10 April. This division was assigned to cooperate with Army Group Center. It consisted of a staff, supply units, the 138th Air Communications Battalion, and the 21st, 34th, 101st (cooperating with the 2nd and 4th Armies), 6th, 10th, 125th, and 133rd (cooperating with the 3rd Panzer and 9th Armies) Air Defense Regiments.

The division – command post Smolensk – distributed its batteries throughout the entire sector. In May, a second division staff was committed, which took command of the 21st, 34th, and 101st Regiments. The new 12th Motorized Air Defense Division was responsible for the 2nd and 4th Army sectors. The 18th Motorized Air Defense Division fought in the areas of the 3rd Panzer and 9th Armies.

The battle for Rzhev was climaxed by the commitment of the air defense batteries. The 15th and 125th Regiments were in the front lines at Rzhev and contributed considerably to the defensive successes of the 9th Army. In November 1942, when the winter battle for Rzhev flared up, the 2 cm, 3.7 cm, and 8.8 cm batteries proved of valuable assistance to the grenadiers. The 10th Air Defense Regiment destroyed 105 Soviet combat vehicles alone during the last two months of 1942 near Rzhev!

The frontal salient at Rzhev got no rest. Luftwaffe reconnaissance aircraft established a concentration of strong enemy forces in the Kalinin-Toropets area in mid-October, for they were making new attack preparations. The objective of this new offensive appeared to be Rzhev itself. The command in the bridgehead had passed to Major General Praun on 21 October. He commanded the 129th ID after Lieutenant General Rittau suffered a soldiers' death. There were two each grenadier regiments of the 6th and 129th ID in the Rzhev bridgehead, as well as the corresponding batteries, engineers, and communications troops. The city itself was a combination of rubble, ruins, and rubbish. The civilian population was starving. It was established that there was even cannibalism taking place. The supply of the German troops with rations and medical equipment was conducted with great difficulty. Spotted Fever broke out, which resulted in the 129th ID suffering more deaths from illness than any other German eastern division.

The winter battle for Rzhev began on 25 November. The "Kalinin Front" attacked, after an enormous preparation by artillery and air, simultaneously on four positions: northeast of Sychevka, west of Rzhev, and north and south of Beliy. Therefore, on the first day, it was obvious that the Soviets wanted to pinch off the Rzhev salient and with it the 9th Army!

The offensive in the Sychevka sector was initiated after a two hour barrage fire at 0715 hours. Eight Soviet rifle divisions and three tank bri-

Chapter 4: The Defense

gades attacked toward the Gzhati confluence and directly into the relief of the 5th Panzer Division by the 78th ID. A 3 kilometer wide penetration appeared on the following day. It was stopped only after the 14th Grenadier Regiment (Colonel Kaether) counterattacked. However, the enemy maintained his superiority. On 27 November, the front was hit a second time. The formerly successful 78th ID (Lieutenant General Voelckers) was cut off. The Russian tanks reached the Rzhev-Sychevka rail line!

The defenders fought courageously and forced the Soviets to pay dearly for each meter of ground. On 11/30, their tankers and infantrymen crossed the rail line near Maloe Krotopovo. Here fought the 5th Panzer Division (Major General Metz). It ultimately held off the assault of the II Soviet Guards Cavalry Corps, during which the subordinate 215th Grenadier Regiment (Major Wesche) particularly distinguished itself.

Generaloberst Model again re-"Modelized" his troops. The XXIII Army Corps (General of Infantry Hilpert), which was in heavy combat, finally mastered the situation by concentrating all of its available combat groups. Major General Praun counterattacked to the rail line with four armored infantry battalions of "Grossdeutschland", the 18th Grenadier Regiment (6th ID), and the motorcycle battalion of the 2nd Panzer Division. On 6 December, his combat group pushed back the farthest penetrating 3rd Soviet Tank Brigade 4 kilometers. Therefore, the rail line was open again and the battle decided!

On the other hand, the battle still raged west of Rzhev. The enemy attack had likewise begun here on 25 November. However, in spite of considerable losses, the committed divisions, "Grossdeutschland", 87th, 206th, 251st, and 253rd, held the main combat line two full days. Then the 9th Army command withdrew the front of 11/28. The Soviets pursued immediately and were able to cross the Volga into the 87th ID sector. However, the heavy snow now influenced the battle. The attack strength of the Soviets began to decrease considerably at the beginning of December. Now they only attacked with individual combat groups.

On 13 December, after a last great attack by the 30th Soviet Army collapsed in the defensive fire of the defenders, the battle faded away here in the snow and ice.

Army Group Center

The most threatened point during the winter battle lay this time on the western front of the 9th Army. The Soviets penetrated on the first day north of Beliy in the 86th and 110th ID areas and entered the Luchessa Valley. There, on 29 November, a combat group from "Grossdeutschland" under Colonel Koehler, who fell shortly thereafter, was able to stop further breakthroughs.

The "Grossdeutschland" Armored Infantry Division opposed the constantly newly committed Soviets with all of its might. However, it all seemed for naught. The Russians were too strong! There were no longer any villages in the Luchessa Valley, only ruins covered by the deep snow. In spite of the icy cold weather, the battle continued until the end of the year; then the strength of the attackers came to an end, as did that of the defenders.

The fiercest portion of the winter battle raged south of Beliy. Two Soviet corps attacked the positions of the XLI Panzer Corps (General of Panzer Troops Harpe) on 25 November and tore through the front on the seam between the 246th ID and the 2nd Luftwaffe Field Division. The breakthrough was expanded on the third day of the battle to a depth of 20 kilometers. The "Grossdeutschland" Fusilier Regiment (Colonel Kaschnitz) was bloodied on the Nacha River. However, their perseverance delayed the Soviet attack considerably, so that the front slowly solidified.

The XXX Army Corps (General of Artillery Fretter-Pico) was deployed from Army Group North, in order to take command of the sector south of Beliy. To the corps was subordinated the newly arrived 19th Panzer Division (Major General Schmidt), the 20th Panzer Division (Major General Baron von Luettwitz), and the 1st SS Cavalry Division (SS Gruppenführer Bittrich).

The German counterattack against the Soviet penetration area began on 7 December, as the snow reached 40 cm deep. From the north advanced (from right to left) the 20th, 19th Panzer Divisions, 1st SS Cavalry Division, while from the south attacked elements of the 1st Panzer Division and the "Grossdeutschland" Fusilier Regiment. The attack was initiated without any artillery preparation, in order to surprise the enemy. The 19th Panzer Division made the best forward progress, in spite of tenacious defense, and stood 10 kilometers deep into the Soviet interior by evening. Two days

Chapter 4: The Defense

later, the lead attack elements of the 1st and 19th Panzer Divisions met. Therefore, the Soviets south of Beliy were encircled. The pocket was compressed and destroyed within six days.

The winter battle of 1942 around the Rzhev salient was over. The 9th Army command reported to the OKH the results: 1847 tanks, 279 guns, 353 anti-tank guns, and air defense guns destroyed. Two Soviet rifle divisions, 7 motorized, and 6 tank brigades no longer existed in the Beliy pocket!

The battle for Rzhev was a question of existence for the army group. After it was over, it was apparent that the Soviets were not satisfied. They already had another objective in mind. Army Group Center was bloodied during the combat of the last few months. Field Marshal von Kluge reported on 2 September a shortage of 42,000 men, which could never be replaced!

On 4 November 1942, Army Group Center had the following formations available:

Front Troops:
11 panzer
5 motorized
1 SS cavalry
1 mountain
49 infantry divisions;

Security Troops:
5 security
3 Luftwaffe Field
1 air
2 construction
2 Royal Hungarian light divisions
2 French volunteer battalions.

In November, these few divisions had to defend an area stretching from Velikie Luki through Rzhev, Orel, Sevsk, and up to the Pripet Marsh. The indented front line was far too long for these exhausted troops, which could

Army Group Center

count on neither reinforcements of personnel nor equipment, while the opposing Soviet "fronts" were continuously reinforced. Here the war shipments from the USA became more and more noticeable.

The area around Velikie Luki, on the extreme left flank of the army group, was another danger point during the winter of 1942, next to the Rzhev salient. The Army Group Center command decided to decisively eliminate the problem around Velikie Luki in conjunction with Army Group North. The German 11th Army, which had deployed before Leningrad in autumn 1942 under Field Marshal von Manstein, was entrusted with this mission after the failure of the attack on the old metropolis of Tsarist Russia. Field Marshal von Manstein summoned his generals to a final briefing at the LIX Army Corps (General of Infantry von der Chevallerie) before the attack on 20 November. However, before the Field Marshal could sign the attack order, he – and the majority of his army – received urgent orders for transport to the southern sector, where the Soviet armies had just initiated the battle of Stalingrad!

The significance of the first battle destroyed the conception of the army group command. At the same time, a second strike brought them closer to their objective, which the "Red Army" would achieve 1 1/2 years later: the separation of Army Groups North and Center. The 3rd Shock Army (Lieutenant General Purkaev), completely equipped and the best trained for winter warfare, attacked on the seam between the two German army groups on 19 November. Here, widely dispersed through the thick forests and marshy terrain, stood the 83rd ID.

The division had the thankless mission of being the connecting link between the central and northern sectors of the Eastern Front. As the only large strong point directly behind the front, they occupied the city of Velikie Luki, whose 30,000 inhabitants had already been an enemy objective for the past year. In November, Velikie Luki had no solid contact with the remaining main combat line to the north nor to the south. The supply of the German formations in and around the city was secured by the 3rd and 28th Armored Trains.

The major Soviet attack hit the 83rd ID with its full weight on 11/19 and, on the first day, blew them apart. The enemy tank battalions did not

Chapter 4: The Defense

halt in front of Velikie Luki, but immediately penetrated to either side of the city to the west. The German combat groups fought bitterly, and despite snow drifting they were unable to prevent a breakthrough.

During the night of 20 November, Velikie Luki was completely encircled. In the city were approximately 7500 men, which belonged to the 277th Grenadier Regiment, 3rd Rocket Launcher Regiment, 17th Observation Battalion, 286th Heeres Air Defense Battalion, 2/736 Heeres Artillery Battalion, 3/183 Artillery Regiment, and to the 70th Artillery Regiment. Lieutenant Colonel von Sass was the "Fortress Commandant."

The news of the encirclement of Velikie Luki alarmed the German leadership. However, nothing could be done about it, because there were no troops available. General of Infantry von der Chevallerie was entrusted with the relief of Velikie Luki. Nevertheless, on 11/20, all he could do was task the 4th Combat Squadron (Lieutenant Colonel Schmidt) with transporting some ammunition, rations, and medical equipment to the encircled troops by air supply.

The 8th Panzer Division – which belonged to Army Group North – the closest formation to Velikie Luki, received the order to attack toward it from the north. In the meantime, the enemy had advanced far beyond Velikie Luki and reached Novo Sokolniki, which was held by a combat group of the 3rd Mountain Division under Colonel Jobsky. The 8th Armored Infantry Regiment – in July 1942, all of the motorized infantry regiments were redesignated as armored infantry regiments – received the following mission:

"The regiment immediately attacks the enemy forces that have already advanced west of Velikie Luki and rescues Novo Sokolniki!"

The German counterattack began on 22 November. The 8th Armored Infantry Regiment (Colonel von Wagner) fought its way to Gorki. The 8/2 Armored Infantry Regiment (Captain von Mizlaff) was able to recapture Glasyri. The strength of the regiment was exhausted. The neighboring 28th Armored Infantry Regiment (Lieutenant Colonel Baron von Wolff) advanced past Gorki. Here it bogged down. The following 10th Panzer Regiment

Army Group Center

(Major Schmidt), equipped with old technology tanks and without time for a rest, failed against the Soviet combat vehicles. Only the 80th Artillery Regiment (Colonel von Scotti) brought any relief to the encircled troops in Novo Sokolniki and Velikie Luki with its artillery fire.

The counterattack of elements of Army Group North had, therefore, collapsed on the second day.

On 22 November, Army Group Center no longer had any large formations available on this frontal sector. The 20th Motorized Infantry Division was in rail transport to Nevel and the 291st ID was marching between Nevel and Demidov. Both divisions were to be transported to Army Group South.

The army group command immediately stopped these two divisions, turned them 180 degrees, and ordered them to counterattack toward Velikie Luki. Major General Jaschke, commander of the 20th Motorized Infantry Division, took charge. His division stood initially on the Lovat' and defended against every Soviet attempt to cross!

However, they could not count on the 20th Motorized Infantry Division and the 291st ID at this time. General of Infantry von der Chevallerie requested to break out the defenders from Velikie Luki. The OKH categorically refused and, on 11/20, ordered:

> "Combat must be conducted in the Velikie Luki area so that contact can be established with the individual combat groups through attack. A withdrawal to the west is out of the question!"

In the next few days, the LIX Army Corps formed two combat groups with formations that were, in the meantime, freed up by the army group, and attacked them toward Velikie Luki and Novo Sokolniki. Major General Jaschke took the northern combat group, which consisted of the 20th Motorized Infantry Division, 291st ID (Major General Goeritz), and the remnants of the 83rd ID. Lieutenant General Wöhler, the Army Group Center Chief of Staff, arrived in the combat area and took the southern group. He had the 331st ID (Lieutenant General Dr. Beyer), 76th Armored Infantry Regiment, 10th Panzer Regiment, 237th Assault Gun Battalion, and elements of the 291st ID. The two combat groups set out on the relief attempt

Chapter 4: The Defense

to the east on 9 December. The enormous superiority of the enemy and the poor weather conditions complicated the attack.

The attack of the combat group of Major General Jaschke came to a halt on 12 December. Three days later, the exhausted men were rallied again. The defenders of Velikie Luki needed help. They were already so weak from losses that they could no longer be described as a unified combat formation. The enemy had penetrated into the city and had split the German defenders in two, and ultimately three small pockets.

The 504th and 506th Grenadier Regiments of the 291st ID reached Burtseva on 20 December. Then their strength was finally at an end. These two regiments opposed three Soviet rifle divisions, two tank, and one ski brigade. The combat report of the 291st ID from 12/22 read:

> "The infantry combat strength of the division is: 26 officers, 118 non-commissioned officers, and 532 men. 504th Grenadier Regiment: 7 officers, 32 non-commissioned officers, 148 men; 505th Grenadier Regiment: 14 officers, 43 non-commissioned officers, 201 men; 506th Grenadier Regiment: 5 officers, 43 non-commissioned officers, 183 men; 291st Engineer Battalion: 1 officer, 2 non-commissioned officers, 24 men! ... Therefore, the grenadier regiments are no longer combat capable. ... All battalion and company commanders have fallen, their positions have been filled by officers that have not led an attack. ... Exhaustion is so prevalent that the troops cannot react to enemy fire. ..."

This was the bitter end of the northern combat group. The group of Lieutenant General Wöhler also got no further. Its lead attack elements approached to within 10 kilometers of the outskirts of Velikie Luki on Christmas Eve. An assault troop of the 331st ID was even able to approach to within 4 kilometers of the ring around the defenders. Then they were stopped.

On 26 December, the Soviets stormed into the city with tanks, eliminating one German nest of resistance after the next. As the year 1942 came to a close, there were two strong points left in Velikie Luki.

427 men held out in the old, long bombed-out citadel, under the leader-

Army Group Center

ship of Captain Darnedde, commander of the 83rd Field Replacement Battalion. They fought in an area 100x250 meters. Another 1000 men held out with Lieutenant Colonel von Sass in the garrison and railroad installation in the eastern quarter of the city.

There was no Christmas or New Years Day for these defenders. They froze, bled, and hoped. Ten men received one loaf of bread per day and one half of tinned meat. Drinking water had to be obtained from frozen pools at threat to life. There was neither the time nor the room to bury the dead. The wounded could not be bandaged, and their blood froze, as well as their bodies.

There were no bells on the last day of the year; instead, on 31 December 1942, almost 3000 Soviet shells rained down on the defenders...

5

THE WITHDRAWAL
The Soviet Offensive 1943

The battle for Velikie Luki lasted until the first two weeks of the new year. The lives, struggles, and deaths of the encircled German defenders grew more horrible day by day. Supply from the air had to be suspended. On the other hand, enemy artillery fire increased. The wounded could no longer be treated. In addition, the chances of being liberated from the outside became impossible.

On 8 January, the Soviets demanded that the defenders surrender. Lieutenant Colonel Baron von Sass did not reply – the battle continued.

Lieutenant General Wöhler, army group Chief of Staff, did not give up hope in making contact with Velikie Luki. He formed a motorized combat group out of elements of the 5th Jaeger Battalion, the 8th and 28th Armored Infantry Regiments, the 1/15 Panzer Regiment, and the 118th Panzer Battalion. Major Tribukait, commander of this combat group, ordered his officers and soldiers: "Drive, drive, do not stop!"

The mixed combat group rolled from Burtseva to the northeast on 9 January at 1410 hours. Exactly an hour later, the lead panzer elements reached Velikie Luki and the citadel! The seemingly impossible breakthrough was achieved!

However, the Soviets immediately closed behind the combat group. Their guns fired without pause on the citadel and, in a short period of time,

Army Group Center

hammered all of the German tanks! Therefore, a breakout was hampered.

The Soviets now strengthened their attacks on both strong points. Lieutenant Colonel von Sass, who commanded in the eastern quarter of Velikie Luki, had to evacuate one nest of resistance after the other. Finally, the defenders held a sector of only 1000x100 meters. The radio station of the encircled troops sent its last message on 14 January:

"Russians attempting to blow up the regimental command post..."

Then contact was lost. The soldiers fought another two days. Lieutenant Colonel von Sass and Major Schwabe surrendered with their last men. They had no more ammunition, no more rations, and, in addition, diphtheria had broken out and there were no medicines available!

The defenders of the citadel of Velikie Luki were likewise at the end of their strength. Major Tribukait, the senior officer, ordered a breakout on 16 January. The wounded and the doctors were left behind in the destroyed casemates.

The last defenders broke out, overran the initial Soviet defensive line in hand-to-hand combat, and then the second and the third lines. It was a hopeless sacrifice. Many soldiers fell into the deep snow from exhaustion, while others were laid low by Russian bullets – and only 186 officers and soldiers reached the advanced strong point of the 331st ID.

The battle for Velikie Luki was over.

At the beginning of 1943, the Soviet leadership turned their attention to the right flank of Army Group Center. After the collapse of Army Group South due to the loss of the battle of Stalingrad, the possibility existed here of rolling over Army Group Center from the south. The penetration into the German front west of Kursk, which was achieved during the past winter, could be the departure point for an offensive that would not only collapse the German frontal salient on either side of Orel, but also the entire army group!

The Soviet Army Group "Briansk Front" (commander: Colonel General Sokolovskiy, War Counsel: Lieutenant General Bulganin, the later President of the USSR) received the mission of conducting this offensive.

Chapter 5: The Withdrawal

The attack of the 13th and 48th Soviet Armies occurred on 12 February and hit the 2nd German Army with all of its weight. The army of Generaloberst von Salmuth (Chief of Staff: Major General Harteneck) had just reached its new positions west of Kursk with great difficulty and was in no way sufficient in number or equipment. The soldiers of the 2nd Army, supported by the few fighter-bombers of the Luftwaffe, resisted the attacking Soviets bitterly.

The "Briansk Front" suppressed the German strong points with difficulty. However, the offensive developed into a fierce battle. The battle lasted for two weeks on the snow covered terrain. The Soviet tank and rifle divisions could only gain 10 to 30 kilometers of terrain at this time. On 24 February, the "Briansk Front" stood on the general line: Novosil-Maloarkhangelsk-Briantsevo.

The Soviet High Command in Moscow had to realize during the first days of the attack that they would not achieve the hoped for success. Therefore, they ordered the "Voronezh Front" (opposite Army Group South) and the "Central Front" to support the "Briansk Front."

The attack of the "Central Front" (commander: Army General Rokossovskiy) began on 15 February. Its 65th, 21st, 70th Armies, and 2nd Tank Army attacked out of the Fatezh-Lgov sector. The 65th Army (Lieutenant General Batov) and the 2nd Tank Army (Major General Rodin) were ordered to attack Orel frontally.

The offensive of the "Central Front" rolled against the 2nd Panzer Army of Generaloberst Schmidt (Chief of Staff: Major General von Kurowski). The soldiers of the army fought just as steadfastly as their comrades in the neighboring 2nd Army. They prevented any enemy penetration into the German main combat line.

The commander of the "Central Front" later wrote the following sentences in his memoirs:

> "The numerous columns of troops, trucks, and tanks moved from the unloading station at Yelets with difficulty along the only highway to the west. Because trucks and horses were in short supply, the soldiers had to carry their heavy machine-guns, anti-tank weapons, and even mortars. The artillery lagged far behind the troops..."

Army Group Center

The Soviet superiority in troops and equipment became noticeable ten days after the beginning of the attack. The 115th Tank Brigade (Colonel Sankovskiy) achieved a penetration into the German front on the extreme left flank of the "Central Front" on 25 February. Army General Rokossovskiy immediately recognized the opportunity and committed the II Cavalry Corps (Major General Kryukov) to the breakthrough.

Therefore, the Soviet tanks had hit the most sensitive point on the German front. Only the 105th Light Hungarian Division was located here, and it had no combat value to speak of and fled from its positions.

The 2nd Panzer Army command immediately advanced the available combat groups of other divisions to counterattack. These were elements of the 5th Mountain Division (Lieutenant General Ringel) and the 221st Security Division (Major General Lendle). These two divisions were almost without heavy weapons and could only offer tentative resistance. Therefore, the army group decided to throw the 4th Panzer Division (Major General Schneider) into the frontal gap.

The forward-most elements of the division arrived in Novgorod-Seversk on 7 March and received orders personally from Field Marshal von Kluge:

> "Attack against the broken-through and by-passed sectors with the objective of blocking the advance of the enemy into the depth of the southern flank of the 2nd Panzer Army and by counterattacking from the Dessna up to the Seim establish contact between the northern flank of the 2nd Army and the southern flank of the 2nd Panzer Army."

The 4th Panzer Division came just in time to prevent the decisive collapse of the front. Nevertheless, it was not able to halt the attack of the II Soviet Cavalry Corps by itself. The Soviets threw back the tenaciously defending Germans and, on 10 March, occupied Novgorod-Seversk.

However, then the strength of the "Central Front" was exhausted. Each additional attack collapsed in the fire of the German batteries, and the Soviets had to suspend their offensive. The STAVKA ordered a halt on 23 March after a German counterattack on Sevsk was successful.

The 2nd Army and the 2nd Panzer Army had defied two enemy army groups and held the strategically important Orel salient!

Chapter 5: The Withdrawal

At the end of March, the Soviet High Command gave up attempting to repeat this offensive on the right flank of Army Group Center!

The emphasis of the operations in spring of 1943 had, in the meantime, been shifted to the north. While in the south of the army group front the Orel salient was being held, the Rzhev salient had to be evacuated.

As the battle of Stalingrad was being lost, Hitler had decided to close the threatening gaps in the south of the Eastern Front. On 6 February, he summoned the commanders of Army Group Center (Field Marshal von Kluge) and the newly formed Army Group Don (Field Marshal von Manstein) to his headquarters. Field Marshal von Manstein was authorized to evacuate the positions on the Mius, while Field Marshal von Kluge was to re-order the 530 kilometer long Rzhev salient.

At the beginning of 1943, the 9th Army (commander: Generaloberst Model, Chief of Staff from 1/30/1943: Colonel Baron von Elverfeldt) still lay with its five corps undisturbed in the salient, which stretched northwest of Dukhovchina through Beliy to Rzhev and from here directly to the east from Gzhatsk and Viazma to Spas Demensk. Committed in this salient from the left to the right were:

XLI Panzer Corps with 197th, 52nd, 246th, 86th, 110th ID;
XXIII Army Corps with 253rd, 206th ID, 14th Mot ID, 251st, 87th, 6th, 129th ID;
XXVII Army Corps with 256th, 72nd, 95th ID;
XXXIX Panzer Corps with 2nd Panzer Division, 102nd, 337th ID, 36th ID, 5th Panzer Division;
IX Army Corps with 342nd, 35th, 252nd, 292nd ID.

The 4th Army (commander: Generaloberst Heinrici, Chief of Staff: Major General Roettiger) held the adjacent sector from Viazma to Spas Demensk. The army had deployed from left to right:

XX Army Corps with 98th, 183rd, 268th ID;
XII Army Corps with 260th, 267th, 183rd ID.

Army Group Center

The evacuation of the Rzhev salient, that much fought-over cornerstone of Army Group Center, was to take place under the cover name of "Operation Bueffel [Buffalo]." Generaloberst Model had already made preparations for this under the designation of "Bueffelbewegung." Not only did he construct the 100 kilometer wide "Bueffel Positions" between Dukhovchina and Spas Demensk in the short time span of seven weeks with the help of 29,000 engineers, construction soldiers, and Hilfswilligen, but he also improved the road situation in the area south of Rzhev. Engineer battalions, construction companies, and RAD detachments constructed 200 kilometers of new road and 600 kilometers of field paths within 10 days! In addition, 1000 kilometers of railroad track, 1300 kilometers of wire, and 450 kilometers of field cable were also laid. The heavy equipment was transported by 200 railroad trains (100,000 tons).

These preparations were not discovered by the enemy.

Another nine full days passed, and then the rear area services, such as hospitals, filed commandants, power companies, etc., withdrew. With them, approximately 60,000 civilians left the Rzhev sector.

On 1 March at 1900 hours, the frontal troops began to evacuate the forward-most positions. The withdrawal was conducted gradually, so that the German main combat line would not be broken. In the first sector, in which seven days were spent, the outer salient between Rzhev and Gzhatsk was evacuated.

The Soviets still did not recognize this initial withdrawal, because the German rear guard companies remained in the old main combat line positions until 2 March at 1800 hours and imitated full occupational forces with heavy fire.

The city of Rzhev was evacuated during the night of 3 March. When the last three grenadier companies of the 129th ID withdrew from the city, the engineer battalion (Captain Rautenberg) blew up the large Volga bridge. At the same time, the bunkers and firing positions were blown into the air. The only two churches left standing served as shelters for the civilians that were no longer capable of being transported.

On 7 March, the front of the 9th Army ran from Beliy through Sychevka to Viazma. On 3/5, the city of Gzhatsk was given up by the IX Army Corps.

Chapter 5: The Withdrawal

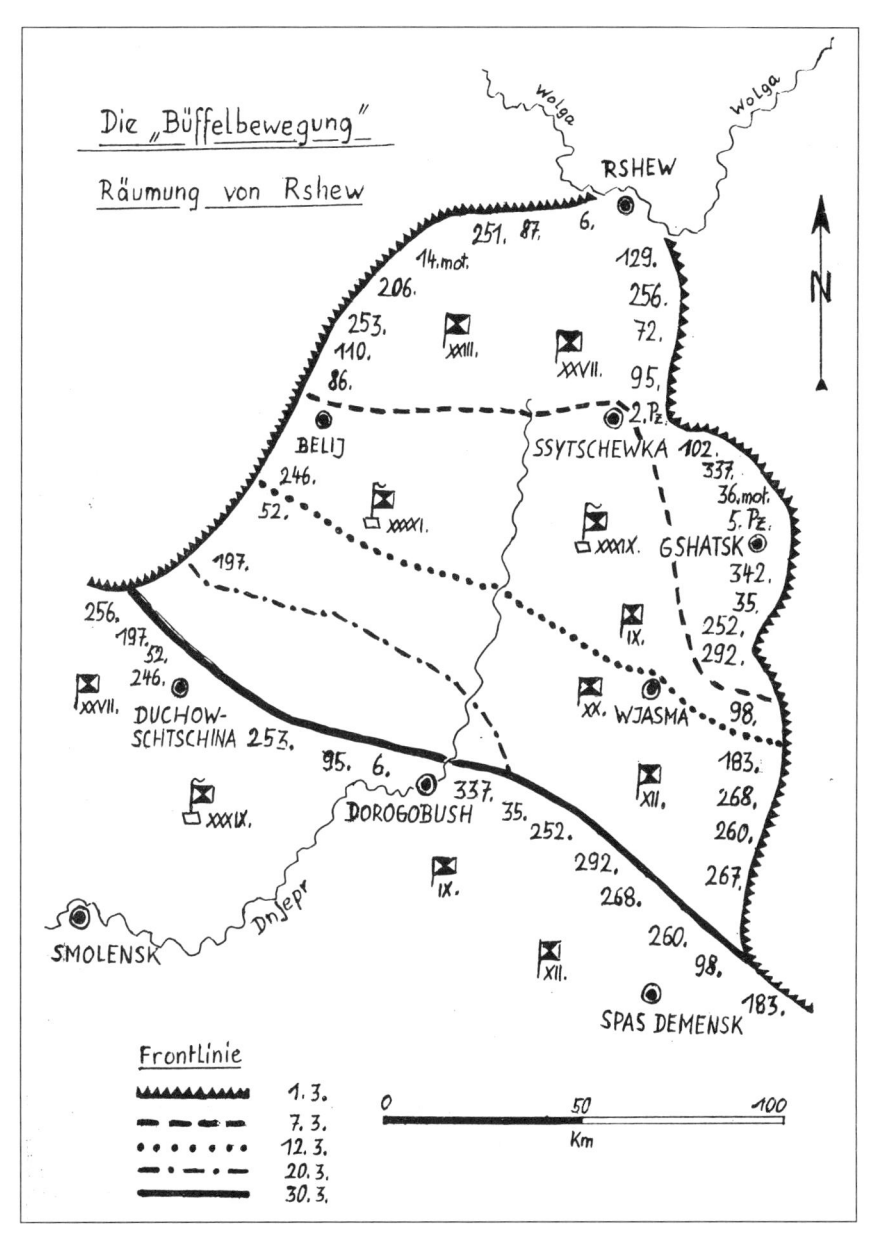

The "Bueffelbewegung"
The Evacuation of Rzhev

Army Group Center

The Soviets just now began to pursue. However, the withdrawal could still be executed as planned. On 3/12, Viazma was evacuated and, on 25 March, "Operation Bueffel" was over!

The new German main combat line ran from the northwest to the southeast directly in front of Dukhovchina-Dorogobush-Spas Demensk. The evacuation of the 160 kilometer deep and 530 kilometer long salient had not only abbreviated the main combat line by 330 kilometers, but it also freed up reserves: one army, 4 corps, 15 infantry, 2 motorized, and 3 panzer divisions.

The end report from the army group command read:

> "The movement went as planned. The enemy could not disrupt the withdrawal. ... The German troops suffered only light casualties. Because of the successful execution of the plan and because of local successes over the enemy, they feel victorious. They have gained a great boost in morale. It was as if they won a battle!"

On 25 March, the 9th Army turned over the XXVII and XXXIX Corps to the 4th Army. Generaloberst Model set up his headquarters in Smolensk.

The evacuation of the Rzhev salient went like clockwork and raised hopes that such withdrawals on other fronts would also spare forces. However, Hitler and the OKH thought otherwise. In 1943, Hitler wanted another offensive, in order to stop the wear on the Army and to strike a blow at the Soviets before they could launch their own offensive.

Therefore, on 13 March, the OKH issued Operation Order Nr. 5: "Instruction for the Conduct of Combat During the Next Few Months." Here we find the words:

> "... if possible before the enemy attacks and seizes the initiative. ... The objective is the destruction of enemy forces in front of the 2nd Army by means of an attack to the north out of the Kharkov area in conjunction with an attack out of the area of the 2nd Panzer Army."

Chapter 5: The Withdrawal

Hitler was fascinated by the courageous defensive combat of the 2nd Army west of Kursk and the 2nd Panzer Army on either side of Orel, as well as by the reconquest of Kharkov and Belgorod. Therefore, this created a situation on the front offering the opportunity to outflank the Soviet frontal wedge, which was extended far to the west, from the north and the south.

Hitler and Generaloberst Zeitzler, Army Chief of the General Staff, arrived at the headquarters of the army group in Minsk on 13 March. Here the decision was made that as soon as the situation on the inner flanks of the 2nd Army and 2nd Panzer Army was cleared up and an attack group was formed from the forces of the 9th Army, the planned operation to the south would be executed.

Ten days later, the army group command ordered Generaloberst Model to make preparations for this attack. Therefore, the 9th Army was redesignated Festungsstab 11 and transferred to Orel on 3/30. The transfer occurred after disagreements between Generaloberst Schmidt and Generaloberst Model were removed. The commander of the 2nd Panzer Army did not want a second army command committed in the sector between the Dessna and Kirov.

The army group had to order the armies to strictly defend, because the main effort of the future operation would lay exclusively in the sector of the 9th Army. The 2nd Panzer Army was ordered to construct a position on the Oka and Bolva, the 4th Army was to construct the Kirov positions, and the 3rd Panzer Army had to fortify the area between the Dnepr and Duena.

On 4/5, the 9th Army occupied its new headquarters in Kiskinka, near Orel. Generaloberst Model presented his proposals for the execution of "Citadel" four days later. The Generaloberst wanted to attack two panzer corps from the north to the south frontally against Kursk, while one panzer corps would protect the right flank and one army corps protected the left flank. The objective was the high ground east of Kursk, because it was the "key for the domination of all east-west communications."

The army group command worked up their own draft based on these proposals and presented it to the OKH on 4/12. This draft saw the mission as:

Army Group Center

"On X-Day, 9th Army breaks through the enemy positions between Trossna and Maloarkhangelsk, with the cooperation of the forces on either side of the Orel-Kursk rail line, and attacks with its main effort...up to the high ground north and east of Kursk, in order to ultimately capture Kursk. ...Contact will be established as soon as possible with the forces of Army Group South, that will be attacking from the south through Oboyan and toward the Tim. ..."

At this time, Generaloberst Model was released from all further work on the plans, because he took over the leadership of Army Group South temporarily for Field Marshal von Manstein, who was on leave. The Generaloberst returned on 19 April from Saporozhe to Orel. Here, in the meantime, Hitler's Operation Order Nr. 6 from 4/15(Nr. 430246/43) had arrived. This order contained the decisive instructions for the new offensive of the Eastern Army:

"I have decided, as soon as the weather allows, to conduct Attack "Citadel" as the first strike of this year. This attack has decisive significance. It must be executed quickly. It must seize for us the initiative for this spring and summer. Therefore, all preparations must be conducted with great circumspection and energy. The best formations, the best weapons, the best commanders, large amounts of ammunition must be committed on the main effort... The victory of Kursk must be as a beacon to the world."

On 4/19, Generaloberst Model summoned all commanding generals and operations officers (1st General Staff Officers) of the panzer divisions to his headquarters. The Generaloberst realized during this meeting that the force distribution for his army was insufficient for the assigned objective. He immediately reported his requests to the army group command: "More tanks! More officers! More artillery! Better training for the attack troops!" The next few days were characterized by arguments between the two operations staffs, so that, on 4/22, Generaloberst Zeitzler visited the headquarters of the 9th Army command. However, Generaloberst Model

Chapter 5: The Withdrawal

was not consoled. On 4/26, he went to Hitler himself and presented his ideas. The Generaloberst recognized the weaknesses of his army (26,442 men), as well as the strongly fortified Soviet positions. Hitler sympathized with these arguments and postponed the start of the attack to 10 May.

The starting date was to be often postponed, because the responsible troop leaders were all of differing opinions. These opinions were bounced off of each other during a meeting of the army group and army commanders and various other high ranking officers in the OKH on 4 May in Munich. Generaloberst Model again set forth his ideas, which were based on the difficulty of breaking through the strong enemy positions. On the other hand, the two army group commanders, Field Marshals von Manstein and von Kluge, as well as the Chief of the General Staff, Generaloberst Zeitzler, disagreed with him. Generaloberst Guderian, the Inspector of Panzer Troops, pointed out the shortages in the reorganization of the panzer branch and spoke for a delay of the offensive.

Hitler decided against Model's arguments, even though he did not want to wait until 1944, as did Guderian. He finally ordered that the attack be postponed until the beginning of June. Army Group Center was to be furnished with all of the available new tanks and assault guns.

The deployment of men and equipment into the sector of the 9th Army was to be considerably increased from now on. At the beginning of June, the army was organized from left to right as follows:

XXIII Army Corps with 383rd, 216th, 78th ID, 8th and 13th Jaeger Bns, 811th and 813th Armored Engineer Companies;
XLI Panzer Corps with 86th ID, 18th Panzer Division, 292nd ID, 656th Anti-tank Regiment, 216th Assault Gun Battalion, 313th, 314th Panzer Companies;
XLVII Panzer Corps with 9th Panzer Division, 6th ID, 2nd, 20th Panzer Division;
XLVI Panzer Corps with 31st ID, 7th Panzer Division, 358th, 102nd ID, 9th, 10th, 11th Jaeger Bns, 505th Panzer Bn, 312th Panzer Company;
XX Army Corps with 72nd, 45th, 137th, 251st ID;

Army Group Center

In reserve: 4th, 12th Panzer Divisions, 10th Armored Infantry Division.

This massing of troops in a small area was unusual for the Eastern Front in 1943. However, the Soviet "Central Front", which stood opposite the 9th Army, was in no way weaker. The army group of Army General Rokossovskiy had:

31 rifle,
9 airborne,
6 artillery divisions,
1 artillery brigade
1 rocket launcher brigade,
1 anti-tank brigade,
4 tank corps and
3 independent tank brigades.

On 11 June, Generaloberst Model returned from his leave to the homeland. He immediately got back to work, so that the 9th Army combat diary laconically reported: "After the return of the commander, a wave of work poured over the entire army area of operations."

Model's newest draft was organized around three points:

1. Break through the enemy positions with infantry only;
2. Three panzer divisions follow in second echelon as the main effort group;
3. Two panzer and one armored infantry division follow in third echelon and attack into the open [operational] area.

The final operation order for "Operation Citadel" was issued by the OKH on 14 June. In it, the corps of the 9th Army were ordered:

XXIII Army Corps and XLI Panzer Corps secure the eastern flank of the panzer wedge.

Chapter 5: The Withdrawal

XLVII Panzer Corps forms the main effort and attacks through to the high ground north of Kursk, continues to attack to the south and makes contact with Army Group South.
XLVI Panzer Corps secures the west flank.
XX Army Corps remains in position and simulates attack.

The preparations for the offensive reached fever pitch in mid-June. The 9th Army received rations for ten days for its 266,000 soldiers; this was 5320 tons. Ammunition deliveries totaled 12,300 tons, feed for the 50,000 horses 6000 tons, fuel 11,182 cubic meters.

The tank situation for the eight panzer divisions and for the 505th Panzer Battalion, which was exclusively equipped with the new "Tigers", totaled 478 tanks. The 5th Panzer Division was the strongest, with 84 heavy tanks. In addition, there were 348 assault guns available, distributed among the 16 committed assault gun battalions.

Luftflotte 6 (Generaloberst Ritter von Greim) had to support the 9th Army during the upcoming attack. Its mission was:

1. Disrupt the enemy's command and control in the Kursk area;
2. Disrupt and paralyze enemy movement.
3. Support the main effort group near Kursk.

All air formations of the 1st Air Division (Lieutenant General Deichmann) were subordinated to the luftflotte. The division had 730 combat, fighter-bomber, reconnaissance, and fighter aircraft that were stationed on 15 airfields around Orel. The mission of the division was the elimination of enemy airfields and the support of the XLVII Panzer Corps.

The 12th Air Defense Division (Lieutenant General Buffa) – command post Orel – had to first secure the airfields and second support the XLVII Panzer Corps in the attack. The 10th Air Defense Brigade (Major General Pawel) – command post Konotop – had to secure the air space in the 2nd Army sector.

The intensive preparations in the Army Group Center area for "Operation Citadel" increased until the end of June/beginning of July. The date of the attack was finally established for 5 July. Hitler issued two orders of the day the day before. The order to the troop commanders began with the words:

"My Commanders!

I have given the order for the first offensive strike of this year.

You and your subordinate soldiers are destined for successful execution under all circumstances. The significance of the first attack strike of this year is extraordinary. This new operation will not only strengthen our own people in the eyes of the rest of the world, but, most importantly, will also instill new self-confidence in the German soldiers themselves. ..."

A second order of the day was directed at the soldiers in the attacking divisions and was to be issued to them in the last hours before the beginning of the attack:

"Soldiers!

Today you will launch a great attack, whose outcome will have decisive significance for the war.

Your victory must strengthen the conviction of the entire world that resisting the German Wehrmacht is useless. ...

The powerful strike, which you will direct at the Soviet armies this morning, must shake them to their roots. ...

The German homeland ... has placed its deepest trust in you!"

The months of attack preparation could not be hidden from Soviet air reconnaissance, outposts, and agents. The first report of the planned German offensive was received by the Soviet High Command on 20 April. The

Chapter 5: The Withdrawal

secret agent installed in Switzerland, "Dora", reported to Moscow on this day:

"Date of German attack against Kursk, which was originally set for the first week of May, has been postponed."

In the next few weeks, the well organized Soviet spy network and its middlemen sent information, including secret attack orders, to Moscow. The Soviet leadership had better information about the re-deployment of the 9th Army than the German division commanders.

After the first reports, the STAVKA alerted its frontal commanders and summoned them to a meeting in Svoboda, near Kursk, in April. The commanders of the "Central" and "Voronezh Fronts" attended with their chiefs of staff and responsible party secretaries and discussed initial defensive measures.

The STAVKA not only reinforced the armies located in the 360 kilometer Kursk salient, but also formed a new army group east of Kursk, which was later designated the "Steppes Front." This army group (commander: Colonel General Konev, Chief of Staff: Lieutenant General Sakharov) was intended to be an attack group that would eventually parry and destroy the German panzer forces that had broken through. Subordinated to it were the 5th Guards Army, the 27th, 47th, 53rd Armies, the 5th Guards Tank Army, the IV Guards Tank Corps, the X Tank Corps, the I Mechanized Corps, the III, V, and VII Guards Cavalry Corps, and the 5th Air Army.

The reinforcement of the troops in the Kursk salient was conducted simultaneously with a reorganization of the "Red Army." Commands for the rifle corps were also formed, which for the period of two years were absent due to the lack of trained staff officers. New uniforms and rank designations, which were reminiscent of the Tsarist Army, were introduced.

At the end of June, 40% of the Soviet field armies were located in the Kursk salient. This strong concentration could not be established by the Germans due to the lack of air reconnaissance!

Army Group "Central Front" (commander: Army General Rokossovskiy, Chief of Staff: Lieutenant General Malinin) stood opposite the German 9th Army. On a 70 kilometers front, they had deployed, from right to left, the 48th, 13th, 70th, 65th, and 60th Armies. Behind them, in second echelon, also from right to left, were the XIX, XVI Tank Corps, 2nd Tank Army, III, and IX Tank Corps.

The 16th Air Army was assigned to cooperate with the "Central Front." Subordinate to it were the III Combat Air, VI Fighter, and VI Combined Air Corps, as well as the 2nd Fighter-bomber, 2nd Combat Air, 5th Fighter, and 1st Combined Air Divisions. The air defense in the Kursk salient was provided by 9 air defense divisions with 40 air defense regiments and 10 air defense armored trains.

The strong Soviet formations were prepared for the attack of the 9th Army during the last weeks before the German offensive. On 1 July, the STAVKA ordered the "Central Front" on alert, because they counted on the attack occurring between the 3rd and 6th of July!

At this time, the German officers and soldiers still did not know when their own barrage fire was to begin!

Shortly after midnight in the early hours of 5 July 1943, the German commanders read Hitler's order of the day.

Shortly after midnight at 0130 hours on 5 July, Army General Rokossovskiy ordered the 600 batteries of his army group to open fire on the German assembly areas!

"Operation Citadel" had begun – however, the first shots were fired by the Soviets!

The combat and stuka squadrons of the 1st Air Division took off at 0330 hours to attack the Soviet lines. The 1st Stuka Squadron under Lieutenant Colonel Pressler attacked the important communications hub of Maloarkhangelsk (this was the largest town on the attack axis of the 9th Army)!

Three hours later, the soldiers from three panzer and two army corps rose from their trenches and attacked the Russian positions. The main effort of the German Luftwaffe and artillery commitment lay first on the left flank, where the enemy positions were to be broken through, in order to open the way for the breakthrough of the XLVII Panzer Corps.

Chapter 5: The Withdrawal

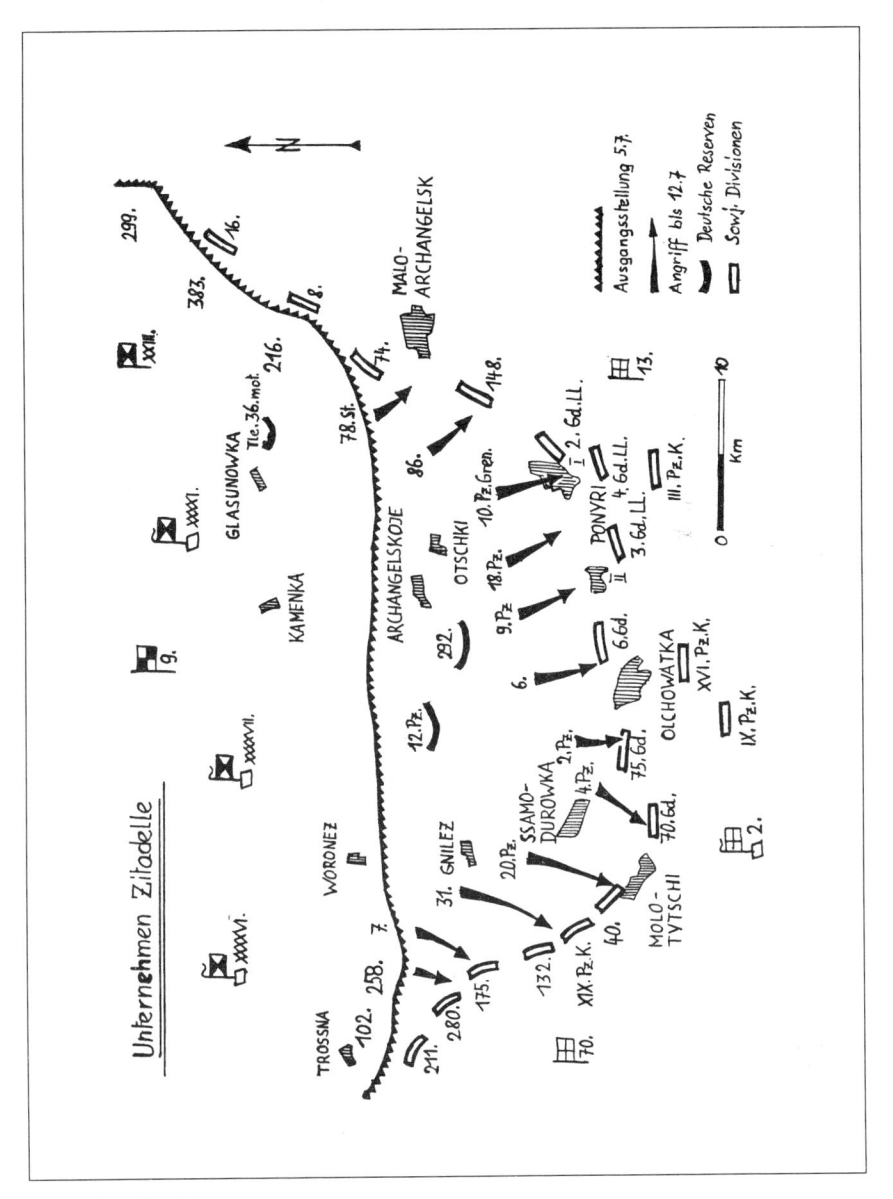

Operation Citadel

Army Group Center

The XXIII Army Corps (Lieutenant General Friessner) penetrated into the initial Soviet positions. The attack, however, only progressed well during the morning. It bogged down at noon in strong Soviet defensive fire. The 383rd ID (Major General Hoffmeister) and the 216th ID (Major General Schack) stopped due to heavy casualties and advanced no further. Only on the right flank was the 78th Assault Division (Lieutenant General Traut) able to gain ground in the afternoon and penetrate into Trossna.

The XLI Panzer Corps (General of Panzer Troops Harpe) had to break the resistance of the 13th Soviet Army (Lieutenant General Pukhov) on the Orel-Kursk rail line, in order to protect the left flank of the XLVII Panzer Corps. The 13th Army was the strongest army in the "Central Front", because the main effort of the German offensive was expected to be here.

The Soviet resistance was correspondingly strong. However, the two infantry divisions of the XLI Panzer Corps were able to fight their way into the initial enemy positions. The 86th ID (Lieutenant General Weidling) advanced into the area southwest of Maloarkhangelsk by evening and the 292nd ID (Major General von Kluge) was able to capture Oserki. The two heavy anti-tank battalions, the 653rd (Major Steinwachs) and 654th (Major Noack), were at the focus of the battle with their new 72 ton heavy "Ferdinand" tanks. These tanks proved to be unworthy and were, therefore, not employed again.

The XLVI Panzer Corps (General of Infantry Zorn) had to cover the right flank of the German attack wedge. The corps had the task of breaking through the Soviet defenses on the Trossna-Kursk rollbahn. The 31st ID (Lieutenant General Hossbach), which was on the left, advanced against fierce resistance toward Tureka and the right flank division (258th ID under Lieutenant General Hoecker) and captured the hills southeast of Obydenki. Then all further attacks here died out.

The XLVII Panzer Corps (General of Panzer Troops Lemelsen), which was on the main effort of the offensive, had committed the 6th ID (Lieutenant General Grossmann) in front on the left and the 20th Panzer Division (Major General von Kessel) on the right. Both divisions bravely attacked the positions of the 70th Soviet Army (Lieutenant General Galanin) and, an hour after the beginning of the attack, threw the 15th and 81st Rifle

Chapter 5: The Withdrawal

Divisions back to the south. As the Soviets withdrew, the new "Tigers" of the 505th Panzer Battalion under Major Sauvant rolled onto the Eastern Front for the first time.

The XLVII Panzer Corps registered the greatest progress by the evening of the first day of the battle. It had pushed back the left flank of the 13th and the right flank of the 70th Soviet Armies and had already penetrated into the second line of Russian resistance. They were on the verge of breaking through here.

Luftflotte 6 supported the advance of the German divisions in rolling sorties. On 5 July, a total of 2088 sorties were flown. The German fighters shot down 163 enemy aircraft, while only 7 German planes were lost!

The 9th Army command was essentially satisfied with the outcome of the first day. Generaloberst Model ordered the commitment of the luftflotte exclusively in support of the XLVII Panzer Corps on the following day. The corps was to be reinforced during the night by the 2nd and 9th Panzer Divisions to attack through to the hills on either side of Olkhovatka on 6 July.

Model's great opponent, Army General Rokossovskiy, had also made his decisions. During the night, he ordered the immediate advance of the 2nd Tank Army and the XVI and XIX Tank Corps.

In the early morning, the German divisions began their attack. However, the Soviet tank brigades rolled from the south and the east within a few hours and stopped the German attack everywhere. In the XXIII Army Corps area of operations, only the 78th Assault Division advanced. The brave Wuerttenberg soldiers fought their way another 5 kilometers in the direction of Maloarkhangelsk and suffered heavy casualties.

The XLI Panzer Corps was engaged in heavy combat on either side of Ponyri. However, the 292nd and, especially, the 86th ID were not discouraged by the Soviet superiority. During the evening, the corps advanced the 18th Panzer Division (Major General von Schlieben).

Army General Rokossovskiy recognized the German main effort and dispatched the XVII Guards Corps and the XVI and XIX Tank Corps from Olkhovatka from the north to counterattack, in order to beat back the XLVII Panzer Corps. At the same time, the majority of the 16th Air Army (Lieutenant General Rudenko) attacked the German corps.

Army Group Center

The 7th of July appeared to be a day of crisis for friend and foe. The Soviets moved the 1st Guards Artillery Division to the hills between Olkhovatka and the 5th Artillery Division to Ponyri to support the rifle divisions on the main effort. The superiority of the enemy artillery forced all of the German divisions into the defense. Only in the XLI Panzer Corps area of operations was the 18th Panzer Division able to gain some ground toward Ponyri, but did not capture the town, however. Here held the 307th Soviet Division (Major General Yenshin) with the support of strong combat air formations.

The XLVII Panzer Corps repulsed strong enemy tank attacks. It could only advance slowly, while suffering heavy losses. The commitment of the 2nd Panzer Division paid off. During the afternoon, the division attacked through the third enemy defensive line and, therefore, gained the chain of hills north of Olkhovatka. This chain was the focal point of the terrain between Orel and Belgorod. Whoever occupied these hills could easily attack into the 125 meter deep Kursk basin!

The air formations of the Luftwaffe conducted 1687 sorties in the costly combat of the 9th Army. They brought some of the ground troops local relief, however, they could not cut up the tenacious enemy defenses. The German aircraft shot down 74 enemy aircraft and destroyed 14 tanks on this day.

On the evening of 7 July, the losses of the 9th Army totaled 10,000 dead, wounded, and missing!

The crisis was still not over, however. In fact, it reached its climax on the following day. The corps of the 9th Army were all forced onto the defensive by the counterattack of the "Central Front."

The XLVII Panzer Corps, which received the 4th Panzer Division (Major General Schneider) from the OKH during the night, still gained some ground to the southwest. General of Panzer Troops Lemelsen assembled the operational tanks of the 2nd and 4th Panzer Divisions into one brigade. The combat group was able to break through the enemy front and advance deep to the south. The tanks reached the hills south of Samodurovka. Then their strength was exhausted.

The attack of the XLVII Panzer Corps to the south opened a gap to the neighboring XLVI Panzer Corps, which could not follow with its left flank.

Chapter 5: The Withdrawal

The 9th Army had planned for the 20th Panzer Division to follow the XLVII Panzer Corps. The army command formed a combat group out of the 20th Panzer Division, the 31st ID and the jäger battalions under the leadership of Lieutenant General Baron von Esebeck. The combat group was inserted into the gap in the afternoon.

The 20th Panzer Division (Major General von Kessel) found a weak spot in the enemy front and captured the town of Samodurovka in a raid. The division continued the attack and advanced toward the dominant chain of hills. Then it started to rain. The tanks bogged down in the mud and the ardently needed stukas and combat aircraft could not take off.

On the evening of 8 July, Generaloberst Model ordered all of his divisions to stop. He then ordered a reorienting and regrouping for the next day. The offensive was to continue on 7/10.

Field Marshal von Kluge, Generaloberst Model, and Generals of Panzer Troops Harpe and Lemelsen met on 7/9 at the XLVII Panzer Corps command post. The Generaloberst had to realize that his army could no longer make an effective strike; he wanted, however, to continue. He ordered in the evening:

"XLVII Panzer Corps has to take the high ground southwest of Olkhovatka. In addition, on 7/10, the main attack will be concentrated on the hills near Molytychi through Teploe."

During the night, the corps formed an armored assault group from the 2nd, 4th, and 20th Panzer Divisions under Lieutenant General Baron von Esebeck. On 7/10, the combat group set out after a short artillery preparation and reached the line Teploe-western edge of Samodurovka. An additional attack to the southwest failed because of the constantly growing enemy counterattacks. The breakthrough could not be forced anywhere.

The enemy had properly estimated the threat of the XLVII Panzer Corps attack. Army General Rokossovskiy organized his tank forces during the night of 7/11 and attacked them into the flank of the XLVII Panzer Corps on the following morning. The 9th Army command tried to save the situation by throwing their last reserve – 10th Armored Infantry Division (Lieutenant General Schmidt, Ia: Lieutenant Colonel de Maiziere, the present

Army Group Center

Inspector General of the Bundeswehr) – into the battle. The division could no longer alter the situation. The Olkhovatka high ground was lost.

During the evening, Generaloberst Model realized that he had lost the battle! However, he wanted to tempt fate one more time, because the OKH had promised him the 12th Panzer Division and the 36th Motorized Infantry Division on the following day. During the night, the Generaloberst signed the new attack order (Nr. 4024/43 gKdos). It was the last of its type...

... Then, a short time later, an alert arrived: A major Soviet attack against the 2nd Panzer Army!

Generaloberst Model saw the danger that this represented for his army. He suspended all attacks – without notifying the army group command or the OKH! The 12th Panzer Division and the 36th Motorized Infantry Division were diverted to the 2nd Panzer Army. The heavy Heeres anti-tank battalions were halted at 0800 hours, removed from the front, and loaded for Orel. During the evening the 18th, 20th Panzer Divisions, and the 848th Heeres Artillery Battalion followed.

During the early afternoon, the OKH ordered the suspension of all attacks by the 9th Army and, at 1745 hours, turned over command of the neighboring 2nd Panzer Army to Generaloberst Model. On 13 July at 1200 hours, the Generaloberst was named commander of the 9th Army and the 2nd Panzer Army, simultaneously. In the meantime, he was flown to Orel.

On this day, Hitler summoned the two army group commanders to give him a situation briefing in his headquarters. The conference ended abruptly: break off "Operation Citadel." The Soviet attack against the Orel frontal salient and the Anglo-American landing in Sicily gave no other choice.

The commander of the Soviet "Central Front" reported to Moscow on 12 July:

"The troops of the Central Front, which stood as a deadly wall against the enemy, displaying Russian steadfastness and tenacity, have stopped his attack in eight days of constant and bitter combat. The first stage of the battle is over!"

The second stage of the battle had already begun. The Soviet leadership, in spite of the German preparations for "Operation Citadel", planned

Chapter 5: The Withdrawal

a major offensive, which was to be the final deathblow to Army Group Center.

The "Red Army" was to attack the Orel salient with three army groups to penetrate and destroy the majority of Army Group Center. Army Group "West Front" (Army General Sokolovskiy) was ordered to cut off Orel in an attack to the south in the direction of Bolkhov and Khotynets. The "Central Front" (Army General Rokossovskiy) had to advance from the southeast, in order to join up with Sokolovskiy's troops. The "Briansk Front" (Colonel General Popov) had to conduct two attacks out of the Novosil area, which were devised to outflank the city of Orel.

Powerful Soviet barrage fire was opened in the early morning of 12 July onto the German positions between Zhisdra and forward of Orel. 80 rifle divisions and 14 tank corps, with 3500 tanks, attacked the front of the 2nd Panzer Army northeast of Orel. The enemy offensive lay in the northern sector, between Zhisdra and Bolkhov. Here, on the first day, the German front was on a width of 28 kilometers. A little later, the front in the east exploded as Soviet combat vehicles were able to penetrate between the 56th and 262nd ID. Then, the front northeast of Bolkhov was torn. Therefore, on 7/12, the entire front of the 2nd Panzer Division was split apart.

What was the use of bravery when the enemy had tanks and artillery? The 11th Guards Army (Lieutenant General Bagramyan) broke through from the north into the positions of the LV Army Corps (General of Infantry Jaschke). The Soviet guards soldiers advanced 25 kilometers deep on this day. The neighboring 61st Army (Lieutenant General Belov) gained 3 kilometers in the direction of Bolkhov. The 3rd Army (Lieutenant General Gorbatov) and the 63rd Army (Lieutenant General Kolpakchi) advanced from the east and split the connection between the LIII German Army Corps (General of Infantry Cloessner) and the XXXV Army Corps (General of Infantry Rendulic).

The XXXV Army Corps was engaged on a 120 kilometer wide front against both enemy armies. From left to right, between Mzensk and east Orel, resisted the 34th (Major General Hochbaum), 56th (Major General Luedecke), 262nd (Major General Karst), and 299th ID (Major General Count von Oriola). General Rendulic's corps prevented the Soviets from attacking through to Orel during the first two days.

Army Group Center

Generaloberst Model, who took command in the Orel salient on the first day of the battle, issued an order of the day on 7/14, in which he said:

"The Red Army ... is attacking on the entire front of the Orel salient. We are facing a battle that will decide everything. In this hour, which will require all our efforts and strength, I have taken command of the combat tested 2nd Panzer Army."

The fourth day of combat showed that the Soviets were able to break through at three locations on the front of the 2nd Panzer Army and gain free ground. The two most threatening penetrations lay on either side of Bolkhov, which was already outflanked by the 11 Guards and 61st Armies. A smaller penetration by the 63rd Army west of Novosil was blocked by the brave efforts of the XXXV Army Corps. Now, the commitment of the first motorized formations became noticeable as they were deployed from the 9th Army. Generaloberst Model committed the panzer divisions into the penetration gaps. The divisions delayed the tempo of the Soviet advance, but they could not stop the offensive.

German resistance stiffened considerably on 7/19. The 46th ID (Lieutenant General Hauffe), 78th Assault Division (Lieutenant General Traut), 2nd Panzer Division (Major General Luebbe), and 12th Panzer Division (Major General Baron von Bodenhausen) particularly distinguished themselves.

The deepest penetration was that southwest of Bolkhov, where the enemy had, in the meantime, inserted the 4th Tank Army. The Soviet lead tank elements aimed in the direction of Karachev and Naryshkino, and they also were located directly east of Briansk. At the end of July, troops of the 9th Army – particularly the XXIII Army Corps (Lieutenant General Friessner) – stabilized the front here. The gaps near Karachev were closed after counterattacks by the 9th Panzer Division (Lieutenant General Scheller), 129th ID (Lieutenant General Praun), and the Central Cavalry Regiment (Lieutenant Colonel Baron von Boeselager).

On 7/23, the lead Soviet attack elements reached the Oka and Optukha rivers. Therefore, the city of Orel was on the front. Three days later,

Chapter 5: The Withdrawal

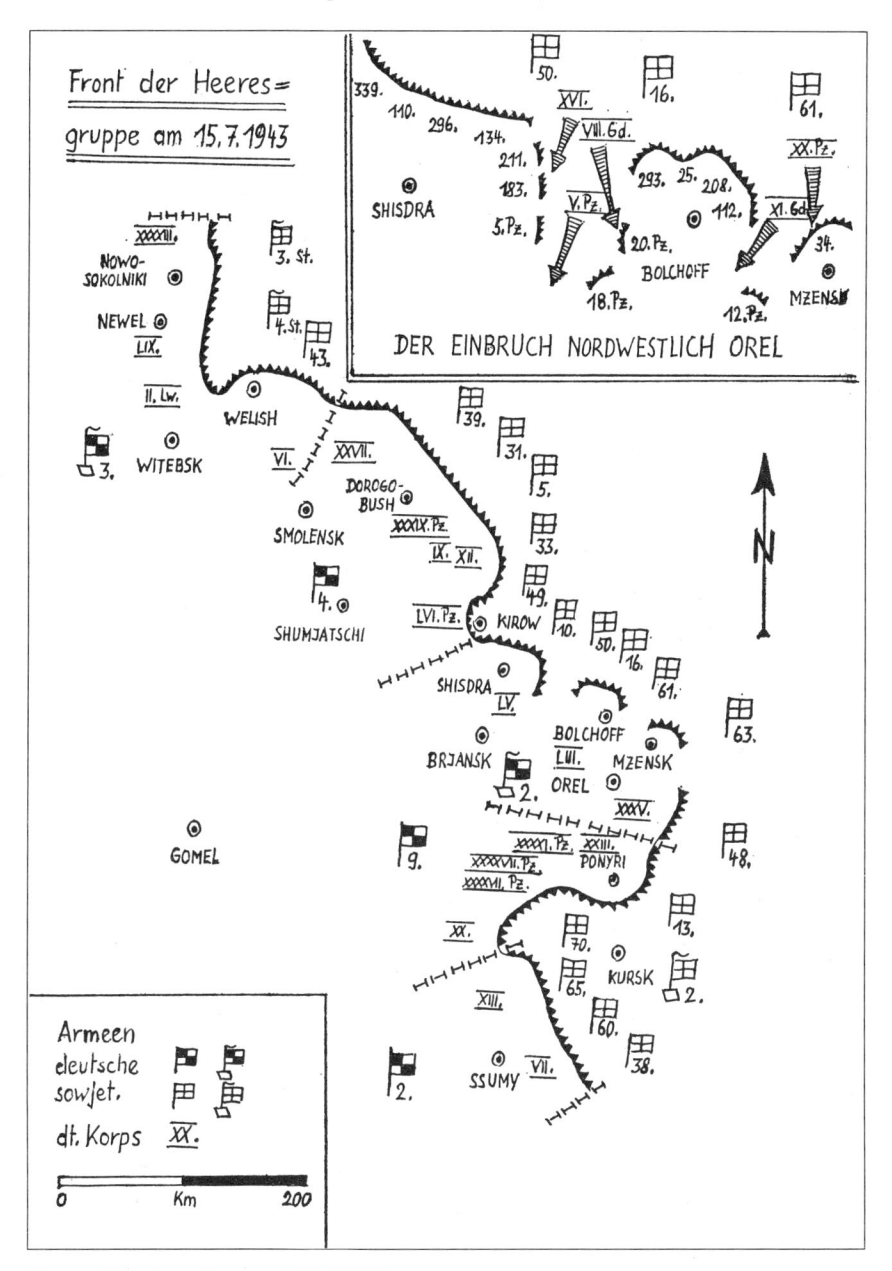

Front of the Army Group on 7/15/1943
Insert: The penetration northwest of Orel

Army Group Center

Generaloberst Model ordered the evacuation of Orel and the withdrawal of the army to the "Hagen Positions." The 2/5 Railroad Engineer Battalion began to evacuate all of the bridges, railroad installations, and railroad stations in Orel.

To cover the withdrawal, a blocking group was formed under the leadership of Lieutenant General Praun. The 8th Panzer Division (Major General Fichter), 293rd ID (Major General Arndt), and the 129th ID (Lieutenant General Praun) stood against the pursuing Soviets on a 37 kilometer wide front.

On 4 August, the advance detachments of the 3rd and 63rd Soviet Armies reached the empty city of Orel. The USSR celebrated this victory on the following day. Stalin issued an order of the day to the "Red Army":

> "Today, 5 August, at 2400 hours, Moscow will salute the brave troops, that have liberated Orel and Belgorod, with 12 salvoes of 120 guns. I Give my heartiest thanks to all troops, that are taking part in the offensive!"

The evacuation of the Orel salient had to be conducted if the fate of the 6th Army in Stalingrad was to be averted by the 9th Army and the 2nd Panzer Army. At the beginning of August, the Soviet offensive grew in size. Now, attacking the 2nd Panzer Army from north to the south were the 11 Guards, 4th Tank, 61st, 63rd, 3rd Guards, 48th, and 13th Armies. The right flank of the "Central Front" participated in the attack and advanced between Olkhovatka and Ponyri to the northwest in the direction of Naryshkino and Kromy.

The German front ran from southwest of Kromy directly east of the city to the north, bent sharply to the northeast at Naryshkino in the direction of Briansk, then ran directly to the north, passing Zhisdra to the east.

The troops of the 2nd Panzer and 9th Armies were ordered to withdraw. Naryshkino, Kromy, Karachev, and Zhisdra were all surrendered between 8/10 and 8/15. Several days later, the exhausted corps stood in the "Hagen Positions", which stretched from north to south between Kirov-Briansk-Sevsk.

Chapter 5: The Withdrawal

At the beginning of August, the "Red Army" expanded its offensive to the north. The "Kalinin Front" (Colonel General Yeremenko) and the "West Front" (Colonel General Sokolovskiy) were ordered to attack in the direction of Yartsevo-Smolensk-Roslavl. Moscow attached such significance to this new attack direction that Stalin even visited the troops of the "West Front." This was the one and only time that Stalin visited the front!

The attack of the two fronts was led by Marshal Voronov. The offensive was launched on 8/7. "West Front" attacked with the 10th Guards (Lieutenant General Trubnikov), 5th (Lieutenant General Polenov) and 33rd Armies (Lieutenant General Gordov) east of Spas Demensk. In spite of the commitment of strong tank troops and air formations from the 1st Air Army (Lieutenant General Gromov), the three armies did not gain more than 4 kilometers. The 2nd Panzer Division, 36th Motorized Infantry Division, and 56th ID repulsed every Soviet penetration into the German positions. The bravery of these three divisions was even noted in the "Red Army's" General Staff Work!

On 8/8, the 5th Army was able to achieve a penetration into the German main combat line north of Kirov. The Soviets immediately shoved their V Mechanized Corps, which was equipped with British tanks, into the gap and followed up with the 68th Army (Lieutenant General Zhuralev).

The resistance of the defenders was fierce and lasted until 8/12, when the order was given by the army group to evacuate Spas Demensk.

The offensive of the "Kalinin Front" began on 8/13 and was directed against the flanks of the 4th Army and 3rd Panzer Army. The will to defend of the German troops was strong and made the attacking 39th (Lieutenant General Sygin) and 43rd Armies (Lieutenant General Golubev) pay for every meter of ground. The Soviets could only gain 6 kilometers in five days, in spite of an enormous superiority of numbers.

Therefore, Moscow ordered a halt. The armies were regrouped and refitted with weapons and equipment during the next two weeks. However, the German defenders also utilized this pause and regrouped.

Army Group Center now stood in combat on a 950 kilometer front with 48 infantry divisions. 8 infantry and 6 panzer and armored infantry divisions were held behind the front in reserve. A report of the army group command on 8/25 revealed the following shortages:

Army Group Center

100,000 men for the infantry,
20,000 men for the panzer and armored infantry forces,
700 heavy anti-tank guns,
150 anti-tank guns and self-propelled weapons,
353 tanks.

The second phase of the Soviet offensive began on the entire width of the front on 26 August. The "Central Front" initiated the attack in the south with powerful artillery fire and strong air support. They committed, from south to north, the 60th, 65th, 2nd Tank, 48th, and 13th Armies. The offensive was directed against the entire 2nd German Army and the right flank of the 9th Army.

The enemy achieved a deep penetration in the Sevsk area on the first day. Here the XX Army Corps (General of Artillery Baron von Roman) fought bitterly with the 86th (Lieutenant General Weidling) and 251st ID (Major General Felzmann). Both divisions, however, were too weak to stand up to the attack of two Soviet Rifle Corps (XVIII and XXVII). The city of Sevsk fell into enemy hands on 8/27 at 1130 hours.

Another main effort in the 2nd Army sector proved to be near Dubovtsy, where the 82nd ID (Major General Heyne) fought meritoriously. The resistance against a far superior enemy could, nevertheless, not hold out for long. On the second day, contact with the neighboring 7th ID (Major General von Rappard) was lost.

On 8/27, the 2nd Army formed a corps group under Lieutenant General von Sauchen (4th Panzer Division, 31st and 251st ID), which was ordered to attack toward Sevsk from the north. This attack did not succeed. The Russian bridgehead near Sevsk was, in the meantime, expanded to a depth of 10 kilometers and a width of 20 kilometers. The 2nd Tank Army (Lieutenant General Bogdanov) entered the bridgehead.

On 8/27 at 2030 hours the new commander of the 2nd Army, Generaloberst Weiss, requested by telephone to withdraw his XIII and XX Army Corps. However, Field Marshal von Kluge categorically refused to allow him to withdraw!

A crisis arose on the right flank of the army group, and a similar threat emerged on the center of its front, where, on 8/28, the "Kalinin" and "West

Chapter 5: The Withdrawal

Fronts" continued their offensive.

The main effort in this sector was well placed by the Soviets, because it was right on the seam between the 4th and 9th Armies (The tanks of the 2nd Army were transferred for further utilization to the Balkans after the evacuation of the Orel salient. Therefore, the 2nd Panzer Army was removed from the order of battle of Army Group Center).

The attacking enemy tank forces ultimately struck the XLI Panzer Corps (General of Panzer Troops Harpe) in the 9th Army sector and the IX Army Corps (General of Infantry Schmidt) in the 4th Army sector. The IX Army Corps could not hold and withdrew to the Ugra.

Field Marshal von Kluge, who went to the Führer Headquarters on this day, urgently pointed out that the army group needed help if it were not to be rolled over from the south. In the meantime, in the 2nd Army area of operations a crisis erupted so that, despite the opposition of its commander, the 12th Panzer Division and 183rd ID had to be given up by the 9th Army.

A similar crisis developed in the 9th Army sector on 8/29, as the 19th Guards Army was able to gain ground south of the Yelnya-Spas Demensk rail line. In spite of an express order to hold from Field Marshal von Kluge, Yelnya was not held, even though the 5th Panzer Division and the 630th Heeres Engineer Battalion struggled bitterly.

On 30 August, the front was torn between the 2nd and 9th Armies! Now the army group command had to order the withdrawal of both armies to a line Putivl-Krolevets-Dessna-Briansk. The enemy was too strong, and German losses totaled 9,000 men in the past five days. Generaloberst Weiss wanted to withdraw his battered army on the entire breadth, but again the Field Marshal said no. The commander of the rear area was tasked with deploying all available forces to the front in the Novgorod area, because a new threat emerged here.

On 9/1, the army group command transferred its headquarters to Orsha.

Contact with Army Group South was lost on this day, as the XIII Army Corps (General of Infantry Straube) gave up Krolevets on the right flank and withdrew to Seim. Another crisis developed in the north in the 4th Army area of operations when an enemy breakthrough occurred in the 252nd ID area of operations and Russian formations occupied Dorogobush.

Army Group Center

Field Marshal von Kluge reported to the OKH:

> "The morale of the troops has been influenced by the costly combat and the clear enemy superiority in equipment and personnel. The specter of apathy and the loss of the will to resist is raising its head."

In the following days, the "Central Front" also pushed the right flank of the 2nd Army further back to the west. Mutino was lost on 9/2, the Nerussa was crossed to the west, and a fierce struggle developed around the Sobich bridgehead. On 9/6 the 2nd Army withdrew across the Dessna. Here, hastily thrown together combat groups held the bridgeheads of Vitemlya, Novgorod-Seversk, Leskonogi, and Ochkin for days.

From 9/1, the "West Front" and "Briansk Front" attacked the exhausted 4th and 9th Armies without pause. The main effort appeared to be in the Smolensk direction. The XXXIX Panzer Corps, under the leadership of General of Artillery Martinek, bitterly defended the Yartsevo-Dorogobush road from 9/2. Similar defensive efforts were being made in the 9th Army sector by the XXXV Army Corps (General of Infantry Rendulic) and by the combat group of General of Panzer Troops Harpe, which was formed to protect the southern flank. The 4th and 9th Armies could not stand up to the continuous enemy attacks and had to withdraw further to the west.

In spite of all the battering, the withdrawal of the two armies was still being conducted while maintaining a unified front. On the other hand, the situation on the right flank became more critical day by day. Contact with Army Group South could not be re-established because the neighboring army group was still being battered. They were quickly evacuating the Ukraine. Therefore, the right flank of Army Group Center hung in the breeze. Strong enemy tank formations had long been attacking into the gap and were able to roll onto the army group from the south. On 9/6, Field Marshal von Kluge ordered all German panzer forces thrown onto the right flank and subordinated to the 2nd Army command. On the following day, he reported to the Führer Headquarters. Generaloberst Reinhardt, commander of the 3rd Panzer Army, which had not yet been attacked, took command of the army group.

Chapter 5: The Withdrawal

On 9/8, the Soviet troops reached the Dessna in the 2nd Army sector and established the first bridgehead south of Muravy, which was, nevertheless, pushed aside on the following day by the XX Army Corps. Now the 2nd Army defended the 170 kilometer long Dessna front with only six infantry divisions!

At the same time, the lead Russian tank elements reached the bank of the Dessna in the 9th Army sector. The XXXV Army Corps was able to hold out for several hours near Monastyrishche. However, on 9/10, the majority of the 9th Army withdrew into the bridgehead around Briansk. The army achieved a success near Roslavl when the combat group of General Harpe was able to surround the II Guards Cavalry Corps! The 505th "Tiger" Battalion particularly distinguished itself at this time.

However, the situation on the southern flank was as critical as before. The 2nd Army command reported on 9/11: "Combat strength of 2nd Army = 6981 men!" The Soviets had already established bridgeheads at six locations on the Dessna. Novgorod-Seversk fell on 9/16 into the hands of the XVIII Soviet Rifle Corps. Then, the army group command ordered an abbreviation of the front of the 2nd Army without first requesting permission from the OKH!

It was at this time that the Russian volunteer battalions mutinied on the Dessna; and the VIII Hungarian Corps decided they no longer wanted to fight in the front lines! The right flank of the 2nd Army was bent further back to the west. The XLVI Panzer Corps evacuated Chernigov on 9/20 to avoid the threatened encirclement. At the end of September, it finally appeared that the combat strength of the "Central Front" was weakening. On the Zozh, which was reached by the Soviets at the end of the month, the enemy transitioned to positional warfare. The 2nd Army was saved, for the time being!

Meanwhile, the combat around Briansk and Smolensk ended. Army Group "Briansk Front" attacked to the west north of Kirov on 9/7 after a powerful artillery and air preparation. The 50th Army (Lieutenant General Boldin) and the II Guards Cavalry Corps (Major General Kryukov) penetrated into the German positions on this day. Four days later, the Soviets had crossed the Dessna and neutralized the Briansk-Smolensk rail line. Fierce combat occurred in the entire sector as the German defenders fought bitterly.

Generaloberst Model spent more and more time forward with the troops and had a decisive influence in the battle. For example, when the II Guards Cavalry Corps surprisingly occupied the important Ordshinikidzegrad railroad base near Briansk, the Generaloberst immediately ordered all available commanders to counterattack. The 129th (Lieutenant General Praun) and the 383rd ID (Lieutenant General Hoffmeister) were the first in position. Then the 707th Security Division (Major General Busich) arrived. Construction battalions and supply troops were alerted. Generaloberst Model personally led elements of the 5th and 20th Panzer Divisions, as well as the combat groups of the 110th ID, and mastered the situation by 9/19.

However, it could be seen that the superiority of the enemy must ultimately lead to their victory. The 11th Guards Army (Lieutenant General Bagramyan) outflanked the city of Briansk on 9/12. Again, the 95th, 110th, 134th, 299th, 339th ID and 707th Security Division distinguished themselves. Nevertheless, they could not prevent Briansk from falling into the hands of the Soviets on 9/17.

The "Briansk Front" crossed the Belorussian border nine days later...

From mid-September on, the 4th Army (Generaloberst Heinrici) was in fierce defensive combat around the most important city of the central sector – Smolensk. The attack of the Soviet "West Front" to conquer this metropolis began on 9/14. The Soviets shifted the main effort into the sector of the XXVII Army Corps (Lieutenant General Schneckenburger). Here the enemy was able to penetrate up to 8 kilometers deep in the 52nd and 197th ID areas of operations. The penetration in the 52nd ID area of operations soon developed into a breakthrough. The 4th Army command proposed withdrawing the front. Field Marshal von Kluge refused.

The combat on 9/14 was only a taste of the battle that would develop on the following day. After a three-quarter hour artillery preparation, the Soviets launched a major attack against the IX Army Corps west of Yelnya. The 78th Assault, 35th, 330th, and 342nd ID were at the focus of the battle.

Chapter 5: The Withdrawal

The German main combat line was lost at 1100 hours. Then the IX Army Corps had to withdraw.

In light of this critical situation, Generaloberst Heinrici ordered the withdrawal of his corps without consulting the army group command. This withdrawal took place in heavy combat, during which the soldiers of the IX, XXVIII Army Corps, and the XXXIX Panzer Corps destroyed 150 enemy combat vehicles and 86 aircraft.

On this day, Field Marshal von Kluge again flew to Hitler and obtained permission to withdraw the army group to the "Panther Positions", which were constructed from the Dessna through Orsha up to Vitebsk.

The 16th of September brought rain and, therefore, flooded roads. This, however, in no way prevented the heavy Soviet tanks from continuing their advance. This time, they achieved a penetration in the 78th Assault, 330th, and 342nd ID areas of operations. The combat around Berniki, Yartsevo, Gorodok, and Dukhovshchina flared up.

On 9/18, Field Marshal von Kluge ordered the leap-frog withdrawal of the armies to the "Panther Positions" by 10 October. The XXVII Army Corps evacuated Dukhovshchina. On this day, an enemy penetration also occurred on the extreme left flank of the 4th Army. The seam between the 256th ID (flanking division of the 4th Army) and the 206th ID (flanking division of the 3rd Panzer Army) was torn.

The 4th Army was able to hold out in the achieved positions for almost three days. It appeared that the enemy had to take a pause in the combat. On 9/22, they attacked further with incredible fury. The lead enemy tank elements crossed the Roslavl-Smolensk rail line. Two days after that, strong enemy forces broke through between the IX Army Corps and the XXXIX Panzer Corps. Motorized formations advanced up to the Smolensk-Monastyrshchina road. the Russian divisions stood before Smolensk! The 4th Army command moved up the 18th Panzer Division and the SS Cavalry Brigade. However, they could not master the situation. During the night of 25 September, the advance detachments of the 5th (Lieutenant General Polenov), 31st (Major General Gluzdovski), and 68th Soviet Armies (Lieutenant General Zhuravlev) penetrated into Smolensk!

Army Group Center was no longer in a position to stop the enemy offensive anywhere. The front of the army group was 700 kilometers long

Army Group Center

and was defended by 42 infantry, 2 armored infantry, 6 panzer, and 4 Luftwaffe field divisions. Of these, at the end of September, only 11 infantry, 1 panzer, and 4 Luftwaffe field divisions were still combat capable!

The fierce combat of the army group was supported by the few forces of the Luftwaffe, as best as the air formations and air defense artillery divisions were able. In spring 1943, the Luftwaffe was reorganized in the central area. The former Air Command East was redesignated as Luftflotte 6 in May 1943. The commander remained Generaloberst Ritter von Greim, and the Chief of Staff was Major General Kless.

The Luftwaffe was committed on every main effort of the ground battle, because they were not strong enough to be committed on all sectors due to their numerical inferiority.

In preparation for "Operation Citadel" they conducted several large-scale bombing attacks on Russian communications installations and industries from April on. For example, in May, combat aircraft and stukas attacked the Kostornoe-Kursk and Arkhangesk-Yelets rail lines. A large attack was conducted on the Gorki tank works by 168 combat aircraft on 6/5. At the same time, German bombs rained down on the railroad stations at Ryasan, Stalinogorsk, and Tula. The attack on the Gorki tank works was repeated on 6/6, 6/14, and 6/22.

However, the Soviet Air Force also conducted harassment attacks deep into the German occupied interior. Thus, combat air formations of six Russian air armies attacked the airfields in central Russia on 6 May. Another major attack was repeated on 8 June, when the airfields at Secha, Briansk, Karachev, Orel, and Bobruisk were to be destroyed.

The German fighter pilots and air defense soldiers were at their posts. The 51st Fighter Squadron under Major Nordmann shot down 51 Russian bombers on 8 June without suffering any losses of their own! To defend against additional Soviet air attacks, the 54th Fighter Squadron was, at times, transferred to airfields in central Russia from the northern sector. Of their pilots, Senior Lieutenant Nowotny particularly distinguished himself when he shot down his 124th enemy aircraft on 6/24.

A reinforced commitment of German fighters occurred at the beginning of "Operation Citadel" and the subsequent Soviet offensive in the

Chapter 5: The Withdrawal

Orel frontal salient. Thus, in the month of July 1943, the 1st Air Division, to which all air formations of Luftflotte 6 were subordinated, reported:

7/5 - Senior Sergeant Strassl shot down 15 enemy aircraft south of Orel,

7/6 - Senior Sergeant Strassl shot down 10 enemy aircraft south of Orel,

7/11 - Major Resch crashed near Orel after 94 kills,

7/16 - Lieutenant Scheel was shot down near Orel after 71 air victories,

7/26 - Lieutenant Jennewein, world ski champion, was shot down east of Orel after 86 air victories,

7/27 - The 51st Fighter Squadron achieved its 6,000 air victory and, therefore, led all other German fighter squadrons.

The air defense artillery achieved greater significance as the war continued as the "loyal helper" and often the "last savior" of the infantry. The 12th and 18th Air Defense Divisions were deployed in the army group sector and participated in the changing fate.

When "Operation Citadel" began, the air defenders were often located in the front lines. The 35th Air Defense Regiment of the 12th Air Defense Division, for example, was able to destroy 137 tanks and shoot down 112 aircraft from 7/5 to 8/11/1943. The subsequent Russian offensive found the air defense batteries in all of the hot spots. The 35th Air Defense Regiment (Colonel Dr. Rudhart), for example, fought east of Yelabuga-Smolensk and defended Smolensk with its guns.

In mid-September, the 18th Air Defense Division (Lieutenant General Heinrich Prinz Reuss) had its three regiments (6th, 10th, 35th) deployed near Orsha and Vitebsk and had a great deal to do with the fact that the fierce winter battle around Vitebsk did not lead to a crisis.

Army Group Center

In October, the air defense forces of the Luftwaffe received command authority with the II Air Defense Corps command. The corps command was formed out of the former III Luftwaffe Field Corps. The commander was General of Air Defense Odebrecht, and his command post was established in Bobruisk.

The major air defense formations were committed as follows:

12th Air Defense Division (command post Bobruisk) in the 2nd and 9th Army sectors,
18th Air Defense Division (command post Orsha) in the 4th Army sector,
10th Air Defense Brigade (command post Vitebsk) in the 3rd Panzer Army sector.

After a short breather, the "Red Army" continued its offensive. On 10/20, the former "Central Front" was redesignated as the "1st Belorussian Front", after its formations established a bridgehead across the Dnepr near Loev.

The attack of the "1st Belorussian Front" began on 10 November with the 48th, 61st, and 65th Armies setting out from the Loev bridgehead. The objective of the armies was the line Gomel-Bobruisk. After five days of fierce combat against the 2nd German Army they were able to sever the Gomel-Kalinovichi railroad line and, on 11/18, occupy Rechitsa.

The right flank of the "1st Belorussian Front" began its offensive on 11/22. The 3rd and 50th Armies attacked out of the Propoisk area to the west with the support of the 16th Air Army. On 11/25, they reached Stariy Bykhov on the Dnepr and crossed the river there.

On the same day, the 48th Army (Lieutenant General Romanenko) crossed the Berezina southeast of Parichi. Therefore, Field Marshal von Kluge had to allow the withdrawal between Zozh and the Dnepr.

On 11/26, the Russian troops entered Gomel. Therefore, the first regional capital of Belorussia was occupied. Stalin ordered a salute of honor!

However, now the strength of the "1st Belorussian Front" was exhausted, and the offensive ceased with the capture of Gomel.

Chapter 5: The Withdrawal

On 14 October, Field Marshal von Kluge wrote to Hitler:

> "The number of combat ineffective divisions is increasing. The reason lies in their commitment against clearly recognized superior enemy forces. Never before has an Army been required to make such physical and mental efforts as during this war..."

However, this was still not the worst hour of the army group, for that was yet to come. As the Field Marshal described, the situation was not good, as is proven in the following statistics:

	AG Center	Red Army in Central Sector
Front Divisions	53	206
Reserve Divisions	1	67
Soldiers on the Front	914,500	1,501,500
Soldiers in the Interior	10,500	162,500
Tanks on the Front	594	1,320
Tanks in the Interior	-	1,740
Guns on the Front	2,577	6,370
Guns in the Interior	-	350

In October, the army group command left its former headquarters in Orsha and occupied a command post in Minsk, which was constructed by "Organization Todt." Field Marshal von Kluge was no longer in charge here. Unfortunately, on 10/28 he was wounded during a trip to the front and had to return to the homeland. Field Marshal Busch, the former commander of the 16th Army (Army Group North), took command of Army Group Center on the following day. Generaloberst Model left his army on 11/3 to command Army Group North Ukraine. The 9th Army was taken over by General of Panzer Troops Harpe.

It was as if the left flank of the army group was spared from all enemy offensives. During the summer 1943, the 3rd Panzer Army (commander:

Army Group Center

Generaloberst Reinhardt, Chief of Staff: Major General Heidkaemper) defended a front 250 kilometers wide, which stretched from Demidov to northwest of Vitebsk. The army consisted of the VI, XLIII, LIX Army Corps, and II Luftwaffe Field Corps, with a total of 292,000 men.

The summer months passed on the front without great event, except for local combat. The great Soviet offensive near Orel on the left flank of the army group became noticeable when the 3rd Panzer Army had to give up the LIX Corps command and the 291st and 330th ID.

On 9/14, the OKH shifted the army group boundary south of Nevel. The XLIII Army Corps, with the 83rd, 205th, and 263rd ID, was subordinated to Army Group North. Thus, the well equipped, but completely unsuitable for ground combat, II Luftwaffe Field Corps (General of Aviation Schlemm) now stood on the threatened seam between the army groups.

The withdrawal to the "Panther Positions", which had to include the 3rd Panzer Army, led to the first serious attacks of the opposing "Kalinin Front." During the course of the withdrawal, the 3rd Panzer Army evacuated Velizh on 9/20 and Demidov two days later. The VI Army Corps (General of Infantry Jordan), which was in charge here, had to repulse constant enemy attacks. The hard pressed 87th and 206th ID were finally relieved by the 14th Motorized Infantry Division and the 246th and 256th ID from the 4th Army.

The 3rd Panzer Army reached the "Panther Positions" with its right flank between Zurazh and Babinovichi at 1110 hours.

The left flank of the army was engaged in a bitter battle for six days. On 6 October, the "Kalinin Front" attacked its 3rd and 4th Shock Armies against the seam of Army Groups Center and North. This attack hit the combat inexperienced 2nd Luftwaffe Field Division in the Budnitsa area. The Luftwaffe soldiers were, indeed, able to repulse the initial attack. Their strength, however, failed in the afternoon. The Soviets tore through the front east of Lake Yeserishche. During the evening, the 2nd Luftwaffe Field Division existed no more, and a gap 18 kilometers wide yawned in the German front!

The 3rd Panzer Army command and the army group command immediately recognized this threat, which would have to lead to the separation

Chapter 5: The Withdrawal

of the two army groups. The 129th ID and the 846th Heeres Artillery Battalion were immediately dispatched to the II Luftwaffe Field Corps. Luftflotte 6 committed all available fighter, fighter-bomber, and stuka squadrons. The 500 German aircraft facilitated the construction of a screening front, if only temporarily.

For six days, the combat groups of the 3rd Panzer Army struggled, and then a somewhat secure line was established between Lake Senitsa and Lobok. There was no longer any contact with Army Group North!

At this time, the situation was even worse for the right flank of the neighboring Army Group North, because here the important communications hub, Nevel, was lost. Generaloberst Reinhardt wanted to clear up the situation, however, Field Marshal von Kluge refused to launch a premature attack to the north. On 9/10, the army group reinforced the 3rd Panzer Army with the IX Army Corps, including the 20th Panzer Division and the 505th "Tiger" Battalion.

The IX Army Corps command (General of Infantry Cloessner) took command in the north of the front. The Germans had only a few days to construct temporary positions. On 10/17, the Soviets continued their offensive to the west and southwest. A penetration on Lake Sadrach was blocked by the cooperation of elements of the 20th Panzer Division, 129th ID, and 505th Panzer Battalion. The 20th Panzer Division even won its old main combat line back.

Field Marshal Busch, who had now commanded the army group for several days, received a report from Generaloberst Reinhardt on 10/23 concerning the continuation of the combat. Therefore, the Field Marshal ordered the removal of the 20th Panzer Division, because a mobile army group reserve was needed. He gave the order for the gradual withdrawal to the "Panther Positions."

On 10/29, the "Kalinin Front" launched a new major attack and widened the gap between the two army groups. In the meantime, the "Kalinin Front" was redesignated as the "1st Baltic Front." The threatening situation intensified practically hour to hour. The enemy was able to advance to the south, west of Lake Obol, and, on 11/9, to occupy Savan. At the same time, their formations reached the Nevel-Polozk rail line and, on 11/10, the

Pustoshka area. The army group command recognized the threat and, on 11/6, deployed the 252nd ID, two each anti-tank, assault gun battalions, one engineer battalion, one heavy artillery battalion, and a rocket launcher regiment.

The OKH now demanded a counterattack to the north to close the gap. Field Marshal Busch was summoned to Hitler's headquarters.

The counterattack began on 11/8 in damp winter weather. The IX Army Corps attacked with the 252nd ID and 20th Panzer Division after a short fire strike. In spite of heavy casualties, especially in the cleverly designed mine fields, the attack advanced quickly at first. The 3/7 Grenadier Regiment (Captain Mueller) distinguished itself. At 2325 hours, the army group command canceled the promising attack, because the 16th Army had not set out in the opposite direction from the north. Generaloberst Reinhardt protested severely.

Then, the Soviets suddenly struck on another frontal sector. Eight rifle divisions and two each rifle, tank, and mechanized brigades attacked Vitebsk frontally from the east on 11/8. They achieved a 3 kilometer wide penetration in the 206th ID area of operations and expanded it to 5 kilometers wide and 3 kilometers deep by evening. An attempt to block it on the following day failed, because the Luftwaffe could not take off due to fog and so the counterattack of the 211th Security Division petered out. The 206th ID had to withdraw. Its 301st Grenadier Regiment was temporarily encircled, but it fought its way out!

The next day was characterized by fierce combat in the VI Army Corps (General of Infantry Jordan) area. Then, on 11/16, the Soviet III Guards Cavalry Corps was able to break through to the south in the direction of Gorodok, west of Lake Ordove. Therefore, the 3rd Panzer Army was outflanked to the rear!

In view of the threatened encirclement, Generaloberst Reinhardt wanted to evacuate the entire Vitebsk salient. Field Marshal Busch, however, turned down this proposal.

The LIII Army Corps took command on the deep western flank of the 3rd Panzer Army. However, they could not assemble a unified resistance to oppose the attacking Soviets with the available construction battalions and supply troops.

Chapter 5: The Withdrawal

Generaloberst Reinhardt was still trying to obtain permission for an evacuation, however, the Field Marshal again turned him down. Finally, the 3rd Panzer Army command prepared for the evacuation of the Lobok passage on their own responsibility, since this was the northern-most tip of the front. When Hitler found out about this, he categorically ordered the evacuation halted and replaced with a counterattack near Gorodok, on Lakes Korosho and Losvida.

Generaloberst Reinhardt had to honor the Führer Order and issued his decree:

> "In this anxious hour, each of us has been called upon by the Führer to hold onto our positions until the last. Difficult weeks lay behind us. In spite of this, we will hold in the decisive hour. I believe in each of you. We must and will succeed!"

On 11/24, a thaw set in and bogged down all attack preparations by friend and foe alike in a sea of mud. The troops could use the breather and began to entrench in the achieved line. On 9 December, when a light frost set in, they had to count on a new enemy attack at any hour.

This began on 12/13, simultaneously by the 4th Shock and 11th Guards Armies against the northern flank of the 3rd Panzer Army. The IX Army Corps, which had been commanded since 12/8 by Lieutenant General Wuthmann, stood on the main effort of the enemy attack. On the first day, the enemy was able to achieve two penetrations, which again forced Generaloberst Reinhardt to request permission to retreat. Field Marshal Busch again refused!

On the next day, the Soviets turned their attack to the west and achieved an additional penetration. In this manner, they attacked through to the Nevel-Gorodok road. The encirclement of the IX Army Corps and its separation from the army was indicated. The situation worsened considerably on 12/15 when lead Soviet tank elements approached from the west and east to within 10 kilometers! They were already standing in the rear of the troops near Lobok!

Then Hitler finally gave permission to withdraw, but the order arrived too late. The 87th ID (Colonel von Strachwitz) was encircled on 12/16. All radio communications with this unit were lost on this day.

The Soviets were not satisfied with this partial success. They wanted more! The V Soviet Tank Corps tore a 3 kilometer wide gap between the 129th ID and 20th Panzer Division on 12/17! Then, the army group command also had to give in, and finally – though much too late – ordered the general withdrawal of the northern flank. It was directed at the 3rd Panzer Army, the 197th ID, 5th Jaeger Division, and "Feldherrnhalle" Armored Infantry Division.

The 87th ID, which was encircled on 12/16, broke the encirclement on the morning of the following day near Malashkinki, with 5000 men under the leadership of their commander, Colonel Baron von Strachwitz. The forward combat group, under Colonel Geissler, who fell in hand-to-hand combat, overran the enemy positions with the "Deutschlandlied [Song of Germany]" on their lips. Nevertheless, the breakthrough was much too expensive with the loss of the heavy weapons and equipment, as well as 45 dead officers and 1496 men.

Shortly before Christmas, the LIII Army Corps took command in the northern sector.

The Soviets also crashed against the German front east of Vitebsk. After a one and one-half hour barrage fire, they attacked on a 12 kilometer front of the 14th Motorized Infantry Division (Major General Floerke). With the help of the 519th Heeres Anti-tank Battalion, the division stopped the first large attack on the 19th, as well as the second on 12/21!

A new attack on 12/23 tore the seam between the 206th and 246th ID and advanced Soviet tanks to the Vitebsk-Zurazh road. The soldiers of the VI Army Corps destroyed 71 combat vehicles on this day.

On Christmas Eve, the fierce combat on the front of the 3rd Panzer Army reached its climax. A breakthrough of the V Soviet Tank Corps between the 129th ID and 3rd Luftwaffe Field Division advanced up to Gorodok, and the city was lost. As the Christmas bells rang in the homeland that evening, the entire army was engaged in a bitter struggle. The 14th Motorized Infantry Division, 3rd and 4th Luftwaffe Field Divisions, and 129th ID withdrew to the Losvida blocking position on Christmas Eve 1943.

Chapter 5: The Withdrawal

Combat did not decrease on the 1st and 2nd days of Christmas. The 6th Luftwaffe Field Division (Lieutenant General Peschel) lay at the center of the battle this time. 37 Soviet rifle, 1 cavalry division, and 15 tank brigades crashed against the thin lines of the 3rd Panzer Army. The newly deployed "Feldherrnhalle" Division stopped an enemy attack on the Vitebsk-Orsha road.

On 29 December, the lead Soviet tank elements reached the area in which the headquarters of the 3rd Panzer Army command was located. Generaloberst Reinhardt moved his staff to Beshenkovichi. During this night, a heavy snow fall occurred, with temperatures of minus 6 degrees.

Thus ended 1943...

The Soviet offensive of 1943 not only signified the withdrawal of the front troops, but also brought great changes in the homeland. On 12 August 1943, Hitler ordered the immediate construction of an East Wall, which received the name "Panther Position." On 8/24, Army Group Center formed the staff of the 2nd Senior Engineer Command, which was given responsibility for the reconnaissance and construction of the "Panther Position." When the armies withdrew to these partially constructed positions in September and October, they not only brought their weapons and vehicles with them, but also transported important industrial machinery and goods, as well as 300,000 horses and 600,000 cattle.

The German Weisruthenien [Belorussian] Generalkommissariat was now the combat area. On 9/20, Hitler ordered that the former command authority of the commanders of the rear area be given over to the army commanders.

On the same day, Field Marshal von Kluge intended to declare the Weisruthenien Generalkommissariat as an operations area. However, Hitler turned down this proposal.

Therefore, Belorussian towns were still governed by Kreiskommissars as part of National Socialist Regions, as Soviet shells slammed into neighboring towns.

6

THE DEFEAT
The Collapse of the Army Group 1944

The new year was not yet five days old when a major attack was unleashed against the German lines southeast of Vitebsk. The enemy achieved a penetration in the sector of the "Feldherrnhalle" Division, but the immediate commitment of the 1/481 Grenadier Regiment of the 256th ID won back the old main combat line. The simultaneous attack to the northwest of Vitebsk led to a penetration in the front of the 6th Luftwaffe Field Division, in spite of the destruction of 47 Russian tanks. Therefore, a limited withdrawal of the IX Army Corps was ordered. On 1/8, the 6th Luftwaffe Field Division totaled only 436 men! Field Marshal Busch visited the battered corps in the morning hours of 7 January. He could not promise any help, but ordered: "Holding is your first duty! A withdrawal is forbidden!"

However, no battles were won with words these days. Already the new commitment of the 5th Soviet Army, which was inserted east of Vitebsk, was becoming noticeable. In this front sector the German divisions were suffering heavy casualties from the constant attacks of the Russian fighter-bombers. The main effort of the attack lay in the "Feldherrnhalle" and 246th ID areas, and 57 tanks were destroyed.

On 1/9, the Russian attack increased in intensity, despite snow storms. 56 rifle, 3 cavalry divisions, 5 rifle, and 22 tank brigades crashed against

Chapter 6: The Defeat

the 18 divisions of the 3rd Panzer Army! The divisions of Generaloberst Reinhardt did not withdraw at all at this time, so the Soviets suspended their attack. The front was quiet for three days, then the tanks with the red stars rolled again. On 1/13, 200 enemy batteries opened fire on the positions of the 6th Luftwaffe Field Division (Lieutenant General Peschel) and the 12th ID (Lieutenant General Baron von Luetzow). The enemy attack was repulsed on either side of Lake Saronovskoe, with the support of the 519th Heeres Anti-tank Battalion!

Soviet losses were high, and they were higher than the defender's. On 1/17, the "1st Baltic Front" ceased their attempts to destroy the 3rd Panzer Army. The front of the army ran from left to right directly north of Sirotino in a great arc to Lake Loswida, and from here to the southeast up to east Vitebsk, then bent in a half circle to the west. The following units were committed here from the left: IX Army Corps (Lieutenant General Wuthmann), with the 252nd ID, elements of the 20th Panzer Division, and 5th Jaeger Division; LIII Army Corps (General of Infantry Gollwitzer), with the 12th ID, 6th Luftwaffe Field Division, elements of the 20th Panzer Division, and 3rd and 4th Luftwaffe Field Divisions; and VI Army Corps (General of Infantry Jordan), with the 197th ID, 14th Motorized Infantry Division, 206th, 131st, and 299th and 256th ID.

After the 1st winter battle for Vitebsk waned, the 3rd Panzer Army had to give up a good portion of these divisions because there were enemy penetrations and breakthroughs occurring on other sectors of the front. Thus, in the next few weeks and months, the 12th and 129th ID, "Feldherrnhalle" Armored Infantry Division, and the 20th Panzer Division left the frontal sector. The 3rd Luftwaffe Field Division was disbanded due to heavy losses.

The Russians appeared to have been waiting for this to happen, and they soon began a new major offensive against Vitebsk. The 11th Guards, 4th Shock, 5th, 33rd, 39th, and 43rd Soviet Armies all attacked on 2/3, after a two and a half hour fire preparation, with the objective of capturing Vitebsk. 20 rifle divisions and 6 tank brigades attacked to the southeast, and a similar number of large formations attacked the city to the northwest. The main effort lay in the southeast in the 131st and 206th ID areas, while the emphasis in the northeast was in the 12th ID and 20th Panzer Division areas.

Army Group Center

The 131st (Major General Weber) and 206th ID (Lieutenant General Hitter) experienced the fiercest fighting of their careers on 2/8. The commitment of the 529th Grenadier Regiment (Lieutenant Colonel Kieszling) and the 299th Artillery Regiment (Lieutenant Colonel Reinking) was exemplary. Besides the infantry units, the two air defense regiments (the 6th and 35th) played a large part in the defense against the enemy attack. On 12 February, the Soviets finally achieved a breakthrough into the German front at the Staroe Selo hills. This success could not be exploited by the enemy, though, because heavy snow drifts set in. All of the attacks ceased, and the 2nd winter battle for Vitebsk ended on 2/17.

At the end of February, the 3rd Panzer Army withdrew its front north of Vitebsk. They had fewer forces, because the 5th Jaeger and 121st ID were transferred to the 9th Army. The months of March and April were spent in see-saw combat, which was mainly played out in the Noviki bridgehead and on the Luchessa. Here, the 197th ID (Lieutenant General Woessner) and the 1/347 Grenadier Regiment (Captain Leipold) achieved local success.

With the start of the mud period, the army group command ordered the formation of "Fortress Vitebsk." General of Infantry Gollwitzer was assigned as the fortress commandant. The deserving commander of the VI Army Corps, General of Infantry Jordan, took command of the 9th Army on 5/20, and his successor was General of Artillery Pfeiffer.

At the end of February, the front of the army group ran – after the end of the 2nd winter battle for Vitebsk – in a straight line from north to south: Lake Neshchedo-northeast Vitebsk-straight to the south up to the Shlobin hills-along the Pripet up to Kovel. Therefore, the most threatened positions lay on the two flanks. After the battle in the north was over, the southern flank gained great significance. Here the "1st Belorussian Front" had attacked far to the west between Army Groups Center and South, aiming at Brest-Litovsk. The city of Kovel was encircled, and the Pripet was crossed to the northwest at several locations.

In March 1944, Kovel was the focal point of all further combat. The encircled defenders (soldiers of the Waffen-SS, police, field railroad men, and other troop units), under the leadership of SS Obergruppenfuehrer Gille,

Chapter 6: The Defeat

prevented the Soviets from capturing this important railroad and road hub since the beginning of March.

Kovel was encircled from four sides. In the south stood the enemy 18th Rifle Brigade; in the southeast was the 175th and 328th Rifle Divisions; in the northeast attacked the 260th and 362nd Rifle Divisions; and from the northwest the 60th Rifle Division also tried advancing on Kovel.

The 2nd Army command (Generaloberst Weiss) attempted to construct a new, if only a strong point-like, line of resistance further to the west with the LVI Panzer Corps (General of Infantry Hossbach). Moreover, the corps was ordered to relieve Kovel with the 5th Panzer Division (Major General Decker), 5th Jaeger Division (Lieutenant General Thumm), and 131st ID.

The attack of the corps began on 22 March out of the area southeast of Brest. General of Infantry Hossbach had given his soldiers a short order: "Forward to Kovel!" A thaw and the resulting melting snow complicated the advance of the combat groups, which strived to move through the Pripet region to the southeast against the enemy's resistance and the mud, which grew deeper daily.

On 25 March, the corps received the 4th Panzer Division (Lieutenant General von Saucken), which was assembled in the Mokrany area, in order to advance directly on Kovel on the right flank of the LVI Panzer Corps. The Soviet resistance strengthened daily. In addition, the flooded region was an unavoidable obstacle. On 3/27, the 5th Jaeger Division was unable to open the Ratno passage through the Pripet source region, and the losses increased. General Hossbach shifted the main effort further to the right, where the 4th and 5th Panzer Divisions were trying to advance near Zdomysl.

After several days of preparation, the attack began on the evening of 3/30 with a fire strike by ten batteries. The 75th Jaeger Regiment of the 5th Jaeger Division attacked the enemy positions near Piaseno. The Soviets recognized the threat and threw everything they could against the division. This gave the 4th and 5th Panzer Divisions breathing space, and they were able to roll to the south.

In a few days, the two panzer divisions overran the Russian infantry positions on the western and southwestern edge of the encirclement front. The 4th Panzer Division, on the extreme right flank, pressed to the southeast and, during the night of 4 April, penetrated into the north of Kovel. The 12th Armored Infantry Regiment, 1/35 Panzer Regiment, and 3/49 Anti-tank Battalion broke through the strongly defended forest north of Nove Koszary in the morning and, in the afternoon, reached the Kovel-Brest rail line. Therefore, the only road to Kovel was in German hands.

The combat group under Colonel Hoffmann set out to break through to Kovel on 5 April at 1200 hours. Six "Panther" tanks of the Waffen-SS and the 1/35 Panzer Regiment formed the lead elements. The enemy was taken by surprise, thrown back, and by 1300 hours Colonel Hoffmann reported to the Kovel commandant, SS Obergruppenfuehrer Gille, that Kovel was liberated!

Elements of the 4th and 5th Panzer Divisions took up positions around the city, established a new main combat line, and repulsed each Soviet attempt to enter Kovel. Meanwhile, Easter had arrived (4/9).

On 20 May, Field Marshal Busch presented two of the plans, which were worked out by his staff, at Führer Headquarters. The first plan was the "Small Solution", and purported that the army group could be ordered to withdraw to the Dnepr. The second plan was designated the "Large Solution", and called for a retreat to the Berezina.

Hitler did not want to hear either of the proposals. He categorically turned down the plans and issued "Führer Order Nr. 11" on 13 March, which created "fortresses" throughout that were to be defended until the last man. Hitler ordered that the cities of Bobruisk, Mogilev, Orsha, Vitebsk, and Minsk be established as "fortresses" in the army group area!

Field Marshal Busch gave up and accepted the directive, which was issued on 23 May: "... Under all circumstances, defend and hold!" Therefore, the divisions were fixed in the old main combat line. Hitler and the OKH did not believe that there would be a Soviet attack against Army Group Center. They assumed that the "Red Army" would direct their attention to the Tarnopol-Kovel area against Army Group North Ukraine. Therefore, in April and May, all available panzer forces were subordinated to Army Group North Ukraine!

This misinterpretation of the strategic situation was to cost Army Group Center dearly in the following weeks and months and bring it to the edge of complete destruction.

Chapter 6: The Defeat

In June 1944, Army Group Center was located in positions forming a half circle from south of Polozk in the north up to northern Kovel in the south. The main combat line was defended from north to south by the 3rd Panzer, 4th, 9th, and 2nd Armies. The organization was as follows:

Army Group command (headquarters Minsk)
Commander: Field Marshal Busch
Chief of Staff: Lieutenant General Krebs
Ia: Colonel von der Groeben
Oberquarteierm: Colonel von Unold

3rd Panzer Army command (headquarters Beshenkovichi) – front length approximately 220 kilometers
Commander: Generaloberst Reinhardt
Chief of Staff: Major General Heidkaemper
Ia: Lieutenant Colonel Ludendorff

IX Army Corps (General of Artillery Wuthmann,
Chief: Colonel Praefke)
with 252nd ID, Corps Detachment D;

LIII AC (General of Infantry Gollwitzer,
Chief: Colonel Schmidt)
with 246th ID, 4th and 6th Luftwaffe Field
Divisions, 206th ID;

VI AC (General of Artillery Pfeiffer,
Chief: Colonel Mantey)
with 197th, 299th, 256th ID; 95th ID in
reserve.

4th Army command (headquarters Orsha) – front length approximately 200 kilometers
Commander: Generaloberst Heinrici

Army Group Center

Chief of Staff:Colonel Dethleffsen
Ia:Colonel Kuehlwein

XXVII AC (General of Infantry Voelckers,
Chief: Colonel Staats)
with 78th Assault, 25th Armored Infantry,
260th ID; 14th Motorized Infantry Division
in reserve;

XXXIX Pz Corps(General of Artillery Martinek,
Chief: Lieutenant Colonel Masius)
with 110th, 337th, 12th, 31st ID;
"Feldherrnhalle" Armored Infantry Division
in reserve;

XII AC (General of Infantry von Tippelskirch,
Chief: Colonel Deyhle)
with 18th Armored Infantry, 257th, 57th ID.

9th Army command (headquarters Bobruisk) – front length approximately 280 kilometers
Commander:General of Infantry Jordan
Chief of Staff:Major General Staedke
Ia:Lieutenant Colonel Schindler

XXXV AC (General of Infantry Wiese,
Chief: Colonel Gundelach)
with 134th, 45th, 296th, 6th, 383rd ID;

XLI Pz Corps (General of Artillery Weidling,
Chief: Colonel Berger)
with 36th Motorized Infantry Division, 35th,
129th ID;

Chapter 6: The Defeat

LV AC (General of Infantry Herrlein,
Chief: Colonel Hoelz)
with 292nd, 102nd ID.

2nd Army command (headquarters Petrikov) – front length approximately 300 kilometers
Commander: Generaloberst Weiss
Chief of Staff: Major General von Tresckow
Ia: Colonel Lassen

XXIII AC (General of Engineers Tiemann,
Chief: Colonel Langmann)
with 203rd Security, 7th ID;

XX AC (General of Artillery Baron von Roman,
Chief: Colonel Wagner)
with 3rd Cavalry Brigade, Corps Detachment E;

VIII AC (General of Infantry Hoehne,
Chief: Colonel von Schoenfeld)
with 12th Hungarian Reserve, 211th ID, 5th
Jaeger Division.

The security of the rear area was conducted by the large formations:

201st Security Division (command post Lepel) = 3rd Pz Army;
286th Security Div. (command post south Orsha) = 4th Army;
707th Security Div. (command post Bobruisk) = 9th Army;
II Hungarian Reserve Corps (command post Kobryn) = 2nd Army.

The I German Cavalry Corps (General of Cavalry Harteneck) – command post Pinsk – was located in the Pinsk Marsh area with the subordinate 4th Cavalry Brigade to clear out the partisans from the rear of the front troops.

Army Group Center

The destruction of these armies, corps, and divisions was the objective of the intensively planned major offensive of the "Red Army" since spring 1944. The preparations were set in force in mid-April and increased during the month of May. The components of the armies assigned for the attack were increased as follows: personnel 60%, armored weapons 30%, artillery 85%, and air 62%. The supply of men, weapons, and equipment continued without pause from May out of the deep interior of Russia to Belorussia. In the first three weeks of the month of June, 75,000 railroad cars made it to the front with supplies.

On 22-23 May, the Soviet commanders went to their last briefing. Then, "Operation Bagratian" was formalized. After that, the Russian army groups opened the offensive against Army Group Center along the entire front. The initial attacks were to capture the "fortresses" of Vitebsk, Orsha, Mogilev, and Bobruisk and, therefore, split the German front. Then, concentrated attacks were to be launched from the Vitebsk and Bobruisk areas to encircle the 4th Army in the Minsk hills. The strongest had to be launched at the northern flank, because the seam between Army Groups North and Center was recognized as being weakly occupied.

The "Red Army" prepared 166 rifle, tank, and cavalry divisions with 2,220,000 men, 31,000 guns, 5,200 tanks, and 6,000 aircraft for this offensive. The divisions belonged to four army groups, of which two were combined into a coordinated group. Marshal Vassilevskiy had responsibility for the northern group, Marshal Zhukov for the southern group. The organization of the army groups and armies at the beginning of June was:

1st Baltic Front Commander: Lieutenant General Bagramyan
Chief: Lieutenant General Kurassov
Counsel: Lieutenant General Leonov
with 4th Shock, 6th Guards, 43rd, 51st and 2nd Guards Armies;

3rd Belorussian Front Commander: Col. Gen. Chernyakhovskiy
Chief: Lt. Gen. Pokrovskiy
Counsel: Lt. Gen. Makarov

Chapter 6: The Defeat

with 39th, 5th, 31st Armies, 5th Guards Tank and 11th Guards Armies;

2nd Belorussian Front Commander: AG Sakharov
Chief: Lt. Gen. Bogulyubov
Counsel: Lt. Gen. Mekhlis
with 33rd, 49th, 50th Armies;

1st Belorussian Front Commander: AG Rokossovskiy
Chief: Col. Gen. Malinin
Counsel: Lt. Gen. Telegin
with 3rd, 48th, 65th, 28th, 61st, 70th, 47th 2nd Tank, 8th Guards, 1st Polish Armies.

This enormous deployment naturally could not be hidden from the German scouts, sentries, [radio] intercept services, and air reconnaissance. On 6/7, the 9th Army command reported that strong Soviet combat formations were assembling on their front. The army group command replied, "That's out of the question!" Three days later, a radio message to partisan groups was intercepted according to which the Orsha-Borissov stretch was to be completely paralyzed on 20 June. Other similar reports followed, so that, on 6/12, finally even the army group command had to realize that an enormous deployment was taking place in front of the 9th Army. Field Marshal Busch then took his first defensive measures. He asked the OKH to remove the civilian administration of the Reichskommissariat Ukraine behind the 2nd Army to create a unified command authority. However, Hitler turned the proposal down.

The first indications of the Russian offensive appeared. Strong Soviet combat air formations attacked the airfields at Brest-Litovsk, Pinsk, Minsk, and Orsha during the night of 14 June. German night fighters and air defenders were able to shoot down 14 aircraft. Three days later, the Soviets probed the German main combat line, in some places in regimental strength.

Field Marshal Busch was still not alarmed by these threatening indications. He was convinced – as was Hitler – that a major attack would not occur. On 19 June, he went home on leave. Exactly 24 hours later, strong partisan formations blew up the Pinsk-Luniniec, Orsha-Borissov, Orsha-Mogilev, and Moledechno-Polozk rail lines. The 1st General Staff Officer of the OKH, Colonel Count Kielmannsegg, called Minsk on the evening of 6/20 and indicated to the army group command that the Soviet main effort lay near Polozk. However, the army group command did not believe him!

30 hours later, the "Red Army" struck!

As the morning of 22 June 1944 dawned, surprisingly strong artillery fire suppressed the German positions in the Vitebsk salient. The Russian shells hammered the earth for only a half hour, and then the tank regiments and rifle divisions broke loose.

The 43rd Army and the 6th Guards Army attacked northwest of Vitebsk against the IX German Army Corps. The 252nd ID, which was holding on the left flank, was overrun by the first assault of the XII Soviet Guards Corps. The Russian tanks rolled over the German lines, tearing a 8 kilometer wide gap to Army Group North and expanding it to a depth of 6 to 8 kilometers. The lead tank elements made it to Sirotino.

The 5th and 39th Armies attacked the VI Army Corps several kilometers further to the southeast out of the bridgehead on the Sukhodrovka. Here, the 299th ID was simply swept aside by the overpowering enemy forces, while the 256th ID could not hold and also had to withdraw. In the afternoon, the Soviets achieved three deep penetrations, which, in spite of the hopeless counterattack of the 95th ID, could not be removed.

Field Marshal Busch, who was advised of the major attack during the morning by telephone, immediately returned to his headquarters in the afternoon. Now he and his staff officers had to realize that the left flank of the army group was threatened with disintegration and that all contact with the neighboring army group in the north was lost. During the evening of the first day of the attack, the OKH approved the proposal of committing the 24th ID and the 909th Assault Gun Brigade to close the gap on the Obol – and to Army Group North.

The combat diary of the army group command pointed out:

"On 6/22 – the 3rd anniversary of the beginning of the war with the Soviet Union – the enemy opened their summer offensive with

Chapter 6: The Defeat

attacks against the front of Army Group Center. In the 2nd Army area of operations, they had the character of reconnaissance attacks, in the 4th Army area of operations they were assessed as pre-attacks to gain assault departure positions. In the 9th Army area of operations it remained quiet on this day. On the other hand, the enemy began the real attack against the 3rd Panzer Division with the main effort against the VI Army Corps southeast of Vitebsk and, surprisingly, also northwest of the city in the IX Army Corps area of operations between Sirotino and the left boundary of the army group. Due to these deep penetrations, considerable stress was placed on these two positions, which led to a crisis in the IX Army Corps area of operations. ... The major attack northwest of Vitebsk came as a complete surprise to the German leadership, because the previous enemy picture did not indicate such an enemy concentration."

The night of 23 June passed in the north of the front with the thunder of fire, the thud of bombs, the explosions of shells, the clattering of tanks, the moaning of the dying, and the flight of the living. As the new day dawned in the east, the Soviet war machine set in motion on all sectors of the army group front.

The Soviets advanced in the north of the front across the Polozk-Vitebsk railroad line deep to the south and penetrated into Vitebsk. In spite of the bitter defense offered by various hastily thrown together combat groups, the tank forces stood only 8 kilometers from army headquarters that evening! Field Marshal Busch issued an unconditional order to hold to the IX Army Corps.

The retreat in the south could no longer be stopped. The VI Army Corps collapsed under the strike of the 39th Soviet Army. The corps defended only in the smallest combat groups and withdrew fighting to Vitebsk or to the west into the forests and marshes. The army intended to evacuate Vitebsk, but Hitler and Field Marshal Busch turned down this proposal. The OKH would only allow the LIII Army Corps to withdraw to the Vitebsk outskirt positions.

While the 3rd Panzer Army was fighting for its very existence, the Soviets now extended their offensive against the 4th and 9th Armies! Fierce

Army Group Center

barrage fire tore up the trenches of the 4th Army, which was led temporarily since 5 June by General of Infantry von Tippelskirch for the ill Generaloberst Heinrici. The major attack had two emphases. The 11th Guards and 31st Armies attacked the XXVII Army Corps east of Orsha, while the armored brigades pushed back the inner flanks of the 78th Assault and 25th Armored Infantry Divisions back along the highway. By evening, the corps had to commit the 14th Motorized Infantry Division and the 667th Assault Gun Brigade to prevent a breakthrough on the first day.

The second emphasis lay east of Mogilev. Here, the 33rd and 49th Armies struck the 337th ID and achieved a deep penetration on the Ryassna-Mogilev road. There was no doubt that the Soviets wanted to make it to Mogilev. When the first and second German trench lines were overrun, the Russian tanks gushed forth into the rear area of the XXXIX Panzer Corps.

Still further to the south, the salvoes of the Russian guns also thudded. The 48th and 65th Armies attacked the XXXV and XLI Panzer Corps south of the Dnepr to the northwest. Two small local penetrations, which were achieved by the 65th Army, were removed. An additional attack north of Zhlobin was directed against the 296th ID, which was also stopped.

Therefore, the great battle in Belorussia began. ...

24 June 1944 brought the great attack against the 9th Army and can be considered the "beginning of the end." Army Group Center was torn apart on this day. Contact with the armies, corps, and divisions was lost and, from the third day of the battle on, German units fought as divisions, companies, or platoons.

The 5th Soviet Army overran the right flank of the 3rd Panzer Army in the north of the front. The 197th and 299th ID were hopelessly dispersed. Through this gap attacked the 39th Soviet Army up to the Duena [Dvina] near Pushkari. Therefore, the lead Russian tank elements stood to the west of Vitebsk. Then, when the 43rd Army came from the north, the LIII Army Corps was separated from the rest of the front. The clocks indicated 1610 hours; that was when "Fortress" Vitebsk was encircled by the enemy!

The enemy penetration north of the city already had a depth of 12 kilometers and a width of 30 kilometers, while in the south the enemy tanks

Chapter 6: The Defeat

rolled 10 kilometers into the depth of the interior. The gap to the right neighbor was 20 kilometers! The remnants of the VI Army Corps stood hopelessly against 20 rifle divisions. Bravery would no longer help. The 197th ID withdrew to the west, the 299th ID no longer existed, and the 256th ID withdrew to the southwest.

At 1830 hours, the army group command issued the order: "LIII Army Corps, leaving a division to defend Vitebsk, will fight its way to German lines!"

The 206th ID (Lieutenant General Hitter) received the order which decided its fate.

On 6/25, the 3rd Panzer Army practically ceased to exist. The VI Army Corps, fighting on the right flank, was fixed by the 5th Guards Tank Army, which had just arrived on the battlefield, was pushed to the southwest and, finally, destroyed in the next few days along the Orsha-Minsk highway. General Pfeiffer, the commander, died a soldier's death. On this day, the 3rd Panzer Army command only had the combat groups of the IX Army Corps left, and they were fighting their way back through the lake and marsh terrain to the west.

The LIII Army Corps command (General of Infantry Gollwitzer), which was encircled in Vitebsk, radioed on 6/25 at 1312 hours:

> "Situation has changed. Completely encircled by the constantly reinforcing enemy. 4th Luftwaffe Field Division exists no longer! 246th ID and 6th Luftwaffe Field Division in heavy combat on several fronts. Various penetrations into the city of Vitebsk. ..."

It was 1500 hours when the following radio message arrived: "Situation at its climax." Therefore, at 1830 hours, the army group command ordered a breakout. However, three minutes later, General Gollwitzer radioed back:

> "The overall situation forces us to concentrate our forces for a breakout to the southwest. Will start 0500 hours in the morning."

Army Group Center

Then the OKH interfered. Hitler ordered that a General Staff officer be sent to Vitebsk in a plane to order General Gollwitzer to hold. Generaloberst Reinhardt angrily refused to execute this order. He called Field Marshal Busch:

> "Tell the Führer that if he stands by his order, there is only one officer in the 3rd Panzer Army that can carry it out, and that is the commander. I am ready to execute this order!"

Field Marshal Busch passed this message on to the OKH. An hour later, Hitler gave in, and he rescinded his order. Then a radio message arrived from Vitebsk:

> "I am responsible for the battle. Gollwitzer."

On the next morning at 0830 hours, German reconnaissance aircraft sighted combat groups of the LIII Army Corps, that had broken out, 10 kilometers southwest of Vitebsk. The corps command radioed at 0915 hours, "206th ID pressured by the enemy outside of Vitebsk." Then they went silent. While the 3rd Panzer Army command hoped that the men of the LIII Army Corps would be able to fight their way out, Field Marshal Busch radioed Vitebsk at 1210 hours that the 206th ID had to fight to the last man!

On 27 June at 0900 hours, the LIII Corps command reported again. General Gollwitzer said that he was located with his combat groups in heavy combat 13 kilometers southwest of Vitebsk. It was the corps' last radio message! Not one officer, not one non-commissioned officer, not one soldier escaped the Russian encirclement! The combat group, where General of Infantry Gollwitzer was located, surrendered on 6/27, as did all of the others. They were 200 men, of which 180 were severely wounded! On this day, the Soviets assaulted the ruins of Vitebsk. They led approximately 10,000 German soldiers away into captivity and buried the 20,000 dead. The commanders of the 4th and 6th Luftwaffe Field Divisions, Lieutenant Generals Pistorius and Peschel, were among them.

The battle of the 3rd Panzer Army was still not at an end.

Chapter 6: The Defeat

On 6/25, the Soviets had hopelessly dispersed the front of the army and reached the Dvina near Ulla. On this day, the former headquarters was lost. Corps Detachment D under Major General Pamberg defended the area around Beshenkovichi to the last bullet. Generaloberst Reinhardt withdrew his operations staff during the night to Berezino.

On 6/27, the remnants of the army withdrew further. The soldiers of the 252nd ID barely made it to the Ulla, in order to save themselves. And the enemy continued to deploy reinforcements here. On this day, the army group command sent the 212th ID to the army, which still could not prevent the enemy from gaining additional ground south of Lake Ussveya.

Generaloberst Reinhardt had a long talk with Field Marshal Busch, which could often lead to serious differences. The Generaloberst requested and demanded the withdrawal of his army. The Field Marshal rigorously turned down these requests.

On 6/28, the remnants of the army had fought their way back into the Lepel area. The gap to the neighboring 16th Army in the north could in no way be closed. The Soviets compressed the last combat groups into an ever decreasing space. Again Generaloberst Reinhardt requested the immediate withdrawal of the army behind the Berezina. His army now had only 70 guns left!

Field Marshal Busch again turned down this request. It was the last order he issued to the 3rd Panzer Army command.

Field Marshal Model had taken command of Army Group Center.

On 6/24, the major Russian attack hit the 4th Army on the entire front, and the army could not offer an energetic resistance. Its heavy weapons were completely demolished in the first three days by the massive attacks of the 4th Soviet Air Army! The XXXIX Panzer Corps, which was to defend the area around Mogilev, was hit hardest, and its front collapsed under the attacks of two Russian armies. The right neighboring XII Army Corps radioed to the 4th Army command at 1400 hours:

"Troops fighting their way to the west. 12th ID defending Mogilev!"

Army Group Center

Then the corps command went silent. General von Tippelskirch had no further contact with them! Then the XXVII Army Corps, which was fighting in the north, also fled to the west toward Orsha, and the commander requested the withdrawal of his army. The army group command categorically turned him down.

The situation intensified practically from hour to hour. On 6/25, there was still no unified front in the 4th Army sector. The left flank of the army was overrun. The 78th Assault Division (Lieutenant General Traut) was ordered to let itself be encircled in Orsha and defend the city as a fortress. However, before the combat groups of the division could move to Orsha, the city was already in Soviet hands! Orsha fell on 6/26.

Therefore, the left flank of the army was pushed away from the Orsha-Borissov-Minsk highway. The few regiments – often only at company strength – had to try fight their way to the west through the extensive forest and marsh region. The Soviets pursued throughout, overtaking the German columns, splitting them apart, and destroying them individually. The last transport trains with wounded, weapons, and equipment had left just before the encirclement of Orsha, however, several kilometers later 25 trains were overtaken by Soviet tanks and destroyed.

It was similar on the right flank of the army. The Russian rifle divisions and tank brigades had long ago severed the Bobruisk-Mogilev road and had gotten into the rear of the defenders. Mogilev was encircled. Major General von Erdmannsdorf defended the city for another several days with hastily thrown together troops. However, on 6/26, the weapons went silent here. The 4th Army no longer had a right flank!

On this day, Field Marshal Busch was at the Führer Headquarters. He proposed to Hitler giving up Bobruisk, Mogilev, and Orsha, after the cities had long been in Russian hands. The Field Marshal believed his army group could be saved if he were allowed to move it behind the Dnepr. Hitler, as always, refused. Then he relieved the Field Marshal.

On 6/27, the 4th Army command still had communications to their corps and ordered – without consulting the OKH – a general retreat. The Soviet tanks were quicker and constantly cut off the individual combat groups. The fighter-bombers hammered at the columns moving to the west with their machine-guns and on-board cannon.

Chapter 6: The Defeat

The XXVII Army Corps was totally dispersed. The division commanders had ordered their combat groups to Borissov, where, eventually, a new defensive line could be occupied. The withdrawing XII Army Corps had the same goal.

On 6/28, the 4th Army command redeployed from Belynichi to Berezino. From this day on, they had no telephone communications with the army group command. The staff officers could only issue orders by "Fieseler Storch." General von Tippelskirch ordered his corps to hastily withdraw to the Berezina over the radio.

The army group command tried to close the threatening gap between the 3rd Panzer and 4th Armies with a combat group. Lieutenant General von Saucken received the mission of holding the enemy on the Berezina with the 5th Panzer Division, the 505th "Tiger" Battalion, police forces, and companies of the Engineer Training Battalion. The 5th Panzer Division was able to stop the lead Soviet tank elements near Zembin.

The combat groups in the east now had to fight their way through, but only a few succeeded. General of Artillery Martinek, commander of the XXXIX Panzer Corps, could no longer advance with many of his officers and soldiers. They remained somewhere in the forests and marshes east of Mogilev, never to be heard from again.

The race to the Berezina began.

The combat group of Lieutenant General von Saucken occupied the bridges near and in Borissov to make it possible for the troops that could break through to cross to the west. The only question was who would make it to the river first: the Soviets or the Germans?

On the evening of 6/28, at 2030 hours, the new commander arrived at the just-redeployed army group headquarters in Lida: Field Marshal Model. In the same hour, the offices of the all-powerful regional commissar of Weisruthenia fled the city of Minsk!

On 6/29, the lead Soviet tank elements reached the Berezina. Engineers threw up the first bridges near Bogushevichi across the river and they advanced further to the west. German combat groups could no longer make it to the Berezina. Undaunted, von Saucken's soldiers held out. They had no news from the XXVII Army Corps. They only knew that the commander, Lieutenant General Schuenemann, had fallen.

Army Group Center

From 1 July on, the Russians expanded their front on the Berezina. Here, from north to south, they attacked Combat Group von Saucken. It was the only bridgehead that still held out on the eastern bank – then stragglers started to show up. The report from one officer read:

> "After a forced march, in spite of many Russian attacks and encirclement attempts and in spite of strong air attacks, we made it into the forest on the edge of the Berezina near Shukovets on 1 July. ... The traffic jam on the small forest trails was so heavy that one would often only advance a few meters, after waiting for several hours. ... The majority crossed on the late afternoon of 2 July. ... The majority of our people were lost. ... We had been without warm rations since 27 June."

The XII Army Corps was overtaken by enemy tanks and could not make it to the Berezina! Lieutenant General Mueller surrendered with the remnants of his divisions in the forest between Mogilev and the Berezina!

However, time was also running out for the entire 4th Army. Combat Group von Saucken was already fighting on all sides and could no longer handle the Soviet tanks that were now advancing in all directions. Borissov was lost on 30 June. In the meantime, the Soviet armies were already located west of the river and were rolling on Minsk. Their tanks reached the only withdrawal road for the 4th Army near Pogost. Therefore, the 4th Army was practically encircled.

There was no longer a way out. The 4th Army came to its end in the forests east of Minsk. The day passed, and the combat stopped. The troops continued to try to escape to the west. Remnants of the XXVII Army Corps tried to break out on 5 July. The report of the 78th Assault Division read:

> "At 2300 hours, the assault began. Some units sang the Deutschlandlied. That night would never be forgotten by any of the participants. Burning villages, guns, and infantry fire, muffled explosions, and detonations mixed in with the thundering Hurras. ..."

On this night, the German front already lay 170 kilometers to the west of the combat groups trying to break out! The report continued:

Chapter 6: The Defeat

"Whoever fell out because of wounds or illness, experienced the horrible fate of the abandoned. ... Marshes, rivers, thick forests, the heat of the sun, hunger, and lack of water had a terrible effect. What drove us on was the unshakable will to reach the German front. ..."

The fate of the 9th Army was not much different. The "1st Belorussian Front" – led by Marshal Zhukov – began their first probing attacks to gain attack departure positions on 6/22. The main effort lay in the 65th Army area, which attacked the XLI Panzer Corps and achieved a penetration near Parichi. Thus, the I Guards Tank Corps was able to be shoved through the front on the very first day, in order to attack through the marshes to the northwest.

The German XXXV Army Corps, which had been led by Lieutenant General von Luetzow for the past few days – the army command had just replaced the commanders of the XXXV and XLI Panzer Corps – was already outflanked to the southwest by enemy tank forces during the first two days of the battle. Because the 3rd Soviet Army was able, simultaneously, to penetrate on the seam between the 4th and 9th Armies, the corps was also outflanked on the north.

Strong enemy forces were discovered in the forest west of the Drut. The 9th Army command, that believed the main effort of the Russian offensive was located here, committed the 20th Panzer Division (Major General von Kessel) in a counterattack. Then the news arrived about the expansion of the Russian breakthrough near Parichi into the south of the front. The 20th Panzer Division was immediately stopped and turned 180 degrees. However, before it could reach the new combat sector, it was too late.

The Russians utilized the penetration area in the north and broke through with their tank brigades across the Mogilev-Bobruisk road to the south. Early on the morning of 6/27, their lead tank elements stood in front of Titovka, 2 kilometers east of the road bridge to Bobruisk. From the south, the Don Guards Tank Corps advanced toward Bobruisk and up to the western edge of the city.

The army group still ordered the army to withdraw to Bobruisk. The IX Soviet Tank Corps stood in the northwest of the city, elements of the 3rd

Army Group Center

Soviet Army advanced in the north, and the Don Tank Corps advanced with the CV Rifle Corps from the south and west toward Bobruisk. The city and the XXXV Army Corps, with the 6th, 45th, 296th, and 383rd Divisions, were encircled on 6/27.

On 6/27, General of Infantry Jordan requested to break out of the encirclement to the northwest. The army group command turned him down! Major General Hammann was designated commandant of the "fortress" of Bobruisk and was ordered to defend the city until the last cartridge.

On 6/27, the XLI Panzer Corps command also transferred to Bobruisk. On the next day at 0100 hours, it radioed the army group:

> "383rd ID is in combat around Bobruisk. Since darkness, troop units from all of the divisions of the XXXV Army Corps have been streaming into Bobruisk, they are disorganized and without heavy weapons. The commander of 134th ID shot himself. The commander of 36th Motorized Infantry Division declared that he no longer has any control over his division. Artillery and heavy weapons were destroyed. There is no radio contact with XXXV Army Corps, which had ordered the destruction of the guns. ..."

When Lieutenant General Hoffmeister, commander of the XLI Panzer Corps, sent this message, there were already 3500 severely wounded in the unprepared casemates of the citadel. The defenders did not know from where they were being fired upon. The enemy stood on all sides, aircraft flew over the smoking ruins; and still hundreds of stragglers streamed into the city.

Chaos dominated, and it finally influenced Hitler in far away East Prussia, as he gave permission to give up Bobruisk at 1245 hours. The defenders broke out of Bobruisk on 6/29. Major General Hamann and 5000 wounded remained behind. The breakout was again stopped and destroyed by the Russians.

Lieutenant General von Luetzow immediately recognized the futility of the combat around Bobruisk. He organized the fleeing divisions for further combat in the south of the city. He collected all that he could and attempted a breakout to the west. Of these men, 14,000 reached the Ger-

Chapter 6: The Defeat

man front without any equipment. Lieutenant General von Luetzow and Major Generals Conrady and Michaelis were not among them.

The defenders of Bobruisk hoped to break through to the northwest. The combat groups made it through Soviet lines and reached the Sovissloch-Oktyabr area on 6/30. However, there were still 74,000 men left behind Russian lines; they died either from fighting, from hunger and exhaustion in the marshy forests, or they were captured.

There was no longer a 9th Army!

The commander, General of Infantry Jordan, was relieved. In his place arrived the former commander of the XLVII Panzer Corps, General of Panzer Troops von Vormann.

The combat diary of the army group command noted on 30 June:

"Today, for the first time in the nine day battle of Belorussia, there was some relief from the tension. The enemy did, indeed, occupy Sluzk after a see-saw battle, however, they were tied down there by the tenacious resistance offered by the weak German forces committed there, which allowed us to make use of the time to unload operational reserves, which had arrived in the Baranovichi area. Also, the enemy mobile formations, which were attacking through Borissov toward Minsk, ran into strong resistance on the Berezina; one of the enemy groups advancing through Bogoml was thrown back. ..."

For the first time in days, Field Marshal Model could take a breath. The fleeing forces of his army group appeared to have been stopped. However, he also had to try to create a reserve with what he received from OKH and Army Group North. The 4th and 7th Panzer Divisions were on the way, the 170th ID arrived, and the 28th Jaeger Division was deploying. Transport trains with 7 march battalions and 3 Heeres anti-tank battalions arrived on 6/29 and 6/30 in Minsk.

On 6/30, the Field Marshal issued the following order to the armies:

4th Army: Divisions immediately behind the Berezina,
9th Army: Stop the enemy in front of Minsk,

Army Group Center

2nd Army: Hold Sluzk - Baranovichi area,
4th Panzer Army (Army Group North Ukraine): Take over the defense of the Brest-Litovsk area.

Minsk was no longer to be held.

The newly organized XXXIX Panzer Corps, which was led by Lieutenant General von Saucken, was the corset rod of the army group, with the 5th Panzer Division (Lieutenant General Decker), 7th Panzer Division (Major General Dr. Mauss), 50th ID (Major General Haus), and 170th ID (Major General Has). However, after the Soviets outflanked the corps on the Berezina, it had to withdraw to the west. On 7/2, the 5th Panzer Division was able to throw back the V Soviet Guards Tank Corps, which was already in the rear, and establish contact with Moledechno.

The way to Minsk was open to the Soviets!

The army group removed all of the necessary goods from the former regional capital. Thus, on 7/1, for example, 8000 wounded left the city. Two days later, 3 more hospital and 43 evacuation trains rolled to the west – then the Soviets arrived.

The 3rd Soviet Army (Lieutenant General Gorbatov) entered Minsk on 3 July 1944 with the I and II Guards Tank Corps!

Field Marshal Model constructed a defensive line west of the city between Baranovichi and Moledechno. The 5th Panzer Division stood north of Minsk on the Vilnius rail line, the 12th Panzer Division assembled southwest of the city, the 4th Panzer Division and the 28th Jaeger Division established a defensive line in front of Baranovichi, and the 170th ID entrenched around Moledechno. This line was to be held until the encircled divisions had fought their way through, but this did not occur.

28 German divisions with 350,000 men were destroyed east of Minsk! The battle west of Minsk continued.

An officer of the 7th Panzer Division wrote in his diary:

> "Confusion reigns on the front, the withdrawal is being conducted by individual troops in complete disarray. The command posts are not kept informed about the situation on the front."

Chapter 6: The Defeat

The Soviet armies continued to attack. On 7/8, they occupied Baranovichi, and on 7/9, Lida; on 7/11, the resistance west of Minsk collapsed; and on 7/12, Soviet tanks rolled on Polish and Lithuanian roads.

Vilnius was the last "fortress" to be lost during these turbulent days.

On 7/2, the alert was sounded here. The evacuation of the 5000 wounded from the hospitals began. A combat group under Colonel Bauch took up the positions on the outskirts of the city. Field Marshal Model issued orders to the combat group on 7/3. Two days later, Vilnius was subordinated to the 3rd Panzer Army command as a "fortress."

Major General Stahel, an air defense officer, was designated fortress commandant on 7/7. On this day, he had the following troops under his command:

399th Grenadier Regiment (Major Soth)
1067th Grenadier Regiment (Lieutenant Colonel Tolksdorff)
16th SS Polizei Regiment (Lieutenant Colonel Tittel)
16th Parachute Regiment (Lieutenant Colonel Schirmer)
Grenadier Brigade (2 battalions) (Major Schubert)
2/240 Artillery Regiment, 256th Anti-tank Battalion, 296th Air Defense Battalion.

The Soviet attack began on 7/8. Soviet tanks and infantrymen attacked across Lake Narocz toward the airfield, which was defended by the paratroops until the last officer fell. At midday, the Soviets entered the city, overran the initial anti-tank obstacles, and destroyed various combat groups. On the following day, the defenders had reported 500 dead and 500 wounded. Vilnius was cut off from the outside world on 7/9, and air supply was initiated.

The superiority of the Russians was too strong. The OKH ordered a breakout on 7/11 at 1800 hours.

On 7/12, the defenders broke contact with the enemy and waded the Viliga during the night of 7/13. On this morning, 2000 men made it to German lines.

The positions of the withdrawing German armies were already on the Nieman. Fierce combat developed, especially between Olita and Grodno.

Army Group Center

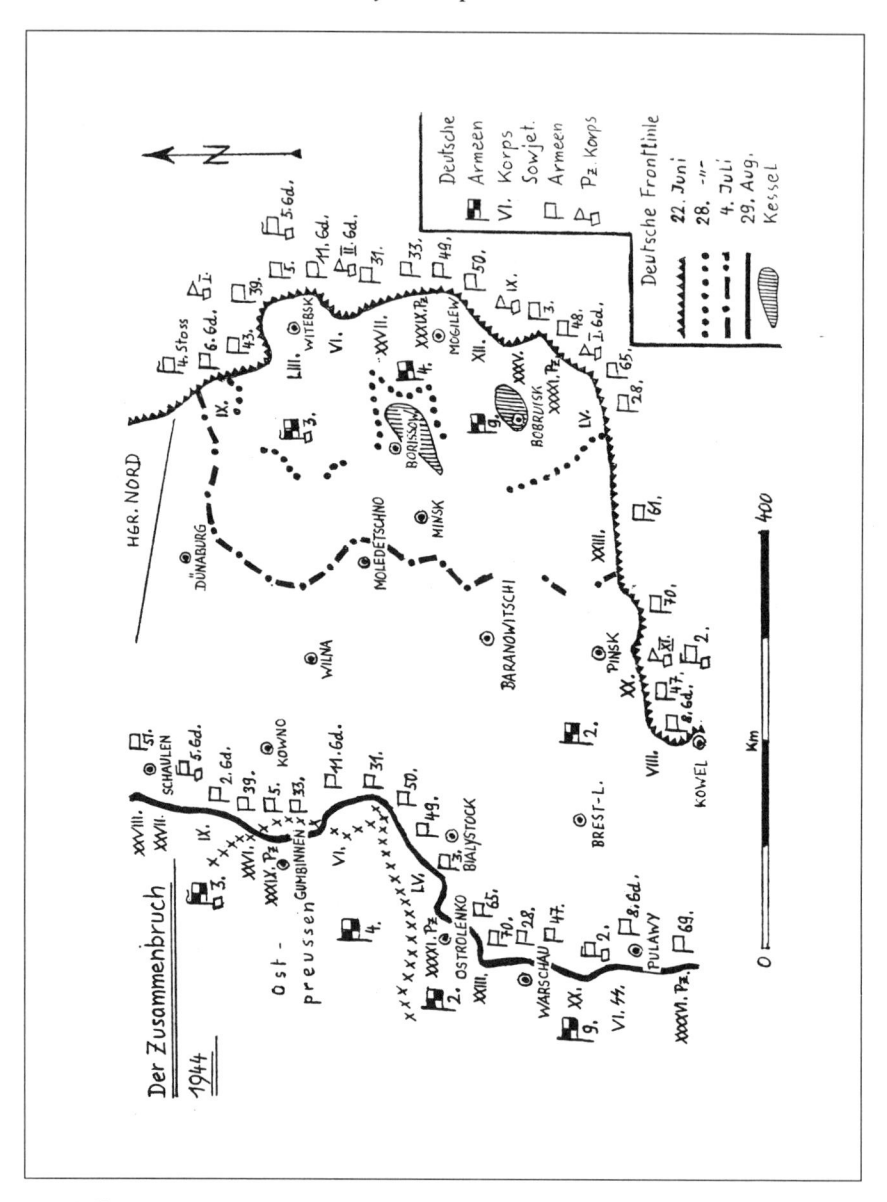

The Collapse 1944

Chapter 6: The Defeat

The city of Grodno fell on 7/16. The XXXIX Panzer Corps was able to temporarily hold a bridgehead between the two cities on the eastern bank of the Nieman with the (from left to right) 7th Panzer Division, 170th ID, 50th ID, 5th Panzer Division, and 50th ID.

The 2nd German Army in the south of the army group was spared the chaos during the first days of the major Soviet offensive. The army remained in its positions in the Pripet area, as a 350 kilometer wide gap was established on its left flank, through which 126 rifle, 6 cavalry, 16 motorized divisions, and 45 tank brigades of the "Red Army" attacked.

The Soviet attack against the 2nd Army began on 7/14. The Russians drove out of the Tarnopol-Kovel area with tank forces and achieved a deep penetration between the 2nd Army and Army Group North Ukraine. The German divisions were outflanked on the following day and had to withdraw to the west and northwest on 7/18.

The Soviet armies pursued immediately. They stuck close to the German combat groups and reached the Bug at the same time they did. On 7/18, the river was crossed by the Soviets near Luboml and Vlodava. The commander of the "1st Belorussian Front", Rokossovskiy, who was promoted to Marshal after the capture of Minsk, ordered as the objective: Brest!

In the second half of July, the Russian formations found themselves deployed in eastern Poland, and their 65th and 28th Armies crossed the Bug. A counterattack by the German 4th Panzer Division and the SS "Wiking" Division on 7/23 from the south forced the 65th Army to evacuate its just won bridgehead. The Soviets were forced on the defensive.

The 2nd Tank Army (Lieutenant General Bogdanov) and the 1st Polish Army (Lieutenant General Berling) occupied Lublin on 7/22 and advanced directly to the Vistula from there.

On 27 July, further to the south, the 28th Army attacked Brest-Litovsk from the north, the 61st Army from the east, and the 70th Army from the south. It was defended by a numerically small combat group under Lieutenant General Scheller, Senior Field Commandant of Brest. The combat group was overrun, and General Scheller fell. The Soviets occupied Brest-Litovsk on 28 July.

At this time, they had reached the old western boundary of the USSR, where the German offensive to the east had begun on 22 June three years prior.

Army Group Center had lost all of the territory that it had won and occupied for three years.

During the past four weeks, it had lost approximately 200,000 dead, including 10 generals, and 85,000 prisoners, including 21 generals. The collapse of Army Group Center in summer of 1944 was worse than Stalingrad for the German Eastern Army.

At the end of July, Field Marshal Model ordered – without consulting the OKH – the immediate withdrawal of troops to the Polish border and the giving up of all "fortresses" and strong points still held. Therefore, a main combat line was constructed again in the Bialystok area, on which all enemy attacks could be repulsed.

This measure did result in getting a handle on the army group's formations, however, the right flank hung in the breeze. There was no longer contact with the neighboring Army Group North Ukraine, which had been redesignated "A."

The Soviet leadership made use of this weakness and forced the gap in the direction of the Vistula. The lead Tank elements of the "Red Army" reached the river on 7/26. Marshal Rokossovskiy forbid its crossing for the time being, because he wanted to wait for the deployment of Russian artillery and the preparation of stronger attack forces.

The 8th Guards Army – this was the army that had defended Stalingrad – attacked on 8/1 under Army General Chuikov. On the first day, a 10 kilometer wide and 3-5 kilometer deep bridgehead was established near Magnuszew.

The German staffs were surprised by the weight of the Russian attack. A counterattack was launched on 8/4. The 19th Panzer Division and the "Hermann Goering" Armored Parachute Division attacked. Somewhat later followed the 17th, 45th ID, and 25th Panzer Division. At the same time, German fighter-bombers joined in the battle for the first time in a long while. The 19th Panzer Division advanced along the Pilica, while the 45th ID and "Hermann Goering" attacked along the Radomka. The IV Soviet Guards Corps was caught in the pincers and pushed back.

Chapter 6: The Defeat

Marshal Rokossovskiy pulled back. He allowed the 69th Army (Lieutenant General Kolpakchi) to cross the Vistula near Pulavy. Therefore, the German defenses were weakened. The German forces were too few. They did not succeed in condensing the two Russian bridgeheads.

Positional warfare began on 10 August – it would continue until January of the next year.

An additional Soviet attack occurred north of Warsaw. The III Soviet Tank Corps marched on Zegrze on the Bug. The army group reacted quickly. The tried and true XXXIX Panzer Corps (General of Panzer Troops von Saucken) was ordered to counterattack.

The "Hermann Goering" Armored Parachute Division was to attack to the northeast on the Prague-Volomin rail line, the 19th Panzer Division followed in the same direction north of the road, while the 4th Panzer Division had to advance on both sides of the Radzymin road to the southwest, immediately followed by the SS "Wiking" Division.

The German attack to encircle the III Tank Corps began on 2 August. The 19th Panzer Division entered Radzymin and established contact with the 4th Panzer Division. Field Marshal Model was located at the head of the attacking 4th Panzer Division! The Soviets were thrown back to Volomin. The paratroopers outflanked the city from the south, the soldiers of the 4th Panzer Division from the east. Volomin was assaulted on 8/3.

The III Soviet Tank Corps was encircled! By 8/11, 6000 men surrendered; 3000 dead Red Army soldiers were left on the battlefield. The German front was thereby stabilized northeast of Warsaw.

The former commander of Army Group Center, Field Marshal Model, was entrusted with the command of the Invasion Front on 17 August. He left the Eastern Front forever. His successor was the admirable commander of the 3rd Panzer Army, Generaloberst Reinhardt, whose army was taken over by Generaloberst Raus, the former commander of the 1st Panzer Army.

Now the Polish capital was the focus of the battle in the east.

The 9th Army command (General of Panzer Troops von Vormann) was able to solidify its front between the Bug and the Radon-Lublin road at the end of July. The army command was transferred to the right flank of the army group after the collapse. They were able to establish contact with the

Army Group Center

4th Panzer Army (Army Group A) and, therefore, create a unified main combat line.

The Soviets were unable to make it through to Warsaw on the first try. A German bridgehead still existed on the eastern bank of the Vistula, and it was held by the 73rd ID. The 9th Army command, therefore, had to be concerned that Warsaw did not become part of the combat zone. Unfortunately, military requirements must often give way to political considerations. The political organs did not care very much for giving up their former powerful positions. Therefore, during the battle for Poland, there did not exist an Army rear area, because the influence of the governors of Warsaw and Radom began right behind the front.

Since 7/26, the 9th Army command received news that it would shortly have to contend with a large scale revolt. Therefore, the garrison, under Lieutenant General (Air Defense) Stahel (since 7/27 the commandant of Warsaw), was placed on alert. The city commandant had available:

4th Grenadier regiment
Warsaw Watch and Alert Regiment
996th, 997th, 998th Landesschuetzen Battalions
225th OFK Grenadier Company
146th Motorized Field Gendarmerie Company
146th Engineer Construction Battalion
475th Tank Destroyer Company
2/743 Anti-tank Battalion.

To these Heeres troops were added 12 battalions of SS and police, which were subordinate to the SS and Police Commander, Gruppenführer Geibel.

The revolt in Warsaw began suddenly on 1 August at 1700 hours. The surprise attack of the Poles was frustrated by the alerted German defenders. They were not able to capture the two Vistula bridges, which were the objectives of the revolt. 2 German officers, 9 non-commissioned officers, and 45 men held the bridges and, therefore, decided the fate of the revolt during the early hours.!

The staff of the Polish Home Army radioed at 2130 hours:

Chapter 6: The Defeat

"We have begun the Battle of Warsaw. ... In view of the fact that the Battle of Warsaw has begun, we propose that the Red Army immediately come to our assistance by attacking from the outside."

The individual German strong points, including the commandanture, were encircled on the first day. Nevertheless, contact was maintained with the outside world by telephone. The Generalgouvernement requested immediate assistance from the army group.

Field Marshal Model, who was still commander at that time, replied:

"This revolt is the result of the corruption and false treatment of the Polish population. My soldiers are too good for that!"

Because the army group had to turn its attention back to the east, the formations of the Reichsführer SS and Chief of the German Police took over suppressing the revolt. Himmler immediately set in march to Warsaw: Police and SS units from the Warthegau under the leadership of SS Gruppenfuehrer Reinefarth, the Dirlewanger Police Regiment from Lyck, and the RONA SS Brigade (Kaminski) out of Chenstochow. The OKH ordered the 608th Security Regiment (Colonel Schmidt) to Warsaw.

SS Gruppenführer von dem Bach-Zelewski, Chief of all anti-partisan formations, arrived in the Polish capital on 8/4 and took command. The systematic suppression of the revolt began on the next day and lasted two whole months. The battle was fought fiercely and inhumanely by both sides. Because the Poles fought until the last cartridge, the Army had to call on the help of mortar batteries, tanks, assault gun battalions, engineer battalions, etc. Several stuka attacks brought death and destruction to Warsaw.

The 9th Army did not participate in the combat, even though the revolt was played out directly behind its front. The army command wanted nothing to do with SS methods. The army combat diary reported sarcastically on 8/5:

"Regiment Kaminski has forced open the Reichsstrasse from the south to the Machorka factory" – and two days later – "...more plundering is being accomplished than advancing."

Army Group Center

Nevertheless, the SS and police troops were not able to overcome the resistance of the Poles. Because the Soviets were making themselves noticed in front of the 9th Army attack sector, the 9th Army command was forced to clear up the situation in their rear.

General of Panzer Troops Baron von Luettwitz, the new commander of the 9th Army, took measures to clear up the revolt. The Reichsführer SS yielded to these measures. He had to realize that his formations would not dominate Poland. The SS regiments had already lost 9000 men!

The 9th Army committed the 19th Panzer Division (Lieutenant General Kaellner) to attack the inner city. The division suppressed the Mokatow quarter in two days with stuka support.

General Bor-Komorowski, commander of the Polish Home Army, had been a worthy opponent. His units had fought bravely, but now he had to surrender. 15,200 dead and missing, as well as 7000 severely wounded, were enough! His representative arrived at the command post of Gruppenführer von dem Bach on 2 October and offered to surrender.

11,000 Polish soldiers were marched into captivity.

Hitler took bitter revenge on the civilian population. He ordered Warsaw to be leveled. Nevertheless, this order was sabotaged by the Army and was never executed. However, the 9th Army could not prevent the 153,810 Polish women, men, and children, and 167,752 other civilians from being transported to concentration camps.

Besides the bitter and bloody struggle in the streets of Warsaw, the 9th Army had to continue to defend against the enemy on the front. At the end of August, the 73rd ID, 1131st Grenadier Brigade, and elements of the 19th Panzer Division fought in the Vistula bridgehead east of the Polish capital. From the beginning of September on, the Soviets tried to compress this bridgehead with strong air support. The defenders experienced extensive artillery fire and a hail of bombs. Only the 52nd Fighter Squadron (Lieutenant Colonel Hrabak) brought any relief. The most successful fighter squadron in the Luftwaffe shot down its 10,000 aircraft on 9/2 over the Vistula bridgehead!

The enemy major attack on the bridgehead occurred on 9/10. The defenders energetically set about the defense, but they could not stand up to

Chapter 6: The Defeat

the superiority. During the night of 9/14, the rear guards of the 73rd ID and the 19th Panzer Division withdrew across the Vistula bridges, which were blown at 0200 hours in the morning.

Hitler was furious. The commander of the 9th Army, General of Panzer Troops von Vormann, was summoned. Hitler punished the 73rd ID by stopping leaves and promotions, even though this division had just suffered unheard of losses and had bravely fought on in spite of that fact.

The 1st Polish Army (Lieutenant General Berling) stood on the banks of the Vistula in Warsaw! After a short barrage fire, the army began the crossing on 9/16. The Germans did not allow one Pole onto the western bank. During the evening, the 1st Polish Army reported 2000 men lost. Then Marshal Rokossovskiy suspended all attacks!

The front of the 9th Army was quiet. In mid-September, the organization of the army was as follows:

Right flank: VIII AC (General of Artillery Hartmann) 17th ID, 45th ID, 6th ID, Corps Detachment E;

Center: XLVI Panzer Corps (General of Panzer Troops Fries)
5th Hungarian Division, 25th Panzer Division, Warsaw Security Regiment, elements of the 19th Panzer Division;

Left flank: IV SS Panzer Corps (SS Obergruppenführer Gille) Bulk of 19th Panzer Division, SS "Totenkopf" Division, SS "Wiking" Division;

Reserves: 73rd ID, "Hermann Goering" Armored Parachute Division.

At the beginning of September, the "Red Army" tried to break through Army Group Center. This time, they set the main effort on the Narev, in order to advance to the northwest to the East Prussian border. They attacked on 9/4 with all of their weight on the right flank of the 2nd Army (Generaloberst Weiss). The 35th and 7th ID were overrun by the enemy despite a bitter defense.

Army Group Center

At the beginning of September, the front of the 2nd Army stretched from the confluence of the Bug into the Narev up to north Lomsha. Here they made contact with the 4th Army, which, at this time, was prepared to defend East Prussia. The 2nd Army command (Generaloberst Weiss) was located in Mockein, southwest of Rozan. The large formations of the army were deployed from right to left as follows:

XX Army Corps - in the Bug confluences area up to west of Ostrov with the 35th ID, 5th Jaeger Division, 211th ID;

XXIII Army Corps - in the area west of Ostrov up to east Rozan with the 541st, 292nd ID and elements of the 35th ID;

I Cavalry Corps - in the area southeast of Ostrolenka with 3rd Cavalry Brigade, 129th ID, 14th Motorized Infantry Division, 102nd ID, 4th Cavalry Brigade;

LV Army Corps - in the area south of Lomsha with the 28th Jaeger Division, 367th ID, 203rd ID.

In front of this main combat line were deployed the enemy forces of the "1st" and "2nd Belorussian Fronts." Since the beginning of September, the Soviets had prepared to attack the 2nd Army with (from left to right) the 65th, 48th, 3rd, 49th, and 50th Armies. The main effort lay on the left flank of the 65th Army, where the VIII Guards Tank, IX Tank, and the I Mechanized Corps were deployed.

The 65th Army (Lieutenant General Batof) reached the Narev near Karnevsk and Pultusk on 9/5. The first attempt to cross near Pultusk (which the German defenders called Ostenburg) was repulsed by the 5th Jaeger Division. A second attempt succeeded. In the evening, elements of three Soviet divisions were located on the German bank.

The XX Army Corps immediately ordered the 5th Jaeger Division, the 252nd, and 254th ID to counterattack. Unfortunately, the bridgehead could no longer be compressed. Therefore, the Russians shoved additional troops

Chapter 6: The Defeat

to the western bank. By 9/9, the enemy bridgehead had a depth of 10 kilometers and a width of 20 kilometers.

The 2nd Army had to do everything in its power to remove this "Boil" in its front – the OKH even deployed reserves. The German counterattack was launched on 4 October. The 252nd ID, SS "Wiking" Division, and 3rd Panzer Division attacked the Russian positions after an artillery preparation.

The German tanks, including the "Tigers", ate their way through the front of the 65th Soviet Army on 9/4 and 9/5 and stood only 3 kilometers before the river by that evening! When the next day dawned, the enemy struck back.

Russian fighter-bombers and newly inserted tank brigades, with the super-heavy "Stalin" tanks, rolled forward, and the German attackers were forced onto the defense. Nevertheless, they did not withdraw, but fought over each farmhouse, intersection, and parcel of woods.

The Soviet leadership, however, played their trump – as they always did during the last two years – and that was their superiority. The Russian 48th Army crossed the Narev near Rozan after a strong artillery preparation!

Therefore, a second bridgehead was established.

The 2nd Army had to break off the battle. The tanks were removed, and the divisions returned to their departure positions. However, the Soviets did not pursue – not yet!

The middle and right flank of the army group began to stabilize in September. On the other hand, the left flank was still a source of concern, as it had been since the beginning of the Soviet summer offensive. Due to the Russian breakthrough north of Vitebsk and, therefore, the resulting separation of Army Groups Center and North, the 3rd Panzer Army got no rest. The gap to the neighboring 16th Army in the north was again supposed to be closed on order of the Führer. However, the forces of the 3rd Panzer and the 16th Armies were too weak.

The 3rd Panzer Army had to defer to the superiority of the Soviets. At the beginning of August, they were forced back to the East Prussian border. On 8/2, the IX Army Corps repulsed the first Soviet attempt to penetrate German territory near Raseinen.

Army Group Center

The new commander was faced with a difficult mission from the day he took command. He was ordered to re-establish contact with Army Group North. The army group was separated from the Eastern Front by the advance of the "1st Baltic Front" (Army General Bagramyan) to the Baltic Sea near Tuckum! The 3rd Panzer Army was to close the gap with new panzer divisions transported up from the southern sector.

This attack began on 16 August under the cover name "Operation Doppelkopf." The army had two panzer corps available. The XXXIX Panzer Corps (General of Panzer Troops von Saucken) assembled around Libau with the 4th, 5th, and 12th Panzer Divisions, as well as the newly formed Strachwitz Panzer Formation (SS Gross Brigade and 101st Panzer Brigade). The XL Panzer Corps (General of Panzer Troops von Knobelsdorff) assembled around Tauroggen with the 1st ID, the 7th and 14th Panzer Divisions, and the "Grossdeutschland" Armored Infantry Division.

The large number of panzer troops assembled by the OKH was an indication of the value placed on this operation, which would determine whether the Eastern Front could again establish a unified front.

The XL Panzer Corps attacked through Kelme-Telshe to the northeast, in order to reach Shaulen. The Russians quickly established the objective of this attack and threw strong tank and air forces against the attacking Germans. The attack of the panzer divisions bogged down on the little Venta River. On 8/17 and 8/18, General von Knobelsdorff regrouped. Now "Grossdeutschland" alone was to make it to Shaulen, while the 14th Panzer Division had to advance to the southeast and fall onto the enemy's flanks. A participant reported:

> "During the night of 8/18, with considerable difficulties caused by mine fields, poor roads, and impassable trails, we marched into the new assembly area. ... Groups of enemy stragglers and infiltrators were scattered throughout the forests, harassing column movement and even paralyzing some."

The new attack of the XL Panzer Corps had some bad luck. Only the 1/26 Panzer Regiment (Captain Count Rothkirch) gained any ground to

Chapter 6: The Defeat

Shaulen on 8/18. All of the other formations were forced onto the defense by the enemy. The XL Panzer Corps advanced no further!

At this time, the XXXIX Panzer Corps was luckier. The panzer formation of Major General Count von Strachwitz, which was located on the left flank, attacked the harbor city of Tuckum in the afternoon hours of 8/19. The formation was able to quickly breech the Soviet resistance and reached Dzukste by nightfall, but it was captured on the next morning. On 20 August, as the clocks struck 0700 hours, fire erupted from the sea. For the first time, German warships joined in a battle with Army Group Center! A naval formation under Vice Admiral Thiele – consisting of the heavy cruiser "Prinz Eugen" and the destroyers "Z-25" and "Z-28" – had arrived from Oesel and stood 25 kilometers off of the coast. 284 naval shells of all calibers opened the way to Tuckum for the panzer formations! It was exactly 1200 hours when Major General Count Strachwitz – riding in the lead tank – reached the security post of the 281st Security Division near Kemmern.

Contact with Army Group North was established.

The city of Tuckum fell into the hands of the panzer formation in the afternoon, and the enemy had no time to withdraw. A large amount of booty, including intact tanks, lay in the streets of the small harbor city.

Unfortunately, Panzer Formation Strachwitz, under its capable commander, could not remain with the 3rd Panzer Army. Major General Count von Strachwitz was transferred to Army Group North, with his formation, which would fight for its existence from Estonia to Kurland.

The establishment of contact between the two army groups created a unified front. The northern boundary of Army Group Center lay directly west of Dobeln. The left flanking division – "Grossdeutschland" Armored Infantry Division – was in contact with the 81st ID of Army Group North.

The army front ran from this junction in an almost straight line to the south to Kursenai, where it bent somewhat to the east toward Shaulen, and then continued on to the southwest. From left to right stood:

XXXIX Panzer Corps with "Grossdeutschland", 12th, 4th and 5th Panzer Divisions;
XL Panzer Corps with 201st Security Division, 551st ID, 7th Panzer

Army Group Center

Division;
XII SS Corps with 548th, 96th, 69th ID.

The army, nevertheless, could not remain long in these positions. In the meantime, new preparations for an enemy offensive were discovered. At the beginning of September, the "Red Army" planned an attack with four "fronts" to finally separate Army Group North from the Eastern Front and destroy it. Unfortunately, the German leadership could not determine the main effort of these plans.

The enemy offensive was launched on 14 September, after an enormous artillery preparation (180 guns per kilometer!), against Army Group North. The enemy main effort was again directed at the left flank of the 3rd Panzer Army.

On 9/15, on order of the OKH, it was subordinated to Army Group North (Generaloberst Schoerner).

The army group command ordered a relief attack by the panzer army in the direction of Dobeln, to relieve the hard-pressed 16th Army. The XXXIX Panzer Corps (General of Panzer Troops von Saucken) attacked to the east. The German troops had to overcome tenacious enemy resistance and could only gain a few kilometers of ground. After several days of hopeless attempts, the army group suspended all attacks.

On 1 October 1944, Army Group Center (headquarters Ortelsburg/East Prussia) lay on a front that ran in an almost straight line from east of Tilsit in the north to southeast of Rarka in the south. The 4th Army (headquarters near Loetzen) defended the East Prussian border up to directly northeast of Lomsha. It consisted of the XXVI, XXVII Army Corps, and XLI Panzer Corps and VI Army Corps, with the following divisions (from north to south): 56th, 1st ID, Schirmer Parachute Regiment, 561st, 547th, 131st, 170th, 558th, 299th ID, SS Combat Group Hannibal, 50th, and the 286th and 203rd ID. Then they closed with the 2nd Army (headquarters Zichenau) with the LV Army Corps, Cavalry Corps, XXIII, and XX Army Corps. To these corps belonged: 367th, 562nd ID, 28th Jaeger Division, 102nd, 129th ID, 14th Motorized Infantry Division, 3rd and 4th Cavalry Brigades, 292nd, 541st ID, 6th Panzer Division, 211th, 7th ID, 5th Jaeger Division, and 542nd

Chapter 6: The Defeat

ID. The 9th Army (headquarters southwest Warsaw) defended the main combat line from north Warsaw up to the junction with Army Group "A" with VI SS Corps, XLVI Panzer Corps and VIII Army Corps. Their divisions were, from left to right: SS "Wiking" Division, SS "Totenkopf" Division, "Hermann Goering" Armored Parachute Division, 19th Panzer Division, 5th Hungarian Division, 251st, 6th, 45th, and 17th ID.

These divisions would only remain in the above named positions for a few days. The Soviet offensive to decisively separate Army Group North from the Reich and occupy East Prussia began on 5 October 1944. The powerful assault of the 4th Soviet Shock, the 6th Guards, 43rd, 5th Guards, 2nd Guards, and 39th Armies (from right to left) tore a 17 kilometer deep and 76 kilometer wide gap in the front of the 3rd Panzer Army between Kursenai and Raseinen on the first day. The next day, the Soviets shoved the 5th Guards Tank Army and the independent I and XIX Tank Corps into and through the gap.

The enemy breakthrough was complete!

On 6 October 1944, there was no longer a German front in Kurland!

The Soviet XXIX Tank Corps (Major General Malkhov) crossed the German border near Krottingen on 9 October!

The battle for East Prussia began!

In the summer of 1944, the superiority of the Soviet Army and air forces was so great that, in spite of the bravery of individual German troop units, any resistance was senseless. Losses could no longer be replaced in the army group or Luftflotte 6.

The few air formations of the luftflotte of Generaloberst Ritter von Greim were utilized as "fireman" during these months and were committed wherever an enemy breakthrough occurred. Therefore, it was possible not to see any aircraft with the iron crosses over many of the combat regions.

The few fighter squadrons that were still available attacked the Russian bomber formations, despite their numerical inferiority. In the time period from 22 June to 15 August, the Luftflotte reported 1571 aircraft shot down, 369 of these by air defense artillery. Totals for the month of September were given as 1280 aircraft.

Army Group Center

The 52nd Fighter Squadron, Lieutenant Colonel Hrabak, registered its 10,000 kill this month. Therefore, it stood in the lead of all other German fighter squadrons. Captain Borchers, commander of the 1/52 Fighter Squadron, accomplished the 10,000th kill for his squadron. At the same time, it was his personal 118th air victory! German losses were heavy. The 51st Fighter Squadron, Major Losigkeit, which had supported the army group from the very first day of the war, lost its most successful pilot in June. Senior Lieutenant Hafner, Staffelkapitaen of the 8th Company of the 51st Fighter Squadron, was shot down after he registered his 204th air victory.

In the time period from 16-28 October – as the first battle of East Prussia was at its climax – Luftflotte 6 reported shooting down 264 aircraft and destroying 189 tanks.

The German fighter-bomber squadrons transitioned more and more to combating the advancing Soviet tank forces and, therefore, were able to give some relief to the infantry. The 2nd "Immelmann" Fighter-bomber Squadron under Colonel Rudel introduced this new type of air-ground operation. Colonel Rudel was the most successful "tank killer" in the Luftwaffe. While he attacked the tanks with his stukas, the II Group of his squadron, under Major Kemmel, provided them with air cover.

The two divisions of the II Air Defense Corps (General of Air Defense Odebrecht) were distributed throughout the entire front of the army group and fought at all of the hot spots. The 18th Air Defense Division (Lieutenant General Heinrich XXXVII Prinz Reuss) broke down into combat groups at the beginning of the major Russian offensive in June. The groups were distributed to the "fortresses." The 34th and 101st Air Defense Regiments fought in and around Bobruisk and died there. The 10th Air Defense Regiment fought in Orsha. The 2/49 Air Defense Regiment was encircled in Vitebsk and, therefore, ceased to exist. The 18th Air Defense Division withdrew to East Prussia and was assigned to work with the 4th Army and 3rd Panzer Army there.

The new division commander, Major General Sachs, was finally appointed Luftwaffe Commander East Prussia on 12/1/1944, and all Luftwaffe forces (except for the flying formations) were subordinated to him. The 6th Air Defense Regiment was encircled in Memel, but it was then transferred

Chapter 6: The Defeat

to East Prussia. The 10th Air Defense Brigade was disbanded and assigned as the 116th Motorized Air Defense Regiment to the 4th Army. The 136th Air Defense Regiment was transported from Kurland to Insterburg for the final battle. The 125th Air Defense Regiment moved into the 3rd Panzer Army sector. The air defense forces were reinforced by the 16th Air Defense Brigade, which was formerly assigned to protect the Führer Headquarters. After the headquarters was removed from Rastenburg, the brigade was transferred into the Rominter Heide.

The air defense of Luftflotte 6 received the following missions in December:

1. Protect against air attack,
2. Form tank blocking positions,
3. Support Army artillery.

At the end of December, the luftflotte finally got the I Air Defense Corps back, which was transferred to the southern sector in spring of 1942. The corps, under General of Air Defense Reimann, was committed on the right flank of the army group. The following air defense batteries were available to the luftflotte:

	heavy	light/medium	search light
23 June	98	103	16
23 August	234	173	21
23 October	229	166	24

In opposition to these numbers, the enemy had the following forces available on 1 December:

1st Air Army (Insterburg area) = 1,500 aircraft
2rd Air Army (Memel area) = 1,800 aircraft
4th Air Army (North Poland) = 1,400 aircraft
16th Air Army (Central Poland) = 1,300 aircraft

Army Group Center

The rapid loss of Belorussia and Eastern Poland alarmed the OKW and the Reich government! Now hasty orders and instructions had to be prepared to put the German Reich on a defensive footing. On 9/1/1944, the OKW formed "Festungsbereich Ost [Fortress Region East]" (commander: Generaloberst Strauss, Chief of Staff: Major General Heider). This staff was responsible for the rapid construction of the so-called "East Wall." The representative for East Prussia was Major General Vierow.

Hitler appointed a Gauleiter for the Reichsverteidigungs- kommissaren [Reich Defensive Commissariate], which was concerned with all military, political, and economic factors. Therefore, the National Socialist Party became directly involved in military matters, which led to differences of opinion between the two agencies. These differences of opinion concerned, for example, the evacuation of regions within the army group combat zone and immediately behind the combat zone, for which the Reichsverteidigungskommissar was responsible. Because neither the OKW nor the government had properly defined the term "combat zone", no one knew where the military and political spheres of influence began and ended.

On 9/25/1944, Hitler ordered the creation of the "Volkssturm" as a type of militia troop to support the Army. SS Obergruppenführer Berger was the Stabsführer, while Major General Kissel functioned as the Chief of Staff. The "Volkssturm" were subordinated to the Gauleiters in their regions of authority, which could issue them commitment orders without consulting the military. The "Volkssturm" were committed to the front without corresponding equipment or weapons. Battalions often had only 10% of their required carbines and these with only 5 rounds per rifle.

The first Volkssturm battalions to face combat came from East Prussia. Here the war struck the first serious wounds on German territory. The East Prussian Gauleiter had ordered all men between the ages of 16 and 65 to construct the "East Wall" on 7/14. At the end of July/beginning of August, the Memel area was evacuated of civilians. It was obvious that East Prussia was the objective of the "Red Army."

The first bombs fell on East Prussia on 8/27/1944. However, they were not Soviet bombers, but British combat aircraft that dropped their loads on Koenigsberg on this day. 1000 dead and 10,000 homeless were the result of this attack. Three days later, the "Royal Air Force" flew a second attack on

Chapter 6: The Defeat

Koenigsberg. They increased the damage of the first attack with 2400 dead and 150,000 homeless.

The war continued to grow nearer! The Landkreis of Tauroggen and the region north of Memel were declared combat zones on 9/22. The first muster of the East Prussian Volkssturm was held on 10/18 by Reichsführer SS Himmler in Preussisch-Eylau. Two days later, 7 Volkssturm battalions went to the front, and they were assigned to the 170th ID. Gauleiter Koch forbid the assimilation of the battalions into the division!

East Prussia had become a theater of war.

The Soviet breakthrough into the front of the XXVIII Army Corps west of Shaulen led not only to an advance to the Baltic Sea within a few days and, therefore, the splitting off of Army Group North, but also to the encirclement of the Memel area on 10 October.

The XXVIII Army Corps (General of Infantry Gollnick) was entrusted with the defense of Memel. At that time, the corps was subordinated to the 3rd Panzer Army, which still belonged to Army Group North. Because the front of the panzer army was torn away, the 3rd Panzer Army command was again subordinated to Army Group Center on 10/10. The army, whose headquarters was located in the Heinrichswalde near Tilsit, was ordered: to recapture the "East Prussian" positions northeast of the Reich border, conduct a counterattack with the "Hermann Goering" Armored Paratroop Division and the 6th Panzer Division, and then hold "Fortress Memel"!

Since 10/7, Memel itself was evacuated by the Navy. On this day, the 14th Security Flotilla, the 15th, 16th, and 22nd minesweepers, which were stationed here, left. On the next day, the 24th U-Boat Flotilla, the floating dock, and two floating cranes followed. The target ship "Goya", as well as the transports "Askari" and "Bolkoburg", left on 10/9. Several destroyers fought their way back into the harbor on 10 October and loaded the rear area services, including 210 female naval assistants. The last naval ship, the air defense ship "Hans Albrecht Wedel", steamed out of Memel to Pillau on 10/12 with the naval service agency and 80 wounded.

On this day, the "fortress" was already being fiercely contested. On 10 October, the Soviet Air Force attacked, just as heavy Russian artillery opened fire. The first enemy tank attacks were repulsed by the 502nd "Tiger" Battalion. In spite of this, Memel was encircled on this day, after which the Soviets were able to occupy Heydekrug.

In the "fortress" remained:

The 58th ID, 7th Panzer Division, "Grossdeutschland" Armored Infantry Division, remnants of the battered 551st ID, 6th Air Defense Regiment, 217th and 227th Naval Air Defense Battalions, 4 security battalions, 2 Volkssturm companies, 21st Naval Replacement Battalion, and the 502nd Panzer Battalion; in addition, there were also approximately 30,000 civilians, who were unable to break out to Tilsit.

The battle for Memel was fought bitterly right from the start. The OKH forbid the defenders to break out. The naval combat group under Vice Admiral Thiele joined in the battle on 10/12 at 2000 hours, with the heavy cruisers "Luetzov" and "Prinz Eugen", as well as the destroyers 16, 25, 36, and the 3rd Torpedo Boat Flotilla. The ships repeated their bombardment of the Russian positions on the following day, at which time the two cruisers alone fired 1318 shells.

On 14 October, the Soviets began the great attack to capture Memel. The encircled troops defended bitterly and were able to repulse the attack, destroying 68 tanks. The naval combat group again joined in the battle on this day and participated in its success. A second Soviet attack on the following day also failed.

On 10/17, the OKH, which had utopian plans as always, ordered the defenders to attack to the north to make contact with Army Group North. However, this operation could not be executed, because Generaloberst Schoerner turned down the plan and directed the attention of the OKH to Gumbinnen, where a new Russian offensive had begun. The change in the situation influenced that in Memel itself. The defenders had to be reduced so that they could be turned over to the threatened Gumbinnen front. Thus, at the end of October, the 7th Panzer Division and the "Grossdeutschland" Armored Infantry Division were transported by ship from Memel to East Prussia. The transports loaded 68 heavy tanks, 23 assault guns, 35 armored cars, 104 trucks, and other equipment.

The 95th ID was transferred from Army Group North to Memel to defend the city and harbor along with the 58th ID. The two infantry divi-

Chapter 6: The Defeat

sions fought bitterly in the following weeks and months and were still not defeated by the end of the year. Nevertheless, the defenders had to slowly withdraw toward Memel because of Soviet superiority. On Christmas Day 1944, the main combat line ran from Karkelbeck in the north in a half circle about 6 kilometers east of Memel then directly to the south, south of Schmelz.

The only contact with the outside world was through the "Naval Harbor Force." These were very small ships, which evacuated the wounded and provided the threatened city with small amounts of rations and weapons. The "Harbor Forces" consisted of 14 launches, 2 air defense, 2 ferries, 11 pinaces, 6 motorized barges, artillery barges 19, 34, 38, and 39, and naval barges 179, 204, 380, 517, 557, and 977.

The Soviet penetration into Memel was the prelude to the battle for East Prussia, which had to be conducted by the 4th Army (Commander: General of Infantry Hossbach, Chief of Staff: Colonel Baron von Varnbühler). In October, the army had to defend a 350 kilometer front, which stretched from Novograd to Memel.

This front was held by five army corps with 13 infantry, 2 security divisions, 2 cavalry brigades, and the SS Polizei Regiment "Hannibal." Committed were: VI Army Corps (General of Infantry Grossmann), XXVI Army Corps (General of Infantry Matzky), XXVII Army Corps (General of Infantry Priess), LV Army Corps (General of Infantry Herrlein), and the XLI Panzer Corps (General of Artillery Weidling).

At the beginning of October, German air reconnaissance established large enemy movements, which appeared to be attack preparations. The "3rd Belorussian Front" assembled to attack toward East Prussia. Its objective was to advance north of the Rominter Heide directly on Koenigsberg, in order to crush the entire defense of East Prussia with one blow. The "front" included the 26th Army (right), 11 Guards Army (center), and 31st Army (left).

40 rifle divisions and several tank brigades launched their attack on the morning of 16 October, after a two hour barrage fire, between Sudauen (Suvalki) and the Memel. The XXVII Army Corps stood on the main axis

Army Group Center

of the attack. Since the enemy intentions were known, the corps evacuated its forward positions during the last night, so that the barrage fire inflicted only a few losses.

The 1st East Prussian ID (Lieutenant General von Krosigk) had to accept the full weight of the initial attack. The East Prussian grenadiers stood steadfastly against the crashing waves and made the Soviets pay dearly for any ground gains. Again they unleashed a powerful barrage fire, reinforced with a constant air attack, onto the brave division. Losses increased horribly. All of the heavy weapons were destroyed. Then the enemy advanced against the division a second time, which suffered their highest losses of the entire war on this day. The 1st ID had to pull back, but it held!

On the following day, the three enemy armies were able to expand the penetration in the XXVI and XXVII Army Corps areas and slowly gain ground to the west toward the Reich border!

The military situation required the immediate evacuation of civilians from the border region. Now even the Kreisleiter realized the threat and immediately issued the evacuation order. The order was issued to Kreis Schlossberg and Goldap on 10/17 and to Kreis Gumbinnen on 10/20. However, these measures were taken too late! Panic ensued. An unorganized flight erupted to the west...

And from the east rolled the Soviet tanks. The city of Schirwindt, which was the cornerstone of the front, was lost on the evening of 10/17. Wirballen fell on the same day. The Soviets stood on the Reich border. The third day of the battle brought even further advances to the west, in spite of the bravery of the German soldiers and the sacrifices made by the fighter-bomber pilots.

Barrage fire and bombing attacks opened the battle on 10/19. Soviet tank and rifle formations had crossed the border, taken Eydtkau, and advanced on either side of the Rominter Heide. The 4th Army could not stand up to the enemy and, since it had no reserves, evacuated the bridgehead near Tilsit. The large Luisen bridge in Tilsit, which was the border crossing into the Baltic provinces, was blown on 10/20!

This was the day on which the 11th Soviet Guards Army (Colonel General Galitski) broke through to the west through Grosswaltersdorf, north of the Rominter Heide! The front of the XXVII Army Corps was torn apart.

Chapter 6: The Defeat

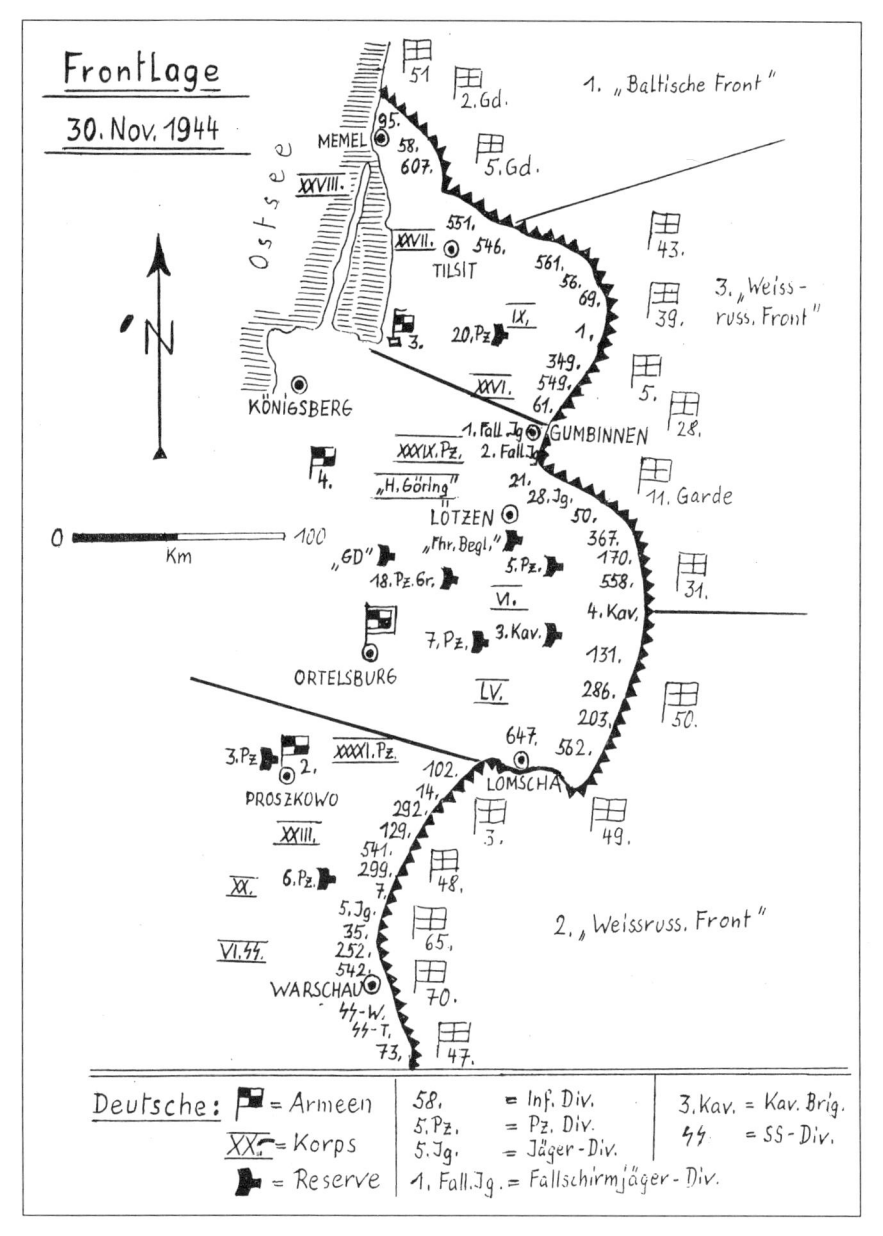

Front Situation 30 November 1944

Army Group Center

The lead Soviet attack elements entered Gumbinnen. On 21 October, there were only the 802nd Air Defense Battalion (Lieutenant Colonel Salomon) and stragglers from the combat groups of the 16th Parachute Regiment here. All enemy breakthrough attempts failed here at this blocking position. The air defense battalion destroyed 28 enemy tanks on this day, while the 1st Battery alone put 21 combat vehicles and 19 anti-tank guns out of commission. Volkssturm companies were thrown into the battle to support the artillerymen and paratroopers. Battalions Goldap and Treuburg distinguished themselves.

The Soviets reached Nemmersdorf on the Angerapp, but they could advance no further!

The 4th Army command had already initiated countermeasures. The 5th Panzer Division (Colonel Lippert) and the "Hermann Goering" Armored Parachute Division (Major General Necker) were deployed from the 3rd Panzer Army, and the combat inexperienced "Führer Grenadier Brigade" (Colonel Kahler) came from the Führer Headquarters.

The counterattack of these divisions began on 10/21. The "Führer Grenadier Brigade" attacked from Goldap to the north in the direction of Grosswaltersdorf. The Russians defended tenaciously. However, the German attack slowly gained ground. Then, the 5th Panzer Division and "Hermann Goering" came from the north. The lead attack elements met near Grosswaltersdorf! The commander of the XXVII Army Corps, General of Infantry Priess, died a soldiers' death at the head of his divisions. The enemy forces, which had broken through, were cut off! They took their revenge out on the civilian population, particularly in Nemmersdorf and Schulzenwalde.

Now the battle of Goldap flared up. The few German defenders resisted without hope. On 10/22, they had to turn the city over to the Russians. Ebenrode fell on 10/26. On the other hand, the 1st ID was able to hold Schlossberg. In all, 616 enemy tanks were destroyed in this area.

The 4th Army command intended to align its front and remove the Russian penetration near Goldap. The XXXIX Panzer Corps, which was deployed from the 3rd Panzer Army and had been commanded by Lieutenant General Decker for the past few days, was entrusted with this counterattack. The corps prepared the 5th Panzer Division and elements of the

Chapter 6: The Defeat

"Führer Grenadier Brigade" for a surprise attack in the north. This attack was launched on the morning of 1/3, without any artillery preparation, and the enemy was taken by surprise. By 0200 hours of the morning the lead elements reached Lake Goldap, and they advanced further to the south. The 50th ID (Major General Haus) met elements of the "Führer Grenadier Brigade" here.

The German lead attack elements met east of Goldap. The divisions immediately transitioned to the defense, oriented to the east and west. Each Russian breakout attempt and each relief attempt collapsed in the German fire! Goldap was reconquered on 11/5. 134 guns, 59 tanks, and many weapons were also captured.

The 4th Army had achieved a great success. It again had a solid front that now ran: Augustovo-Filipovo-eastern edge of Goldap-Grosswaltersdorf-Trakehnen-Schlossberg up to Memel and here along the river to the Kurish harbors. The attack of 40 Soviet divisions was parried. Nevertheless, the enemy remained in control of a 150 kilometer wide and 40 kilometer deep parcel of German territory.

At the beginning of November, the "Red Army" suspended the battle against Army Group Center throughout. The 2nd Army defended the right flank from directly north of Warsaw, along the Narev, to Novograd. A Russian bridgehead emerged in the German front near Pultusk to the northwest. The 4th Army held a frontal salient to the east, which ran from Novograd on the Narev along the Bobr and the Rospuda up to Filipovo, from here back into East Prussian territory, through Gumbinnen, and from Schlossberg up to Kurland, where it met up with the 3rd Panzer Army.

The 9th Army, which had fought in the army group area of operations since June 1941, was turned over to Army Group "A." The organization of Army Group Center on its 600 kilometer long front was as follows:

2nd Army (Generaloberst Weiss, Chief: Colonel Macher)
IV SS Corps with SS "Totenkopf" Division, SS "Wiking" Division, 542nd ID;
XX Army Corps with 252nd, 35th ID, 5th Jaeger Division;
XXIII Army Corps with 7th, 299th, 541st ID;

Army Group Center

XLI Panzer Corps with 129th, 292nd ID, 14th Motorized Infantry Division, 102nd ID;

4th Army (General of Infantry Hossbach, Chief: Colonel Baron von Varnbühler)
LV Army Corps with 547th, 562nd, 203rd, 286th ID;
I Cavalry Corps with 131st ID, SS Polizei Regiment Hannibal, 3rd and 4th Cavalry Brigades;
VI Army Corps with 558th, 170th, 367th ID;
"Goering" Armored Parachute Corps with 28th Jaeger, 21st ID, 1st and 2nd Parachute Division;

3rd Panzer Army (Generaloberst Raus, Chief: Colonel Mueller-Hillebrand)
XXVI Army Corps with 61st, 549th, 349th, 1st, 69th ID;
IX Army Corps with 56th, 561st, 548th ID;
XXVIII Army Corps with 551st, Center and West Blocking Formation, 64th Security Regiment.

On 12/1, the army group had available in reserve: 3rd, 5th, 6th, 7th, 20th Panzer Divisions, 18th Armored Infantry Division, "Grossdeutschland" Armored Infantry Division, and the "Führer Grenadier Brigade."

In December, the main effort of the Eastern War lay exclusively on the southern front. Thus, in November, the army group had to give up the 211th ID, 5th Cavalry Brigade, and "Führer Escort Division." During December, their former reserves were taken, including the SS divisions and the IV SS Corps, XXXIX Panzer Corps, and I Cavalry Corps.

These transfers occurred at a point in time when the deputy Gauleiter of East Prussia bragged in a radio speech: "East Prussia will remain forever German!" and as Stalin issued his basic Order Nr. 220:

> "The encirclement of Hitler's Germany will be complete. The Red Army and the armies of our allies have occupied the departure positions for the decisive advance into the heartland of Germany!"

7

THE INTERIOR
Military and Civilian Administration - Partisan Warfare

The war planned by the Reich leadership against the Soviet Union required not only military preparations, but also preparations in the political sphere. The campaign was not conducted only to defeat the "Red Army." It had to be conducted to exploit the economic resources for the German war economy. This included the task of occupying the land, in order to later absorb it into the German Reich. This far reaching objective could not be secured by the frontal troops alone. So, early on, governmental organizations were established within the OKW to later provide military protection of the occupied territories of the USSR, administer them politically, and exploit them economically.

Utilizing experience from the 1st World War, the OKH worked out proposals for a military administration in January 1941. Hitler glossed over these proposals and issued "Principles for the Special Regions..." on 3/31/1941.

The principles specified that the rear of the military operations area would be occupied and a political administration had to be established here, which would be subordinated to a newly created Reich ministry. Military affairs would be seen to by a Wehrmacht commander in the rank of a commanding general.

Army Group Center

The Wehrmacht commander would have the following tasks:

"1. Cooperate with the Reichskommissar;
2. Utilize the land and secure its economic value for the benefit of the German economy;
3. Utilize the land to supply the troops;
4. Secure the region militarily;
5. regulate road traffic;
6. Provide shelter for the Wehrmacht, police, and prisoners of war."

When the army group took command of the 4th and 9th Armies and the 2nd and 3rd Panzer Groups in spring of 1941, the "Staff of the Commanding General of the 102nd Rear Area" was already established. The command had authority over the security formations and rear area elements of the army group and, after the beginning of the campaign, administered the occupied area militarily.

The OKH ordered that the area crossed by the frontal troops be administered by the field and local commandanturas. Each army had 3 to 4 commandanturas in its rear area, which received their instructions from the commandants of the army rear areas, who in turn were subordinated to the commander of the Heeres Rear Area. They had far reaching independence, however, they were bound by the instructions of the OKH. The Heeres Rear Area, in general, was the region from the front up to a depth of 200 kilometers.

The commander of the 102nd Heeres Rear Area, therefore, was responsible for the military administration of the Army Group Center rear area. The staff was established from Military District XI and utilized forces from the reorganized 213th ID.

The commander was General of Infantry von Schenckendorff, the former commander of the XXXV Army Corps. His deputy was General of Cavalry Koch-Erpach. As corps troops, the staff had available:

825th Supply Company
213th Electric Power Company

Chapter 7: The Interior

587th Bakery Company
587th Butcher Company
745th Rations depot
808th Ambulance Platoon
213th Veterinary Company
690th Motorized Field Gendarmerie Battalion
758th Motorized Field Post Office
12th Land Construction Company.

Four security divisions belonged to the command region. These divisions followed the four armies/panzer groups. They formed regimental strength formations that followed directly behind the field troops to track down the concealed Soviet formations and engage them. The remaining division troops had to maintain order on roads and railroads; they also had to provide security for industrial operations, important communications hubs, and Wehrmacht shelters.

The security divisions were supported by construction engineer battalions, Landesschuetzen units, police forces, and detachments of the Reichsarbeitsdienste.

The formations of the commander in the Heeres Rear Area crossed the Reich border approximately eight days after the beginning of the war, in order to execute their many-faceted mission. They advanced further to the east every day, just as the frontal divisions gained territory. At the end of July, the former Bialystok administration district was taken from the army group command and incorporated into the administration organization of the province of East Prussia.

At the beginning of August 1941, the area of the security forces of the army group was defined in the west by the province of East Prussia (directly north of Grodno-east of Volkovysk-Bug east of Biala). In the north, the boundary ran along the former Russian-Lithuanian border up to Drissa. From here it bent sharply to the south, encompassed Borissov (headquarters of the army group command), went south of the highway back to Minsk and, from here, directly south up to Davidgrudeck, where it made contact with the rear area of Army Group South. General of Infantry von

Army Group Center

Schenckendorff had his headquarters in Baranovichi. He had the following security divisions committed on 8/6:

The 286th Security Division stood outside the area of authority behind Army Group Center. Its forces secured along the highway from Minsk to Smolensk. The 403rd Security Division followed the front troops to the north and made it to the marshland north of Vileika. The 221st Security Division occupied the area south of Baranovichi. The 339th Security Division followed the 2nd Panzer Group. The region did not change in the north and in the center during the next few weeks. Only the southern sector was shifted about 8 kilometers west of Unecha at the end of September. The command occupied quarters in Smolensk, while the Senior SS and Polizei Commander settled in Baranovichi.

The Heeres Rear Area expanded considerably to the east after the beginning of the Moscow offensive. At the end of October, its eastern boundary ran on a line: Toropets (in the north)-Velizh-Demidov-Krichev-Klintsy (in the south). The areas of the security divisions were:

403rd Security Division: Vitebsk - Velikie Luki;
286th Security Division: Orsha - Borissov;
339th Security Division: Bobruisk - Sluzk;
221st Security Division: Gomel - Mogilev.

The German formations were reinforced at this time by local forces. These were Soviet prisoners that had crossed over to the Germans voluntarily. The so-called East battalions emerged. They were used more and more to secure rail stretches and bridges. At the end of October, the 601st, 602nd, 604th, and 605th East Battalions were in the Heeres Rear Area and were committed to guard bridges along the rivers Berezina, Dnepr, and the northern Volga.

The Soviet winter offensive of 1941/42 not only caused a withdrawal of the eastern boundary of the Heeres Rear Area, but also an active commitment of the security divisions to the front. With the increase in partisan activity, additional combat groups had to be committed to combat this new enemy force.

Chapter 7: The Interior

Because their own formations were not sufficient, the German leadership was forced in 1942 to commit more and more foreign troops to the partisan battle.

Thus, it was possible to designate the former expelled Pole Kaminski as governor of the region south of Briansk with the mission of maintaining the Navlyam-Lokotiy-Dmitrovsk area free of partisans. Kaminski executed this mission with his own army, which was designated the "Russkaya Osvoboditelnaya Narodnaya Armiya" [Russian People's Liberation Army] (known as RONA for short). In March 1942, the RONA consisted of six infantry battalions, one artillery battalion with 20 guns, and one tank company with 12 combat vehicles. Kaminski's army effectively kept the area free of partisans. (His army withdrew to the west in 1943 with approximately 30,000 civilians, along with the German Army. The RONA was later designated the "Kaminski Brigade", and was noted for sadism and terror.)

Besides the Russian volunteer battalions, there were divisions of the Royal Hungarian Army, which were committed in the interior as security troops. In late summer 1942, the 2nd Hungarian Army stood in the front lines. It was then realized that its officers and soldiers were not ready for combat and were incapable of resistance when compared to the German divisions.

Therefore, the 2nd Hungarian Army was removed from the front and transferred to the interior. The redesignation of the 2nd Royal Hungarian Army into the "Royal Hungarian Defensive Force Command" occurred on 5/1/1943. Their headquarters was in Pinsk. The commander was Colonel General Jany, who was relieved on 5/18/1943 by Lieutenant General Lakatos.

Lieutenant General Lakatos led two corps. The VII Royal Hungarian Army Corps lay in the interior behind Army Group South. The VIII Royal Hungarian Army Corps was located in the southern sector of the Central Heeres Rear Area. The VIII Corps consisted of five light divisions, of which the 1st and 102nd Light Divisions were stationed in the rear area of the 2nd Army.

Army Group Center

The Commander of Security Troops and the Commander of Heeres Rear Area – which from 1942 was the same designation for the senior command authority in the interior – had control over the following troops in his area in April 1943:

203rd Security Division (command post Bobruisk),
221st Security Division (command post Gomel),
286th Security Division (command post Orsha),
390th Field Construction Division (command post Mogilev),
VIII Royal Hungarian Army Corps (command post Chernigov),
102nd Light Division (command post Novgorod-Seversk),
105th Light Division (command post Nezhin),
108th Light Division (command post Starodub),
East Troop Command (command post Berezino).

The headquarters of the commander was located in Mogilev from 1943. From 7/22/1943, the commander was General of Mountain Troops Kuebler. Besides the above named security divisions, he commanded an additional 56 independent security battalions, which were subordinated to the commander of East Troops.

These 56 battalions were distributed throughout the entire area of operations. In May 1943, there existed a total of 23 German Landesschuetzen, 4 German Polizei, 15 Hungarian, 1 French, and 13 Russian battalions. Of these, 36 battalions were to guard the railroads, 8 were to secure roads, and 12 were committed to guard economic installations.

The situation behind the front worsened considerably after summer 1943, and above all, after the army group began its retreat. The important lines of communication could only be partially secured. Thus, every 200 meters on the roads and the railroad lines there were constructed small strong points with bunkers, which were occupied by a squad or a platoon. At night, these strong points could not be left, because of the numerical superiority of the partisan formations.

In addition, since early autumn 1943, the first signs of the disintegration of the Russian battalions became apparent. First mutinied the 1/1 Geor-

Chapter 7: The Interior

gian Battalion, and it spread from there. At all locations, German officers and drill instructors were being murdered. The army group command, therefore, repeatedly requested the OKH to remove the East battalions or, at least, transfer them to the west.

In autumn 1943, the setbacks on the front caused a change in the Heeres Rear Area. The front itself was withdrawn back to the boundary of the Weissruthenien Generalkommissariat and, more or less, into the German area of authority.

Therefore, on 10/1/1943, the agencies in the Heeres Rear Area were disbanded. The security divisions and independent security battalions were subordinated to the Wehrmacht Commander of Weissruthenia.

This staff was formed out of the former headquarters of the Commander of the Rear Area of Army Group "B." On 10/8/1943, the commander was Lieutenant General (from 1/1/1944, General of Cavalry) Count von Rothkirch und Trach.

From January 1944 to the collapse of the army group, the commander had available, other than local Landesschuetzen battalions, only the 221st Security Division and the 2nd Cycle Security Regiment. The remaining security divisions were located in the rear areas of the armies: 201st Security Division in the 3rd Panzer Army area, 286th Security Division in the 4th Army area, 707th Security Division in the 9th Army area, and the 203rd Security Division in the 2nd Army area.

The Commander of the Heeres Rear Area was not only responsible for the military protection of the area, but he also had to care for the economic, social, and political well-being of the German troops located there. He also had to secure and organize the supply of men and equipment for the front troops.

Therefore, there were many agencies and commands subordinate to him, of which we will only point out a few here:

The Group Heeres Patrol Service was created in the Heeres Rear Area on 9/10/1941 from Military District VII. The personnel came from the 61st Infantry Replacement Battalion in Munich. In January, this group was reinforced by four additional officers, which were obtained from Military

Army Group Center

Districts IV and VII. On 6/25/1942, the group was redesignated as a "General Purpose" staff. The staff from Military District III arrived with personnel from the 67th Infantry Replacement Battalion in Berlin-Spandau. On 3/1/1943, this staff received additional reinforcement by the creation of a group of field police directors. This staff was organized in Military District XXI, while the men originated from the 600th Infantry replacement Battalion in Lissa/Wartheland.

The railroad was an important connection between the homeland and the front. From the beginning of the Eastern campaign, the military leadership knew that the vast regions could only be controlled by a smoothly running rail system, which could also supply the army groups.

The 2nd Field Railroad Command was responsible for Army Group Center. In 1943, the command managed a railroad network of 2039 kilometers length, as well as 261 locomotives and 1599 railroad cars. In addition, the personnel necessary to run this system included 11,388 German and 22,576 Russian workers.

In 1943, this service was subordinated to the General of Transport in the Army Group Center area of operations. In 1943/44, Colonel Teske commanded a total of 86,000 German and Russian railroad personnel, a railroad engineer brigade with 14,800 men, a railroad communications regiment with 1,500 men, a field waterway detachment with 1,170 men, a transport security regiment with 8,600 men, and a light air defense detachment with 600 men.

Besides these military and economic-political missions, there was also the ideological well-being of the troops, as well as the political monitoring of the local populations. These missions were conducted by the so-called propaganda companies (known as PK for short).

Army Group center, as well as Luftflotte 2 (later 6), had Front PK, while the Wehrmacht Commander had his own propaganda detachment in the interior. At the beginning of the campaign, there was one PK for each army command. Thus:

612th PK belonged to the 9th Army,
670th PK belonged to the 2nd Army,

Chapter 7: The Interior

689th PK belonged to the 4th Army,
693rd PK belonged to the 2nd Panzer Group (only for a time),
697th PK belonged to the 3rd Panzer Group.

Luftflotte 2, the later Luftwaffe Command East, and Luftflotte 6 had five Luftwaffe PK and a combat reporting platoon in their areas of operations. The individual commitment areas of these propaganda units were:

> 1st Luftwaffe PK (Major Weinschenck) was subordinated to Luftwaffe Command East after April 1942, it was committed in Smolensk (previously Paris), from October 1942 it was transferred into the southern sector to Kharkov. The 3rd Luftwaffe PK (Captain Reuschle, from October 1941 Captain Baron von Gemmingen) was subordinate to the Commander of the Luftwaffe Units of the Army Group (Koluft). In February 1942, it was transferred to Paris. The 5th Luftwaffe PK (Major Hirz) was subordinate to Luftflotte 6 from May 1942. In November 1942, it was transferred to Brussels, in spring 1943 it was brought back to the central sector and in July 1943 disbanded. The 6th Luftwaffe PK (Captain Wiebe, Captain Raubuechl, Captain Reuschle) belonged to the II Air Corps and was transported with them to Sicily in November 1941. The 8th Luftwaffe PK (Captain Renner) was subordinate to the VIII Air Corps and was transferred to the southern sector of the Eastern Front in March 1942.

While the front PK had the mission of taking care of the field units (making sure that they were mentioned in the German press and on the German radio), the Weissruthenien Propaganda Detachment influenced the civilian population with their propaganda.

The Propaganda Detachment (commander Major Kost) had its seat in Smolensk in the old city hall in Glinka Park. Among others, it operated the soldiers transmitter "Siegfried", which beamed its programs to Moscow with a strength of 610 khz on a frequency of 491.8 (It is interesting that the transmitter of the National Committee of "Free Germany" in Moscow used this same frequency after August 1943). The detachment operated other

Army Group Center

transmitters in Klintsy, Mogilev, Bobruisk, and Sluzk. The "Siegfried" transmitter had nothing to do with the Reich radio station in Minsk, which was operated by the civilian Reichskommissariat.

The emphasis of the propaganda work was centered on the press. The Propaganda Detachment operated a total of eleven newspapers with a circulation of 440,000. The largest circulation was enjoyed by the bi-weekly newspaper "Rul'" [The Rudder], which was exclusively directed at the Russian civilian population.

The front PK also published newspapers. These were the following:

697th PK (3rd Panzer Army):
Army Newspaper "Panzerfaust" = 58,000,
News Pamphlet "Panzerfaust" = 35,000,
Leave Newspaper "Panzerfaust" = 20,000;

612th PK (9th Army):
Army Newspaper "Der Durchbruch" = 70,000,
News Pamphlet "Das Neueste" = 50,000,
Leave Newspaper "Im SF-Zug" = 55,000;

689th PK (4th Army):
Army Newspaper "Der Stosstrupp" = 60,000,
News Pamphlet "Der Stosstrupp" = 45,000,
Leave Newspaper "Bahnsteig" = 20,000;

670th PK (2nd Army:
Army Newspaper = "Der Sieg" = 38,000,
News Pamphlet = "Der Sieg" = 35,—.

The front theater groups, which worked on the basis of the premise "strength through pleasure", were an important factor for the morale of the troops. These frontal theater groups played far forward. Thus, for example, on New Years Day 1943, one such group played only 30 meters behind the front in the Rzhev combat sector. Front theater with fixed seats existed in

Chapter 7: The Interior

the great theaters in the rear area. The theater groups often held out for as long as possible as the front began to withdraw into the rear area. The players would then become interspersed with the soldiers and, thereby, became involved in the maelstrom of events in summer 1944.

The occupied Russian territory was administered up to a depth of 200 kilometers behind the front by the senior military authority. All regions west of here were subordinate to the civilian authorities, which did not administer the regions in accordance with the combat situation, but only on the basis of political principles.

The necessary principles were established before the beginning of the Eastern Campaign. At the same time as the first plans of the military operation came into being, the political plans for the occupation of Russian territory were drawn up in the Reich ministries.

The government of the Reich created their own ministry. The "Reich Ministry for the Occupation of the Eastern territories" was to administer the newly conquered territory politically, exploit it economically, and impress National Socialism onto the population.

In the draft plans of Reichsminister Rosenberg, the entire region of European Russia was seen as coming under German administration. He wanted to establish three Reichskommissariats: Ostland, with the Generalkommissariats of Estonia, Latvia, Lithuania, and Belorussia; Ukraine, with the Generalkommissariats of Zhitomir, Chernigov, Kiev, Kharkov, and Voronezh; and Moscow, with the Generalkommissariats of Leningrad, Tula, Moscow, and Kasan. A Caucasus Reichskommissariat was to be established later.

The region occupied by Army Group Center was assigned to Reichskommissariat Ostland under the name "Weissruthenia." The boundary of this new German Generalkommissariat was already determined before one German soldier set foot on Russian territory. The boundary was to run in the east, east of Smolensk, in the south directly north of Briansk up to the Generalgouvernement, in the west to the province of East Prussia, and in the north it was to border on the Latvian Generalkommissariat. A Generalkommissar was also selected for this area. Gauleiter Kube was selected on 6/17 – five days before the beginning of the campaign.

Army Group Center

The official take over by the political administration occurred at a later point in time. The Reichskommissar Ostland set up its offices on 7/17/1941 and issued its first orders on 8/18.

On 8/18/1941, the boundary of the Generalkommissariat ran: in the north, southeast of Orany, around Vilnius, east of Duenaburg, south of the Sebezh-Yetsina rail line; and in the east, south of Zhukovka, 20 kilometers directly to the west north of the Briansk-Brest rail line and up to the East Prussian border northeast of Brest.

The majority of the Belorussian Socialist Soviet Republic was turned over to the Generalkommissar by the military administration on 9/1/41. Gauleiter Kube took his seat in Minsk. The Weissruthenien Generalbezirk, at this time, encompassed five city districts (Minsk, Mogilev, Bobruisk, Vitebsk, and Smolensk) and five main districts (Baranovichi, Minsk, Mogilev, Vitebsk, and Smolensk). The five main districts were organized into 37 Kreisgebiete.

Therefore, the Weissruthenien Generalbezirk had reached its greatest extent. The eastern main districts – Smolensk, Vitebsk, and Mogilev – had to be returned to military administration because of the events of 1941/42. From then on, these districts belonged to the army group rear area.

In 1942, the Generalkommissariat had an area of 53,662 square kilometers, which was inhabited by 2,411,333 people. The region was divided into a Stadtkreis (Minsk), with 10 main districts and 69 Landkreisen, which were administered by German authorities (mostly political leaders of the NSDAP).

The main mission of the German civil administration was to create measures to further the war effort in the occupied region.

The dissolution of the Soviet Kolkhoz economy occurred in February 1942. A so-called "Gemeinwirtschaft" was instituted in its place. This was a transitional form of private enterprise, in which the farmer could work his own land. Nevertheless, the German Kreislandwirte controlled these Gemeinwirtschaften. On 6/3/1943, Reichsminister Rosenberg issued a declaration concerning the introduction of private property. However, before this re-privatization could be fully introduced, the war returned to Weissruthenia.

Chapter 7: The Interior

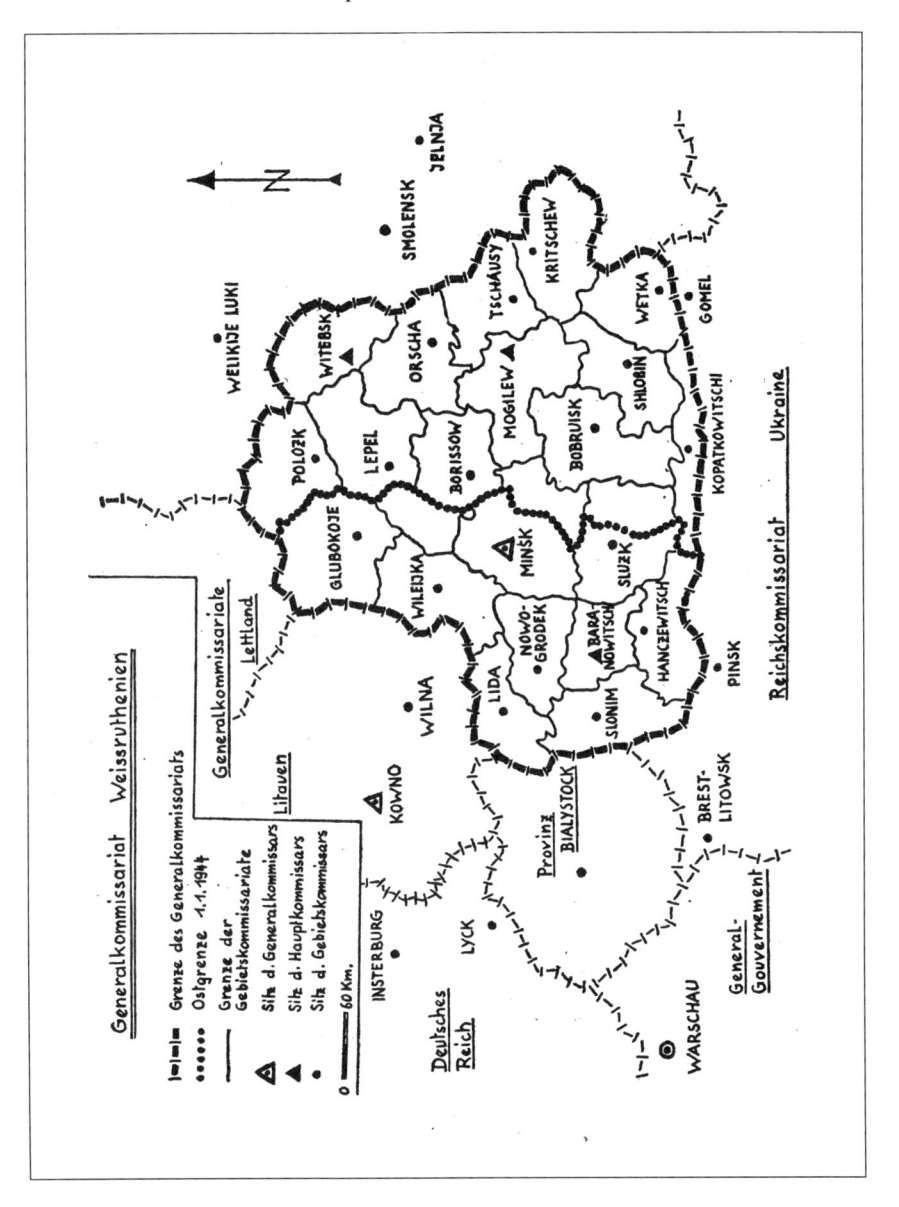

Army Group Center

The German civil administration also created a somewhat freer cultural life, although they also did not allow much private initiative here.

Therefore, the opening of the municipal theaters in Minsk in July 1941 caused a sensation. In March 1943, the "German Soldatentheater" was created out of the "German Front theater" in Minsk. In 1942, the "Ostland-Film-GmbH" was founded in Minsk. The first Belorussian movie theater was opened in Minsk in May 1942; a year later there were five theaters for local films, one for German, and one soldiers' theater.

The Minsk long wave transmitter (frequency 1442) and the Baranovichi medium wave transmitter (577) went into operation in November 1941. The "Reichsrundfunk Transmitter Minsk" was incorporated into the "Grossdeutschen Rundfunk."

Education was seen to by the opening of Volksschulen in November 1941. Instruction in trades began in the following year. Thus, for example, in the main district of Minsk, there existed a total of 3288 Volksschulen, of which 5 contained German children.

In summer 1942, the Generalkommissariat established the "German House" in Minsk as the focal point of cultural life. In the same year, two art expositions were conducted in the city and, on 4/15/1942, the first issue of "Minsker Zeitung; Deutsches Tageblatt fuer Weissruthenien" was published.

Beside business and culture, the Generalkommissariat placed its third emphasis on lines of communications. On 1/1/1942, the Reichsverkehrsministerium took over from the military administration the operation of the rail lines directly behind the front. The main Minsk Railroad Directorate was directly subordinated to the ministry and, on 12/1/1942, was expanded to a Reichsverkehrsdirektion.

The efforts of the Reichsverkehrsdirektion Minsk had resulted in the following statistics by 9/3/1943: 124 restored bridges with a total length of 4860 meters, 457 newly constructed bridges with a length of 4486 meters, 9055 kilometers of track traced, 868 kilometers of track restored, and 340 kilometers of new track laid. During summer of 1943, the Reichsverkehrsdirektion consisted of 81,486 personnel, had 723 locomotives and 1771 railroad cars available for a rail network of 5707 kilometers. In given months of the year 1943, the following trains traveled over this network:

Chapter 7: The Interior

	Supply trains	Troop transports	Freight trains
April	1146	885	339
June	1114	768	321
August	1025	1134	348
October	630	722	154
December	785	947	112

The Generalkommissariat instilled the National Socialist Volkssturm politics rigorously into the people's lives. The political mission, as maintained by Gauleiter Kube, was "Priority Nr. 1" of all work in Weissruthenia.

The Jewish people became the target of these politics. Shortly after the occupation of Weissruthenia by the civilian administration, extermination began. The political police organs were given a free hand by order on 1/12/1942.

The 1st Platoon of the Special Purpose Battalion of the Waffen-SS was committed in the Reichskommissariat Ostland, in order to liquidate the Jewish people. The 2nd Platoon was located in Minsk, Vileika, and Baranovichi. They reported the following statistics:

5/11/1942 - 1000 Jews shot near Minsk
6/15/1942 - 1000 Jews shot near Minsk
6/27/1942 - 4000 Jews shot in Slonim
7/28/1942 - 6000 Jews shot in Minsk, and so forth.

These measures ultimately led to the initial sympathy of the poor rural populations being turned against the Germans in a short period of time. Therefore, the German civil administration opened the way for the partisan formations. Resistance against the German occupation authorities grew from month to month and could no longer be stopped.

The greatest strike by the partisans occurred during the night of 9/22/1943, when the three partisans Masanik, Drozd, and Troyan, as well as their helper Ossipova, succeeded in killing Gauleiter Kube with a mine!

SS Gruppenführer and Lieutenant General of Police von Gottberg, the former Senior SS and Polizei Commander in Weissruthenia, was his successor.

Army Group Center

The new Generalkommissar, who did not originate from the National Socialist hierarchy, attempted to renew German prestige. However, he did not have the time. SS Gruppenführer Gottberg did create defenses out of farms, as the front approached the Generalkommissariat. The farmers were given the land as private property and tried to defend it with their own weapons.

Gottberg's efforts finally led to the formation of a "Weissruthenien Zantralausschuss", which emerged from the "Weissruthenien Zentralrat" under Professor Ostrovski on 12/21/1943. This Zentralrat was to evolve into an independent government for Weissruthenia and was to be concerned with the social and cultural affairs under the control of the Generalkommissar.

However, before the Zentralrat could fully develop – its constitution was ratified on 3/19/1944 – the war returned to Weissruthenia.

On 4/1/1944, the Generalkommissariat was dissolved by the Reichskommissariat Ostland and it was directly subordinated to the "Reich Ministry for the Occupied Eastern Territories." Three months later, all civil work ended in Weissruthenia – Army Group Center no longer controlled it. Soviet tanks were again stationed there, where the war had begun on 6/22/1941!

Military concerns in the Generalkommissariat were handled by the Wehrmacht Commander Ostland. The commander's seat was in Riga. His orders and instructions were directed at senior field and field commandanturas.

Three senior commandanturas, 7 field commandanturas, and one independent Wehrmacht local commandantura were located in Weissruthenia:

OFK [Senior Commandantura] 392 Vilnius with FK [Field Commandantura] 660 Postavy, FK 812 Molodechno, FK 814 Vilnius;
OFK 399 Pinsk with FK 199 Brest-Litovsk;
OFK 400 Baranovichi with
FK 184 Sluzk
FK 250 Slonim
FK 551 Lida

Chapter 7: The Interior

Wehrmacht Local Commandantura Minsk.

Construction units and Landesschuetzen formations were only subordinated to these local commandanturas and field commandanturas at certain times. Thus, for example, on 1/5/1944, the following Heeres formations were located in Weissruthenia:

LXI Reserve Corps (Vilnius) with
52nd Field Construction Division
141st Reserve Division
151st Reserve Division
360th Reserve Division

I Royal Hungarian Army Corps (Pinsk) with
1st Light Division
5th Light Division
29th Light Division.

As its senior command authority, the Luftwaffe had the XXV Field Luftgau Command (General of Aviation Fischer) with headquarters in Minsk. This Field Luftgau Command held the imposing title of "Luftgau Command Moscow" during the first few months of the campaign – however, it was returned under the command of Smolensk!

The Wehrmacht units did not interfere in the politics of the Generalkommissariats. This is what the formations of the Central Senior SS and Polizei Commander were for. The SS and polizai detachments operated according to special instructions from the Reichsführer SS and Chief of German Police. No Wehrmacht agency had any influence over them.

On 6/22/1941, as Army Group Center crossed the border, the special formations of the "Kommandostabes Reichsführer SS" followed. These were the 1st and 2nd SS Motorized Brigades, 1st and 2nd SS Cavalry Regiment, "Reichsführer SS" Escort Battalion, and the "Hamburg" SS Freiwilligen Standarte.

Army Group Center

From 6/23/1941, the units were subordinated to the XLII Army Corps of the 9th Army to clear the rear area. However, on 6/27, the Reichsführer SS refused to allow them to be subordinated to Army formations and forbid it from happening from then on. On 7/10/1941, he placed SS Gruppenführer von dem Bach in charge of all SS and polizei units from his command post in Baranovichi.

SS Gruppenführer von dem Bach led the battalions and regiments in the interior to combat the partisan detachments, which were composed of soldiers from the regular army that had been overtaken by the rapid advance of the German troops and had fled into the forests and marshes. The two cavalry regiments were organized into an SS Cavalry Brigade and committed in the Pripet Marsh. By 8/13/1941, they reported executing 13,788 "plunderers" and 714 prisoners!

The SS Cavalry Brigade (SS Standartenführer Fegelein) was subordinated to the commander of the Heeres Rear Area in October 1941 and, in December, was committed to the front on the left flank of the 9th Army, where they fought bravely and successfully near Rzhev.

In 1942, SS Gruppenführer von dem Bach received the designation "Senior SS and Polizei Commander Central Russia." He was responsible for the security of the entire region in the rear of the army group and the Generalkommissariat of Weissruthenia. Because his region was infested with partisan activity, he was "empowered by the Reichsführer SS to combat partisans" on 10/3/1942 and, on 6/21/1943, designated "Chief of Partisan Combat Formations." Since September 1941, the headquarters had been located in Mogilev, and it was transferred to Minsk between February and May of 1943. After that, the emphasis of the commitment of the polizei formations had shifted to the partisan battle and a Special Purpose Senior SS and Polizei Command (SS Gruppenführer von Gottberg) was formed for the police mission in the Generalkommissariat.

The utilization of police in Weissruthenia was directed by the SS Polizei Standortfuehrern, which were established in Smolensk, Baranovichi, Mogilev, and Vitebsk. The Ordnungsdienste were manned by the Kommandos der Ordnungspolizei. They were stationed in Glebokoe, Vileika, Minsk, Lida, Slonim, and Baranovichi.

Chapter 7: The Interior

The local national police forces – at least, those that were not utilized as local police – were organized into Schutzmannschafts Battalions. In Weissruthenia in 1942 there were 5 such battalions, in 1943 there were 13, and in 1944 there were 23, as well as one Cossack Cavalry Battalion. The Schutzmannschafts Battalions were organized into the 30th Waffen Grenadier Division of the SS in July 1944, which was committed in Warsaw and later on the Western Front.

A special unit of the Senior SS and Polizei Command Central Russia was the SS Special Battalion Dirlewanger, which engaged the partisans without mercy from February 1942. The battalion consisted of 50% convicts, 40% Russian volunteers, and 10% detainees. The special battalion was later expanded to a brigade, which fought in Warsaw and on the Oder front.

Gradually, German polizei regiments, which received the designation "SS Polizei Regiment" on 2/24/1943, were committed to secure the Generalkommissariat and combat partisans. Their creation, their commitment, and their demise is reflected in the table below:

Rgt Nr.	Year and loc Created	Battalions	Commitment	End
2	1942 Tilsit (Koenigsberg)	11, 13, 22	Heeres rear area	June 1944 near Polozk
13	1942 Minsk	6 (Hannover) 301 (Braun-schweig)	Heeres rear area	Transferred to Ober-krain 1944 85 (Magdeburg)
14	1942 Minsk	51 (Mannheim) 122 (Ludwigs-hafen) 313 (Augsburg)	Heeres rear area	Transferred to Ukraine in 1943
22	1942 Warsaw	41 (Danzig) 43 (Bromberg)	Heeres rear area	(Unknown)

Army Group Center

24 1942 Lemberg 83 General-July 1944
153 kommissariat near Minsk

26 1942 Drontheim 251 (Dresden) General-Transferred
255 (Sudeten-kommissariatto the land) Carpathians in 1943

31 1943 Hamburg 1/12 Heeres rear August 1944
2/31 area Belorussia
3/31

36 1943 Minsk 2/1 Heeres rear July/August
2/36 area 1944 near
3/36 Minsk

Stalin's call on the Russian people to defend their homeland, as well as the barbaric German occupation politics, resulted in the gradual worsening of relations between the Germans and the Belorussian people.

On 5/22/1943, when the commander of Army Group Center, Field Marshal von Kluge, sent a letter to the then Chief of the German General Staff, it was high time that the Belorussian people were won over to the German cause. Field Marshal von Kluge wrote:

> "The development of the overall situation indicates a clear policy directed against the Russian people, whose support ... must be won over. The former methods have failed. There is still time to correct this, it is high tome to correct this. ... They (the Belorussians) must know why they are fighting – or ultimately, they will be fighting against us!"

They were already!

On 6/30/1941, the Central Committee of the Communist Party of Belorussia issued its Directive Nr. 1, in which secret regional committees were set up throughout the land to make contact with Red Army stragglers. Thus emerged the first partisan detachments behind the front. The CPSU Directive from 7/1/1941 supplied instructions on organizing these bands.

Chapter 7: The Interior

Two days later, the Moscow government established the "Central Headquarters of the Partisan Movement" under Marshal Voroshilov. The Secretary of the Central Committee of the CP in Belorussia, Ponomarenko, was its Chief of Staff and, at the same time, commander of all partisan detachments in Belorussia.

The activities of partisan groups in the rear area of Army Group Center became more noticeable after August 1941. According to Russian sources, during this month there were 231 detachments committed with 12,000 men, and there were 55 detachments in the Smolensk-Moscow-Tula area alone. The first major sabotage activities occurred in September. The first transport train with German troops was derailed between Minsk and Bobruisk and 180 locomotives were blown up in the Orsha area!

This war in the rear of the front – for which the German Army leadership was unprepared – resulted in a secret memo from the OKW on 9/16/1941:

"... in accordance with the following guidelines:

a) Each case of revolt against the German occupation authority ... must be tied in to Communist origins.

b) The most effective means must be taken to prevent it from happening again. ... In atonement for a German soldier's life, 50 to 100 communists must be put to death. ..."

The army group did not have sufficient forces to master this unrest. The units of the commander of the Heeres Rear Area had to secure the supply of the armies. Thus, in autumn 1941, there was only the "Kommandostab of the Reichsfuehrers SS" with its SS formations. The 1st Motorized SS Brigade was to clear up the Glukhov-Novgorod Sevesk-Konotop area. A report from the brigade related:

"From 11/14-11/21 shot in combat: 59 partisans, after conviction: 47 partisans."

Army Group Center

The year 1942 brought a general increase in partisan activity throughout the Heeres Rear Area and in the Generalkommissariat. Thus, for example, the approximately 18,000 partisans in the Viazma-Briansk area were influential in the 490 villages there. On 2/15/1942, partisan formations occupied Dorogobush and held the city for five days.

The army group command had to form partisan search commands out of field troops, which searched out reported Russian units. In addition, the army group had to give up the Hungarian divisions.

The 105th Royal Hungarian Division was in combat against the partisan detachment of the communist leader Kofpak southwest of Glukhov. On 2/28/1942, the Hungarians were able to encircle the detachment near Veesloe. The partisans made use of their knowledge of the land and broke out of the encirclement. The situation was similar everywhere!

23,000 partisans, which were organized into 227 detachments and 19 brigades, operated in Belorussia during the first six months of 1942. The most notorious of these brigades were: 1st Belorussian (commander Shmyrev), 2nd Belorussian (commander Dyachkov), "Death to Fascism" Brigade (commander Melnikov), "Dzershinski" (commander Korotkin), "Voroshilov" (commander Kapusta), and "Chekist" (commander Kipich).

The Chief of the Feldpolizei reported to the OKH the following partisan threatened areas on 7/31/1942: west of Viazma-north of Glusha-east of Pochep-north of Bobruisk-Klintsy-either side of Smolensk-northeast of Polozk-northwest of Orsha-east of Vitebsk -south of Orsha-south of Mogilev, etc.

The partisan situation worsened after the headquarters of the "Belorussian Partisan Formations" was created on 9/9/1942, which centralized the operations of the individual groups from Moscow. The senior leadership of the "Red Army" issued the following summons:

> "The Red Army High Command requires all commanders, political workers, and fighters in the partisan movement to carry the battle further and stronger into the enemy's interior, constantly maintaining pressure on the fascists and giving them no time to take a breath!"

Chapter 7: The Interior

In Moscow, Kalinin took command of the Belorussian partisan brigades. In early autumn, he commanded 52 brigades with approximately 58,000 men. The emphasis of the commitment was on four locations: Polozk-Nevel, Vitebsk-Minsk, the Briansk area, and the Bobruisk area. In the Heeres Rear Area 30,200 partisans also operated in the Kalinin, Smolensk, and Orel areas.

Strikes against transport installations increased. From July to November 1942, 597 trains were derailed, 473 bridges were blown, and 855 vehicles were destroyed in the Generalkommissariat alone. A report from the army group command to the OKH revealed:

> "Strikes against the railroad during the day have increased. Thus, on 9/22/1942, on the Polozk-Smolensk stretch, the double track section was put out of commission for 21 hours and the single track section for 10 additional hours; on 9/23, on the Minsk-Orsha-Smolensk stretch, the double track section was put out of commission for 28 hours, and the single track section for over 35 hours!"

Even worse than the railroad sabotage was the destruction of important bridges. Thus, three detachments destroyed the bridge across the Ptich; here, 18 days passed before the first train could pass. In mid-November, the "Partisan Detachment Briansky Les" left their hiding places in the forests and crossed the Dnepr and Pripet to the Mosyr-Zhitomir rollbahn. During the night of 11/15/1942, the partisans attacked the Slovakian bridge guards near Perenivka and blew up the 100 meter long bridge!

German defensive measures were first centrally coordinated when, on 10/3/1942, SS Gruppenfuehrer von dem Bach was designated "Authority of the Reichsfuehrer SS for the Combat of Partisans." Before that, the army commanders in the rear of the front or the field commandanturas in the Generalkommissariat had to fend for themselves.

On 2/25/1942, the IX Army Corps formed an anti-partisan command from corps troops. The command consisted of the headquarters staff of the 78th ID and three companies. In July and August, the commander of the Heeres Rear Area conducted several operations with elements of the 707th

Army Group Center

Security Division, the 102nd and 108th Royal Hungarian Divisions, and the 38th Grenadier Regiment against the partisans in the forests near Briansk. An additional operation was initiated in the Revna area on the Dessna between 9/6 and 9/15, during which 556 prisoners, 5 guns, 8 anti-tank guns, 41 machine-guns, and 15 mortars were captured.

After October, the formations of the Senior SS and Polizei Commander took over combating the partisan detachments. SS Gruppenfuehrer Gottberg laconically reported after a battle north of Postavy on 11/23/1942:

"Town burned to the ground and the population treated specially!"

By the beginning of 1943, the partisan threat increased, in spite of all of the German defensive measures. The most significant results were achieved in the Briansk area. Here stood 48 partisan detachments with 9,776 men, 83 independent groups with 7,449 men, as well as 3,600 men from the Ukrainian partisan movement. They were able to occupy a total of 500 villages and create a partisan republic extending 260x50 kilometers! The leader of this republic took over the illegal Communist Party Regional Committee in Orel.

The partisan formations received a continuous flow of men, weapons, and equipment. The flow was maintained by the infiltration of combat and supply groups through the German front and by supply flights conducted by the Soviet Air Force. In February alone, 600 aircraft flew equipment into the area behind the army group, and in May 1943 there were 2000 aircraft!

The partisans could thank this support from the outside and the flow of men from the interior lands for allowing them to conduct more and more successful strikes. During the night of 1/22/1943, 5,885 tracks were blown on the Orel-Briansk stretch in one strike! On 3/8, the 160 meter long Dessna bridge near Wygonichi was blown into the air. The Briansk-Gomel rail line remained blocked for eight days. Several days later, on 3/21, the Dessna bridge on the Smolensk-Briansk stretch was dropped into the water and, on the next day, explosives were detonated on the Dessna bridge between Krichev and Unecha.

Chapter 7: The Interior

The Belorussian partisans reported: In the time from 1/1-5/1/1943: 634 trains derailed; from 8/3-8/15/1943: 94,477 tracks blown up; from 5/2-8/31/1943: 1,014 trains derailed, 804 locomotives destroyed, 72 bridges destroyed, and 70 supply installations blown up!

These successes led to Hitler's issuance of "Basic Order Nr. 14 for Partisan Combat" on 4/27/1943. This order charged the army group and army commanders with conducting the war against the partisans as intensively as before. Point 8 of the order read:

> "While combating the partisans, it is also necessary to strike at the partisan helpers."

The army commanders were forced to remove more and more troops from the front and commit them to missions in the interior. Thus, for example, a combat group fought under the command of the 293rd ID headquarters at the end of April on the Briansk-Duderovski rail line. At the beginning of May 1943, the headquarters of the XLVII Panzer Corps conducted an operation in the vicinity of Vitemlya with the 292nd ID, the 9th Armored Reconnaissance Battalion, and a battalion from "Brandenburg."

The partisan situation in the rear area of the 9th Army had become a real threat in June 1943, because of the planned "Operation Citadel." Therefore, the 9th Army command had to remove this threat from the source.

From mid-May, three operations were conducted against the partisan brigades in the Briansk area. The 4th Army command conducted Operation "Nachbarhilfe [Neighbor Assistance]." Here, on 5/16, they were able to encircle and destroy an enemy group between Mglin and Kletnya with a Luftwaffe field regiment, four German, and two East battalions.

On 5/21, the 2nd Panzer Army command began Operation "Freischuetz" in the region northwest of Briansk. Here, under the leadership of the LV Army Corps, participated the 6th ID, a regimental group from the 5th Panzer Division, a combat group of the 31st ID, the 747th Grenadier Regiment, and the 455th Oststab. In fierce, tenacious combat, with German losses of 22 dead and 70 wounded, 420 prisoners were taken, 17 machine-guns, and 20 machine-pistols were captured. The partisans lost approximately 1400 dead. The third operation – "Zigeunerbaron [Gypsy Baron]" – took place during the time period from 5/15-6/6/1943 between Briansk and Trubchevsk. The headquarters of the XLVII Panzer Corps led the operation, in which elements of the 4th and 18th Panzer Divisions, the 10th Motorized Infantry Division, and the 7th ID participated.

During the beginning of "Operation Citadel", which was expected to change the course of the war (according to the Wehrmacht leadership), the partisans struck. the "Hero of the Soviet Union", Fedorov, had taken command of the partisan brigades behind the army group. His brigades and detachments wanted to block supply traffic in the rear area. The operation was directed by the command posts of the Soviet fronts and armies, which indicated where the partisans should be committed.

The commander of the "Central Front" ordered on 8/26:

> "The flow of reserves to the front on the railroad and main routes is to be tied up and paralyzed in the rear of the enemy in the Briansk-Lokot, Briansk-Gomel, Krichev-Unecha sectors!"

The month of August was the most successful for the partisans. Alone during the night of 8/3, mines were detonated on 8,422 sectors of railroad track. Several days later, partisans blew up 7,200 near Kalinin, 8,300 around Smolensk, and 13,700 in the vicinity of Orel. The Belorussian detachments destroyed a total of 95,000 sections of track and paralyzed the Molodechno-Minsk, Kovel-Sarny, Brest-Pinsk, Kovel-Brest, and Kovel-Kholm stretches for several days.

The combat was conducted without mercy by both sides and without regard to women and children. The partisans often used women and children to seek out mines in newly reconquered villages.

The Communist Party centralization was often apparent in the organization of the partisan war. In Weissruthenia alone there were 8 illegal regional, 103 district, and 184 territorial Party committees. The propaganda was spread not only by word of mouth, but also by newspapers and pamphlets. In 1943 there were 139 illegal communist newspapers in the German Generalkommissariats!

Luftwaffe support to the army group's defensive battle

The few fighter squadrons, that were still available in 1943, took off in spite of poor conditions, in order to help the infantry.

One of the "silent heroes", which the Wehrmacht reports never mentioned. The "Fieseler Storch" was the jack of all trades; it was a reconnaissance, transport and command aircraft.

An 8.8 cm air defense gun in position. The "Eight-Eight" was the best gun in the 2nd World War. Originally intended for air defense, it proved, above all, to be an anti-tank gun.

Combat aircraft – they were seldom seen after the summer of 1943 – prepare to take off from a temporary airfield.

The most reliable aircraft in the war was the "Good old Aunt Ju." The "Ju 52", which had already been committed in 1936 in Spain as a bomber, carried paratroops, weapons, ammunition, and fuel to the Eastern Front and flew wounded to the homeland.

This is the face of the "Landser", who, in the summer of 1944, was fighting the fourth year of the war against the Soviets. He is a "man without a name"; however, he was just one of the millions that was fulfilling his "damned duty." The cigarette in June 1944 was often worth more than medals or shoulder-boards.

Heavy anti-tank guns secure a withdrawal road near Vitebsk. However, often the Soviet tanks were faster, over-taking and overrunning the columns.

The Collapse of the Army Group 1944

The great offensive of the "Red Army" between Vitebsk and Bobruisk lead to the collapse of the army group and the loss of Belorussia in a few weeks. Now and then, the Russian penetrations were blocked by counterattacks – here by the "Tigers" of the "Grossdeutschland" Division.

The Loss of Belorussia

Resistance against the superior enemy is hopeless. The last houses were blown up and burned.

Moving to the west. Heavy weapons were left behind. Only horse-drawn carts made it. Thus it was in the north near Vitebsk...

And so it was in the south in the Pripet Marsh. The "Landser" attempted to fight their way to freedom through the forests in groups.

The Russian border is crossed to the west. The columns strive to make over the bottomless Polish roads to the homeland.

The East Prussian border is reached. The exhausted grenadiers of the 4th Army establish themselves in temporary positions to fight to the last. They are tired, hungry and without hope...

Combat on the German Eastern Border

In late summer 1944, thousands of East Prussians were called up to construct border positions...

...however, the Soviet tanks were faster. German refugees fled for the first time out of East Prussia and Wartheland to the west.

German refugees from Nemmersdorf were overtaken by the Bolsheviks, and they were plundered and destroyed. The remnants lay on the side of the road.

Soviet tank troops roll through Muehlhausen.

During the two-day tank battle south of Gumbinnen, 114 Soviet tanks were destroyed by the Hermann Goering Armored Parachute Regiment alone.

The "forest of signs", recognized by all "Landser", directly behind the front. A "snapshot" near Smolensk.

Daily Life Behind the Front and in the Occupied Area

Directly behind the combat divisions followed the construction and supply troops, the units of the OT [Organization Todt] and the RAD. Railroad engineers repair a bridge across the Dnepr.

The local and field commandanturas set up soldiers homes, soldiers movie theaters and music halls. However, the "Landser" only left the main combat line rarely...

... then they came as wounded to the hospitals and awaited transport to the hospitals in the homeland.

In spite of considerable difficulties and constant sabotage, these transports were conducted in silence and without transparent heroism by the blue and gray men of the field railroad services.

While the German front soldier quickly won the trust of the local population ...

The German Generalkommissariat – the "Golden Phesants" – quickly turned this trust into mistrust. The photograph shows a German "Landwirtschaftsfuehrer" participating in a harvest festival in a Belorussian village.

Forced labor — here women, children, and elderly constructing positions — ultimately turned the mistrust into hate, which led to the gruesome partisan war.

SS Einsatzkommandos capture a Russian partisan. There is no hope for her...

... German security troops pause at another partisan position. A mounted police column discovers a partisan shelter.

At the end of 1944, the Volkssturm was the last "secret weapon" mobilized. All men that had already experienced the 1st World War and all youths were called on to hold the front. An Upper Silesian Volkssturm battalion carries anti-tank weapons to the front.

The Final Battle of Army Groups Center, North, and Vistula in Germany

A company of "Hitler Youth" led by experienced front soldiers distinguish themselves during combat in Pomerania in February 1945.

From the Baltic Sea to Silesia Germany is a Theater of War

With the loss of Koenigsberg, Army Group North ceased to exist. The German defenders are led off to captivity.

Fortress Kuestrin. Here a four-barreled air defense gun on the Oder, is defended until March 1944. Then the Soviets established a bridgehead from which they launched the attack on Berlin on 16 April.

The Silesian city of Lauban was reconquered by German troops. Throughout the streets of the city lay the ruins of burned out Bolshevik tanks, almost all of them destroyed by grenadiers with anti-tank weapons.

The defenders of Breslau held out for a month against an entire army and surrendered only after they no longer had any rations or ammunition.

After the horrible allied air bombing in February 1945, Dresden is a pile of ruins. However, the German defenders still held out for two days before surrendering to the Soviets. The destroyed Elbe bridge.

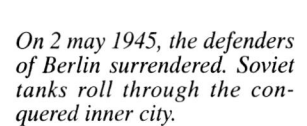

On 2 may 1945, the defenders of Berlin surrendered. Soviet tanks roll through the conquered inner city.

American and Soviet officers discuss the demarcation line between their armies – Germany no longer exists!

That is the end of Army Group Center. Defeated after years of combat, the soldiers are marched off to captivity. For many it was a one way trip.

Chapter 7: The Interior

The year 1944 brought a new high to the partisan war, which flourished during the collapse of Army Group Center. The emphasis in spring 1944 was placed on the Minsk area and in the Pripet area.

The largest partisan strike against Army Group Center occurred during the night of 6/20/1944 when various detachments blew up 10,500 railroad track sections within a few hours directly behind the German front. These were all of the lines connecting the front with the rear area!

This sabotage and others in the rear area, as well as in the Generalkommissariat, contributed to the collapse of the army group. As the last formations of Army Group Center tried to struggle through the forests and marshes to the west, hundreds of German soldiers were sacrificed to the partisans-or was it thousands?

Will we ever know?

The struggle of Army Group Center in and around Belorussia was over – it was lost. ..

Field Marshal von Kluge had described in his already mentioned letter in 1943:

> "The Russian people will know which political objectives the German Reich has in store for Russia. ... They will remember, for example, if a political objective for the future was the propagation of friendship between Germany and a Russian Reich. This would include future cooperation between the highly cultured and economically advanced Europe with greater Russia as a powerful, independent agricultural territory."

However – as with many chapters of the 2nd World War – the words "too late!" have to be added to this one. The vastness of Russia was fought over with strength and power; however, the German politicians and soldiers failed to win the souls of the Russian people!

8

THE SURRENDER
The Final Battle in Germany 1945

"The East must fend for itself and do with what it has!"

These were the words of the Senior Commander of the Wehrmacht to the Army Chief of the General Staff. On 9 January 1945, in the Führer Headquarters in Berlin, Generaloberst Guderian gave a briefing on the renewed attack preparations of the "Red Army" along the Vistula. He reqüsted reserves from the west and the south. The Generaloberst saw the greatest threat in the anticipated Soviet breakthrough into eastern Germany.

At this point in time, Army Group Center lay like an umbrella in front of the Reich border. In January, its 570 kilometer front ran from Kurischen Haff south of Memel up to the confluence of the Narev into the Bug. On 11 January, the army group's troop units were distributed along this front:

Army Group command (headquarters Ortelsburg)

3rd Panzer Army (headquarters Liebenfelde)
XXVIII Army Corps in the Memel area with 95th, 58th ID;
607th Special Purpose Division (Kurisch Spit);
IX Army Corps between Kurischen Haff and the Inster
with 286th, 551st, 548th, 561st ID;

Chapter 8: The Surrender

XXVI Army Corps between the Inster and west of Ebenrode with 56th, 69th, 349th, 549th ID;

4th Army (headquarters Angerburg)
XLI Panzer Corps between west Ebenrode and north Treuburg with 61st ID, 2nd Parachute Division, 21st ID, 28th Jaeger Division, 50th, 367th ID;
VI Army Corps between north Treuburg and Osowiec with 170th, 558th, 131st ID, Group Hannibal, 541st ID;
LV Army Corps between Osowiec and confluence of the Pisa into the Narev with 203rd, 562nd, 547th ID;

2nd Army (headquarters Proszkowo)
XX Army Corps from the confluence of the Pisa to south of Scharfenwiese with 102nd ID, 14th Motorized Infantry Division;
XXIII Army Corps from south of Scharfenwiese to Ostenburg (Pultusk) with 292nd, 129th, 299th, 7th ID;
XXVII Army Corps from Ostenburg to the confluence of the Narev into the Bug with 5th Jaeger Division, 252nd, 542nd ID.

Because the main effort on the Eastern Front lay in the south since October 1944, from the beginning of December on the army group had to give up divisions, mainly to Hungary. Thus, in the meantime, panzer and SS divisions left East Prussia. Therefore, the newly formed "Grossdeutschland" Panzer Division, the "Grossdeutschland" and "Brandenburg" Armored Infantry Divisions, the 24th Panzer Division (which was battered in Hungary), and the 10th Wheeled Brigade were deployed from the homeland. In addition, the 1st, 23rd, 83rd ID, and 18th Armored Infantry Division were either reconsitituted behind the front or newly organized. In reserve stood as the following: 5th and 7th Panzer Divisions, and the "Hermann Goering" Armored Parachute Division.

Army Group Center

The army group command placed these reserves and newly arrived formations behind the front positions in anticipation of the new Soviet offensive, which had long been established by air reconnaissance. Thus, the 5th Panzer Division was inserted toward Breitstein, and the 24th Panzer Division toward Rastenburg in the 3rd Panzer Army area. The "Hermann Goering" Armored Parachute Division moved into the Gumbinnen area, and the 18th Armored Infantry Division moved toward Johannisburg as a reserve of the 4th Army. The 7th Panzer Division moved toward Zichenau behind the 2nd Army.

As before, Luftflotte 6 cooperated with the army group, although its area of responsibility was extended to include that of Army Group "A" between Warsaw and the Carpathians. On 6 January, the luftflotte had 7 fighter-bomber groups, each with 32 aircraft, and 5 fighter groups, each with 28 aircraft, available. The II Air Defense Corps committed, from north to south, the newly formed 27th Air Defense Division, the 18th Air Defense Division, 15th Air Defense Brigade, and 12th Air Defense Division.

At this time, reconnaissance established the following "Red Army" concentrations before the front:

1st Belorussian Front (commander: Marshal Zhukov),
Chief: Colonel General Malinin)
with 31 rifle divisions, 5 tank corps;
2nd Belorussian Front (commander: Marshal Rokossovskiy,
Chief: Lieutenant General Bogolyubov)
with 54 rifle divisions, 6 tank and 1 cavalry corps;
3rd Belorussian front (commander: Army General
Chernyakovskiy, Chief: Colonel General Prokofskiy)
with 54 rifle divisions, 2 tank corps.

The attack preparations of the three Soviet army groups were not directed solely at Army Group Center, but also against Army Group "A", which was in central Poland. The "Red Army" wanted to destroy both army groups with one powerful offensive.

The main effort of the new offensive, during the initial phase, was directed against Army Group "A", which occupied positions from Narev east

Chapter 8: The Surrender

of Modlin up to Kaschau on the eastern edge of the Slovakian Erzgebirge. The army group (commander: Generaloberst Harpe) commanded from left to right: 9th Army (since November 1944) (commander: General of Panzer Troops von Luettwitz), 4th Panzer Army (commander: General of Panzer Troops Graeser), 17th Army (commander: General of Infantry Schulz), and 1st Panzer Army (commander: Generaloberst Heinrici).

The Soviet plan to destroy Army Group "A" had two parts. The first strike was to be directed on the line Lodz-Chestochow, in order to collapse the front of the army group. The second strike was to open the way to Berlin through Warsaw and Posen. The "Red Army" committed the "1st Ukrainian Front" under Marshal Konev (Chief of Staff: Army General Sokolovskiy) for the first phase. Available to the "front" were: the 5th, 6th, 13th, 21st, 52nd, 59th, 60th Armies, 3rd Guards Army, the 3rd and 4th Guards Tank Armies, and the 2nd Air Army.

During the first weeks of January, the attack troops of the "1st Ukrainian front" assembled in the bridgehead near Baranov, which could no longer be compressed by the German troops during the past year. The offensive was to be launched from here in the direction of Lodz (Litzmannstadt).

The "1st Belorussian Front" under Marshal Zhukov moved into the two bridgeheads near Magnuszew and Pulawy south of Warsaw, in order to attack from here to the German border. Marshal Zhukov had the 8th Guards Army, 3rd and 5th Shock Armies, 33rd, 47th, 61st, 69th Armies, 1st and 2nd Guards Tank Armies, 1st Polish Army, and the 16th Air Army for his operation.

The two "fronts" consisted of 163 rifle divisions and tank brigades with 32,134 guns, 6,460 tanks, and 4,772 aircraft. There were a total of 2,200,000 men preparing for an attack in the icy cold January weather into the heart of Germany. The ratios of Russian to German forces were 11:1 in infantry, 7:1 in tanks, and 20:1 in artillery.

It was 0330 hours in the morning of 12 January 1945 when hundreds of guns sent their fiery greetings from the Baranov bridgehead. Thousands of shells of all calibers were hurled onto the positions of the 4th Panzer and 17th Armies. Fire and smoke soon covered the land west of the Vistula. The frozen ground was torn up in hundreds of places, houses were set ablaze as if they were made of cardboard, bunkers collapsed, roads were torn up, and men were shredded. The fire raged for three hours over the German positions. Then the fighter-bombers roared in from the east and leveled everything that moved with their on-board cannon and machine-guns. At the same time, hundreds of tank engines rumbled and filled the air with ear-shattering noise.

The battle in the foreground of the German Reich made its bloody debut!

14 Soviet rifle divisions and 2 tank corps attacked the German main combat line in the first echelon. The still intact guns of the Army and the air defense still fired, while here and there cracked the discharge of an anti-tank gun or the tatter of machine-guns. However, these were just remnants of German divisions that opposed the enormous weight of the enemy assaulting out of the east on this morning.

This powerful machinery hit two German army corps. One was the XLVIII Panzer Corps under General of Panzer Troops Baron von Edelsheim. The corps had three infantry divisions, the 304th, 168th, and 68th (from right to left). The corps stood with its right flank on the Vistula and with the left adjacent to the Lysa Gora mountain chain. Adjacent to it, on the left, lay the XLII Army Corps under General of Infantry Recknagel, between Lagow-Daleszyce and the Vistula north of Sandomierz.

Two Russian tank corps broke through the German front during the morning, and they expanded their penetration on both sides simultaneously. Therefore, room was made for the 4th Soviet Tank Army. The Russian tanks found their first resistance in the artillery positions. However, this was also removed by the massive commitment of the 2nd Air Army. During the afternoon, the Soviet combat vehicles rolled over the 2nd and 3rd German lines and achieved a breakthrough 35 kilometers wide and 30 kilometers deep.

As night fell on the first day of the battle, 200 tanks – "T-34" and "Stalin" – did, indeed, lay as burning wrecks on the plain west of the Vistula; however, the enemy breakthrough was complete. During the night, the enemy shoved additional formations into the gap and prepared the 4th Tank Army (Colonel General Lelyushenko), the 3rd Guards Tank Army (Colonel General Gordof), and the 13th Army (Colonel General Pukhof) for a new attack on the following morning.

Chapter 8: The Surrender

The commander of the 4th Panzer Army had no reserves to come to the aid of the severely battered XLVIII Panzer Corps. The only reserve was east of Kielce and could only be committed with the approval of the OKH. The order to counterattack did not arrive until evening, when there was already no longer a front.

The XXIV Panzer Corps (General of Panzer Troops Nehring) advanced during the night with the 16th Panzer Division (Major General von Mueller), 17th Panzer Division (Colonel Lux), 20th Armored Infantry Division (Lieutenant General Jauer), and the 424th "Tiger" Battalion (Major von Legat).

A participant reported:

> "It was too late. The intended counterattack advanced disjointedly and widely separated. The remnants of the battered infantry divisions fled past the tanks to the west; all cohesion was lost, their leaders were gone. ..."

The counterattack of the XXIV Panzer Corps fizzled out. The corps itself had to withdraw during the night to save itself. The Soviet tanks had already outflanked the right flank of the corps (17th Panzer Division and 424th "Tiger" Battalion). In the morning, General Nehring received the order: "Corner-stone Kielce is to be held!"

The 13th of January brought the widening of the breakthrough gap. The 3rd and 4th Guards Tank Armies advanced 45 kilometers to the west and entered Kielce from the south. The way for additional enemy forces to the west in the direction of Chestochow was open!

The XXIV Panzer Corps and XLII Army Corps, which held their main combat lines with difficulty, were encircled around Kielce on 1/14! They no longer had contact with the army command or with their neighbors. Then, an order from the 9th Army was intercepted that instructed its divisions to withdraw. Therefore, Kielce lay outside of the German front. On 1/15, General Nehring evacuated the city. He ordered his divisions, which had suffered heavy losses, to conduct a delaying action, in order to hold the way open for the XLII Army Corps that was withdrawing to the west. After

Army Group Center

the infantry divisions were removed from the main combat line, General Nehring ordered the breakout of both corps to the north.

The venture took place on the night of 17 January. From then on, the corps marched like a "wandering pocket." Daily, they defended themselves from Soviet attacks on all sides, in order to be able to resume their march during the snowy nights. The XLII Army Corps met the lead elements of the XXIV Panzer Corps near Bialaczow.

Nevertheless, there was no longer a XLII Army Corps. The commander, General of Infantry Recknagel, and the Chief of Staff, Lieutenant Colonel von Drabich-Waechter, had fallen along with hundreds of their soldiers. The infantry divisions only consisted of combat groups that had broken through individually.

Only the 342nd ID (Major General Nickel) was still intact. The other divisions – 72nd (Lieutenant General John), 88th (Colonel Anders), 168th (Colonel Rosskopf), and 291st (Major General Finger) – were no longer combat capable.

General of Panzer Troops Nehring immediately absorbed the remnants of the XLII Army Corps. He regrouped his formations and attacked to the west on the morning of 19 January. In the lead were the 16th and 17th Panzer Divisions and the 342nd ID, followed by the rest of the combat groups. Thus was Pilica reached. The engineers under Colonel von Ahlfen constructed a wooden bridge to cross the vehicles.

The next day, the radio finally brought the first good news. The OKH ordered contact to be established with the "Grossdeutschland" Panzer Corps near Lodz. The lead elements of the "wandering pocket" met up with an armored scout troop from "Grossdeutschland" on the afternoon of 1/21. The scout troop reported that its corps was holding open a bridgehead on the Warta near Chojne for the withdrawal of the XXIV Panzer Corps and the XLII Army Corps.

The last kilometers to the west were the most difficult. The Russians pressured the German combat groups, which still had to suffer additional casualties. Then, the 16th Panzer Division won a bridge near Kol. Grabia over the Grabia. The columns moved across here. In the early morning of 1/22, after a 250 kilometer march, the 16th Panzer Division reached the

Chapter 8: The Surrender

"Brandenburg" Armored Infantry Division. This division (Major General Schulte-Heuthaus) had held open the bridge on the Warta.

General Nehring was through with his divisions!

The majority of the German formations, which were thrown back by the enormous enemy power during these cold January days and were still stuck in southern and central Poland, were either destroyed or captured. For many of the officers and soldiers of Army Group "A" there would be no homecoming. Thus did the East Prussian "Elk Division" – the 291st ID – meet its end somewhere on the Pilica. The last order given by Major General Finger read: "Save yourself if you can! The objective is Upper Silesia!" Only 1000 men from this division made it to Germany; the General was not among them.

Generaloberst Guderian wrote years later:

> "Only the wandering pocket of the XXIV Panzer Corps and the 'Grossdeutschland' Panzer Corps unswervingly fought their way to the west. Generals Nehring and von Saucken had accomplished quite a military feat during these days!"

The two corps were no longer able to stop the collapse! After the fall of Kielce, the army group had nothing left to oppose the enemy with. The Russian tank corps and rifle divisions marched on a wide front to the west. Chestochow fell on 1/17. The 59th (Lieutenant General Korovniko) and the 60th Armies (Colonel General Kurochkin) defeated the 17th German Army, bypassed Krakow, and, on 19 January, entered the city. The seat of the Generalgouvernement in Poland was now in Russian hands! The 3rd Guards Tank Army (Colonel General Rybalko) and the 52nd Army (Colonel General Koroteev) crossed the Silesian border on 1/19! Three days later, the lead elements of the 5th Guards Army (Colonel General Zhadov) stood on the Oder!

Army Group "A" had ceased to exist. Hitler relieved its commander, Generaloberst Harpe, and replaced him with Generaloberst Schoerner, who came from Kurland, bringing with him his Chief of Staff, Major General Natzmer. On 25 January, Army Group "A" received the designation of Army Group Center.

Army Group Center

The earlier Army Group Center, which had held this designation since 1941, no longer existed from this time on!

The battle against the army group began on 13 January. The Soviet objective was to isolate Army Group Center from the Reich in East Prussia with the "2nd" and "3rd Belorussian Fronts", while the "1st Belorussian Front" advanced out of the Vistula bridgeheads in the direction of Berlin!

On 1/13, the "3rd Belorussian Front" opened this powerful offensive with a frontal attack against East Prussia. The 4th Army, however, was able to repulse all attacks. The 28th Soviet Army (Lieutenant General Luchinski) was only able to gain 7 kilometers of ground. The attack of the "3rd Belorussian Front" bogged down!

The "2nd Belorussian Front" of Field Marshal Rokossovskiy attacked on 1/14 out of the Narev bridgeheads with the 5th Guards Tank, 2nd Shock, 48th, 49th, 65th, and 70th Armies, III Guards Cavalry, VII Mechanized, and I and VIII Guards Tank Corps. The objective of the "front" was the Elbing-Frisches Haff area.

The German defenders fought bitterly, but it was hopeless from the beginning. The superiority of the Soviets was too great. The 2nd Soviet Shock Army captured Pultusk on 1/16 and the 65th Army Nasielsk. The XXIII German Army Corps (Lieutenant General Melzer) and the XXVIII Army Corps (General of Artillery Felzmann) evacuated their positions on the Narev and fought their way back to the northwest.

The unity of the divisions disintegrated, as did that of Army Group "A." The greatly inferior troops of the 2nd Army could not hold out in spite of all resistance and local limited counterattacks. During these decisive days, their strength was weakened by the OKH itself. On 1/16, Hitler ordered the transfer of the 6th SS Panzer Army out of the west to Hungary and the transport of the "Grossdeutschland" Panzer Corps to Lodz, against the wishes of the Chief of the General Staff.

The divisions of the 2nd Army withdrew to the northwest. Because Marshal Rokossovskiy shifted the main effort to the right flank of the "front", the lead Soviet tank elements bored through in the direction of Elbing. On 23 January, the 7th Panzer Division (Major General Dr. Mauss) engaged the enemy in an old style tank battle near Deutsch-Eylau. However, what

Chapter 8: The Surrender

could 20 German combat vehicles do against 200 Russian combat vehicles? On this day, the 25th Panzer Regiment perished along with its commander, Major von Petersdorff-Kampen.

On 1/24 there was heavy defensive combat by the 2nd Army east of Graudenz and near Marienwerder. The remnants of the 2nd Army were pushed back so far that they stood with their backs to the Vistula. The Russian tanks arrived there at the same time as they did, as did the 354th Rifle Division (Major General Dzhanhgava).

The 5th Guards Tank Army attacked through the withdrawing German combat groups through Osterode and Elbing to the coast! The tank formations of Colonel General Volski entered Elbing on 1/26. They left it on the same day, however, and reached the Baltic Sea near Tolkemit!

The 4th Army and the 3rd Panzer Army were, therefore, separated from the Reich in East Prussia! Army Group Center was split apart!

The forces encircled in East Prussia were designated Army Group North.

The German 9th Army, which was located on the Vistula in central Poland, was the objective of the "1st Belorussian Front" in January 1945. The attack also occurred on 14 January. On this day, a two and a half hour artillery strike of all calibers tore up the German trenches, bunkers, and lines of communication. Then the rifle and tank formations attacked from out of two Russian bridgeheads. Indeed, the Soviet forces were able to achieve wide penetrations, though they did not achieve a breakthrough of the army front on the first day!

On 1/15, the enemy barrage fire struck the defenders again for 40 minutes before the assault was unleashed. This time they broke through. The 47th Army (Lieutenant General Perkhorovich) crossed the Vistula north of Warsaw and outflanked the Polish capital from the north. The 1st (Colonel General Katukov) and the 2nd Guards Tank Armies (Colonel General Bogdanov) immediately followed and expanded the gap to 120 kilometers wide and 40 kilometers deep.

The 1st Polish Army (Lieutenant General Berling) advanced from the south in the direction of Warsaw. The 61st Army (Colonel General Belov) followed on the left. Therefore, the pincers began to close around Warsaw on the second day of the battle.

Army Group Center

General of Panzer Troops von Luettwitz, commander of the 9th Army, proposed surrendering Warsaw on 1/15. Hitler refused! However, Generaloberst Harpe ignored the Führer order and, on 1/16 at 2013 hours, gave permission to evacuate the Polish capital of all non-essential troops, rear area services, and equipment.

Warsaw could not be defended; on 1/16, it was already cut off from the outside world. Then Generaloberst Guderian also decided to ignore Hitler's fortress order. He agreed to give Warsaw up. Hitler first learned of this order a day later. He did not remove Guderian for this unauthorized action. The commander of the 9th Army, General of Panzer Troops von Luettwitz, was relieved on 1/20. General of Infantry Busse, the former commander of I Army Corps, replaced him. The officers in the operations branch of the OKH (Colonel Bonin and Lieutenant Colonels von dem Knesebeck and von Christen) were arrested.

On 17 January, the 1st Polish Army entered Warsaw.

Now, the resistance in the Warsaw area was senseless. The XLVI Panzer Corps (General of Panzer Troops Fries) withdrew to the northwest. Therefore, a gap emerged in the German front, which Marshal Zhukov made use of by rushing his tank forces into it. The commander of the XLVI Panzer Corps was also relieved by Hitler and replaced by General of Infantry Gareis.

Marshal Zhukov gave his troops the objective of Posen.

On 1/19 the "Ostdeutscher Beobachter" had as its headline: "Warthegau Remains German!" However, on the next day, the Wehrmacht commander in Military District XXI sounded the fortress alarm. The Russian tanks rolled on. By 2400 hours, the civilian population had to evacuate the city. The surrounding districts received the evacuation order even sooner. This was no organized flight. The combat vehicles with the five pointed red stars were quicker!

Two enemy guards tank corps crossed the Warthe near Treskau on 1/22. The newly appointed fortress commandant, Major General Mattern, issued his first order of the day:

> "The enemy attack on the fortress of Posen has begun. The fortress will be defended in accordance with the Führer's order and the prin-

Chapter 8: The Surrender

ciples of soldierly duty, it will be held to the last man. ... We are given the opportunity to do our duty. We are ready!"

The 8th Soviet Guards and the 1st Tank Armies moved in from the north and south, ringing the city on 1/23. The German defenders held out for four whole weeks against a numerically far superior enemy. Major General Gonell, commander of the infantry school, was appointed the new fortress commandant on 1/28. He opposed the attacking Soviets energetically with his combat groups. An ultimatum from the 8th Guards Army was not answered. Then the enemy guard divisions continued to attack. On 2/12, except for the citadel and a few districts in the east, the city of Posen was in enemy hands. The defenders of the citadel were systematically destroyed by heavy guns fired at close range. However, they still stood! The Russian General Staff study later recalled:

"... as an important communications hub, it blocked the supply of ammunition and fuel to the Oder!"

On 2/22, Major General Gonell ordered a breakout. However, none made it through. The combat groups were wiped out, destroyed, and split apart. General Gonell fell. Then, Major General Mattern had to surrender along with the last 6000 men!

Three weeks earlier, "Fortress Thorn" had ceased fighting. The city had been defended since 21 January by the 73rd ID (Lieutenant General Schlieper). The division, police, fortification troops, and military school fought for eight days. On 1/30, a deep frost and snow fall occurred. On 2/2, the defenders reached the Vistula and the German front.

Now they held out as the only German fortress on the Vistula beside Graudenz. The defenders under Major General Fricke fought until 6 March, as the front was pushed back further to the west and the north.

The 9th Army withdrew to the Oder ...

Contact between Berlin and Danzig and East Prussia was broken on 29 January.

The 9th Army was forced back to the Oder. They no longer had any contact with the 2nd Army. An enormous gap yawned between the two German armies.

The way to Germany was now open to the Soviets!

The gap on the Oder was a mortal threat for the German Reich. There were only the untrained and poorly equipped Volkssturm battalions of Military Districts XX (Danzig), XXI (Posen), and, from 1/22, Military District III (Berlin) available. At the end of January, the OKH hastily transferred divisions from all other fronts, including the west, into Pommerania. The 25th Armored Infantry Division, 344th, 354th, 559th, 712th ID, and the SS Divisions "Das Reich" and "Frundsberg" were to close the gap between the 2nd and 9th Armies.

On 21 January, Hitler issued the order to create the army group command "Vistula":

"a) ... which has to close the gap between Army Groups A and Center, prevent the breakthrough of the enemy in the direction of Danzig and Posen and, therefore, the isolation of east Prussia and secure the deployment of the newly arrived forces.

b) ... has to organize the national defense behind the entire Eastern Front on German territory."

Generaloberst Guderian proposed Field Marshal Baron von Weichs as the new commander. Hitler turned this proposal down and named the Reichsfuehrer SS and Chief of the German Police, Himmler, as the commander of the new army group. His Chief of Staff was also an SS commander, SS Brigadefuehrer Lammerding; the Ia was Colonel Eismann, a General Staff officer. On 1/24, Himmler arrived in Deutsch-Krone in his special train. Here he established his headquarters. He wanted to hold the Oder front and the Vistula front. Before he could issue his first order, the enemy was already there!

The Soviets stood before Schneidemuehl, which was defended by the 5th Lehr [Training] Artillery Regiment. On 1/23 they captured Bromberg. Their 1st and 2nd Guards Tank Armies, the 8th Guards, 5th Shock, and

Chapter 8: The Surrender

61st Armies were already between Frankfurt and Stettin, and were advancing toward the Oder. The III Corps immediately ordered the Oder-Warthe Positions, which were built before the Polish Campaign of 1939, to be occupied by Volkssturm units. However, before the Volkssturm and replacement battalions arrived, the Russian tanks had already broken through these positions.

The 2nd Guards Tank Army and the 5th Shock Army (Lieutenant General Bersarin) reached the Oder north of Kuestrin on 3 February! Major General Raegener temporarily organized the defense of the city. He created two fortress regiments from alert and replacement units from the Army, the Luftwaffe, the police, and two Volkssturm battalions, with which he repulsed the initial Russian attacks on the Oder bridges near and in Kuestrin.

However, the Soviets did not allow this to stop their advance. In the next few days, they crossed the Oder at four locations: north of Fuerstenberg near Vogelsang, south of Kuestrin near Goeritz, north of Kuestrin near Schaumburg-Kienitz, and south of Frankfurt near Schwetzig.

The newly formed army group could not prevent the enemy from crossing at any of these locations. They really had no troop formations to speak of. Only the stukas of the 2nd Fighter-bomber Squadron under Colonel Rudel and Captain Gandermann attacked the Russian tanks near Kuestrin at this time.

The 9th Army tried desperately to hold out on the Oder. Nevertheless, they could not prevent their left flank from hanging in the breeze. On 2/13, Schwetz was lost, and on 2/15 Konitz, Schneidemuehl, and Tuchel were lost as well. A gap of 150 kilometers still existed between them and the 2nd Army, which was subordinated to Army Group "Vistula" on 1/24!

At the beginning of February, the OKH removed the III SS Panzer Corps command (SS Obergruppenfuehrer Steiner) from Kurland and reorganized it into the 11th Panzer Army command. The new army command was ordered to close this gap. It was to counterattack its divisions into Pommerania, striking the Soviet attack wedge on the Oder in the flank. Generaloberst Guderian did not trust the leadership ability of the Reichsfuehrer SS and SS Obergruppenfuehrer Steiner. The Generaloberst convinced Hitler that his first assistant, General of Panzer Troops Wenck, should be entrusted with the command.

Army Group Center

On 2/17, Unfortunately, General Wenck had an accident on his way to the front. SS Obergruppenfuehrer Steiner took command of the 4th SS Polizei Division, 8th SS Panzer Division "Holstein", 10th SS Panzer Division "Frundsberg", and the "Führer Escort Division." The attack began after a short fire strike on 2/19. It bogged down after an 8 kilometer gain in the enemy's artillery fire and under his bombing attacks. The Soviet troops immediately counterattacked and pushed the Germans back to a line Greifenhagen-Arnswalde.

The first attack of Army Group Vistula failed. The 11th Panzer Army command, which had its headquarters near Falkenburg, ordered its formations back into the defense. The army front was reinforced by the 402nd ID, 5th Jaeger Division, and SS "Nederlande" Division between Falkenburg and Schwedt.

The most threatening penetration of the Soviet troops was, as before, on either side of Kuestrin. Here, in a very small area, stood the 2nd Guards Tank, 5th Shock, 8th Guards, and 1st Guards Tank Armies from north to south.

It was obvious that the enemy must launch the last attack from here onto Berlin. The Soviet leadership planned the destruction of "Fortress Kuestrin" as a prerequisite that it had pointed as a dagger between the 8th Guards and 5th Shock Armies since mid-March.

On 3/22, the two armies began their attack to destroy the city and fortress. After a four day air preparation, the 8th Guards Army advanced out of the Kienitz area, and the 5th Shock Army marched opposite them from the north. The two armies met near Golzow. Therefore, Kuestrin was encircled!

Marshal Zhukov carefully prepared for the final attack. On 28 March, after several days of preparation, the 82nd Guards and 35th Guards Divisions attacked. The Russian combat squadrons, in the meantime, had attacked the last defensive works in Schutt and Asche without pause. On 3/29, all of the artillery of the 8th Guards Army fired a 40 minute barrage fire. Then the guardsmen attacked.

The German defenders surrendered on the same day!

Hitler was so disappointed by this news and the failed relief attempt

Chapter 8: The Surrender

that he dismissed his General Staff Chief, Generaloberst Guderian – the creator of the German panzer branch – on 3/28.

The last bulwark in front of Berlin had fallen!

The strength of the German front in Pommerania was increased at the beginning of March by the removal of the 3rd Panzer Army command (Generaloberst Raus) from East Prussia. It relieved the 11th Panzer Army command, which was transferred to the west.

Reichsfuehrer SS Himmler had become more and more withdrawn from his duties as army group commander and Generaloberst Guderian had suggested that he be replaced on "health grounds." Hitler finally gave in. At Guderian's suggestion, he named the commander of the 1st Panzer Army, Generaloberst Heinrici, as the new commander of Army Group "Vistula" on 20 March.

The final battle for East Prussia began on 13 January 1945. The "2nd Belorussian Front" of Marshal Rokossovskiy and the "3rd Belorussian Front" under Army General Chernyakovskiy set out from the Narev bridgeheads and attacked the 2nd and 4th German Armies frontally along the East Prussian border. The talented commander of the "3rd Belorussian Front", Army General Chernyakovskiy, had issued the following order of the day to his soldiers:

> "Now we stand before the Hell from which the fascist aggressor had attacked us. After we clear them out we must show no mercy. ... The land of the fascists must be laid waste."

After a three-hour artillery preparation, the 5th, 28th, and 39th Armies of the "3rd Belorussian Front" attacked. The soldiers of the 4th Army were able to repulse the enemy tank and rifle formations almost everywhere. Only the 28th Army was able to achieve a 7 kilometer deep penetration.

At first, Generaloberst Reinhardt hoped that the Russian offensive could be stopped with his 1.8 million soldiers and 67,000 Volkssturm people. However, when the attack against the 2nd Army began on the Narev on the following day, he realized the threat. He described the seriousness of the

Army Group Center

situation to Hitler that evening in a telephone conversation. From the Führer Headquarters only came the laconic reply: "Hold to the last man!" Then, the strongest reserve, the "Grossdeutschland" Panzer Corps, was ordered to Lodz.

From 1/16 on the Soviets committed their air forces en masse. The Russian pilots flew 3,486 sorties over East Prussia on this day. The commander of the army group requested pulling back the 4th Army to either side of Goldap on 1/17. Hitler again refused.

The German soldiers held off the Soviet assault for six days. Then they ran out of strength. The "3rd Belorussian Front" broke through the main combat line north of Gumbinnen on a 65 kilometer wide front. The 11th Guards Army was immediately shoved into the gap to assault Koenigsberg.

On 1/17, after the 2nd Army withdrew from their Narev positions and lost contact with the 9th Army two days later, the "2nd Belorussian Front" stood on the flanks of the 4th Army. The army of General Hossbach was in danger of being outflanked from 1/20. On 1/21, when General Reinhardt pointed out this situation to Hitler, the OKH finally recognized the seriousness of the situation. Hitler ordered the evacuation of Memel and the withdrawal of the 4th Army.

On 1/23, Generaloberst Reinhardt undertook the creation of an East Prussian Military Authority, in order to organize the withdrawal of the 3rd Panzer and 4th Armies and the battle for East Prussia to the corresponding military point of view. East Prussian Gauleiter Koch immediately complained because he was being passed over. Hitler gave in; for him the "show-off" Koch was more important!

On 1/21, the major enemy attack had already caused a recognizable separation between the 2nd and 4th Armies, which could no longer be removed. At the same time, the frontal attack continued. Insterburg and Allenstein fell into the hands of the Soviets on 1/22. The "Tannenberg Monument" was blown up, although five towers were left standing because the army did not have enough explosives available. The sarcophagi of Field Marshal von Hindenburg and his wife were rescued and transported to Germany on the small cruiser "Emden" from Koenigsberg.

General of Infantry Hossbach, commander of the 4th Army, summoned his commanders to a meeting on 1/22 in Borken. The army commander

Chapter 8: The Surrender

briefed the generals on the intent to break the army out to the west, in order to make contact with the 2nd Army. He had already prepared the corresponding order.

General of Infantry Grossmann, with the staff of the VI Army Corps, was immediately moved to Lake Masurisch. The corps command took over the 28th Jaeger Division, 131st, 170th, and 547th and 558th ID, which were to form the lead elements of the attack wedge in the Wormditt-Guttstadt area.

The XXVI Corps command (General of Infantry Matzky) was forced to leave the front by the withdrawal of the 3rd Panzer Army. It was transferred by the 4th Army command to Mehlsack to block the straggler elements of the 2nd Army and, at the same time, protect the northern flank of the breakout wedge. The VII Panzer Corps (Lieutenant General von Kessel), which had been subordinate to the 4th Army for several weeks, had to secure the southern flank.

Before this regrouping and preparation was over, the "Red Army" dictated the course of the battle. On 1/24, the Soviet tanks entered into the Loetzen fortification area and elements of the "2nd Belorussian Front" drove through Deutsch-Eylau-Osterode-Elbing to the Baltic Sea.

On 1/25, the army group command was redesignated as Army Group North. On the same day, Generaloberst Reinhardt suffered a head wound during a visit to the front in the sector of the 28th Jaeger Division, which was preparing to breakout near Wormditt.

The 4th Army had to break out if it was not going to suffer the same fate as did the 6th Army in Stalingrad.

As twilight fell on East Prussia on 1/26, the 131st (Colonel Schulze) and 170th ID (Lieutenant General Hass) attacked to the west. They were to create a gap through which the army could pass.

Enemy resistance was fierce. The German combat groups were thrown back, dispersed, and repulsed. In spite of this, the 131st ID advanced up to Liebstadt. They could go no further! Only the 2/431 Grenadier Regiment (Captain Heinrici) made it to Preussisch-Holland and attacked through to the elements of the 2nd Army. The 170th ID forced the crossing of the Passarge near Sportehnen, where they ultimately bogged down. On the other hand, a battalion-strength group of the 83rd Jaeger Regiment under

Army Group Center

Captain Homburg and a reconnaissance squadron under Cavalry Captain Count von Finckenstein (both from the 28th Jaeger Division) were able to break through to Elbing before the Soviet tanks entered this city.

The army's main effort was directed due west. The superior enemy forces pressured from the east, so that the front quickly had to be withdrawn to a line from Lake Masurisch to Wehlau and Labiau. Johannisburg, Loetzen, Angerburg, Liebenfelde, Labiau, and many small cities and towns in east Prussia were lost. The main combat line of Army Group North stretched from Frischen Haff halfway between Elbing and Braunsberg in a southerly direction, ran east from Allenstein and Ortelsburg, turned here to the west coast of Lake Spirding, while from there it went almost due north toward Drengfurth on the northern shore of Lake Mauer, and from here in a northwestern direction up to approximately 20 kilometers east of Koenigsberg, crossed the Pregel, and advanced west of Labiau to Kurische Haff.

The 4th Army command, which led the breakout from Glandau southwest of Landsberg, shoved the 24th Panzer Division (Major General von Nostitz-Wallwitz) and the 18th Armored Infantry Division (Colonel Rauch) from the eastern front to the western, in order to still be able to reach the lines of the 2nd Army near Elbing, between Preussisch-Holland and Wormditt.

When the preparations for the breakout and, therefore, hoped-for rescue of the 4th Army and 3rd Panzer Army were completed, Gauleiter Koch sent Hitler the following telegram:

> "4th Army is in flight to the Reich. They are cowardly trying to fight their way to the west. I am continuing to defend East Prussia with the Volkssturm!"

Hitler believed this report. In this critical hour for East Prussia, he relieved the military leadership. On 1/27 at 1300 hours, Generaloberst Reinhardt turned over command of the army group to the former commander of Army Group Kurland, Generaloberst Rendulic. The new commander took up his headquarters in Zinten and established telephonic communications with the 4th Army during the night of 1/30:

Chapter 8: The Surrender

"The attack to the west is to be immediately suspended! The panzer and armored infantry divisions are to be dispatched to the 3rd Panzer Army near Koenigsberg. The 4th Army is to defend where it stands! General Hossbach is transferred to the Führer Reserve. The command of the 4th Army will be taken over by General of Infantry Mueller, who is arriving by plane from Führer Headquarters tonight."

General of Infantry Hossbach yielded to the "Führer Order" and ceased all further attacks to the west on 30 January at 1100 hours. Two hours later, General of Infantry Mueller, the former commander of LXVIII Army Corps in the Greek Isles, took command of the army.

The 4th Army (headquarters near Bartenstein) transitioned to the defense throughout on this day. The XXVI Army Corps stood directly west of Braunsberg. The VI Army Corps held the front west of Bartenstein. The VII Panzer Corps lay northeast of Allenstein. The XX Army Corps fought on the southern front between Ortelsburg and Lake Spirding, while the LV Army Corps defended the western bank of Lake Masurisch, closing on the XLI Panzer Corps of the 3rd Panzer Army. Mobile troop movements, which were required for defense and counterattacks, were ultimately prevented by the endless columns of refugees. Frequently, the National Socialist authorities fled, leaving the civilian population helpless in their villages waiting for the Wehrmacht to conduct the evacuations that were supposed to be secured by the National Socialist Gauleitung.

At this point in time, the 3rd Panzer Army had available the XLI Panzer Corps (right), the IX Army Corps (left), and the 607th Special Purpose Division, which occupied the Kurisch Isthmus. The XXVIII Army Corps, which was formerly fighting in Memel, organized the defense of Samland. Since the beginning of the Soviet offensive, Generaloberst Reinhardt had tried several times to evacuate "Fortress Memel."

On 1/21, Hitler issued the corresponding order. Two days later, the steamer "Venus" and two torpedo boats loaded the first shipment of personnel from the harbor. The Volkssturm companies were transferred to the land bridge. The evacuation of the city by the front troops occurred on the evening of 1/24. The infantry rear guards defended the foreground until 1/27, and then they withdrew into the city. The last naval barges left Memel at 0400 hours on the morning of 1/28, with elements of the 1/154 Grenadier Regiment.

The XXVIII Army Corps began to withdraw from the land bridge to Samland on 1/30. Nidden was given up on 1/31. The formations of the XXVIII Army Corps were directed to new defenses east of Cranz.

However, then the battle of Koenigsberg flared up.

The 11th Soviet Guards Army had broken through the German front east of the city on 1/20 and, since then, were marching unhindered toward Koenigsberg. The express train, which left the Koenigsberg Main Railroad Station on 1/22, was the last to make it through to the west! The military leadership thoughtlessly fled from the city. On the express orders of the army group, Corps Command von Fischhausen returned to Koenigsberg.

In the city itself there were no regular troops other than reserves and training units. There were only Volkssturm battalions (approximately 10,000 men) occupying the temporary defenses in front of the East Prussian capital. Deputy Gauleiter Grossherr defended the Pregel bridge near Palmberg with one battalion. Kreisleiter Wagner stood near Neuhausen with weak forces and made the advancing tanks pay for the airfield. A Volkssturm commander won the Knight's Cross here by destroying tanks.

All of the resistance did not help! The Soviets assaulted past Koenigsberg to the south and took the harbor. An immediate commitment of combat groups of the "Grossdeutschland" Armored Infantry Division re-established contact with the city on 1/30, but the contact was lost again on the following day. The Russians again reached the harbor through Metgethen and outflanked Koenigsberg from the north!

The outspoken Gauleiter, who had declared the cowardice of the 4th Army several days before, had left his headquarters on 1/28.

According to the "Führer Order" of 1/29, the city of Koenigsberg was to be held at all costs! The city was surrounded by four Soviet armies at the end of the month. In the north lay the 43rd Army, in the northeast the 39th Army, in the east the 11th Guards Army, and in the south the 5th Army. Major General Schittnig, commander of the 1st ID, took over command in Koenigsberg. He was replaced three days later by General of Infantry Lasch, the former commander of the I Corps command. He immediately took con-

Chapter 8: The Surrender

trol with a strong hand. Within a short time, General Lasch had the political agencies back in their areas of responsibility. The highest priority was the care for the several hundred thousand refugees and civilians. The Wehrmacht concentrated on the defense.

Elements of the 1st ID and the Volkssturm occupied the 12 forts of the former fortress. The 561st ID (Major General Gorn) defended the city in the east between Palmburg and the Baeckerberg. There was loose contact with the 367th ID (Major General Haehnle) on the left here, while the 5th Panzer Division (Major General Hoffmann-Schoenborn) offered resistance to the 5th Soviet Army south of the Pregel up to the harbor.

After the Soviets had broken through to the coast, there was only contact with Pillau by water, and this was the only harbor that the thousands of refugees, civilians, and wounded could be taken to from the threatened zone. The Army leadership had to take steps to re-integrate Koenigsberg into the front.

The fortress commandant, General of Infantry Lasch, issued an order of the day on 2/5:

> "... The Fatherland requires all of our efforts. Only if we stick together in this decision will we have a future. ...Offer assistance like true German comrades, protect the weak. We will fight as the Fatherland demands: if not for our lives, then for the glory! I call on each of you: uphold the German soldierly tradition!"

The 4th Army could not render assistance to the hard-pressed city of Koenigsberg. Because the army group took away its panzer divisions, the exhausted regiments could not stand for long. Therefore, to defend throughout the front, the army command had to withdraw the defensive lines into the foreground of the harbor. At the end of January/beginning of February, the army strived to accomplish its assigned mission: first, to establish a protective wall for the fleeing women, children, and elderly and, second, to defend East Prussia.

The 4th Army command remained in East Prussia. On 2/8, the 3rd Panzer Army was transferred to Pommerania. At the same time, Army De-

Army Group Center

tachment Samland was formed from the XXVIII Army Corps. General of Infantry Gollnik was responsible for the defense of Samland, including Koenigsberg. The supply of the Wehrmacht was secured by the army group Wirtschaftfuehrer in Rosenberg and the Senior Quartermaster in Pillau.

February brought fierce combat to the entire 4th Army sector. The 28th Jaeger (Major General Koenig), 170th ID (Lieutenant General Hass), and 10th Cycle Brigade (Lieutenant Colonel Briegleb) were bloodied on the Passarge. The 131st ID (Colonel Schulze) bitterly defended Wormditt until 2/11. Fierce combat raged for days around Zinten, and after that Bartenstein and Preussisch-Eylau were evacuated. Gradually, the army withdrew to the harbor. On 2/21, a line was reached which ran out of the area 10 kilometers southwest of Braunsberg and Zinten up to the harbor coast near Brandenburg (southwest of Koenigsberg). The army headquarters was located in Heiligenbeil.

The newly created Army Detachment Samland had as its most important mission the liberation of fortress Koenigsberg. The army detachment (headquarters Pillau) only had the IX Army Corps (General of Artillery Wuthmann) available. On 2/12, the corps was located in positions stretching from the coast east of Neu-Kuhren through Pobethen, Auerhof, Kojehnen, Norgau, and Wischenen to the southwest, and from here to the southeast up to Zimerbude. From left to right were committed on this front: 551st, 95th, 93rd, 58th, and 548th ID. The Koenigsberg fortress commandant had available elements of the 5th Panzer Division, as well as the 1st, 69th, and 367th and 561st ID, which still held a ring around Koenigsberg that stretched approximately 5-10 kilometers in front of the city. For heavy weapons, they had available the Luftwaffe air defense batteries and those of the RAD.

The army group planned an attack of Army Detachment Samland from west to east, while an attack had to be conducted out of Koenigsberg simultaneously from east to west. The attack began on 2/19 at 0530 hours, with the support of heavy artillery from the armored ship "Admiral Scheer" (Naval Captain Thienemann). The 58th (Major General Siewert), 93rd (Major General Lang), and 548th ID (Major General Sudau) attacked from the west. The enemy defended bitterly. He defended the Galtgraben Hills tenaciously. The grenadiers slowly bored their way to the east.

Chapter 8: The Surrender

The 5th Panzer Division (Colonel Herzog) and elements of the 1st ID attacked out of Koenigsberg. Metgethen was reconquered and Seerappen was liberated. The lead attack elements of the 5th Panzer Division advanced on the rail line toward Pillau and the initial companies of the IX Army Corps. Koenigsberg was relieved. There was now an open route – if only 10 kilometers wide – for the numerous civilian refugees, which now streamed toward Pillau.

Fortress Koenigsberg now had some breathing space. However, combat continued to rage around the city. The 5th Panzer Division and the brave 1st ID, whose peacetime garrison was Koenigsberg, had to leave the city. They were transferred to Samland because a Soviet offensive was anticipated here. The commander of the "3rd Belorussian Front", Army General Chernyakovskiy, fell on 2/20 as he was inspecting his troops in front of the city. His successor was the Chief of the STAVKA, Marshal Vassilevskiy.

The tragedy of the battle of East Prussia was played out by the misery of the refugees. Many did not make it to the homeland because their ships were torpedoed by Russian submarines. The German Wehrmacht leadership was concerned about transporting as many of the civilians as possible before the Soviets encircled Koenigsberg for the third time and cut off their withdrawal route to the sea. On 2/7, the army group formed an engineer landing formation under Major General Henke with 42 landing craft, 6 ferries, and 3 motor boats, which could transport either 5,700 men, 56 tanks, or 106 trucks. On 2/16 alone there were 50,000 men in Pillau and 150,000 men in Koenigsberg awaiting transport. In Pillau the steamers "Stadt Memel", "Samland", "Schliekmann", "Natus", and the house boats "Elbing" and "Schmelz" were prepared to take on refugees. A second portion of refugees was led directly across the ice by engineers and men of the Organisation Todt.

Generaloberst Weiss, the former commander of the 2nd Army, became the new commander of Army Group North on 12 March. The 2nd Army was taken over by General of Panzer Troops von Saucken.

It was the conscientious duty of both commanders to hold the routes open with their troops, in order to allow as many women, children, and elderly to flee into the German Reich. There was not much time left, since

Army Group Center

the Soviet Armies attacked without pause against the withdrawing German divisions.

Seven Soviet armies (from left to right: 48th, 3rd, 50th, 31st, 2nd Guards, 28th, and 5th Guards Armies) crashed against the front of the 4th Army, which had withdrawn into the so-called Heiligenbeil pocket. On 12 March, the front ran from directly east of Frauenburg am Haff, south of Braunsberg across the Breitlinde autobahn, and from here between Zinten and Konradswalde back along the autobahn and turned to the west at Kobbelbude toward Heidemaulen.

The following corps and divisions stood on this main combat line (from right to left): VI Army Corps with 349th ID, 24th Panzer Division, 131st ID; XX Army Corps with 541st, 61st ID, 14th Motorized Infantry Division, 292nd, 56th ID; XLI Panzer Corps with 170th ID, 28th Jaeger Division, 256th, 50th ID, "Hermann Goering" Armored Parachute Division, 562nd ID, and the "Grossdeutschland" Armored Infantry Division.

The major enemy attack against the Heiligenbeil pocket occurred on 13 March. Every hungry, exhausted, hollow-cheeked, and drenched soldier knew that the final battle for East Prussia, the final battle of his division, yes, even the final battle of the war had begun. Hundreds of Soviet tanks rolled forward, followed by thousands of soldiers, screaming their dreadful "Urrah."

The Russian main effort appeared during the first day to be in the 24th Panzer Division (Major General von Nostitz-Wallwitz), 131st ID (Colonel Schulze), and the "Grossdeutschland" Armored Infantry Division (Major General Lorenz) sectors. Near Brandenburg on das Haff, the Soviets were able to sever the lines of communication with Koenigsberg for a third time! In spite of the bitter commitment of the last anti-tank battalions and air defense batteries, the German defenders had to withdraw. On 18 March, Wermten, Waltersdorf, Rehfeld, Koenigsdorf, Bladiau, Pottlitten, and Ludwigsort were lost. Braunsberg had to be evacuated two days later. On 3/21, the defensive line ran from Ruhnenberg through Rossen, Heiligenbeil, and Juerkendorf to Wolittnick.

The German area on the Haff grew narrower and narrower. Heiligenbeil became a front city. The remnants of the 131st ID crawled into the ruins of

Chapter 8: The Surrender

the blazing city. The grenadiers held out for three long days; then they had to withdraw. The next day, 25 March, was clear and sunny – and, therefore, from the early morning until late in the evening, enemy air forces were committed without pause. In the meantime, guns of all calibers plowed up every square meter of ground. The combat groups of the 4th Army still held out – however, for how long? On this day, the front ran east of Rosenberg, Gross-Hoppenbruch, and Wolittnick.

The harbor of Rosenberg was the last crystallization point of the battle. From here, it was only possible to cross to Samland by small ships and boats. The last guns of the 116th and 125th Air Defense Regiments were stationary. Fregattenkapitaen Brauneis directed the naval transport. He had 124 pontoons, 52 assault boats, 15 motor boats, 250 rafts, and 10 ferries available, Therefore, by 3/27, 300,000 civilians, 60,285 wounded, 86 guns, 302 trucks, and 11,000 tons of equipment were rescued!

The army group had already made nine requests to the OKH to evacuate the pocket; however, each time the answer "No!" was received. On the morning of 3/26 at 2330 hours, Generaloberst Weiss sent a radio message:

"4th Army operational freedom is limited by constant fire, a hail of bombs, and continuous enemy attack!"

The OKH reply was:

"Mission of 4th Army is to defend a unified front and, therefore, must transport strong elements of the army to the Frische Isthmus!"

However, the army no longer had any strong elements. On 3/27, the remnants of the 61st, 170th, 562nd ID, and 24th Panzer Division were defending in a small bridgehead around Rosenberg, Balga, and Kahlholz. An officer wrote in his diary:

"The Russians are again attacking with tanks. We have no anti-tank guns. Here individual soldiers, all East Prussians, are making efforts that the world will never hear of. It is an unequal battle; Man against tank. Women and young girls help in the front lines, treating the wounded. However, they also carry ammunition forward. And they die like soldiers. ..."

The battle for Balga ended on 28 March. The last 2,530 soldiers, 2,830 wounded, and 3,300 Hilfswillige left the mainland on the last boats on this day. Only a small rear guard from the 562nd ID remained behind for protection. The division commander, Colonel Hufenbach (he was subsequently promoted to Major General), died with his people, sacrificed for their comrades!

Fortress Koenigsberg was the next Soviet objective. A report written later reads:

"On 6 April, the final battle began. At 0730 hours, an extremely strong barrage fire was launched against the southern front, it was repeated against the northern front at 0830 hours. The enemy hammered at the defenders with thousands of guns, mortars, and Stalin Organs. Alarming numbers of bomber squadrons circled without pause over Koenigsberg and dropped tons of their crushing loads onto the unfortunate city. Fighter-bombers continued to hunt, firing out of all tubes at anything that moved in the positions or on the roads. The city sank into ruins. ..."

The 39th, 50th Armies, and 11th Guards Army attacked the positions of the 61st, 69th, 548th, and 561st ID. The positions of the 548th (Major General Sudau) and 561st ID (Colonel Becker) were broken through in the north on the first day. The 69th ID (Colonel Voelker) and the Polizei Combat Group of Major of Police Schuberth, which were defending in the south, had to withdraw to the main railroad station. The battle continued unabated on 4/7. The German resistance began to weaken. The Russians reached the harbor and wharf area.

On the evening of the second day, there was only a narrow contact with the neighboring 1st ID, which was bloodied near Seerappen. General of Infantry Lasch intended to break out. The 4th Army command turned him

Chapter 8: The Surrender

down! A breakout attempt on the third day of the battle was repulsed. Only assault troops were able to establish any contact, so that civilians could get through.

The fortress commandant then committed elements of the 61st ID (Lieutenant General Sperl) and 548th ID (Lieutenant General Sudau). The preparations were delayed by the enemy artillery fire and the continuous bombing, so that they could not set out until the morning of 4/8 at 0200 hours. The breakout did not succeed, because thousands of refugees jammed the roads and prevented any movement. The Russian artillery blanketed the combat groups with grape-shot. Deputy Gauleiter Grossherr and Major General Sudau fell. The troops and civilians streamed back into the city leaderless. Then General Lasch decided to surrender!

He dispatched Steinke and Georges with a letter. The two, which were under a flag of truce, were mortally wounded by their own soldiers near the post office. A second flag of truce (Lieutenant Wildscheck) was also shot by party functionaries. Therefore, General Lasch sent a third flag of truce, this time with Lieutenant Colonel Kerwin and Lieutenant Colonel Cranz. They entered the positions of the 11th Soviet Guards Panzer Regiment on 4/9 at 1900 hours. Marshal Vassilevskiy accepted the surrender!

The combat in Koenigsberg was still not over. Volkssturm companies under SA Führer Wachtholz fought in the palace, and the citadel was defended until 10 April by SS and policemen under the leadership of SS Oberfuehrer Boehme and Major of Police Voigt. Then they also laid their weapons down here!

The surrender of Koenigsberg provoked Hitler to take revenge on the responsible officers. General of Infantry Lasch was condemned to death, and his family was put in Sippenhaft. The commander of the 4th Army, General of Infantry Mueller, had to report to Berlin. On the other hand, nothing happened to Gauleiter Koch. He had been in Pillau for some time and, from here, he fled to Schievenhorst at the mouth of the Vistula. Then, at the end of April, he ran off to Copenhagen dressed as a civilian.

On 31 March, the OKH issued an order (OKH/Gen.St.d.H./Op.Abt. Ia Nr. 450 247/45 g.Kdos. Chefs):

Army Group Center

"The decisive changes in the former combat area around the Bay of Danzig and the independent surrender of fighting troops in the Hela, Gotenhafen, and Danzig areas, has made new regulations necessary:

1. The defenders of Hela, Oxhoefter Kaempe, and Danzig will be subordinated to the XVIII Mountain Corps of the 4th Army near Stutthof – the 2nd Army is directly subordinate to the OKH as of 4/2 at 2400 hours.

2. Formations in the Frische Isthmus, Koenigsberg, and Samland are subordinate to the 4th Army.

3. From 4/3, the army group command is to prepare for transport into the Reich. ..."

Several days later, General of Panzer Troops von Saucken took command of all Wehrmacht elements between Hela and Samland with his 2nd Army command, which was redesignated as Army Command East Prussia on 4/7. He had a difficult job. Koenigsberg fell within the next few days. On 3/28, Danzig was already in the hands of the 65th Soviet Army. (Even though there was still fighting in the streets and in the harbor area for another six days!) On 3/28, Gotenhafen was occupied by the 70th Soviet Army. There was no longer a unified front on the Baltic Sea coast. The only strong point in East Prussia was "Fortress Pillau", where the commander of the LV Army Corps, Lieutenant General Chill, was in command.

The Luftwaffe units, such as they were, were organized under the command of Luftwaffe Command East Prussia, which was formed from the disbanded I Luftgau Command. Major General Uebe, who was relieved by Major General Sachs on 4/26, led the formations of the East Prussian Fighter Command (Colonel Nordmann). He also had the 18th Air Defense Division and the remnants of the 27th Air Defense Division. The 51st Fighter Squadron (Major Lange) was located with its last aircraft on the Pillau-Neitief airfield.

General von Saucken set up his headquarters in Neukrug. His army consisted of, from left to right:

Chapter 8: The Surrender

Samland and Fortress Pillau:
IX Army Corps with 32nd, 93rd, 95th ID, and 5th Panzer Division;
XXVI Army Corps, with the 28th Jaeger Division, 21st, and 61st and 558th ID;

Isthmus:
VI Army Corps with 50th ID, 14th Motorized Infantry Division;

Coast between Stutthof and Boehnsack:
XVIII Mountain Corps with 7th, 129th ID;
XXIII Army Corps with 23rd, 35th, 252nd ID, 4th panzer Division, 12th Luftwaffe Field Division;

Hela peninsula:
Hela Corps with 31st, 83rd, 203rd ID, 4th SS Polizei Division.

The divisions were, naturally, no longer the divisions that were deployed against Russia in 1941. They could only be considered combat groups. The four divisions committed on Hela, for example, reported the following numbers on 4/12:

31st ID = 3454 men
83rd ID = 5190 men
203rd ID = 3048 men
SS Polizei Div = 3110 men.

These divisions had 346 machine-guns, 30 mortars, 28 guns, 21 infantry guns, 4 anti-tank guns, and no assault guns!

Before the new army commander could regroup his troops, the battle in Samland and on the isthmus began. The artillery from four Soviet Armies opened fire on the positions of the German defenders on 16 April. Combat squadrons with 500 aircraft attacked every half hour. All combat became impossible and all resistance senseless. Resistance collapsed during the first hours of the day. The troops began to disintegrate.

Army Group Center

The glorious 1st East Prussian ID, whose commander, Lieutenant General von Thadden, was mortally wounded, found its end in this bloody hell. The remnants of the 93rd ID (Major General Domansky) defended Gut Gaffken to their last cartridge. Combat groups of the 28th Jaeger Division (Major General Verhein) desperately held the Peyse peninsula. The tried and true 5th Panzer Division, whose commander, Colonel Herzog, was also severely wounded, gave up after their last tank was blown up.

The German combat groups quickly withdrew to Pillau. The remnants, which could not make contact, surrendered on 4/17 near Fischhausen. Not very many made it through. The 21st ID totaled 500 men, the 95th and 558th ID together had 300 men, the 28th Jaeger Division had 400, and the 5th Panzer Division had 1200 men.

The battle for Pillau began on 4/20. The "Naval Commandant East Prussia", Naval Captain Strobel, arrived and took command over all naval formations. The coastal batteries immediately became the focus of the battle. The Lochstaedt and St. Adalbertkreuz Batteries fired until they ran out of shells. Then the artillerymen fought with blank weapons until none of them lived!

The defenders of Pillau had to hold out, because there were still numerous refugees to be transported into the Reich. The headquarters of the 609th Artillery Regiment (Colonel Wanke) was responsible for the transport of troop units and Wehrmacht equipment. The army command recognized the significance of Pillau and transferred elements of the 83rd ID from Hela on 4/24.

The combat groups of this division – which had already been defeated once in Velikie Luki – were immediately thrown into the focal point of the battle. The division commander and winner of the Oak Leaves, Major General Wengler, died a soldiers' death on 4/26. The battle for Pillau ended on this day.

The Moevenhaken Battery radioed at 1530 hours: "Ammunition gone. Guns destroyed. Secret documents destroyed." The Kaddig Battery ceased firing at 2200 hours. The artillerymen defended for another two hours in hand-to-hand combat; then it was over. The still intact Lehmberg Battery, whose commander, Korvettenkapitaen Ruthenberg, fell, was the last Ger-

Chapter 8: The Surrender

man strong point in Pillau. Major General Henke assembled the stragglers around the battery. The combat group was encircled. An offer of surrender was turned down. When the last gun fell to volley fire, bitter hand-to-hand combat erupted, which could only end in death. Major General Henke, who had delivered thousands of soldiers and civilians to safety with his landing engineers, shot himself so that he would not be captured.

Now German soldiers were only fighting on the 32 kilometer long Isthmus. Here General of Infantry Grossmann had taken command. He had the 14th Motorized Infantry Division (Colonel Schulze) and remnants of various battered divisions (21st, 83rd, 170th ID, 5th Panzer Division, 28th Jaeger Division) available. The coast of the Isthmus was secured on the harbor side by barges and fishing boats and on the sea side by artillery barges and combat cutters. On 4 May, General of Artillery Wuthmann took command of the troops on the Isthmus. The German defenders continued to withdraw to the southwest. On 4 May, the last piece of East Prussian territory was lost!

The XVIII Mountain Corps (General of Infantry Hochbaum), which, since 4/26, held the sea bridgehead east of the mouth of the Vistula, assembled the formations that were withdrawing from the isthmus. The XXIII Army Corps (General of Infantry Melzer) stood to the left of the Vistula in the Danzig spar. This later bridgehead was about 20 kilometers long and 8 kilometers deep.

General of Panzer Troops von Saucken intended to evacuate these bridgeheads as quickly as possible. First all of the wounded and refugees had to be transported, and then, finally, the combat formations. The evacuation had to be conducted by the Navy if it was to be successful.

A radio message from the Admiralty of the Eastern Baltic Sea on 3 May read:

> "A total of 225,000 soldiers and 25,000 refugees were transported out of the Army Command East Prussia area. Over 175,000 were transported from Hela. The rest are still in the Vistula Estuary.

On the same day, Vice Admiral Thiele radioed the Naval High Command:

Army Group Center

"Due to the complete cessation of eastern traffic to Hela, over 200,000 men are massed in a small area. This will provoke a collapse. Request immediately the commitment of ships to conduct the transport!"

Grossadmiral Doenitz ordered all war ships to Hela and the Vistula Estuary. They were to prevent as many German soldiers and civilians from falling into the hands of the Russians as possible. Therefore, on 5 May, all minesweepers and patrol boats were dispatched. With them steamed the still operational destroyers and torpedo boats, as well as the steamers "Linz", "Ceuta", "Pompeji", and the cruiser "Hansa", to Hela. A strong flotilla under Naval Captain Baron von Wangenheim (the destroyers 25, 34, 38, 39, "Karl Galster", "Theodor Riedel", "Friedrich Ihn", and torpedo boats 23, 28, 33 and 35) took on-board several thousand men and returned to Copenhagen on the following day, which was already occupied by the British Army.

On 6 May, German ships rescued another 42,901 people from Schievenhorst and Hela. During the night of 7 May, 1035 wounded, 775 refugees, and 14,950 soldiers were transported from the Vistula Estuary to Hela, and, during the following night, another 16,105 soldiers, 320 civilians, and 1,205 wounded. The last German ships left from Hela at midnight of 8/9 May. These were the destroyers 25 and "Karl Galster" and torpedo boat 33. ...

From the beginning of the great Soviet offensive to the surrender, the Navy had transported 2,022,602 refugees, wounded, and soldiers back to the homeland. 614,000 German civilians had been killed in East Prussia at this time! Almost 350,000 elderly, women, and children were carted off to Russia; and with them were hundreds of thousands of German soldiers.

Then the land grew silent...

Pommerania and East Brandenburg had been theaters of war since January. On 1/20, the II Provisional Corps gave the alarm to the replacement and training units. The formations were to occupy the Oder-Warthe positions between Landsberg and Crossen. The positions, the so-called

Chapter 8: The Surrender

"Tirschtiegel Block", were constructed in the 30's, but they were never used.

The Soviet tanks were quicker. The OKW Combat Diary noted under 30 January:

> "Russians in front of the Oder-Warthe positions. German forces have still not arrived to occupy these positions!"

On 2/1, the lead enemy attack elements were able to enter the positions without a fight and, on the following day, establish their first bridgehead near Goeritz.

Now the OKH sounded the alarm for all troop units east of the line Wittstock-Nauen-Treuenbrietzen, as well as for all schools in Military Districts II and III. Military District III (Berlin-Brandenburg) formed the CI Corps and subordinated the 303rd "Doeberitz" and 309th "Berlin" Training Divisions to it. The "Jueterbog" and "Muencheberg" Panzer Divisions were also alerted; however, they were not combat capable until March.

General of Artillery Berlin, commander of the CI Army Corps, took command of the Oder front. Beside the above named training and replacement divisions he only had Volkssturm battalions from Brandenburg, Oberdonnau, Munich, Lueneburg, Mainfranken, and Dresden. In addition, a "Corps Oder" (Lieutenant General Hagemann) was formed to which the SS and police units, as well as the 1st Naval Infantry Division, were subordinated to protect the mouth of the Oder.

The organization of Army Group "Vistula" on 1 March (beside the still subordinate 2nd Army) reflected:

9th Army (General of Infantry Busse)
V SS Mountain Corps with 391st ID, 32nd SS Panzer Division, Raegener Division (Fortress Kuestrin) and Fortress Frankfurt;
XI SS Corps with 712th ID, 25th Armored Infantry Division and "Kurmark" Armored Infantry Division;
CI Army Corps with "Berlin", "Doeberitz" and 606th ID;
Corps Oder with 1st Naval Infantry Division, Combat Groups Oberndorff and Klessek.

Army Group Center

3rd Panzer Army (General of Panzer Troops von Manteuffel)
II Provisional Corps command with 9th Parachute Division;
III SS Panzer Corps with 261st ID, 11th, 23rd, 27th, 28th SS Divisions;
X SS Corps with 5th Jaeger Division, 163rd, 402nd ID;
Corps Tettau with 15th, 33rd SS Divisions, "Baerwalde" and "Pommern" Replacement Divisions.

The army group had two panzer divisions (10th SS and "Holstein"), as well as the French volunteer division "Charlemagne" established as reserves behind the main combat line.

Generaloberst Heinrici, the long-time commander of the 4th Army, had taken over command of Army Group "Vistula" on 22 March. The Generaloberst did not hold up in his headquarters, but immediately visited his two armies and was on the road daily. The new commander saw the greatest threat to be east of Berlin, where the 9th Army was unable to penetrate the Russian bridgehead near Kuestrin. He ordered all divisions that had fought their way from Pommerania to refit behind the Frankfurt-Kuestrin sector and be committed on the defensive front.

The Generaloberst demanded new formations from the OKW and OKH if he were to guarantee the security of the Reich capital. Therefore, on 6 April, he was ordered into the Führer Headquarters in the Reich Chancellory. Here the Generaloberst explained the threatening situation, to which neither Hitler nor his closest advisors were exposed to. However, the Generaloberst finally got his way. Hitler recognized that the Oder front had to be held. The Luftwaffe High Command would make available 100,000 men, the Naval High Command 12,000, and the Reichsfuehrer SS 25,000 men. Of these promised forces, however, only 30,000 completely untrained replacements would later show up without weapons!

In the meantime, the Soviets prepared a powerful offensive against the German Oder front. They had assembled three "fronts" ("1st Ukrainian Front" under Marshal Konev, the "1st Belorussian Front" under Marshal Zhukov, and the "2nd Belorussian Front" under Marshal Rokossovskiy). Marshal Konev's troops had the mission of crossing the Neisse and reaching a line Wittenberg-Dresden. The ten armies of Marshal Zhukov received

Chapter 8: The Surrender

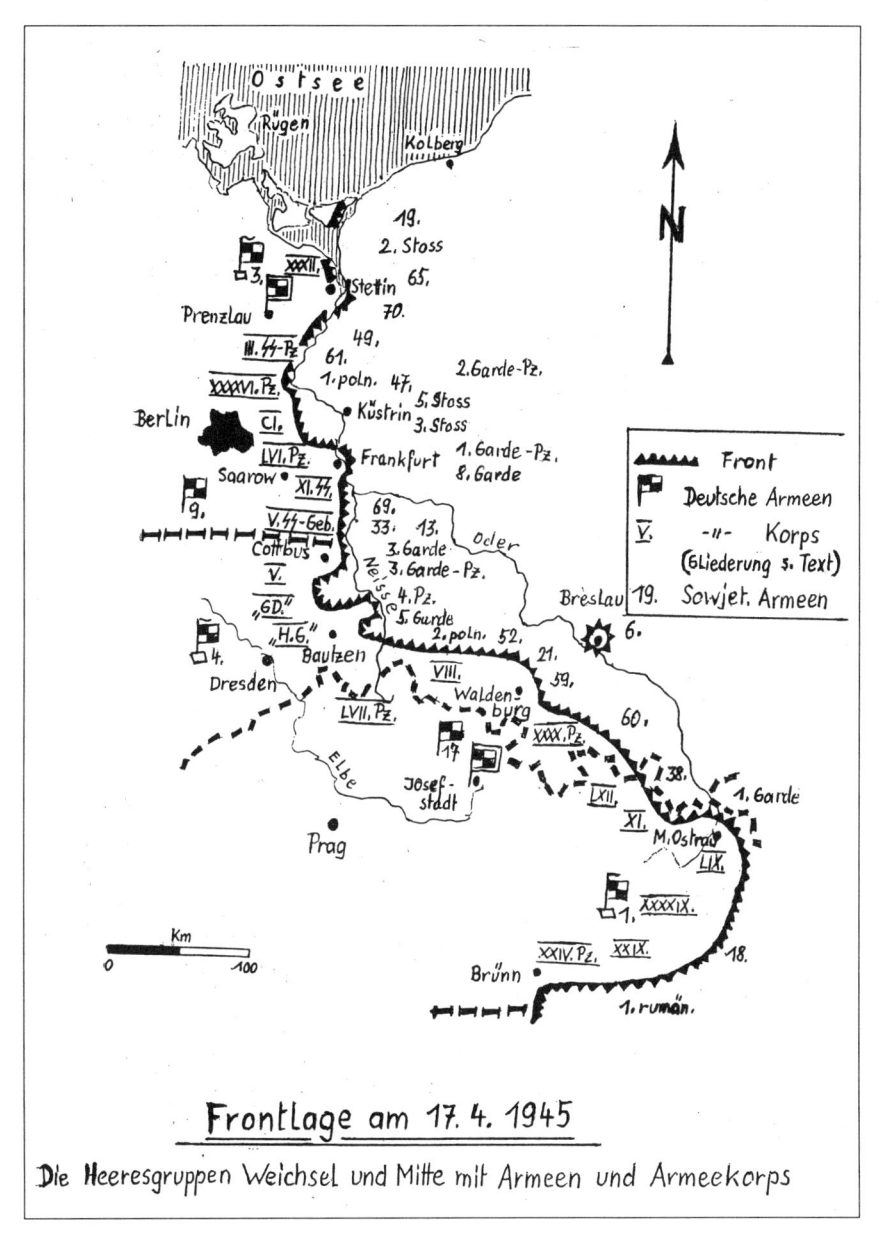

Front Situation on 4/17/1945
Army Groups Vistula and center with armies and army corps

Army Group Center

Berlin as their objective, while Marshal Rokossovskiy was to cross the Oder with his three armies and five motorized corps and advance on Mecklenburg.

For this operation, the "Red Army" had a total of 1,506,700 men, 6,300 tanks, 40,160 guns, and 8,000 aircraft available. Against these forces stood the 235,000 soldiers, 4000 guns, and 300 aircraft of the 9th German Army. The contrast could not have been greater!

The organization of the 9th Army shortly before the beginning of the attack:

Army headquarters in Fürstenwalde;
V SS Mountain Corps (SS Obergruppenfuehrer Jeckeln) with 337th ID, 32nd SS Div., 286th ID;

Fortress Frankfurt (Colonel Biehler);
XI SS Corps (SS Gruppenfuehrer Kleinheisterkamp) with "Muenchburg" Panzer Div., 712th, 169th ID, 9th Parachute Div.;
CI Army Corps (General of Artillery Berlin) with 309th, 303rd, 606th ID, 5th Jaeger Div.;

Army reserves: "Kurmark" Panzer Div., 25th Armored Infantry Division.

16 April 1945 arrived. Everyone who was on the Oder front would remember that day. The "1st Belorussian Front" initiated its attack on Berlin with a fire strike as had not been experienced during the entire war. 22,000 guns, including 400 Stalin Organs, rained death and destruction onto the German positions. 140 large spotlights illuminated the terrain. Their rays illuminated each German bunker, each machine-gun nest, and pointed out every movement to their own artillery observers. At the same time, the air was filled with the droning of 6,500 fighter-bombers and bombers.

After a 35 minute long fiery hell that engulfed the defenders, silence returned to the battlefield. However, only for a few seconds; then the tank

Chapter 8: The Surrender

motors roared to life. The steel behemoths creaked toward the patch-work positions of the 9th Army. Suddenly, machine-guns nattered, anti-tank guns roared, and air defense fire bellowed. The V SS Mountain Corps repulsed all of the enemy's attacks. The remaining two corps of the army were able to hold their positions until midday, but by then their strength was exhausted.

The German divisions and combat groups withdrew three to eight kilometers to the west. No further! Then they entrenched into the ground, took up their carbines, machine-guns, and hand grenades and set to the defense. The enormous forces of Marshal Zhukov, including three tank armies, did not get any further on this day!

The Soviet leadership regrouped during the night. The commissars again read Marshal Zhukov's order of the day to the soldiers:

> "You stand on the border of the cursed Germany! ... Revenge yourselves! Make sure that the breakthrough of our armies will not only be in the memories of today's Germans, but also in that of all future Germans! ..."

On 16 April, Hitler also issued an order of the day, which had much the same tone:

> "The mortal Jewish-Bolshevik enemy is setting to attack one last time with his masses. He is trying to destroy Germany and exterminate our people. ... This time, the Bolsheviks witness the fate of Asia, that means they must bloody the German Reich before its capital. ... Berlin remains German, Vienna will again be German, and Europe will never be Russian! ..."

The horror of this day did not only fall onto the defenders on the Oder, but also hit the neighboring 4th Panzer Army of Army Group Center under Generaloberst Schoerner. Here, the three Soviet armies (13th Army, 5th Guards, and 4th Guards Tank Armies) crossed the Neisse and were able to break through the front of the 4th Panzer Army between Muskau and Guben by evening to a depth of 13 kilometers and a width of 26 kilometers. There-

Army Group Center

fore, on the first day of the battle, the right flank of the 9th Army was already in danger of being outflanked.

The battle on the western hills of the Oder see-sawed during the night of 4/17. The German defenders gave ground slowly. Only the "Muencheberg" Panzer Division under Lieutenant General Mummert was able to defy the Soviets. The infantry divisions could do no more on the second day of the battle. Contact was lost between CI Army Corps and XI SS Corps. The CI Army Corps had to withdraw, and then the army group released the LVI Panzer Corps (General of Artillery Weidling). The corps was to close the existing gap. The SS "Nordland" Division (SS Brigadefuehrer Ziegler) and the 18th Armored Infantry Division (Colonel Rauch) were shoved into the front near Wriezen. However, even these forces were insufficient to stem the massive assault of the Soviet rifle, tank, and motorized divisions.

The German front broke on 18 April!

The "1st Ukrainian Front" broke through the positions of the V Army Corps of the 4th Panzer Army in the south near Cottbus and advanced to the west. In the north the "1st Belorussian Front" had thrown back the CI Army Corps. The 9th Army was dispersed. The LVI Panzer Corps gradually withdrew to Berlin!

The Russian tanks followed close on their heels. On 4/19 they captured Strausberg and crossed the Spree near Spremberg. Soviet batteries fired on Berlin...

Generaloberst Heinrici proposed withdrawing the 9th Army. Hitler still refused!

On 20 April, the "1st Ukrainian Front" stood deep in the rear of the 9th Army. The Soviet 3rd Guards Tank and 4th Tank Armies pressed south of Luebbenau and Luebben to the northwest. Berlin was the decisive objective of this attack axis. The OKH was cleverly withdrawn on the "Führer's Birthday" to the former headquarters in Zossen and then on to Potsdam-Eiche.

On this day, the 9th Army received the V Army Corps with the 35th and 36th SS Divisions, 342nd ID, and 391st Security Division. The divisions, however, no longer had any combat strength and withdrew in a delaying action into the Luebben area.

Chapter 8: The Surrender

The army command had transferred the XI SS Corps into the Fürstenwalde sector to protect the northern flank. Here, the exhausted formations had to be committed against the 3rd and 69th Armies, as well as elements of the 8th Guards Army. Nevertheless, the grenadiers, engineers, artillerymen, radiomen, and drivers could not prevent the Soviets from gaining more ground to the southwest.

The lead attack elements of the "1st Ukrainian Front" and "1st Belorussian Front" reached Koenigswusterhausen on 21 April. The 9th Army was encircled between Guben-Muellrose-Fürstenwalde-Koenigswusterhausen-Luebben!

The eastern front of the army still held out on the Oder between Frankfurt and Gube. "Fortress Frankfurt", 286th ID, 32nd SS Division, 391st Security Division, and the 35th SS Division continued to repulse all enemy attempts to cross. However, on this day, the 33rd Soviet Army was able to get a foothold on the western bank. The front withdrew. Only "Fortress Frankfurt" held out as the last strong point on the Oder. Colonel Biehler commanded about 30,000 men from various units. For heavy weapons they had 100 Russian, Yugoslavian, and French guns, and there were an additional 25 immobile tanks that were entrenched.

Generaloberst Heinrici continued to request the withdrawal of the 9th Army, which was now defending on all sides. In the north, it was being pressured by the 3rd and 69th Armies, in the east assaulted the 33rd Army, in the south attacked the 52nd Army, and from the west the 28th Army and 3rd Guards Tank Army.

The OKH finally approved the withdrawal of the 9th Army on 4/23 and, a day later, the order to evacuate "Fortress Frankfurt" arrived. The army could now remove its divisions from the Oder. On 4/24, the front line ran from Fürstenwalde in the north, directly west of Beeskow, and turned near Luebbenau sharply to the northwest through Luebben, Halbe to Zossen.

On 4/25 the enemy shoved strong forces between Berlin and Zossen. Therefore, the army had to bend its northern flank far to the south. It was now compressed into the small area of Luebben-Halbe-Zossen. Among the Wehrmacht columns were thousands of refugees that wanted to avoid being ravished by the Russians.

The army had practically ceased to exist.

Army Group Center

The Oder had become a stream in the rear of the "Red Army." However, the "2nd Belorussian Front" had begun its attack at the same time as did the "1st Belorussian Front." They had orders to conquer Pommerania and, thereby, occupy the Baltic Sea coast up to Luebeck.

Pommerania itself had already been a theater of war since January. The evacuation of the civilian population had begun on 24 January; the battle of Pommerania had, therefore, already been engaged.

The first counterattack of the German troops was conducted by the newly formed 11th Army of SS Obergruppenfuehrer Steiner. This limited counterattack indeed threw back the 47th Soviet Army almost 12 kilometers and was able to liberate Pyritz. However, it did not have much effect on the overall situation.

On 2/28, the "2nd Belorussian Front" captured Neustettin. Three days later, the III Guards Tank Corps reached the Baltic Sea near Lage and Wusseken. On 3/5, when Koeslin fell, which was defended for two days by the "Karl der Grosse [Charlemagne]" Infantry Brigade and the SS "Juetland" and "Niederland" Battalions, the front of the army group was torn.

In the meantime, the 3rd Panzer Army command had arrived from East Prussia to take command over all German forces in Pommerania.

However, what chance did a German army have against the overwhelming strength of five Soviet armies that had been shoved into the gap between the 2nd Army around Danzig and the 3rd Panzer Army since the beginning of March? The 1st Soviet Guards Tank Army advanced on a wide front between Ruegenwalde and Wladdievenow. Here, only Kolberg was still in German hands. The 2nd Guards Tank Army marched north of Stettin in the direction of the Isle of Wollin. The 3rd Shock and 61st Armies attacked the Stettin Oder bridgehead, while the 47th Army reached the Oder south of Stettin near Fiddikow.

The city of Kolberg contained 35,000 residents in peacetime. Now, there were more than 50,000 refugees in the city, which still hoped to be rescued from the Soviets. On 3/7, Kolberg was surrounded by Soviet tanks. Colonel Fullriede took command over the remnants of the 163rd and 402nd ID. There were still 3,300 men from the Army, Navy, Luftwaffe, Volkssturm, and Hitler Youth that took up the battle against two Russian tank and three Polish rifle divisions.

Chapter 8: The Surrender

The brave defenders fought a hopeless battle for ten days. Their perseverance allowed the Navy to evacuate 68,000 civilians and 1,223 wounded. The final battle for Kolberg took place on the 1,800 meter long and 400 meter wide strip of sand dunes. Colonel Fullriede did not fight "to the last man" as the "Führer Order" demanded. During the night of 3/18, he withdrew his 2,200 men by ship.

The battle in eastern Pommerania, therefore, came to an end. Indeed, there were still stragglers behind the front that were trying to fight their way to the west and cross the Oder. A participant reported:

"Our group had already been underway in the interior of Pommerania for ten days. During the day we hid in thickets, during the night we marched across country by compass and map. Whenever possible, we avoided making contact with enemy troops. Our only rations consisted of several slices of bread and bacon, which were rummaged from overrun refugee columns or abandoned forest houses. We first set out in the direction of Dievenow, because we understood that there was supposed to be a German bridgehead there east of the Oder. However, when we approached the Stepenitz area, we heard from other stragglers that the bridgehead had already been evacuated. German troops were still forward of the Oder only near Altdamm east of Stettin, however, they were already involved in fierce combat. ..."

In March, the 47th and 61st Soviet Armies crashed against Stettin. The city and the eastern bank were defended by the III SS Panzer Corps, along with the 10th SS Panzer Division "Frundsberg", the 4th SS Polizei Division, and the 8th Panzer Division since February. Later, the 1st SS Polizei Jaeger Brigade (Colonel von Braunschweig) was deployed. The combat in March ultimately saw other formations moved up to the Stettin area, including the 1st and 2nd Marine Divisions, as well as the 104th Heeres Anti-tank Brigade.

The German defenders finally had to evacuate the bridgehead up to Altdamm and Gollnow. The 3rd Panzer Army command wanted to keep this bridgehead open for the thousands of refugees that were still coming out of the east.

Army Group Center

Stettin had lost all strategic significance as a city and harbor. Now Swinemuende was the only large port of transshipment for the Navy. On 28 March, the army group formed the so-called Defensive Region Swinemuende, which was occupied by a corps command. Lieutenant General Ansat, the former Senior Artillery Officer (Harko) of the 3rd Panzer Army was the commander. He received the remnants of the 402nd ID and the new 3rd Marine Division.

The Soviets recognized the significance of Swinemuende. They requested their Anglo-American allies to destroy the city and the harbor with a bombing attack. The first large-scale attack on Swinemuende occurred on 3/12 with 400 aircraft. It was certain that the "2nd Belorussian Front" would attack Stettin after regrouping its forces. The city was declared a "fortress." Major General Bruehl was the fortress commandant.

The 3rd Panzer Army – which had been commanded by General of Panzer Troops Manteuffel (Chief of Staff: Colonel Peissner) since 3/15 – was organized for its last battle as follows:

Defensive Region Swinemuende (Lieutenant General Ansat)
with 402nd ID on the Isle of Usedom, 3rd Marine Div.
and 324th Fusilier Battalion on the Isle of Wollin;

XXXII Army Corps (Lieutenant General Neumann) - the corps command was deployed from Norway -
with Combat Group Colonel Ledebour on the coast,
549th ID north, 281st ID in and 610th ID south of Stettin;

Corps Command "Oder" (Lieutenant General Hagemann)
with SS and Polizei combat groups south of Stettin;

III SS Panzer Corps (SS Obergruppenfuehrer Steiner)
with SS Combat Group SS Standartenfuehrer Mueller,
27th SS Armored Infantry Division "Langemarck",
28th SS Armored Infantry Division "Wallonie" in the Greifenhagen area;

Chapter 8: The Surrender

XLVI Panzer Corps (General of Infantry Gareis) with 547th ID and 1st Marine Division between Schwedt and Angermuende;

406th Volks Artillery Corps (Colonel Bartels) was committed behind the XLVI Panzer Corps.

The army defended the Oder front with these weak forces on a breadth of 105 kilometers. 105,000 men and 1,850 guns were to stop the advance of the "2nd Belorussian Front." The troops of Marshal Rokossovskiy had completed their preparations by mid-April. The attack began after a powerful fire preparation on 20 April. the enemy batteries – 238 guns per kilometer of front – opened their barrage fire on the German river positions at 0630 hours. At the same time, assault engineers crossed the river in boats.

The defenders struck back. The Russian formations were wrapped up by counterattacks and prevented from expanding their bridgeheads. The 281st ID (Lieutenant General Ortner) resisted the attack of the CV Rifle Corps, which was to have captured Stettin on this day. The second main axis proved to be in the III SS Panzer Corps area. Here, the 27th SS Armored Infantry Division "Langemarck" (SS Gruppenfuehrer Berger) did not let the enemy advance. The battle raged for two days without moving. Then the Soviets gained the upper hand. While Marshal Rokossovskiy was able to direct new divisions, corps, and armies across the Oder, General of Panzer Troops Manteuffel had no reserves. The main effort in the Stettin area was reinforced. Here, the 2nd Shock and 65th Armies attacked the German positions on the edge of the city on 4/24.

Because the 3rd Panzer Army was now in danger of being overrun on its right flank due to the enemy breakthrough east of Berlin, Generaloberst Heinrici took it upon himself to order a withdrawal! "Fortress Stettin" was evacuated by the German troops and, on 4/26, surrendered to the Soviets by the civilian authorities. Therefore, the Soviets stood in a bridgehead west of the Oder that was 20 kilometers wide and 10 kilometers deep. On this day, Marshal Rokossovskiy decided to attack along the Baltic Sea coast.

Now the OKW, combined with the OKH since 4/25, interfered directly in the control of the 3rd Panzer Army. The III SS Panzer Corps was re-

Army Group Center

moved from the front and hastened to the south. Here it was expanded to Army Detachment Steiner, which had to launch a relief attack on Berlin. Because this attack had priority, the 3rd Panzer Army was to secure the flank to the east and remain on the Oder.

In the meantime, the OKW formed an additional army command. The staff was taken from the 4th Army command, which came from East Prussia. General of Infantry von Tippelskirch was the commander of this new 21st Army, with Colonel von Varnbuehler as his Chief of Staff. The army, which had no large combat capable formations available, was to close the gap between the 3rd Panzer Army and 9th Army!

The front of the 3rd Panzer Army could no longer be held by the categorical orders emanating from the "Führer Headquarters." After the last motorized units were removed for the futile relief attack on Berlin, the thin security lines of the infantry and SS divisions were torn. On 4/30, the Soviet troops captured Demmin. On 5/2, the III Guards Tank Corps entered Rostock and, on 5/4, the Russians stood in Swinemuende. Here, on 4/16, the cruiser "Luetzow" was severely damaged by British bombs and was half sunk. It still fired its intact guns, however, onto the advancing enemy tanks!

At this time, the 3rd Panzer Army stood on a line Lake Plauen-Goldberg-Sternberg.

Pommerania was lost – and with it 50% of the German population, which could anticipate a horrible fate. Death, rape, plunder, and pillage were the order of the day, so that even the army newspaper "Krasnaya Zvezda [Red Star]" had to report the atrocities committed by their own soldiers and the lack of military discipline of the "Red Army"!

Silesia was the third Reichsgau to fall into the hands of the "Red Army" after East Prussia and Pommerania.

Army Group Center – which emerged out of the former Army Group "A" on 1/25 – stood in a hopeless battle against the "1st" and "4th Ukrainian Fronts" since January. The Soviet offensive, which was launched out of the Baranow bridgehead on 1/16, brought the enemy's tanks up to the German Reich border within a few days. Military District VIII (Silesia)

Chapter 8: The Surrender

directed the first mobilized units – 4 regimental staffs, 14 combat groups, and 3 battalions – immediately to construct border defensive positions. However, before most of the units could arrive in the assigned areas, they were overrun by Russian tanks. Military District IV (Saxony) dispatched 20 combat groups into the Liegnitz area at the same time.

On 1/17, the Soviet troops captured Krakau – one of the residences of the Generalgouvernement. Two days later, the 21st Soviet Army (Colonel General Gussev) advanced across the Warthe and attacked into Upper Silesia. The Breslau-Kattowitz road was severed.

The German civilian population still did not want to recognize the threat. The industrial region still had to work, even as the factories and smokestacks came under fire from Russian artillery.

Hitler had entrusted Generaloberst Schoerner with the command of the army group. On 1/20, when the Generaloberst arrived at his headquarters in Oppeln, the lead enemy attack elements were only an hour away to the east of the city. Three days later, the 3rd Soviet Guards Tank Army (Colonel General Rybalko) entered Oppeln.

Generaloberst Schoerner assigned the 17th Army command (General of Infantry Schulz) with the defense of Upper Silesia. The army command formerly was in charge of the sector between the Carpathians and the Vistula. The 1st Panzer Army command (Generaloberst Heinrici) took over this front. Nevertheless, it had to deal with enormous difficulties, because the 1st Hungarian Army began to disintegrate under the battering of the Soviets and their positions had to be secured by their own troops.

The Russian attack was still not stopped. The tanks and infantry forced their way over the Oder near Steinau at the end of January! A counterattack by the "Grossdeutschland" Panzer Corps under General of Panzer Troops von Saucken was immediately ordered by the army group, but it failed. Generaloberst Schoerner, therefore, relieved the meritorious commander; however, Generaloberst Guderian summoned von Saucken to Danzig and convinced Hitler to assign him command of the 2nd Army.

On 1/27, the 3rd Guards Tank and 21st Armies closed the ring around the 17th Army near Rybnik. Kattowitz fell into the hands of the Soviets on the next day. The 17th Army was encircled and was ordered by Hitler – as always – to "defend to the last man."

Army Group Center

Generaloberst Schoerner disregarded this "Führer Order" – it was not the first time – and ordered the withdrawal of the 17th Army to the Oder between Ratibor and Cosel. After he was certain that the order was being carried out, he reported to the OKH:

> "Mein Führer! I have just ordered the evacuation of the Upper Silesian industrial area. The troops have been bitterly battered for 14 days; they can do no more. If we do not evacuate, we will lose the entire army! The way to Moravia will be open. We are withdrawing to the Oder. We will hold there!"

Marshal Konev had his troops immediately pursue them. He established the main axis on Breslau with his tank armies. The attack began on 2/8 out of the Steinau bridgehead. Two days later, the 3rd Guards Tank Army captured Liegnitz, while the 5th Guards Army (Colonel General Zhadov) and the 6th Army (Lieutenant General Gluzdovskiy) concentrated their attacks on Breslau. The lead attack elements of the "front" reached the Oder below Breslau on a 50 kilometer wide front on 11 February!

Therefore, the 4th German Panzer Army fell under the weight of the attack of the "1st Ukrainian Front." The army of General of Panzer Troops Graeser had to fight its way in costly combat from the Baranov bridgehead through Radomsko and Wielun to Silesia. In February 1945, the army was deployed as follows from north to south:

XL Panzer Corps with 100th Brigade, SS Brigade Dirlewanger, Division Matterstock, 608th ID;

XXIV Panzer Corps with 342nd, 72nd ID, 16th and 25th Panzer Division;

"Grossdeutschland" Panzer Corps with Division "Brandenburg", 1st Armored Parachute Division "Hermann Goering", 20th Armored Infantry Division;

Chapter 8: The Surrender

Corps Group Lieutenant General Friedrich with 21st, 6th, 17th Panzer Divisions.

The 4th Panzer Army command was responsible for "Fortress Breslau", where Major General von Ahlfen was established as the fortress commandant on 2/1. Several days later, the fortress was encircled. The Soviets forced their way over the Oder northwest of Breslau in the Regnitz-Laubus area and turned sharply to the south. Therefore, Breslau was outflanked to the west. At the same time, between 1/31 and 2/5, when strong enemy forces crossed the Oder north of Brieg, the Silesian capital was also closed off from the south. On 15 February, Breslau was cut off from the German front. Therefore, it now lay behind Soviet lines.

The defenders of the fortress were a randomly assembled collection of combat groups that now had to be organized by Major General von Ahlfen. In mid-February, the following large formations and combat groups were located in the fortress: The 609th ID (Major General Ruff) defended the front in the southeast of the city on either side of the Oder. To the right was located the 269th ID (Major General Wagner). On the right flank of the 269th ID was a combat group formed from airfield companies, Luftwaffe generator units, and ground personnel, all under Colonel Wehl. Regiment Colonel Goellnitz, which was formed out of replacement and training units, covered to the west, where they met up with a regiment under SS Obersturmbannfuehrer Besslein, which reached the Oder. Between the Oder and the Oels rail line was the 49th Jaeger Training and Replacement Battalion (Colonel Sauer), and from here to the 609th ID fought another regiment formed from replacement units under Major Mohr.

The battle for Fortress Breslau began in mid-February and lasted until the surrender of the Wehrmacht. There were approximately 50,000 soldiers from the Army, the Luftwaffe, the Navy, Waffen-SS, Polizei, Hitler Youth, and Volkssturm that stood against the superior enemy forces, against fire, hunger, and death, during a three month battle. Lieutenant General Niehoff, commander of the 371st ID and winner of the Swords and Oak Leaves, became the new fortress commandant on 9 March. He directed the bitter battle, during which the civilian population suffered horrendous losses, "until the bitter end."

Army Group Center

What words could describe this costly, enormous and, ultimately, senseless battle for Breslau? The unemotional passages from the OKW reports will have to suffice in this circumstance:

19 February: "The defenders of Breslau are conducting a decisive defense against enemy forces attacking from the south and west."

23 February: "The enemy made insignificant progress on the Breslau southern front."

12 March: "The defenders of Breslau held their positions in bitter house to house combat against the Soviets, who have been attacking without success into the southern sector of the city for weeks. During the time period from 10 to 28 February, 41 enemy tanks, 239 guns and anti-tank guns were destroyed in these battles. Moreover, the enemy has suffered high casualties, including approximately 6,700 dead."

27 March: "Again yesterday the enemy assault against the brave defenders of Breslau collapsed against the tenacious resistance of the defenders, who have been engaged in glorious combat since 12 February. Again they inflicted heavy casualties on the Soviets and destroyed 64 tanks."

4 April: "The enemy continues his attacks against Fortress Breslau with strong forces. On the western front, penetrating Russians were removed after fierce combat."

11 April: "The defenders of Breslau repulsed strong attacks against the southern and western fronts of the fortress. Penetrations into the St. Bernhardin Cemetery and west of Manfred von Richthofen Platz were blocked."

9 May: "The defenders of Breslau, that have stood over two months against Soviet attacks, succumbed in the last hours to the enemy's superiority."

Chapter 8: The Surrender

While the defenders of Breslau – they lost 6,000 dead and 23,000 wounded – defended against the 6th Soviet Army for months, the remaining armies of the "1st Ukrainian Front" continued to pressure Army Group Center further toward Silesia and finally back to Moravia. In mid-February, the Soviet tanks reached the area north of Goerlitz. Here they were stopped by the 4th Panzer Army on a line Goerlitz-Schweidnitz. The front situation began to quiet down somewhat in the Silesian region at the end of February. The "Red Army" suspended their advance after gaining a bridgehead near Cosel, but at the same time their forces persisted in the Ratibor-Rybnik sector.

Army Group Center ordered the construction of rear area positions as far back as Bohemia. The resistance of the front troops at the beginning of March on a line were as follows: western bank of the Neisse at Guben-east of Goerlitz-Loewenberg-Striegau-Strehlen-Oppeln-Cosel-Ratibor-Rybnik-Boelitz-Tatra Mountains was considered to be necessary for the many refugees that were still coming from the east.

The army group command committed combat groups at various sectors to straighten out the front and reconquer important locations. A special effort was made by a panzer group under the command of General of Panzer Troops Nehring, which was composed of elements of the XXXIX Panzer Corps (General of Panzer Troops Decker) and the LVII Panzer Corps (General of Panzer Troops Kirchner). In the time period from 1 to 5 March, this combat group was able to recapture Lauban, encircle the Soviet XCIX Motorized Corps, and completely destroy it in a battle lasting several days! During this operation, the 208th ID (Colonel Berger), in cooperation with the 31st SS Division "Boehmen-Maehren" (SS Brigadefuehrer Lombard), was able to recapture Striegau and advance the main combat line up to there!

Ten days later, the "1st" and "4th Ukrainian Fronts" struck back. Their 21st Army and 4th Tank Army set out to the south from the Grottkau area on 3/15 and the 59th and 60th Armies left the Ratibor area for the west. The LVI Panzer Corps (General of Cavalry Koch-Erpach), which was located here, could not prevent their encirclement near Neustadt and came to its end in Upper Silesia west of the Oder.

Army Group Center

Therefore, the German Oder front in Silesia was decisively broken. Only the fortresses of Breslau under Lieutenant General Niehoff and Glogau under Major General Schade still held on. The defenders of Glogau resisted the superior enemy forces until 2 April, and then their resistance collapsed. Major General Schade and many of his officers had fallen.

With the conquest of Upper Silesia, the objective of the Soviets was shifted to Moravia. However, here the corps and divisions of the 1st Panzer Army opposed the Soviets. General of Panzer Troops Nehring took command of the 1st Panzer Army after Generaloberst Heinrici was summoned to command Army Group Vistula. His Chief of Staff was Colonel von Weitershausen.

The 1st panzer Army defended its positions east of the Moldau and prevented practically every attempt of the "Red Army" to advance across the Moravian Valley into Moravia until the beginning of May.

On 12 April, the army was organized as follows:

XXIV Panzer Corps with 344th, 254th ID, 78th Assault Div., 10th Motorized Infantry Div.;

XI Army Corps with 158th ID, 1st Ski Jaeger Div., 97th Jaeger Div., 371st, 68th ID;

LIX Panzer Corps with 544th ID, 16th Panzer Div., 19th Panzer Div., 715th ID, 4th Mountain Div.;

XLIX Mountain Corps with 3rd Mountain Div., 253rd, 304th ID, 16th Hungarian Div., Combat Group Bader, 320th ID;

XXIX Army Corps with 76th, 8th, 15th, 153rd ID;

Reserves: 8th, 17th Panzer Divisions, 75th, 154th ID.

The southern flank of the army had held the Carpathian passes since October 1944 and had fought defensive battles around Kaschau, in the

Chapter 8: The Surrender

western Carpathians, and Beskids at the beginning of 1945. In April, the army was located in positions forward of the Moravian Valley and in the Altvatergebirge. The 1st Panzer Army would be defending in the same sector when the war came to an end.

On the day the "Red Army" initiated its last great offensive against the German Reich, the front of Army Group Center ran from the mouth of the Neisse generally to the southeast up to Maehrish-Ostrau, from here it turned in a great bend to the west into the Bruenn area, where it made contact with the 8th Army of Army Group South.

The headquarters of the army group command was located in Josefstadt on 17 April.

The dispositions of the armies from north to south were:

4th Panzer Army - headquarters Meschwitz - (General of Panzer Troops Graeser)
V Army Corps with 35th SS Div., 214th ID, 36th SS Div.,
275th ID, 342nd ID (between Guben - Forst -
Cottbus);
"Grossdeutschland" Panzer Corps with 344th ID, 21st
Panzer Div., 10th SS panzer Div. (between Cottbus
and Spremberg);
"Hermann Goering" Armored Parachute Corps with "Führer
Escort" Div., 545th, 615th ID, "Brandenburg" Div.
(between Spremberg - Weisswasser - Niesky);
LVII Panzer Corps with 20th Panzer Div., 1st Armored
Parachute Div., 404th, 72nd ID (between Niesky and
the area east of Goerlitz);

17th Army - headquarters Waldenburg - (General of Infantry Schulz)
VIII Army Corps with 6th, 17th ID, 100th Jaeger Div.,
208th, 359th ID (between east of Goerlitz to east
of Schweidnitz);
XL Panzer Corps with 269th ID, 31st SS Div., 45th ID
(from east of Schweidnitz to west of Neisse);

Army Group Center

LXXII Army Corps with 168th, 254th ID, 78th Assault Div., (from west of Neisse to east of Jaegerndorf);
XI Army Corps with 10th Armored Infantry Div., 1st Ski Jaeger Div., 158th ID, 17th Panzer Div., 97th Jaeger Div. (from east of Jaegerndorf to north of Maehrisch - Ostrau).

The adjacent 1st Panzer Army (headquarters near Freiberg) was located with the above mentioned organization from north of Maehrisch-Ostrau to south of Bruenn. From left to right were committed the LIX Army Corps, XLIX Mountain Corps, XXIX Army Corps, and XXIV Panzer Corps.

The opposing formations of the "Red Army" belonged to the "1st" and "4th Ukrainian Fronts." Operating here (from right to left) were the 3rd Guards, 13th, 3rd Guards Tank, 4th Tank, 5th Guards, 2nd Polish, 52nd, 21st, 59th, 60th, 38th, 1st Guards, 18th, and 1st Rumanian Armies. The Soviet 6th Army continued to surround "Fortress Breslau." The Soviet main effort incontestably lay in the great Neisse bridgehead between Forst and Weisswasser. This wedge extended to the west up to the Cottbus-Spremberg area. The Russians had three armies located here, while two stood ready east of the Neisse in reserve.

The attack of the "1st Ukrainian Front" began on 4/16 out of this bridgehead. The 3rd, 3rd Guards Tank, and 4th Tank Armies penetrated into the German front after a long artillery and air preparation. On the first evening, it was already apparent that the strength of the defenders was insufficient against this superior enemy might. The V Army Corps proved to be particularly weak, as its front was torn through this day.

During the next two days, the V Army Corps was broken through, separated from the remaining armies, and thrown back to the northwest toward Luebben. Because contact was lost on the right a threatening gap emerged, through which the Soviet 3rd Guards Tank Army attacked.

The city of Spremberg had to be given up. The 10th SS Panzer Division (SS Brigadefuehrer Harmel) and the "Führer Escort" Division (Major General Remer) could not prevent the breakthrough in spite of all of their efforts. The Russian tanks attacked to the north past Spremberg in the di-

Chapter 8: The Surrender

rection of Kalau. Therefore, they now had an open route to the northwest toward Berlin!

While the left flank of the 4th Panzer Army staggered, a second enemy attack was directed at the center and, therefore, toward Saxony. Soviet and Polish rifle and tank corps attacked out of the bridgehead near Niesky to the west. Their attack reached Bautzen and the Elbe on either side of Dresden.

A several-day battle developed in the Bautzen and Kamenz area. The German formations offered bitter resistance to the advancing enemy and were even able to throw them back in some places. In the battle around Ostsachsen, the 20th Panzer Division (Major General von Oppeln-Bronikowski), the "Hermann Goering" Armored Parachute Division (Major General Walther), and the 100th Assault Gun Brigade defended particularly well. A corps group under General of Artillery Moser (193rd, 404th, and 363rd ID) also fought bravely.

The city of Bautzen fell into the hands of the Soviets on 4/21. On the other hand, the German counterattack on the next day was able to liberate Kamenz again. Then, however, the front of the 4th Panzer Army collapsed.

Soviet tanks attacked through the last combat groups to the Elbe, which was reached on a wide front between Dresden and Torgau. General of Infantry Baron von und zu Gilsa was appointed as the commandant of "Fortress Dresden." However, "Fortress Dresden" was already laid in ruin by allied bombers. Also, there were no troops to defend the one-time residence of Saxon Kings. On 4/24, Soviet tanks encircled Dresden (General Baron von und zu Gilsa surrendered on 8 May).

In the meantime, 26 April had dawned...

An assault troop of the 69th U.S. Division, under the leadership of First Lieutenant Kotzebue (son of a tsarist general!) met a Cossack assault troop of the 175th Rifle Regiment of the 58th Soviet Guards Division at exactly 1200 hours. For the first time during this war, American and Soviet soldiers greeted each other. Their meeting point was Strehla on the Elbe, south of Torgau. An additional American assault troop advanced toward Torgau up to the Elbe bridge, where they were shot at by the Soviets. On the other hand, at 1645 hours of the same day, a strong officer scout troop,

Army Group Center

under the leadership of Major Craig of the 69th U.S. Division, made a third contact with the Soviets.

On the next day, Stalin issued an order to all units of the "Red Army":

> "The troops of the "1st Ukrainian Front" and the allied English-American troops have split the front of the German troops by an attack from the east and the west and have made contact in the center of Germany in the area of the city of Torgau. Therefore, the German troops in northern Germany are cut off from the German troops in the south! ..."

The OKW, which still remained, for the time being, in Berlin with Hitler, reacted to this new situation with a categorical order to the Army Group Center command:

> "After this situation is clarified, attack to the north between Bautzen and Dresden to help Berlin!"

However, Army Group Center was in no shape to execute this order. Its commander, Schoerner – who was promoted to Field Marshal on 4/5 – did not agree with this. He gave a counter order allowing the 4th Panzer Army to withdraw to the Erzgebirge, in order to establish a final defensive wall there.

At the end of April, Army Group Center was surrounded on all sides. The offensive of the "4th Ukrainian Front" had separated the right flank of the 1st Panzer Army from the neighboring 8th Army. Therefore, contact with Army Group South was lost. The XXIV Panzer Corps (General of Artillery Hartmann) had to evacuate Bruenn on 4/26.

The "Red Army" regrouped their troops between the Elbe, the Carpathians, and southern Moravia and, on 6 May, launched a concentrated attack from all three sides. 3 tank armies, 5 guards armies, 12 rifle armies, one each Polish and Rumanian army, and 1 Czech corps attacked between Riesa and Bruenn. The fronts of all three German armies had to withdraw. The 4th Panzer Army fought back to the slopes of the Erzgebirge, the 17th Army withdrew across the Silesian mountains toward Bohemia,

Chapter 8: The Surrender

and the 1st Panzer Army had to give up their months-long defense of the Carpathians.

A danger of the first order had developed in the rear of the army group on 5 May. The Czech population rebelled against the German occupation authorities in Prague. This led to bloody riots as neither side gave any quarter. There were no regular German troops stationed in Prague that could put this revolt down.

Then the army group decided to commit its last reserves. This decision was in response to the bitter mischief that was being visited on the Germans in Prague. The 1st Wlassow Division (Major General Bunitschenko) was dispatched to Prague. This division was organized in 1944 in the Muensingen Military Training Area out of the former East Battalions. The members of the division knew that their mission made no sense after the collapse of the German front, so they made common cause with the Czechs so that they would have an alibi for later on.

When General Wlassow learned of the army group command's psychological blunder, he ordered his division to immediately withdraw to the west. Major General Bunitschenko did not carry this order out. A wave of hatred broke out over Prague, there were cold-blooded murders, horrible rapes, and senseless torture such as the "Golden City" had never seen. Order was not restored until 10 May, when the 3rd Soviet Guards Tank Army (Generaloberst Rybalko) marched into Prague.

Army Group Center no longer existed on this day. The German leadership had strived, during the past few days, to hold open the routes to the west and the American troops for as many soldiers and civilians as possible. All negotiations with U.S. Army commanders were coldly rejected!

Officers and soldiers of Army Group Center had to be taken prisoner by the Russians – for hundreds of thousands, this was a one way trip!

The defeat of Army Group Center at the beginning of May 1945 in the Bohemian and Moravian region also indicated the simultaneous defeat of the Luftwaffe, which had faithfully supported the divisions of the Army since 22 June 1941.

The Luftflotte 6 command (Generaloberst Ritter von Greim) had established its headquarters in Cottbus in February 1945. To the command

Army Group Center

was subordinated the I and II Air Defense Corps with the 10th, 11th, 12th, 17th, 18th, 23rd, and 27th Air Defense Divisions, as well as the XXV Feld Luftgaukommando and the I Luftgaukommando, which came from the East Prussian Luftwaffe Command.

The I Air Defense Corps (General of Air Defense Reimann) committed the 11th Air Defense Division in the sector of the 1st Panzer Army, the 10th Air Defense Division in the 17th Army area of operations, and the 17th Air Defense Division behind the 4th Panzer Army. The II Air Defense Corps (General of Air Defense Odebrecht) fought with the 23rd and 27th Air Defense Divisions on the Oder front. The 12th and 18th Air Defense Divisions supported Army Group North in East Prussia and on the Vistula.

In the meantime, the batteries of the divisions had become "jacks of all trades." They were committed in an anti-tank role in the forward lines, engaged Russian aircraft, and fired on the waves of Anglo-American aircraft, which attacked the German cities between the Baltic Sea and the Erzgebirge with stronger forces week by week.

The most powerful and, at the same time, most horrible air attack hit the loveliest city in Germany: Dresden. On 10/17/1944 and 1/16/1945, the city had already endured two normal attacks, which killed 811 civilians. On 13 February at 2155 hours, as the alarm sirens wailed, no one could have known that 995 combat aircraft would drop 3,000 high explosive and 400,000 incendiary bombs in 1 1/2 hours. After a pause of only 90 minutes, during which the flames continued to blaze, the houses to collapse, and the wounded to scream, another 529 combat aircraft arrived. This time they dropped 5,000 high explosive and 200,000 incendiary bombs. Dresden was a sea of flame, a hell shining as bright as the sun. The clocks struck 1300 hours when the third attack occurred. This time no sirens wailed, for there were none left. 311 American combat aircraft and 210 fighters flew over the city, and another 2,000 high explosive and 50,000 incendiary bombs fell.

Dresden was a hell!

Later totals included 29,000 dead, 75,000 destroyed and 99,000 damaged residences, 28 burned out churches, 40 hospitals, 35 schools, and 110 public buildings!

Dresden no longer existed!

Chapter 8: The Surrender

There was no air defense available to oppose the overwhelming bomber formations of the British and Americans. During this night of Dresden's fire-bombing, only 18 German night fighters took off – there were no more in the central German area.

The still combat capable fighter squadrons were subordinate to the I Fighter Corps (Lieutenant General Huth) in Treuenbrietzen. The 1st Fighter Division (Doeberitz) had 15 fighter, 1 pursuit-interceptor, and 8 night fighter groups available, which, however, had to be committed against American, British, and Russian air formations.

In the sector of the two Army Groups Vistula and Center the 4th Air Division (Major General Reuss) was active, commanding several fighter and pursuit-interceptor squadrons. The 4th Air Division was responsible for, among other things, the commitment of the "Rammkommando Elbe." The Rammkommando, formed from volunteers, was the last desperate levy of the German Luftwaffe. The first commitment of the "Rammkommando Elbe" under Major Koehnke took place over Hannover on 4/9. With a total loss of 77 German pilots, 51 American four-engine bombers were destroyed by ramming.

Since February, Luftflotte 6 had received additional headquarters, however, most of them were formed from staffs that were no longer combat capable. Thus, for example, Luftgaukommando VIII was transferred from Breslau to Prague on 2/8/1945 and took command of the remnants of the grounded air units from Silesia and Bohemia. Luftgaukommando XVII remained in Moravia. Both of these staffs were united with the VIII Air Corps command into Luftwaffenkommando 8 (General of Aviation Seidemann) on 4/29/1945.

Luftwaffenkommando 4 – which evolved from the former Luftflotte 4 and was committed in the Balkans, Hungary, and Slovakia – was also subordinated to Luftflotte 6 in mid-April. The commander, Generaloberst Dessloch, took command of Luftflotte 6 on 4/27/1945. Generaloberst Ritter von Greim was promoted to Field Marshal and appointed as Senior Commander of the Luftwaffe. General of Aviation Deichmann was the new commander of Luftwaffenkommando 4.

However, as the month of May drew across the land, when Army Group Vistula was defeated, Berlin had to surrender, and Army Group Center set

Army Group Center

out to fight its last battle against three Soviet "fronts", there was no longer a German Luftwaffe. The aircraft lay burning, destroyed, and blown up on the airfields; the communications equipment was destroyed and the last intact air defense guns had ejected their last shells into the air.

In April 1945, the main effort of all of the Soviet attacks lay in the center of the front: Berlin. Since 4/16, Marshal Zhukov's "1st Belorussian Front" concentrated 10 armies here! On the day of the attack, the commander issued an order:

"... The time has come to decisively defeat the enemy and end the war victoriously!"

On 16 April, 50 rifle and tank divisions set out from the Kuestrin bridgehead. The numerically inferior German defenders resisted bitterly. The commander of the 8th Soviet Guards Army wrote years later: "No one had counted on such fierce enemy resistance!"

The breakthrough east of Berlin occurred on 19 April!

On the next day, the attack began on the Reich capital. The few troops that still stood east of the city were overrun. The lead Russian tank elements reached Bernau, Jaenickendorf, and Fuerstenwalde on 4/20.

Generaloberst Heinrici, commander of Army Group Vistula, asked the OKW to declare Berlin an "Open City." However, Hitler and the OKW refused! Berlin was to remain a "fortress", in which he – Hitler – would be victorious or die. Therefore, the OKW ordered the LVI Panzer Corps (General of Artillery Weidling) into the city, despite protests from the army group.

Reichsvertidigungskommissar Goebbels organized the resistance in Berlin. Nevertheless, he never coordinated anything with the military commanders and, therefore, was fighting his own war. On 4/20, the following troop units were committed in Berlin:

12 Heeres battalions (replacement and training),
69 Volkssturm battalions,
9 Heeres batteries,

Chapter 8: The Surrender

41 air defense batteries and
66 air defense troops with a total of 41,253 men.

The LVI Panzer Corps now had to construct the defense of the city. On 4/23, the Soviet troops had cut Berlin off from the outside world. On 4/24, the lead elements of the "1st Belorussian" and the "1st Ukrainian Fronts" met near Ketzin west of Berlin.

Marshal Voronov took command over all Soviet troops. He positioned 25,000 guns – that is 610 guns per kilometer! Thousands of shells rained down on the mortally wounded city. At the same time, on 4/25, the 16th Air Army attacked Berlin with 1,486 combat aircraft. By then, Berlin had become the hardest pressed city in the German Reich. Berlin had to endure 400 major attacks, which finally turned it into an inferno!

General of Artillery Weidling took over responsibility for the city, as far as the politicians and the OKW would allow! Weidling divided the city into defensive sectors. Sectors A and B were taken over by the only still combat capable unit – the "Muenchberg" Panzer Division under Major General Mummert. The "Nordland" SS Division (SS Brigadefuehrer Ziegler) was transferred to the southeast of the city into Sector C. The artillery commander of the LVI Panzer Corps, Colonel Woehlermann, commanded Sector D on either side of Tempelhof airfield. Sector E in the Grunewald was occupied by the remnants of the 20th Armored Infantry Division (Major General Schulze) and the 18th Armored Infantry Division (Major General Rauch). Replacement and training units, under the command of Lieutenant Colonel Eder, were directed into Sector F between Spandau and Charlottenburg. The two northern sectors, G and H, were taken over by the 9th Parachute Division under Colonel Herrmann. A Sector Z was organized in the center of the city. Here were exclusively SS and Polizei troops under SS Brigadefuehrer Mohnke. They were also entrusted with the security of the government quarter. The air defense detachments were subordinate to the 1st Air Defense Division (Major General Sydow).

While the first Russian assault battalions were entering Berlin from the north and the first districts were being occupied by Soviet troops, the OKW was still thinking in grand strategic terms. Hitler removed the III SS Panzer

Army Group Center

Corps from the 3rd Panzer Army sector, designated it Army Detachment Steiner, and ordered Steiner on 4/21:

> "The exclusive mission of Army Detachment Steiner is to establish contact with the LVI Panzer Corps by attacking from the north with the 4th SS Polizei Division and as strong elements as possible from the 5th Jaeger Division and 25th Armored Infantry Division, which are to be freed up by the 3rd Marine Division. Withdrawal to the west is strictly forbidden for all units! Officers, that do not strictly adhere to this order, are to be detained and shot. ... The fate of the German Reich capital depends on the success of your mission!"

On 4/22, Field Marshal Keitel, Chief of the OKW, sent a similar order to General of Panzer Troops Wenck, commander of the 12th Army, which was just formed from the Army Group North command. The 12th Army practically existed only on paper. At this time, it commanded divisions that were still forming. In the north lay the XLI Panzer Corps (Lieutenant General Holste). The main combat line ran along the Elbe to Havelberg, through Fehrbellin, Rathenow, Genthin, and Brandenburg. Its combat groups had no solid contact to the right or left.

The second corps of the army – XX Army Corps (General of Cavalry Koehler) – defended the Elbe from Zerbst to Wittenberg and from here to Belzig. Only the "Scharnhorst" Division was located west of Dessau in a defensive position. The remaining divisions, "Ulrich von Hutten", "Theodor Koerner", and "Friedrich Ludwig Jahn", were still assembling their units.

Field Marshal Keitel delivered the "Führer Order" that had the army attack across the line Wittenberg-Niemegk to the east up to Jueterbog. However, General of Panzer Troops Wenck and his Chief of Staff, Colonel Reichhelm, ignored this order in their headquarters, which was located in the Dessau-Rosslau Engineer School. They decided not to attack to the east, but through Belzig to the north in the direction of Beelitz-Ferch. The army command ordered the XLVIII Panzer Corps (General of Panzer Troops Baron von Edelsheim), which was located between Wittenberg and Torgau, to prepare a defense on the Schwarzen Elster as flank protection for the army attacking to the north.

Chapter 8: The Surrender

The attack toward Berlin occurred on 4/24. The "Theodor Koerner" Division (Lieutenant General Frankewitz) assaulted Treuenbrietzen on this day. The "Ulrich von Hutten" Division (Lieutenant General Engel) threw three Soviet divisions back near Wittenberg and established a bridgehead here. Nevertheless, three days later, this had to be evacuated. After the departure positions were achieved, the army received the XXXIX Panzer Corps (Lieutenant General Arndt) with the "Clausewitz" Division (Lieutenant General Unrein) and the 84th ID in the area of Brandenburg to protect the northern flank.

On 4/28, the army set out to break through to Berlin. The XX Army Corps attacked with the "Ferdinand Schill" Division (Lieutenant Colonel Mueller) on the left and the "Ulrich von Hutten" Division on the right. The "Schill" Assault Gun Brigade (Major Nebel) paved the way through the Lehnin Forest. The division ran into fierce resistance. However, by evening they had broken through the enemy front near Belzig and had advanced to within 15 kilometers southwest of Potsdam.

The 12th Army command sent a radio message to the German troops in the Potsdam area – which were designated as "Army Group Spree" (Lieutenant General Reymann):

> "XX Army Corps has reached Ferch. Make every effort to make contact and attack through to the 12th Army!"

The Soviets recognized the danger and energetically set to countermeasures. However, Lieutenant General Reymann and the defenders of Potsdam were able to cross Lake Schwielow in row boats and establish contact with the "Schill" Division. The forces of the army could go no further. General of Panzer Troops Wenck radioed the OKW:

> "The army and, in particular, the XX Army Corps, which has temporarily made contact with the defenders of Potsdam and can absorb them, has been forced into the defense on the entire front, therefore, the attack to Berlin is no longer possible!"

Army Group Center

The attention of the 12th Army was again directed to the east, where the 9th Army began to fight its way through. On 4/21, the army was still defending in the Guben-Muellrose-Koenigswusterhausen-Luebben area. Then it fought its way back to Halbe, in order to break through the fronts of the 3rd Guards and 4th Tank Armies to the west and make contact with the 12th Army.

The remnants of the battered army were further decimated by the constant Russian air attacks and artillery strikes. General of Infantry Busse ordered the columns of refugees be directed to the west, so that they could be better protected. The army gathered all of its combat capable forces in the Halbe area during the night of 1 May and broke out to the west at dawn!

Soviet guns continuously fired on the marching troops and civilian columns. The Chief of Staff, Major General Holz, fell with many of his soldiers, women, and children. The lead attack elements of the army, however, reached the Wagnis!

Lieutenant General Hagemann, commander of the Oder Corps, rode in the only tank in the army at the head of the column. Then lights were noted between Treuenbrietzen and Beelitz. The 9th Army had run into the "Scharnhorst" Division (Major General Goetz).

The breakthrough succeeded! 30,000 soldiers and 5,000 civilians were taken in by the 12th Army!

The Soviet formations attacked into these elements. On 2 May, they tore through the northern flank of the XX Army Corps and advanced to Havelberg on the Elbe. There, the 12th Army was in danger of being encircled itself. General of Panzer Troops Wenck gave the order to withdraw.

The relief of the hard-pressed defenders of Berlin was no longer possible.

The second relief attack for Berlin, which Hitler had assigned to Army Detachment Steiner on 4/21, would not begin. Indeed, SS Obergruppenfuehrer Steiner had three formerly active divisions available. However, these divisions had long ago ceased being divisions. They were not even regiments, but only combat groups without any heavy weapons and without artillery. SS Obergruppenfuehrer Steiner did not even think of executing the attack. He later wrote: "This attack was senseless and meant certain death!"

Chapter 8: The Surrender

Berlin was left on its own.

On 4/23, the Soviet troops occupied Karlshorst, Schoeneweide, and Koepenick. On the following day, they stood on the Schoenefeld airfield, and a day later, the XXVIII Guards Rifle Corps reached the Tempelhof airfield.

More than 5,000 guns opened fire in support of the great attack on the city's center on 4/27 at 0500 hours. The houses on Potsdamer Platz, the ruins on the Hohenzollerndamm, on Leipziger Strasse, and on Alexander Platz were turned to rubble. Major General Baerenfaenger, the youngest general in the Army, fell during hand-to-hand combat with an anti-tank weapon in his hand.

A counterattack in Tempelhof failed. The "Nordland" SS Division withdrew across Leipziger Strasse to the Spittelmarkt. The "Muencheberg" Panzer Division defended in the Leipziger, Priz-Albrecht, and Koethener Strasse sector. The 18th and 20th Armored Infantry Divisions were dispersed. The remnants of the 20th Armored Infantry Division were able to fight their way to Potsdam.

During these turbulent days, Hitler named Field Marshal Ritter von Greim, who was flown in by the world renowned pilot Hanna Reitsch, as Senior Commander of the Luftwaffe. The aircraft had to land on the Ost-West Achse. Engineers had to cut down the trees.

On 4/28, General Weidling proposed to Hitler to make a breakout attempt, which his staff officers had worked out in detail. Hitler turned the plan down! On the same day, the commander of the 5th Shock Army, Colonel General Bersarin, issued his "Order Nr. 1":

> "Today I will be named the Chief of the Occupation and City Commandant of Berlin!"

The combat continued. The Soviets reached the Olympic stadium. Their tanks fired on Charlottenburg Palace and the Charite. There were street battles on Hermannstrasse and at the Zoo.

The remnants of the French volunteer division "Charlemagne" (SS Brigadefuehrer Krukenberg) were bloodied on 4/29 in hand-to-hand combat with enemy tanks on Belle-Alliance Platz. The Frenchmen fought bravely until they ran out of ammunition. The Latvians, Danes, and Norwegians of the "Nordland" SS Division and the Spaniards of the two Legionaire Companies fought and died just as bravely, coming to their end in the ruins of the Reichskanzlei.

The 29th of April brought still more concentrated attacks by the 8th Guards Army from the south, the 3rd Shock and 5th Shock Armies from the north and east, and the 2nd Tank Army from the west. The defenders were compressed into the railroad station, on Hermann Goering Strasse, at the Zoo, and in the government quarter. At 2300 hours, Hitler sent the OKW, which was in Dobbin Quarter, a radio message:

"Report to me immediately: 1. Where are Wenck's lead elements? 2. When will he renew the attack? 3. Where is the 9th Army? 4. To where did the 9th Army breakout? 5. Where are Holste's lead elements?"

The OKW radioed back at 0100 hours:

"1. Wenck's lead elements lay just south of Lake Schwielow.
2. 12th Army cannot continue attack toward Berlin.
3. The majority of 9th Army is encircled.
4. Corps Holste has been forced into the defense."

General of Artillery Weidling no longer had contact with the Reich Chancellory on this day. He ordered his sector commandants to breakout during the coming night with all means available to them. However, again the Soviets were faster. Their 380th, 674th, and 756th Rifle Regiments assaulted the Reichstag at midday on 4/30!

It was 1530 hours on this day, when a single shot cracked in the Führer Bunker under the Reich Chancellory, then the news: Adolf Hitler has taken his own life! He abandoned his soldiers to their own fate ...

General Weidling, who was later informed of the situation by the new Reich Chancellor, Goebbels, faced the consequences. On the next day, he sent the following message into the ether:

"LVI Panzer Corps here!

Chapter 8: The Surrender

We request a cease-fire! At 0050 hours, Berlin time, we will send out a flag of truce to the Potsdamer Bridge. It can be recognized as a white flag in front of a red light! We request a reply! We are waiting!"

The commander of the Soviet 8th Guards Army answered. Then after midnight on 2 May, the Chief of Staff of the LVI Panzer Corps, Colonel von Duvfing, crossed the fire line. He was taken to army headquarters on the Schulenburgring by Russian officers in an armored car. Army General Chuikov, the defender of Stalingrad, had only one question:

"Unconditional surrender? Yes or no?"

The German colonel answered:

"Yes!"

The end arrived. There was no longer an OKH! Army Group "Vistula" was broken. Even though neither Army Detachment Steiner nor the 12th Army could relieve Berlin and the 3rd Panzer Army was ordered to withdraw, Field Marshal Keitel, the highest ranking officer in the Wehrmacht, still believed fate could be changed. On 4/29, he went to Army Group "Vistula." Generaloberst Heinrici and General of Panzer Troops Manteuffel met the Field Marshal on the side of the road near Neustrelitz.

Here the two generals indicated to the Field Marshal that they were defeatists! General of Panzer Troops Manteuffel refused to accept command of the army group! General of Infantry von Tippelskirch was entrusted with the command of the army group, which no longer existed.

On 1 May, the 3rd Panzer Army stood on a line of lakes: Plauen-Goldberg-Sternberg. The 21st Army lay southwest of Lake Plauen. General von Tippelskirch had no troops!

On 5/2, the Soviets captured Rostock and Warnemuende, and Stralsund had fallen three days before. Therefore, Army Group "Vistula" was cut off from the sea. General von Tippelskirch's only chance was to make contact with the American Army, in order to save as many of his soldiers and civilians from Russian captivity as possible (The last commander of the army

Army Group Center

group, Generaloberst Student – the creator of the German paratroops – was unable to make it from the west to his headquarters. On the way, he was captured by the Americans)!

However, the U.S. Army categorically refused to accept their surrender. General von Tippelskirch had to face this icy refusal in northern Germany, as did the 12th Army in the middle of the Reich and General of Panzer Troops Nehring in Moravia.

The German front soldiers were abandoned to the Soviets...

Still the war continued...

On 9 May 1945, Stalin spoke over the Russian transmitters:

"... From now on, the great banner of the peoples' freedom and the peoples' peace will wave over Europe! ... The period of war in Europe is past! The period of peace has begun!..."

There was peace; however, there were no bells in Germany to ring it in! Today we again have bells – however, there is still no peace!

Appendixes

Army Group Center

APPENDIX 1
Organization of the Army Group 1941-1945

21. 6. 1941
Heeresgruppenkommando
  Reserven: LIII. AK. mit 293. ID.

Panzergruppe 2
  Reserve: 255. ID.
    XII. AK.   mit 31., 34., 45. ID.
    XXIV. AK.mot. mit 3., 4. PD., 10. ID.mot., 267. ID., 1. Kav.D.
    XXXXVI. AK.mot. mit 10. PD., SS-D., „Das Reich",
                    IR. „Großdeutschland"
    XXXXVII. AK.mot. mit 17., 18. PD., 29. ID.mot., 167. ID.

4. Armee
  Reserve: 286. Sich.D.
    VII. AK. mit 7., 23., 258., 268. ID., 221. Sich.D.
    IX. AK. mit 137., 263., 292. ID.
    XIII. AK. mit 17., 78. ID.
    XXXXIII. AK. mit 131., 134., 252. ID.

9. Armee
  Reserve: 403. Sich.D.
    VIII. AK. mit 8., 28., 161. ID.
    XX. AK. mit 162., 256. ID.
    XXXXII. AK. mit 87., 102., 129. ID.

Panzergruppe 3
    V. AK.   mit 5., 35. ID.
    VI. AK.   mit 6., 26. ID.
    XXXIX. AK.mot. mit 7., 20. PD., 14., 20. ID.mot.
    LVII. AK.mot. mit 12., 18., 19. PD.

Appendixes

8. 6. 1942
Heeresgruppenkommando

2. *Armee*
    Reserven: VII. AK. mit 88. ID.
        LV. AK. mit 45., 95., 299. ID., SS-Brig. 1

4. *Armee*
    Reserven: 442. ID.
        XII. AK. mit 52., 98., 260., 263., 268. ID.
    XXXXIII. AK. mit 19. PD., 31., 34., 131., 137. ID.
        LVI. Pz.K. mit 10. ID.mot., 267., 331. ID.

9. *Armee*
    Reserven: 87. ID., SS-D. „Das Reich"
        VI. AK. mit 6., 26., 256. ID.
        XXIII. AK. mit 1. PD., 102., 110., 129., 253. ID.
        XXVII. AK. mit 14. ID.mot., 86., 206., 251. ID.
        XXXXI. Pz.K. mit 36. ID.mot., 161., 342. ID.
Kampfgr. Esebeck mit 2. PD., 246., 328. ID.

2. *Panzerarmee*
    Reserven: 707. Sich.D.
        XXXV. AK. mit 4. PD., 262., 293. ID.
        LIII. AK. mit 25. ID.mot., 56., 112., 134., 296. ID.
    XXXXVII. Pz.K. mit 17., 18. PD., 208., 211, 339. ID.

3. *Panzerarmee*
        IX. AK. mit 7., 35., 78., 252., 258., 292. ID.
        XX. AK. mit 183., 255. ID.
    XXXXVI. Pz.K. mit 5. PD., 342. ID.

1. 1. 1943
Heeresgruppenkommando

2. *Armee*
        VII. AK. mit 57., 75., 323. ID.
        XIII. AK. mit 68., 82., 340., 377. ID.
        LV. AK. mit 45., 88., 299., 383. ID.

4. *Armee*
    Reserven: 331., 442. ID.
        XII. AK. mit 260., 268. ID.
    XXXXIII. AK. mit 34., 137., 263. ID.
        LVI. Pz.K. mit 10. ID.mot., 131., 267., 321. ID.

Army Group Center

9. *Armee*
  VI. AK. mit 197., 205., 330. ID., 7. Fallsch.Jäg.D.
  XXIII. AK. mit 12., 20. PD., 86., 110., 206., 253. ID.
  XXVII. AK. mit 9. PD., 14. ID.mot., 6., 72., 87., 95., 251., 256. ID
  XXXIX. Pz.K. mit 2. PD., 102., 216., 337. ID.
  XXXXI. Pz.K. mit 52., 246. ID., SS-Kav.D., 2. Luftw.Feld-D.

2. *Panzerarmee*
  Reserven: 707. Sich.D.
  XXXV. AK. mit 4. PD., 56., 262. ID.
  LIII. AK. mit 25. ID.mot., 112., 134., 293., 296. ID.
  XXXXVII. Pz.K. mit 18. PD., 208., 211., 339. ID.
  Korück 532 mit 102. königl.ungar., 108. königl.ungar. D.

3. *Panzerarmee*
  IX. AK. mit 7., 35., 98., 252., 258., 292. ID.
  XX. AK. mit 31., 183., 255. ID.
  XXXXVI. Pz.K. mit 5. PD., 36. ID.mot., 342. ID.

15. 6. 1944
Heeresgruppenkommando

2. *Armee*
  Reserven: 4. Kav.D., 1. königl.ungar. Kav.D., 5. und
    23. königl.ungar. Res.D.
  VIII. AK. mit 5., 211. ID.
  XX. AK. mit Korps-Gr. E, 3. Kav.D.
  XXIII. AK. mit 7., 203. ID.

4. *Armee*
  Reserve: 286. ID.
  XII. AK. mit 18. Pz.Gren.D., 267. ID.
  XXVII. AK. mit 25. Pz.Gren.D., 78. Sturm-D., 260. ID.
  XXXIX. Pz.K. mit 12., 31., 110., 337. ID.

9. *Armee*
  XXXV. AK. mit 6., 45., 134., 296., 383. ID.
  LV. AK. mit 102., 292. ID.
  XXXXI. Pz.K. mit 35., 129. ID., 36. ID.mot.

3. *Panzerarmee*
  Reserven: 95., 201. ID.
  VI. AK. mit 197., 256., 299. ID.
  IX. AK. mit Korps-Gr. D., 252. ID.
  LIII. AK. mit 206., 246. ID., 4. und 6. Luftw.Feld-D.

Appendixes

12. 4. 1945
Heeresgruppe Mitte
Heeresgruppenkommando
Reserven: Führer-Begleit-D., Div.St.zbV. 601, 602, Festung Olmütz

17. Armee
Reserven: 1. Fallsch.PD., Reste 18. SS-Pz.Gren.-D.,
  Reste 20. SS-Gren.-D., Div.St.zbV. 603
VIII. AK. mit 17., 208. ID., 100. Jäg.D.
XVII. AK. mit 359. ID., Kampfgr. 269. ID., Kampfgr. 31. SS-D.
XXXX. Pz.K. mit 20. PD., 45., 168. ID.

1. Panzerarmee
Reserven: 8., 17. PD., 75., 154. ID.
XI. AK.   mit 68., 158., 371. ID., 97. Jäg.D., 1. Ski-Jäg.D.
XXIX. AK.   mit 15., 76., 153. ID., 8. Jäg.D.
LIX. AK.   mit 16., 19. PD., 544., 715. ID., 4. Geb.D.
XXXXIX. Geb.K. mit 253., 304., 320. ID., 3. Geb.D., 16. ungar. D.,
  Kampfgr. Bader

4. Panzerarmee
V. AK.   mit 214., 275, 344. ID., 35. und 36. SS-D.
LVII. Pz.K. mit 6., 72., 545. ID., Div.St.zbV. 615,
  Pz.Gren.D. „Brandenburg", Pz.Verb. „Böhmen"
Korps-Gr. Moser mit 193., 404., 463. ID.

Heeresgruppe Weichsel
Heeresgruppenkommando
Reserven: 156., 541. ID., Pz.Verb. „Ostsee"

9. Armee
Reserven: LVI. Pz.K. mit PD. „Müncheberg", 25. Pz.Gren.D.,
  Ausb.D. 286
CI. AK.   mit ID. „Groß-Berlin", 5. Jäg.D., Div.zbV. 606
XI. SS-K.   mit 20. Pz.Gren.D., 169., 303., 712. ID.,
  9. Fallsch.D., Pz.Brig. „Kurmark"
V. SS-Geb.K. mit 32. SS-Pz.Gren.D., Div. Raegener,
  Div.St.zbV. 391, Festung Frankfurt

3. Panzerarmee
Reserven: III. SS-Pz.K. mit 11. und 23. SS-Pz.Gren.D.,
  28. und 29. SS-D.
XXXII. AK.   mit 281., 549. ID., Festung Stettin, Kampfgr. Voigt

Army Group Center

XXXXVI. Pz.K.   mit 547. ID., 1. Marine-ID.
   Korps Oder   mit Div.St.zbV. 610, Kampfgr. Klosseck,
Vert.Bereich Swinemünde mit 3. Marine-ID., Ausb.D. 402,
               See-Kdt. Swinemünde

Armee-Oberkommando Ostpreußen

2. Armee
    Reserven: Stäbe 102., 607. ID., 10. Radf.Jäg.Br.
      VI. AK.   mit 129., 170. ID.
      IX. AK.   mit 93., 95., 551. ID.,
                  Pz.Gren.D. „Großdeutschland", 14. ID.mot.
    XXIII. AK.   mit 4. PD., 23.,32., 35., 252. ID.,12. Luftw.Feld-D.
    XXVI. AK.   mit 5. PD., 1., 21., 58. ID., 28. Jäg.D.
    XVIII. Geb.K.   mit 7. ID.
    Gen.Kdo. Hela   mit 7. PD., 31., 83., 203. ID., 4. SS-Pol.D.

Appendixes

APPENDIX 2

Organization of the Luftwaffe in the Central Area 1941-1945

22. 6. 1941
Luftflottenkommando 2
(direkt unterstellt:)
        Jagd-Geschw. 53
        Aufkl.Gruppe (F)/122
        Luftgau-Kdo. Posen
Fliegerkorps II
        Stab Nahkampffliegerführer II
        Schlacht-Geschw. 210
        Kampf-Geschw. 3
        Kampf-Geschw. 53
        Stuka-Geschw. 77
        Jagd-Geschw. 51
        Kampf-Gr.zbV. 102
Fliegerkorps VIII
        Stuka-Geschw. 1
        Stuka-Geschw. 2
        Zerstörer-Geschw. 26
        Jagd-Geschw. 27
        IV./Kampf-Geschw. zbV. 1
        Aufkl.Staffel 2 (F)/11
Flakkorps I
        Flak-Rgt. 101
        Flak-Rgt. 104

4. 7. 1943
Luftflottenkommando 6
(direkt unterstellt:)
        Nachtjagdgruppe
        Fernaufkl.Gr.

Army Group Center

1. *Flieger-Division*
    - Kampf-Geschw. 3
    - Kampf-Geschw. 4
    - Kampf-Geschw. 54
    - Jagd-Geschw. 1
    - Jagd-Geschw. 51
    - Jagd-Geschw. 54
    - Schlacht-Geschw. 1
    - Schlacht-Geschw. 2
    - Schlacht-Geschw. 3
    - Zerstörer-Geschw. 1

12. *Flak-Division*
    - Flak-Rgt. 21
    - Flak-Rgt. 101
    - Flak-Rgt. 162

10. *Flak-Brigade*
    - 5 gemischte Abteilungen

12. 1. 1945

Luftflottenkommando 6
I. *Jagdflieger-Korps* (teilw.)
    1. Jagdflieger-Division (teilw.)

4. *Flieger-Division*
    - Jagd-Geschw. 6
    - Schlacht-Geschw. 4
    - II./Schlacht-Geschw. 2

Luftwaffen-Kommando 8
  I. Flak-Korps mit 10. Flakdivision
                     11. Flakdivision
                     17. Flakdivision

Luftwaffen-Kommando Oder
  II. Flak-Korps mit 1. Flakdivision
                     23. Flakdivision
                     14. Flak-Brigade
                     16. Flak-Brigade

Luftwaffen-Kommando Ostpreußen
  Jagdfliegerführer Ostpreußen (Jagd-G. 51)
  12. Flakdivision
  18. Flakdivision
  27. Flakdivision

Appendixes

APPENDIX 3

Organization of the Navy in the Northern and Vistula Areas 1945

(Schwimmende Einheiten der Kriegsmarine sind nicht aufgeführt, da ihr Einsatz unregelmäßig war und die Verbände stetig wechselten.)

Kommandierender Admiral östliche Ostsee
    Kommand.Admiral: Admiral Burchardi
                                  Vizeadmiral Thiele (seit April 1945)
    Chef d. Stabes: Freg.Kapt. Forstmann

Kommandant der Seeverteidigung Pommern
    Seekommandant: Kapt.z.S. Magnus
                                Kapt.z.S. Rieve (seit Januar 1945)
    Chef d. Stabes: Freg.Kapt. Stavenhagen
    (unterstellt:) Marinefestungspionierstab 7 (Rügen)
                    Marinefestungspionierstab 8 (Swinemünde)
                    Kommandant Abschnitt Stralsund
                    Kommandant Abschnitt Rügen-Hiddensee
                    Hafenkommandant Swinemünde
                    Marine-Artillerie-Abt. 536 (Wollin)
                  Marine-Artillerie-Abt. 537
                  3. Marine-Flak-Rgt. (Swinemünde)
                      mit Flak-Abt. 227, 233, 711, 713
                  3. Marineflugmelde-Abt.
                  3. Marinekraftfahr-Abt.
                  Marinefestungspionier-Btl. 311

Kommandant der Seeverteidigung Ost- und Westpreußen
    Seekommandant: Konteradmiral Stange
                                Kpt.z.S. Jerchel (ab Dez. 1944)
    Chef d. Stabes: Kapt.z.S. Jerchel
                                Freg.Kapt. Schwarz (ab Dez. 1944)

Army Group Center

Kommandant der Seeverteidigung Ostpreußen (ab Januar 1945)
    Seekommandant: Kapt.z.S: Jerchel
                              Kapt.z.S. Möller (seit Februar 1945)
                              Kapt.z.S. Strobel (seit April 1945)
    Chef d. Stabes: Freg.Kapt. Schwarz
    (unterstellt:) Hafenkapitän Pillau
                     Marine-Artillerie-Abt. 533 (Pillau)
                     Marine-Flak-Abt. 215 (Pillau)
                     Marine-Flak-Abt. 225 (Pillau)

Kommandant der Seeverteidigung Westpreußen (ab Januar 1945)
    Seekommandant: Konteradmiral Sorge
    Chef d. Stabes: Korv.Kapt. Meyer
                            Korv.Kapt. Carstanjen (seit April 1945)
                            Freg.Kapt. Gutsch (Mai 1945)
    (unterstellt:) Marinefestungspionierstab Gotenhafen
                     Hafenkapitän Gotenhafen
                     Marine-Art.-Abt. 531 (Gotenhafen)
                   Marine-Art.-Abt. 629 (Gotenhafen)
                   9. Marine-Flak-Rgt. (Gotenhafen)
                       mit Flak-Abt. 219, 249, 259, 818
                   1. Marine-Nebel-Abt. (Gotenhafen)
                   9. Marine-Feuersch.-Abt. (Gotenhafen)

Kommandant im Abschnitt Memel (nur bis Januar 1945)
    Marinefestungskommandant: Kapt.z.S. Goetz
                            Kapt.z.S. Möller (ab September 1944)
    Chef d. Stabes: Freg.Kapt. Bartholdy
    (unterstellt:) Hafenkapitän Memel
                     Marine-Flak-Abt. 217
                   Marine-Flak-Abt. 218

Appendixes

APPENDIX 4
Organization of the Red Army 1941-1943

— Heer —

22. 6. 1941
Westlicher Besonderer Militärbezirk
(Hauptquartier Minsk)
        Oberbefehlshaber: Armeegeneral Pawlov
        Chef d. Gen.St.:   Generalmajor Klimowskich
        Kriegsrat: Korpskommissar Fominych
R e s e r v e n :   X. Schützenkorps (Moledetschno)
                  mit 24., 75. Schtz.D., 50. Pz.Brig.

3. Armee
(Hauptquartier Grodno)
        Oberbefehlshaber: Generalleutnant Kusnezov
        R e s e r v e n :
        150., 184., 194. Schtz.D., 5., 22., 28. Pz.Brig., 29. Kav.D.
        XI. Schtz.K. (Olita)   mit 23., 84., 188. Schtz.D.,
                                128. mech.Brig.
        XXIX. Schtz.K. (Grodno)
                  mit 27., 56., 143. Schtz.D.

4. Armee
(Hauptquartier Kobrin)
        Oberbefehlshaber: Generalmajor Korobkov
        R e s e r v e n :   45., 120., 121. Schtz.D.
        IV. Schtz.K. (Brest-Litowsk)
                  mit 10., 40., 85., 141. Schtz.D.,
                  54. Pz.Brig.
        VII. Schtz.K. (Kobrin)
                  mit 13., 49., Schtz.D., 11. Kav.D.

Army Group Center

10. *Armee*
(Hauptquartier Bialystock)
Oberbefehlshaber: Generalmajor Golubjov
R e s e r v e n :   III. Schtz.K. (Slonim)
mit 5., 34., 89., 129., 145. Schtz.D.,
12. Kav.D.
XII. Schtz.K. (Bialystock)
mit 30. Schtz.D., 2. mech.Brig.,
4. Kav.D.
VI. mech.K. (Bialystock)
mit 86. Schtz.D., 9., 23., 29. Pz.Brig.,
1. und 2. Kav.D.
VI. Kav.K. (Lomscha)
mit 6., 14. Kav.D., 146. Schtz.D.

1. 7. 1943
Heeresgruppe „Zentralfront"
R e s e r v e n : IX. Pz.K.
mit 95., 108., 109. Pz.Brig.,
26. Schtz.Brig.mot.
XIX. Pz.K.   mit 79., 101., 102. Pz.Brig.,
23. Schtz.Brig.mot.
VI. Garde-Kav.K.   mit 229., 259. Pz.Rgt.
12., 15. Flak-D.

1. Garde-Pionier-Brig.
14. Pionier-Brig.
2. Garde-Werfer-Brig.

13. *Armee*
XV. Schtz.K.   mit 8., 74., 148. Schtz.D.
XXIX. Schtz.K.   mit 15., 81., 307. Schtz.D.
XVII. Garde-Schtz.K. mit 6., 70., 75. Garde-Schtz.D.
XVIII. Garde-Schtz.K. mit 2., 3., 4. Garde-Luftl.D.
IV. Art.K.   mit 1., 3. Garde-Art.D., 5., 12. Art.D.

48. *Armee* (keine Korpsstäbe)
16., 73., 170. Schtz.D.;
137., 143.,399. Schtz.D.,2. Art.Brig.mot.

60. *Armee*
XXIV. Schtz.K.   mit 112., 129., 141., 248., 322. Schtz.D.;
[selbst.:]   121. Schtz.D.,
42. Schtz.Brig.,
14., 150. Pz.Brig., 26. Pz.Abw.Brig.

Appendixes

65. *Armee* (keine Korpsstäbe)
                        69., 115., 149., 194., 246., 354. Schtz.D.;
                        37. Gd.Schtz.D., 60. Schtz.D.,
                        11. Gd.Pz.Brig.

70. *Armee* (keine Korpsstäbe)
                        102., 106., 132., 211., 280. Schtz.D.;
                        140., 162., 175., 181. Schtz.D.,
                        27. Pz.Brig., 3. Pz.Abw.Brig.

2. *Panzerarmee*
    III. Pz.K.   mit 50., 51., 103. Pz.Brig.,
                          57. Schtz.Brig.mot.
    XVI. Pz.K.   mit 104., 107., 164. Pz.Brig.,
                          15. Schtz.Brig.mot.

— Luftwaffe —
(Luftwaffe war kein selbständiger Wehrmachtteil, Streitkräfte unterstanden den „Fronten")

1. 12. 1941
Westfront
    Kampffliegerdivisionen   12, 23, 28, 38, 43, 47, 77, 146
    Jagdfliegerdivisionen   10, 46
    Nahkampffliegerdivision   31

Südwestfront
    Jagdfliegerdivisionen   11, 61

direkt dem Oberkommando (STAVKA) unterstellt:
    Fernkampffliegerdivisionen 26, 40, 42, 51, 52, 81, 133

1. 7. 1943
1. *Luftarmee* (bei „Westfront")
    II. Kampfflieger-Korps mit 213. Kampffl.D.
    II. Schlachtflieger-Korps mit 224., 233. Schlachtfl.D.
    VIII. Jagdflieger-Korps

15. *Luftarmee* (bei „Brjansker Front")
    I. Garde-Flieger-Korps mit 3., 4. Gardefl.D., 10., 315.Jagdfl.-
                                           D., 204., 241., 284. Kampffl.D.
    III. Schlachtflieger-Korps mit 225., 308. Schlachtfl.D.

16. *Luftarmee* (bei „Zentralfront")
    III. Kampfflieger-Korps mit 271., 301. Kampffl.D.
    VI. Schlachtflieger-Korps mit 2. Garde-, 299. Schlachtfl.D.
    VI. Jagdflieger-Korps mit 1. Garde-, 279., 282., 283.,
                                     286. Jagdfl.D.

Army Group Center

APPENDIX 5
Commanders of the Army Group and Armies

Heeresgruppe Mitte:

Feldmarschall von Bock	Sommer 1940 — 18. 12. 1941
Feldmarschall von Kluge	19. 12. 1941 — 28. 10. 1943
Feldmarschall Busch	29. 10. 1943 — 27. 6. 1944
Feldmarschall Model	28. 6. 1944 — 16. 8. 1944
Generaloberst Reinhardt	17. 8. 1944 — 17. 1. 1945

(Umbenennung der „Heeresgruppe Mitte" in „Heeresgruppe Nord" — siehe dort — Neuaufstellung des Oberkommandos aus „Heeresgruppenkommando A")

Feldmarschall Schörner	18. 1. 1945 — Ende

Heeresgruppe Weichsel:

Reichsführer-SS Himmler	15. 1. 1945 — 20. 3. 1945
Generaloberst Heinrici	21. 3. 1945 — 28. 4. 1945
General d. Inf. von Tippelskirch	29. 4. 1945 — 30. 4. 1945
Generaloberst Student	1. 5. 1945 — Ende

Heeresgruppe Nord:

Generaloberst Reinhardt	18. 1. 1945 — 26. 1. 1945
Generaloberst Rendulic	27. 1. 1945 — 9. 3. 1945
Generaloberst Weiß	10. 3. 1945 — 5. 4. 1945

(Auflösung der Heeresgruppe)

2. Armee:

Generaloberst Frhr. von Weichs	20. 10. 1939 — 14. 11. 1941
Generaloberst Schmidt	15. 11. 1941 — 13. 7. 1942
Generaloberst von Salmuth	14. 7. 1942 — 3. 2. 1943
Generaloberst Weiß	4. 2. 1943 — 9. 3. 1945
General d. Pz.Tr. von Saucken	10. 3. 1945 — Ende

Appendixes

4. Armee:
Feldmarschall von Kluge	1. 8. 1939 — 25. 12. 1941
General d. Geb.Tr. Kübler	26. 12. 1941 — 19. 1. 1942
Generaloberst Heinrici	20. 1. 1942 — 4. 6. 1944
General d. Inf. von Tippelskirch	5. 6. 1944 — 18. 7. 1944
General d. Inf. Hoßbach	19. 7. 1944 — 29. 1. 1945
General d. Inf. Müller	30. 1. 1945 — Ende

9. Armee:
Generaloberst Strauß	30. 5. 1940 — 14. 1. 1942
Generaloberst Model	15. 1. 1942 — 3. 11. 1943
General d. Pz.Tr. Harpe	4. 11. 1943 — 19. 5. 1944
General d. Inf. Jordan	20. 5. 1944 — 27. 6. 1944
General d. Pz.Tr. von Vormann	28. 6. 1944 — 21. 9. 1944
General d. Pz.Tr. von Lüttwitz	22. 9. 1944 — 19. 1. 1945
General d. Inf. Busse	20. 1. 1945 — Ende

2. Panzerarmee:
Generaloberst Guderian	16. 11. 1940 — 21. 12. 1941
Generaloberst Schmidt	22. 12. 1941 — 14. 7. 1943
Generaloberst Model	15. 7. 1943 — 15. 8. 1943

(zugleich Oberbefehlshaber 9. Armee)
(Verlegung der 2. Panzerarmee auf den Balkan)

3. Panzerarmee:
Generaloberst Hoth	16. 11. 1940 — 7. 10. 1941
Generaloberst Reinhardt	8. 10. 1941 — 15. 8. 1944
Generaloberst Raus	16. 8. 1944 — 9. 3. 1945
General d. Pz.Tr. v. Manteuffel	10. 3. 1945 — Ende

(vorübergehend unterstellt:)
4. Panzerarmee:
Generaloberst Hoepner	16. 11. 1940 — 8. 1. 1942
Generaloberst Ruoff	9. 1. 1942 — 31. 5. 1942

(Verlegung der 4. Panzerarmee zur Heeresgruppe Süd)

(bei Heeresgruppe Mitte 1945:)
1. Panzerarmee:
Generaloberst Heinrici	19. 8. 1944 — 19. 3. 1945
General d. Pz.Tr. Nehring	20. 3. 1945 — Ende

4. Panzerarmee:
General d.Pz.Tr. Graeser	21. 9. 1944 — Ende

Army Group Center

17. Armee:
    General d. Inf. Schulz   25. 7. 1944 — 29. 3. 1945
    General d. Inf. Hasse   30. 3. 1945 — Ende

(bei Heeresgruppe Weichsel 1945)
3. Panzerarmee:
    (siehe dort)

9. Armee:
    (siehe dort)

11. Armee:
    SS-Obergruppenführer Steiner   26. 1. 1945 — 28. 2. 1945
    (Verlegung zur Heeresgruppe B)

21. Armee:
    General d. Inf. von Tippelskirch   27. 4. 1945 — Ende

Appendixes

APPENDIX 6
Chiefs of Staff of Army Group Center and Weichsel

Anlage f)

GENERALSTABCHEFS DER HEERESGRUPPE MITTE

Generalmajor von Greiffenberg	Sommer 1940 — 31. 3. 1942
Generalleutnant Wöhler	1. 4. 1942 — 28. 2. 1943
Generalleutnant Krebs	1. 3. 1943 — 31. 8. 1944
Generalleutnant Heidkämper	1. 9. 1944 — 24. 1. 1945
Generallt. Ritter v. Xylander	25. 1. 1945 — 15. 2. 1945
Generalleutnant von Natzmer	16. 2. 1945 — Ende

GENERALSTABCHEFS DER HEERESGRUPPE WEICHSEL

SS-Gruppenführer Lammerding	15. 1. 1945 — 20. 3. 1945
Generalleutnant Kinzel	21. 3. 1945 — 19. 4. 1945
Generalmajor von Trotha	20. 4. 1945 — 30. 4. 1945
Generalleutnant Dethleffsen	1. 5. 1945 — Ende

Army Group Center

APPENDIX 7
Duty Positions in the Army Group Staff 1941-1945

	22. 6. 1941	1. 3. 1942	1. 6. 1944
Oberbefehlshaber:	von Bock Feldmarschall	von Kluge Feldmarschall	Busch Feldmarschall
Chef. d. Gen.Stabes:	v. Greiffenberg Generalmajor	v. Greiffenberg Generalmajor	Krebs Generalleutnant
1. Gen.St.Offz. (Ia):	von Tresckow Oberstlt. i.G.	von Tresckow Oberstlt. i.G.	von der Groeben Oberst i.G.
General d. Transportw.:	Goeritz Oberst i.G.	Goeritz Generalmajor	Teske Oberst i.G.
Höh. Pionierführer:	Cantzler Generalmajor	Dr. Meise Generalleutnant	Lüdecke Generalleutnant
Höh. Nachrichtenführer:	Oberhäußer Generalmajor	Oberhäußer Generalmajor	Kohlhauer Generalmajor
General zbV. (Feldpol.):	— —	Suttner Generalleutnant	Veith Generalleutnant
Oberquartiermeister:	Eckstein Major i.G.	Eckstein Oberstlt. i.G.	von Unold Oberst i.G.
Führer d. Wirtsch.St.:	Niedenführ Generalmajor	Niedenführ Generalmajor	Bruch Generalleutnant

STELLENBESETZUNG HEERESGRUPPE MITTE
1. 5. 1945

Oberbefehlshaber:	Feldmarschall Schörner
Chef d. Gen.Stabes:	Generalleutnant von Natzmer
1. Gen.Stabsoffz. (Ia):	Oberst i.G. Schindler
Ia/Führung:	Oberstleutnant i.G. Bennecke
Ic/Abwehr:	Oberst i.G. Stephanus
Oberquartiermeister:	Oberst i.G. Leutheuser
General d. Pioniere:	Generalleutnant Boehringer
General d. Transportw.:	Oberst i.G. Meinhardt
Stabsoffizier Artillerie:	Oberst Bamler
HGr.-Arzt:	Generalstabsarzt Dr. Jaeckel
HGr.-Veterinär:	Generalstabsveterinär Dr. Schäfer

Appendixes

STELLENBESETZUNG HEERESGRUPPE WEICHSEL
1. 5. 1945

Oberbefehlshaber:	Generaloberst (Lw.) Student
Chef d. Gen.Stabes:	Generalleutnant Dethleffsen
1. Generalstabsoffz. (Ia):	Oberst i.G. Eismann
Ia/Führung:	Oberstleutnant i.G. Harnack
Ic/Abwehr:	Oberst i.G. von Harling
Oberquartiermeister:	Oberst i.G. von Rucker
General d. Pioniere:	Generalleutnant Dinter
General d. Transportw.:	Oberst i.G. Hamberger
Höh. Nachrichtenführer:	Generalleutnant Meltzer
Stabsoffz. Artillerie:	Oberst Voigt
HGr.-Veterinär:	Generalstabsveterinär Dr. Rathsmann

Army Group Center

APPENDIX 8
Commanders of the Rear Area

Befehlshaber d. rückw. Heeresgebiets 102
General d.Inf. von Schenckendorff
General d.Geb.Tr. Kübler (ab 22. 7. 1943)
(Dienststelle am 1. 10. 1943 aufgelöst)

Befehlshaber d. rückw. Gebiets Weißruthenien
General d.Kav. Graf von Rothkirch und Trach
(Dienststelle am 1. 7. 1944 aufgelöst)

Kommandanten d. rückw. Armeegebiete (Korück)
532 bei 2. *Panzerarmee:*
Generalleutnant Bernhard
(Dienststelle nach Abzug 2. Panzerarmee zur 9. Armee)

559 bei 4. *Armee:*
Generalleutnant von Unruh
Generalleutnant Carp (ab 6. 5. 1942)
Generalmajor Pawel (ab 17. 4. 1943)
Generalleutnant von Altrock (ab 5. 3. 1944)
Generalmajor Liegmann (ab 1. 8. 1944)
Generalleutnant Krampf (ab 15. 8. 1944)

580 bei 2. *Armee:*
Generalleutnant Müller
Generalleutnant Agricola (ab 17. 12. 1941)

585 bei 4. *Panzerarmee:* (hier nur 1945):
Generalleutnant Kratzert

590 bei 3. *Panzerarmee:*
Generalleutnant Schmidt-Kolbow
Generalmajor Deindl (ab 1. 2. 1943)
Generalleutnant Stahl (ab 7. 3. 1943)
Generalleutnant Boettcher (ab 7. 5. 1943)
(Dienststelle am 5. 9. 1944 aufgelöst)

Appendixes

APPENDIX 9
Senior Artillery Commanders

Harko 308 (2. Armee):	Generalleutnant **Müller**
Harko 302 (4. Armee):	Generalleutnant **Wagner**
Harko 307 (9. Armee):	Generalleutnant **Wissmath**
	Oberst **Schräpler** (ab 10. 4. 1945)
Harko 304 (17. Armee):	Generalleutnant **Wintergast**
Harko 311 (1. Panzerarmee):	Generalleutnant **Prinner**
Harko 305 (2. Panzerarmee):	Generalmajor **Leeb**
Harko 313 (3. Panzerarmee):	Generalleutnant **Ansat**
	Generalmajor **Frölich** (ab 1. 4. 1945)
Harko 312 (4. Panzerarmee):	Generalleutnant **Friedrich**

Army Group Center

APPENDIX 10
Duty Positions of the Luftwaffe Operations Staff

1941
Luftflottenkommando 2
Oberbefehlshaber: Feldmarschall **Kesselring**
Chef d. Gen.Stabes: Generalmajor **Seidemann**
Ia: Oberst i.G. **Loebel**; (später)
Oberst i.G. **Uebe**

II. Fliegerkorps
Kommand.General General d. Flieger **Loerzer**
Chef d. Gen.Stabes: Oberst i.G. **Deichmann**

VIII. Fliegerkorps
Kommand.General: General d. Flieger Frhr. von **Richthofen**
Chef d. Gen.Stabes: Oberst i.G. Meister

I. Flakkorps
Kommand.General: Generalmajor von **Axthelm**
Chef d. Gen.Stabes: Major i.G. Groepler

II. Flakkorps
Kommand.General: Generalmajor **Dessloch**
Chef d. Gen.Stabes: Oberstleutnant i.G. **Jebens**

Appendixes

1945

Luftflottenkommando 6
Oberbefehlshaber: Generaloberst Ritter von Greim
Generaloberst Dessloch (ab 25. 4. 1945)
Chef d. Gen.Stabes: Generalmajor Kless

Luftwaffenkommando 4
Kommand.General: Generaloberst Dessloch
General d. Flieger Deichmann (ab 25. 4. 1945)

Luftwaffenkommando 8
Kommand.General: General d. Flieger Seidemann

Luftwaffenkommando Ostpreußen
Kommand.General: Generalmajor Uebe
Generalmajor Sachs (ab 26. 4. 1945)

Luftwaffenkommando Nordost
Kommand.General: General d. Flieger Fiebig

I. Flakkorps
Kommand.General: General d. Flak Reimann
General d. Flak Deichmann (ab 1. 3. 1945)

II. Flakkorps
Kommand.General: General d. Flak Odebrecht

I. Jagdfliegerkorps
Kommand.General: Generalleutnant Huth

1. Fliegerdivision
Kommandeur: Generalmajor Fuchs

4. Fliegerdivision
Kommandeur: Generalmajor Reuss

Jagdfliegerführer Ostpreußen
Kommandeur: Oberst Nordmann

Army Group Center

APPENDIX 11
Duty Positions of Red Army Senior Commands 1941-1945

5. Dezember 1941

„Westfront"
Oberbefehlshaber: Armeegeneral Shukow
Chef d. Gen.Stabes: Generalleutnant Sokolovskij
Kriegsrat: Divisionskommissar Bulganin

„Kalininer Front"
Oberbefehlshaber: Generaloberst Konjev
Chef d. Gen.Stabes: Oberst Kasnelson
Kriegsrat   Korpskommissar Leonov

„Südwestfront"
Oberbefehlshaber: Marschall Timoschenko
Chef d. Gen.Stabes: Generalleutnant Boldin
Kriegsrat: Divisionskommissar Chruschtschow

Armeen: Oberbefehlshaber:
 1. Stoßarmee   Generalleutnant Kusnezov
 3. Armee   Generalmajor Krejser
 5. Armee   Generalleutnant Govorov
10. Armee   Generalleutnant Golikov
13. Armee   Generalmajor Gorodnjanskij
16. Armee   Generalleutnant Rokossovskij
20. Armee   Generalleutnant Wlassow
22. Armee   Generalmajor Vostruchov
24. Armee   Generalmajor Rakutin
29. Armee   Generalmajor Masslennikov
30. Armee   Generalmajor Leljuschenko
31. Armee   Generalmajor Juschkevitsch
33. Armee   Generalleutnant Efremov

43. Armee	Generalmajor Golubev
49. Armee	Generalleutnant Zacharkin
50. Armee	Generalleutnant Boldin
61. Armee	Generaloberst Kusnezow
I. Garde-Kav.Korps	Generalleutnant Belov
II. Garde-Kav.Korps	Generalmajor Dowator
III. Garde-Kav.Korps	Generalmajor Krjutschenkin
Moskauer Verteidigungskorps	Generalleutnant Schuravljev
VI. Luftverteidigungskorps	Oberst Mitenkov

16. Januar 1945

„*1. Weißrussische Front*"
Oberbefehlshaber:	Marschall Shukow
Chef d. Gen.Stabes:	Generaloberst Malinin
Kriegsrat:	Generalleutnant Telegin
mit 8. Garde-Armee	Generaloberst Tschuikov
33. Armee	Generaloberst Zwetajev
47. Armee	Generalleutnant Perchorovitsch
61. Armee	Generaloberst Belov
69. Armee	Generaloberst Kolpaktschi
3. Stoß-Armee	Generaloberst Simonjak
5. Stoß-Armee	Generalleutnant Bersarin
1. Garde-Panzerarmee	Generaloberst Katukov
2. Garde-Panzerarmee	Generaloberst Bogdanov
1. Polnische Armee	General Poplawskij
16. Luftarmee	Generaloberst Rudenko

„*2. Weißrussische Front*"
Oberbefehlshaber:	Marschall Rokossowskij
Chef. d. Gen.Stabes:	Generalleutnant Bogoljubov
Kriegsrat:	Generalleutnant Subbotin
mit 49. Armee	Generalleutnant Grischin
65. Armee	Generalleutnant Batov
70. Armee	Generaloberst Popov
2. Stoß-Armee	Generaloberst Fedjuninskij
5. Garde-Panzerarmee	Generaloberst Wolski
4. Luftarmee	Generaloberst Werschinin

„*3. Weißrussische Front*"
Oberbefehlshaber:	Armeegeneral Tschernjakovskij
Chef. d. Gen.Stabes:	Generaloberst Prokovskij
Kriegsrat:	Generalleutnant Makarov

Army Group Center

mit 11. Garde-Armee	Generaloberst Galitzkij
5. Armee	Generalleutnant Schafranov
28. Armee	Generalleutnant Letschinskij
39. Armee	Generalleutnant Ljudnikov
43. Armee	Generaloberst Beloborodov
1. Luftarmee	Generaloberst Chrjukin

„1. Ukrainische Front"
Oberbefehlshaber: Marschall Konjev
Chef d. Gen.Stabes: Generaloberst Sokolovskij
Kriegsrat: Generalleutnant Krainjukov

mit 3. Garde-Armee	Generaloberst Gordov
6. Armee	Generaloberst Gludsovskij
13. Armee	Generaloberst Puchov
21. Armee	Generaloberst Gussjev
52. Armee	Generaloberst Korotejev
59. Armee	Generalleutnant Korovniko
60. Armee	Generaloberst Kurotschkin
3. Garde-Panzerarmee	Generaloberst Rybalko
4. Garde-Panzerarmee	Generaloberst Leljuschenko
2. Luftarmee	Generaloberst Krassovskij

APPENDIX 12
Commitment of Air Defense (Flak) Divisions in the Central Area

Div.Nr.	Kommandeur	Einsatz: Jahr und Raum
1.	Generalmajor Sydow	1945 Oderfront und Berlin
10.	Generalmajor Engel	1944 Südpolen
		1945 Schlesien und Sachsen
12.	Generalleutnant Buffa	1942 — 1944 in Front und im rückw. Gebiet Mitte
	Generalleutnant Prellberg (ab 1. 5. 1944)	1945 Ost- und Westpreußen
17.	Generalmajor Köppen	1944 Mittel- und Westpolen
		1945 Schlesien und Sachsen
18.	Generalmajor Reimann	1942 — 1944 in Front bei Heeresgruppe
	Generalleutnant Prinz Reuss (ab 1. 4. 1943)	
	Generalmajor Wolf (ab 1. 3. 1944)	1944 — 1945 Ostpreußen
	Generalmajor Sachs (ab 1. 10. 1944)	
23.	Oberst Fichter	1943 rückw. Gebiet Mitte
	Generalmajor Andersen (ab 1. 4. 1944)	1944 Wartheland
		1945 Oderfront und Berlin
27.	Generalleutnant Kathmann	1944 — 1945 Ostpreußen
	Generalmajor Uhl	
	Generalleutnant Kressmann	

Army Group Center

APPENDIX 13
Highest Awards in the Central Area

Das Eichenlaub mit Schwertern und Brillanten zum Ritterkreuz des Eisernen Kreuzes wurde während des 2. Weltkrieges an 27 Offiziere der Wehrmacht als höchste Tapferkeitsauszeichnung verliehen. Davon erhielten folgende Offiziere der Heeresgruppe und der Luftflotten im Bereich Mitte diese Auszeichnung:

Lfd. Nr.	Dienstgrad, Name, Dienststellung	Datum d. Verleihung
1	Oberst Mölders, Kommodore Jagd-G. 51	16. 7. 1941
10	Oberleutnant Rudel, Kdr. III./Schlacht-G. 2	29. 3. 1944
12	SS-Gruppenfhr. Gille, Kdr. SS-D. „Wiking"	20. 4. 1944
17	Feldmarschall Model, Oberbefehlshaber	17. 8. 1944
26	Generalleutnant Dr. Mauss, Kdr. 7. Pz.Div.	15. 4. 1945
27	General d.Pz.Tr. von Saucken, Oberbefehlshaber AOK Ostpreußen	9. 5. 1945

Appendixes

APPENDIX 14
Combat and Battle Calendar

1. Doppelschlacht bei Bialystock und Minsk	22. 6. — 10. 7. 1941
2. Schlacht am Dnjepr und Düna	2. 7. — 15. 7. 1941
3. Schlacht bei Smolensk	8. 7. — 5. 8. 1941
4. Schlacht bei Roslawl	1. 8. — 9. 8. 1941
5. Abwehrschlacht bei Jelnja und Smolensk	26. 7. — 1. 10. 1941
6. Schlacht bei Kritschew und bei Gomel	9. 8. — 20. 8. 1941
7. Schlacht bei Kiew	21. 8. — 27. 9. 1941
8. Schlacht bei Welikije Luki	22. 8. — 27. 8. 1941
9. Doppelschlacht bei Wjasma und Brjansk	2. 10. — 20. 10. 1941
10. Vorstoß gegen Moskau und Woronesh	4. 10. — 5. 12. 1941
11. Abwehrkämpfe um Kalinin	18. 11. — 14. 12. 1941
12. Abwehrschlachten vor Moskau	5. 12. 1941 — 18. 4. 1942
13. Stellungskämpfe im Bereich Heeresgr.	19. 4. 1942 — 4. 7. 1943
14. Abwehrschlachten im Osten	5. 7. — 27. 12. 1943
15. Abwehrkämpfe im Pripjet-Gebiet und Weißrußland	12. 12. 1943 — 19. 4. 1944
16. Stellungskämpfe im Bereich Heeresgruppe	20. 4. — 4. 5. 1944
17. Abwehr- und Rückzugsschlachten während der Sommeroffensive	22. 6. — 31. 8. 1944
18. Abwehrkämpfe an Weichsel und Narew	1. 9. 1944 — 12. 1. 1945
19. Abwehrkämpfe in Ostpreußen	13. 1. 1945 — 9. 4. 1945
20. Abwehr- und Rückzugskämpfe im Wartheland	16. 1. — 30. 1. 1945
21. Abwehrkämpfe in Schlesien und Böhmen	21. 1. — 9. 5. 1945
22. Abwehr- und Stellungskämpfe an der Oder	31. 1. — 15. 4. 1945
23. Abwehrkämpfe in Pommern	10. 2. — 9. 5. 1945
24. Abwehrkämpfe in der Danziger Bucht	23. 3. — 9. 5. 1945
25. Schlacht in Mitteldeutschland	16. 4. — 9. 5. 1945
26. Schlacht um Berlin	25. 4. — 9. 5. 1945

APPENDIX 15
Generalkommissariate Belorussia 1943

a) *Dienststelle Generalkommissar*

Generalkommissar:	Gauleiter Kube
	SS-Gruppenfhr. von Gottberg
	(ab 22. 9. 1943)
Abteilungsleiter I (Politik):	Oberdienstleiter Bauer,
	Oberdienstleiter Dr. Lübbe
Abteilungsleiter II (Verwaltung):	Regierungsrat Dr. Kaiser
Abteilungsleiter III (Wirtschaft):	Regierungsrat Freitag
Abteilungsleiter IV (Arbeit):	Kriegsverwaltungsrat Osbelt
Bezirksleiter der NSDAP:	Oberbereichsleiter Wurzer

b) *Geographische Einteilung*

Generalbezirke/ Kreisgebiete	Stadt- kreise	Land- kreise	Fläche in qkm	Einwohner
Minsk-Stadt	1	—	42	103 110
Minsk-Land	—	9	5 429	304 241
Slonim	—	5	4 704	171 563
Sluzk	—	8	5 242	220 603
Wilejka	—	8	7 530	299 553
Lida	—	8	4 641	278 508
Borissow (Barisau)	—	5	1 248	32 717
Hancewitze	—	4	6 085	114 595
Glubokoje	—	10	8 746	340 217
Baranowitschi	—	7	5 694	341 522
Nowogrodek	—	5	4 301	194 504
	1	69	53 662	2 411 333

Appendixes

APPENDIX 16
Abbreviations

Zusammengesetzte Abkürzungen sind nicht aufgeführt, können aber selbständig aufgeschlüsselt werden.

AA.	— Aufklärungs-Abteilung	GR.	— Grenadier-Regiment
Abt.	— Abteilung	Gren.D.	— Grenadier-Division
Adm.	— Admiral	Gruf.	— Gruppenführer
AK.	— Armeekorps	H./Harko.	— Heeres-Höherer Artillerie-Kommandeur
AOK.	— Armee-Oberkommando		
AR.	— Artillerie-Regiment	HGr.	— Heeresgruppe
Arko.	— Artilleriekommandeur	HKL.	— Hauptkampflinie
		Hptm.	— Hauptmann
Art.	— Artillerie-	HQu.	— Hauptquartier
Aufkl.	— Aufklärung	I	— Infanterie-
Batt.	— Batterie	ID.	— Infanteriedivision
Befh.	— Befehlshaber	ID.mot.	— Infanteriedivision motorisiert
Br.	— Brigade	IG.	— Infanteriegeschütz
Brig.Fhr.	— Brigadeführer	i.G.	— im Generalstab
Btl.	— Bataillon	Inf.	— Infanterie-
D.	— Division	IR.	— Infanterie-Regiment
F.d.M.	— Führer d. Minensuchkräfte	JG.	— Jäger-
		K.	— Jagdgeschwader
F.d.T.	— Führer d. Torpedoboote	Jäg.	— Korps
		K.Adm.	— Konteradmiral
F.Kapt.	— Fregattenkapitän	Kapt.	— Kapitän
Fla.	— Heeresflak	Kaptlt.	— Kapitänleutnant
Füs.	— Füsilier-	Kdr.	— Kommandeur
Fw.	— Feldwebel	Kdtr.	— Kommandantur
G.	— Geschwader	Kfz.	— Kraftfahrzeug
Gd.	— Garde-	KG.	— Kampffliegergeschwader
Geb.	— Gebirgs-		
Gefr.	— Gefreiter	KGr.	— Kampffliegergruppe
Gen.Adm.	— Generaladmiral	K.Kapt.	— Korvettenkapitän
Gen.d.	— General d.	Komm.Gen.	— Kommandierender General
Gen.Kdo.	— Generalkommando		
Gen.Ob.	— Generaloberst	Kp.	— Kompanie
Gen.St.	— Generalstab	lFH.	— leichte Feldhaubitze
Glt.	— Generalleutnant	Lkw.	— Lastkraftwagen
Gm.	— Generalmajor	Lt.	— Leutnant

Army Group Center

Lw.	— Luftwaffe	Pz.Jäg.	— Panzerjäger
Lw.FD.	— Luftwaffen-Felddivision	Pz.K.	— Panzerkorps
		R.	— Panzertruppe
mech.	— mechanisiert		— Regiment (nur bei
MG.	— Maschinengewehr	Pz.Tr.	Zusammensetzungen)
mot.	— motorisiert		
MPi.	— Maschinenpistole	RAD.	— Reichsarbeitsdienst
Nachr.	— Nachrichten-	Radf.	— Radfahrer-
OB.	— Oberbefehlshaber	Rgt.	— Regiment
Ob.	— Oberst	rückw.	— rückwärtig
Oberstlt.	— Oberstleutnant	San.	— Sanitäts-
Oblt.	— Oberleutnant	Schlacht-G.	— Schlachtgeschwader
Ofw.	— Oberfeldwebel	schw.	— schwer
OGruf.	— Obergruppenführer	SD.	— Sicherheitsdienst
OKH.	— Oberkommado d. Heeres	sFH.	— schwere Feldhaubitze
		Sfl.	— Selbstfahrlafette
OKL.	— Oberkommando d. Luftwaffe	Sich.D.	— Sicherungsdivision
		Skl.	— Seekriegsleitung
OKM.	— Oberkommando d. Kriegsmarine	sowj.	— sowjetisch
		SS.	— Waffen-SS
OKW.	— Oberkommando d. Wehrmacht	SS-Pol.D.	— SS-Polizeidivision
		SS-T.D.	— SS-Totenkopfdivision
OQu.	— Oberquartiermeister	Stand.Fhr.	— Standartenführer
OT.	— **Organisation Todt**	Sturmbannf.	— Sturmbannführer
PD.	— Panzerdivision	Uffz.	— Unteroffizier
Pi.	— Pionier-	V.-Abt.	— Vorausabteilung
PK.	— Propagandakompanie	V.-Adm.	— Vizeadmiral
Pol.	— Polizei-	VB.	— Vorgeschobener Beobachter
Pz.	— Panzer-		
Pz.Gren.	— Panzergrenadier-	z.S.	— zur See

Bezeichnungen der Schiffsgattungen:

M	— Minensuchboot
R	— **Räumboot**
S	— Schnellboot
T	— Torpedoboot
U	— Unterseeboot
UJ	— Unterseebootsjäger
V	— Vorpostenboot
Z	— Zerstörer

Also from the Publisher

SCORCHED EARTH Paul Carell. The classic! This new edition of Paul Carell's eastern front study picks up where *Hitler Moves East* left off. Beginning with the battle of Kursk in July 1943, Carell traverses the vast expanse of the Russian War, from the siege of Leningrad and the fierce battles of the northern front, to the fourth battle of Kharkov, and the evacuation of the Crimea, a withdrawal forbidden by Hitler. The book ends in June of 1944 when the Soviet Armies reach the East Prussian frontier. Hundreds of photographs, situation and campaign maps, complete index, and comprehensive bibliography add to this impressive account. This edition includes a new preface by the author. Paul Carell is also the author of *Foxes of the Desert*; *Invasion! They're Coming*; *Operation Barbarossa In Photographs*; and *Stalingrad - The Defeat of the German 6th Army* (all four titles are available from Schiffer Military/Aviation History).
Size: 6" x 9"
b/w photographs, maps   600 pages, hard cover
ISBN: 0-88740-598-3 $39.95

RETREAT FROM LENINGRAD: ARMY GROUP NORTH 1944/1945 STEVEN H. NEWTON. Most histories of the northern sector of the Russian front concentrate on the siege of Leningrad, and focus little attention on the heavy fighting during the Wehrmacht's withdrawal into the Baltic countries. *Retreat from Leningrad* begins where those books end, with the massive January 1944 Soviet offensive which was designed not only to break the siege completely but also to destroy Army Group North. Enjoying huge superiorities in men and material, the Red Army attempted to crush two German armies which lacked more than a handful of tanks, contained a high percentage of unreliable foreign volunteers, and were hampered by Adolph Hitler's inflexible "no retreat" strategy. This untold story is recovered here in great detail, primarily as told by the German officers who served as commanders and chiefs of staff for Army Group North and its constituent armies. Their accounts were drafted soon after the war ended at the request of the United States Army, but have languished in poorly translated manuscripts until Professor Steven H. Newton re-translated, corrected, and annotated them, as well as providing substantial amounts of new material direct from the army group's operational records. The result is the most comprehensive and detailed operational study of sustained combat in the northern sector of the Russian front ever published in English.
Size: 6" x 9" maps
328 pages, hard cover
ISBN: 0-88740-806-0 $24.95

GERMAN BATTLE TACTICS ON THE RUSSIAN FRONT, 1941-1945 Steven H. Newton. In this new book, Professor Steven H. Newton has retrieved, retranslated, and annotated the detailed tactical accounts of combat in Russia that German officers provided their American captors after the war. In this collection of ten essays, the Chief of Staff of the XXXXI Panzer Corps describes the final furious dash toward Moscow. One of the commanders of the relief force narrates the rescue of the troops trapped in the Demyansk pocket. A corps commander on Manstein's right flank at Kursk analyzes the tactical failures of the battle. And in one of the more controversial documents in the early cold war, the last commander of Army Group South recalls his futile attempt to interest General Patton in assisting in the war against the Soviets. A wide variety of tactical situations – from winter warfare to desperate infantry defenses, and unit types – from panzer divisions to cavalry brigades – are covered in this collection.
Size: 6" x 9"
20 maps 320 pages, hard cover
ISBN: 0-88740-582-7 $24.95

RED ARMY TANK COMMANDERS: THE ARMORED GUARDS Colonel Richard N. Armstrong. This new book profiles six Soviet commanders who rose to lead six tank armies created by the Red Army on the eastern front during the Second World War: Mikhail Efimov Katukov, Semen Il'ich Bogdanov, Pavel Semenovich Rybalko, Dmitri Danilovich Lelyushenko, Pavel Alekseevich Rotmistrov, and Andrei Grigorevich Kravchenko. Each tank commanders' combat career is examined, as is the rise of Red Army forces, and reveals these lesser known leaders and their operations to western military history readers.
Size: 6" x 9" 15 b/w photos, maps
476 pages, hard cover
ISBN: 0-88740-581-9 $24.95

RED ARMY LEGACIES: ESSAYS ON FORCES, CAPABILITIES & PERSONALITIES RICHARD N. ARMSTRONG. For twenty-five years, it was the author's job to watch and examine the Soviet Army for a possible conflict, and to understand the Soviet Army's use of its combat experience. In Richard Armstrong's new book, *Red Army Legacies: Essays on Forces, Capabilities & Personalities*, eleven essays show how the Soviet Army used its "Red Army Legacy." Among the subjects covered are: **Part I - Forces**; Chapter One - Guards of Destruction; Chapter Two - The Bukrin Drop: Limits to Creativity; Chapter Three - Tank Corps Commander; Chapter Four - Mobile Groups: Prologue to MG; **Part II - Capabilities**; Chapter Five - Hunting Tongues; Chapter Six - Battlefield Agility: The Soviet Legacy; Chapter Seven - Red Army Indicators; Chapter Eight - Repelling Counterattacks and Counterstrikes; **Part III - Personalities**; Chapter Nine - Nachalnik Razvedki: The Red Two; Chapter Ten - Popel: The Fighting Commissar; Chapter Eleven - Radzievskii: The Thinking Warrior.
Size: 6" x 9" maps
256 pages, hard cover
ISBN: 0-88740-805-2 $24.95

STALINGRAD The Defeat of the German 6TH Army Paul Carell. In this 50th Anniversary book, Paul Carell updates and revises the Stalingrad sections of *Hitler Moves East* and *Scorched Earth,* and reappraises the operations of the 6th Army from the 1942 German summer offensive, through the fighting in the streets of Stalingrad to the final defeat in January 1943.
Size: 7" x 10"
Hard cover, 352 pages, 190 color and b/w photographs, 27 maps
ISBN: 0-88740-469-3 $29.95

ASSAULT ON MOSCOW 1941: The Offensive • The Battle • The Set-Back Werner Haupt. Over 50 years ago, the great battle for the Soviet capital occurred and in which, for the first time in two years of war, the victorious German armies and air fleets were handed a defeat from which the Wehrmacht never recovered. The battle for Moscow was one of the turning points of the Second World War! *Assault on Moscow* is a work that covers the vast scope of war on the Eastern Front. Detailed unit operations and individual accounts make for absorbing reading, and a rare chance for the reader to examine an early, yet very important, Russian front battle.
Size: 6" x 9" over 140 b/w and color photographs
304 pages, hard cover
ISBN: 0-7643-0127-6 $35.00

ARMY GROUP NORTH: The Wehrmacht in Russia 1941-1945 Werner Haupt. After long years of studying sources and literature, Werner Haupt presents the military history of one of the larger theaters of World War II. The completion of the history of "Army Group North" is the result of the author's utilization of all available German and Russian literature, as well as those combat diaries and documents of the committed troop units that are available in German archives. In addition, the author was assisted in clearing up several questions by the advice of former members of the army group – from commanders to drivers. This series by Werner Haupt will continue with a volume each on Army Group Center and Army Group South. The author served in the German Army as a soldier and officer in the northern sector of the Eastern Front during the Second World War. He is also the author of *Assault on Moscow - 1941* (available from Schiffer Publishing Ltd.).
Size: 6" x 9", 45 b/w photographs, 3 maps
416 pages, hard cover
ISBN: 0-7643-0182-9 $35.00